2004 SPORTING
KNIVES

Edited by
JOE KERTZMAN

SPORTING KNIVES 2004 STAFF

Editorial Comments and Suggestions

We're always looking for feedback on our books. Please let us know what you like about this edition. If you have suggestions for articles you'd like to see in future editions, please contact

Joe Kertzman/Sporting Knives
700 East State St.
Iola, WI 54990
email: kertzmanj@krause.com

Published by

krause publications
An F&W Publications Company

700 East State Street • Iola, WI 54990-0001
715-445-2214 • 888-457-2873
www.krause.com

Please call or write for our free catalog of publications. Our toll-free number to place an order or obtain a free catalog is 800-258-0929 or please use our regular business telephone, 715-445-2214.

Library of Congress Catalog Number: 2001086713

ISBN: 0-87349-595-0

Edited by Joe Kertzman
Designed by Ethel Thulien and Patsy Howell

INTRODUCTION

The great cutlery tradition of the United States of America continues. This isn't about marketing knives. There's nothing "corporate America" about this script. This isn't Wall Street, nor are we in Hollywood trying to make a movie, or knives, or movie prop knives for that matter. This isn't about money, Honey. We're not greasing anybody's palms.

The great cutlery tradition of the U.S. of A. takes into account men and women who spent years sitting in chairs that hurt the eyes long before they hurt their backs. They hunched over abrasive wheels the size of monster truck tires grinding steel knife blades before dropping them one by one into inspection bins. The great American cutlery tradition begins with steel makers working in temperatures hotter than Hades and atmospheres louder than pounding drums. A summary of the American pocketknife involves the steel finishing process, you know, the time when folks with the patience of Job sat and sanded steel by hand until there were no pits or imperfections, and knife blades folded in and out of handles as sweetly as honey from a pot. These particular knives of the United States belong in trousers and bib overalls pockets, in toolboxes and Ford truck glove compartments. These aren't sissy slicers, they're the real deal, the kind of fixed-blade camp and hunting knives you sharpen in circular motions on soapstones, not in the slots of electric can openers. They're bowies and skinners and cleavers and fillets.

Knives that define our history weren't all made in the USA. No, some were borrowed from Germany, France, Spain, Norway, Sweden, India, Japan, Brazil, China or Africa. They passed through the hands of Americans. They worked, or they didn't. They cut, or they couldn't cut it. Edges were subjected to leather, wood, bark, plastic, rubber, rope, carpet, cardboard, bone and wire. Blade bevels bit hard and did their jobs. There were nicks and notches, cuts and scratches, chips and gashes.

The saga never ended. You might as well move the personal belongings of the knife company owner into his office, warehouse or factory, because that's where he spends all of his time. "There just has to be a better way to manufacture this tactical knife so that it won't fail in combat situations." "No, look closely. Right there. Yes, that's what I mean. You can't have the handle edge digging into the hands of the guy who uses the knife to skin deer. Round off that corner." "Do you think a flat or hollow grind will work better on this blade configuration?" "Maybe we should design two types of boot knives and let the local cops wear them on the job for a few months and give us their suggestions." "If the blade breaks by bending it in a vise, then it will break when a fireman is using it to pry open a window during a house fire." "No, that steel will rust in salt water, and the SEALs were promised corrosion-resistant cutters."

The finest in factory knives are becoming more high-tech, exciting and drop-dead gorgeous everyday, thanks to advances in steels, technologies, machinery and methodologies. Turning the pages of this book is like turning the pages of knife history and getting a complete overview in one sitting. Knife companies with 100-year legacies are featured alongside cutlery giants that grew up overnight by utilizing the ultimate in high-tech, high-speed, tight-tolerance, computerized, digitized and stylized machines available. Buck and Benchmade, Spyderco and Schrade, Cold Steel and Gerber, Microtech and Masters of Defense. They're all represented, respected and accounted for, because each offers a style of knife unlike their competitor, even if in the smallest way.

The knife industry had benefited because it is still a small-niche market with high competition. So, sit back, relax and enjoy the knife show. You're sure to come away with a better appreciation for the factory knife and all that went into its history and making. No grinding wheels or steel mills, but a lot of cool cutters and some real slick sheaths to keep them in, too!

Joe Kertzman

Sporting Knives 2004
CONTENTS

Schrade Cutlery: Celebrating 100 Years of Quality and Value 1904-2004

2003 Schrade D'Holder   SDH02

The second in the five-piece Schrade Centennial series designed by master custom knifemaker D'Alton Holder, the SDH02 artfully blends the themes of steel and the outdoor world. This superb drop point hunter takes the Rocky Mountain bighorn ram as its inspiration. The 8-1/2-inch, integral design blade is crafted from 440C stainless steel. Natural ram's horn is the material of choice for the contoured finger-grooved handle. Nestled in the bolster, a beautiful ram's head relief designed by wildlife sculptor Bruce Shaw completes the piece. Limited to only 500 pieces. Priced at $450.00

X-Timer Fixed Blade   XT2B

Fixed blades have gone extreme! The new line of X-Timer fixed blades offers high-tech styling, heavy-duty functionality and the quality that you'd expect from Schrade. The knives are equipped with beefy stainless steel blades, epoxy coated and laser-etched with the X-Timer logo. The 5-inch handles, crafted with textured TPR for a great grip, are well-balanced, precision-engineered and easy on the hands. Carried in the unique wrap-around ballistic belt pouch, this is a great knife for chores around the camp, dressing game in the field or any other tough job encountered by sportsmen. Priced at $64.95

Schrade Walden Cigar Box Knife   CSW296

Saluting the company's storied Schrade Walden heritage from the early 1900s, this finely crafted folder features genuine bone handles and polished bolsters. Packed in a handsome cigar box, this beautiful collectible is also a versatile tool, sporting two blades forged from Schrade's legendary tough stainless steel. Whether carried for daily use or set out for display, this classic trapper model is sure to please any discriminating blade enthusiast. Priced at $60.00

Spitfire LTD   SPF1LTD

The new Spitfire LTD demonstrates Schrade's commitment to innovative design and the finest materials available. This bold and efficient folder boasts Schrade's new patent pending, ambidextrous locking mechanism, treated with titanium for added strength and durability. Hidden in a 3-1/8-inch G-10 handle, the 2-inch blade is crafted from ATS-34 stainless steel. Also new is the quick-release lanyard—a simple squeeze and the knife is free in your hand and ready for any job. Priced at $115.00

Uncle Henry Golden Spike Fixed Blade   153UH

A tough knives for tough chores, the Golden Spike features a rust-resistant 9-1/4-inch stainless steel blade that will hold an edge cut after cut. The attractive handle is also nearly indestructible. Crafted from Staglon® it features finger grooves for maximum control and comfort. Fitted with solid brass guard and butt piece and shipped with a genuine leather sheath. Made in the U.S.A. and backed by a limited lifetime warranty. Priced at $67.95

Old Timer Golden Bear Lockback   6OT

Measuring 6 inches long closed, the Golden Bear is the outdoorsman's choice for an all-around lockback blade. Features a rust-resistant Schrade+ stainless steel blade. The handles are virtually indestructible—crafted from Delrin® they carry a saw-cut pattern for non-slip use. Includes a genuine leather sheath. Backed by a limited lifetime warranty. Priced at $49.95

Old Timer Middleman Pocket Knife   34OT

America's best-selling pocket knife! Measuring only 3-3/16 inches closed, the knife features three blades crafted from high-carbon steel—guaranteed to hold a great edge. The Delrin® handles offer supreme durability and nonslip use. Solid nickel silver bolsters. Made in the U.S.A. and backed by limited lifetime warranty. Priced at $31.95

Diamond Machining Technology

In 2002 Diamond Machining Technology, Inc. (DMT®) marked its 26th year as the leader in and innovator of manual diamond sharpening technology for people and industries that depend on performance edges. Incorporating the diamond's ability to abrade hard materials, DMT's engineering and product development expertise and patented processes have evolved to service industrial, commercial and consumer markets. The company offers sharpening solutions for everyone from do-it-yourselfers to large commercial operations. DMT's specialized, precision sharpening systems function to easily and efficiently sharpen, hone, lap or deburr in the production, maintenance and repair cycles of a myriad of products.

DMT produces their entire family of products, including the new Dia-Sharp® line of continuous diamond surfaced sharpeners in the company's facility in Marlborough, Massachusetts. Home to the company since 1983, the facility accommodates DMT's sales, marketing and production departments. The recently expanded production area houses first-of-its-kind injection molding systems complete with robotics to produce its patented DuoSharp® line as well as its internationally recognized polka dot patterned Diamond Whetstone™ line.

In manufacturing innovative products of exceptional quality—known worldwide for their durability, performance and precision—DMT is also a responsible, community-oriented corporate citizen. Currently, DMT works with the Commonwealth of Massachusetts in a three-year pilot program for workplace education to train the incumbent workforce in new technologies. Additionally, creating employment opportunities, DMT contracts with local work programs for the mentally and physically challenged to employ workers in assembling and packaging DMT products. With a high commitment to local and state environmental standard in their production processes, DMT developed a closed loop water treatment system of their own design to eliminate any industrial discharge.

DMT was founded in 1976 by Elizabeth and David Powell, former college professor and aeronautical engineer, respectively. Their entrepreneurial success story began in Hudson, Massachusetts, on the third floor of an old mill where the Powells first developed and produced diamond saw blades used for cutting blocks of granite. With a 1978 change in U.S. foreign policy, America released a significant part of the stockpile of industrial diamond to Israel, causing world prices to plummet and DMT sales to plunge to near zero. Faced with the need to diversify, and putting their Yankee ingenuity to the test, the Powell's "Eureka moment" came from a rather unlikely discovery.

From a round, four-inch, discarded center punch-out of a diamond grinding wheel, grew the potential for a new tool. This diamond-surfaced plastic, perforated punch-out was transformed from waste material to sharpening innovation. It was an unbreakable, clean cutting, super-fast sharpener requiring no oil as a lubricant. It was a tool that could sharpen any material, including the toughest composites, any metal, including tungsten carbide and even polycrystalline diamond (PCD) inserts without mechanical assistance, i.e. by hand.

Sending a sample to L.L. Bean, one purchasing manager extolled the product's sharpening performance and suggested DMT consider a non-circular shape. With the reshaping to a rectangular stone and the development of manufacturing and plating technologies to serve the sharpening needs of many markets, the company was on the course to becoming the recognized leader and industry standard in diamond honing hand tools.

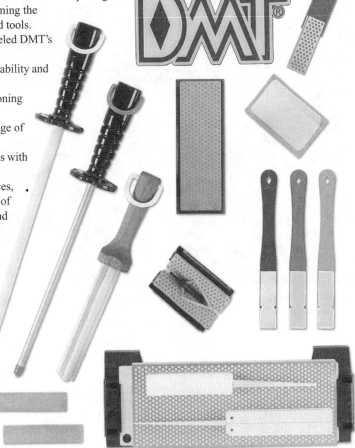

A variety of successful new products in receptive markets fueled DMT's growth. Innovative firsts now copied, but never equaled, are:

The Crystal Saver® — Rescues fine crystal, restoring serviceability and beauty by smoothing rough and chipped edges.

The Diamond Whetstone™ — Facilitates quick, precision honing of all tools in every market.

The Diafold® Serrated Knife Sharpener — Sharpens the range of serrated blades in both outdoor and culinary markets.

DMT's unprecedented engineering abilities provide customers with sharpening tools for processes requiring extraordinarily precise tolerances. To insure incredibly flat and stable sharpening surfaces, DMT has invented a unique mold design that allows the mating of perforated steel inserts to engineered grade resins. DMT diamond surface flatness exceeds that of ground steel plates—a precision standard not attained by other manufacturers or sharpeners.

DMT's ever evolving line now numbers some 300 different products targeted at markets as varied as culinary, lawn and garden, woodworking and carving, outdoor, speed skate/ski/snowboard, fresh and saltwater fishing, industrial, commercial and home improvement (DIY). Entering international markets in the 1980s, this progressive company introduced five-language packaging and marketing materials to present and promote the DMT brand globally. DMT now realizes 30% of their sales internationally.

With David Powell's retirement in 2001, Christine Miller, former Vice President of Operations, was promoted to President. Chris joins Elizabeth Powell, Chair and Treasurer, in managing this woman-owned company. These businesswomen are setting the goals and meeting the challenges of leveraging the company's cutting-edge competencies to continue the innovative success of DMT.

Kids and Knives:

Zero Tolerance is Mindless Apathy

In giving a kid a knife, remember to teach the lessons that go along with owning it

By James Ayres

Small kid, big knife. A six-year-old cleans a Randall Model 1 in a mountain creek after dressing out a rabbit.

"I used that Scout knife to cut fishing poles, clean fish, shave kindling, and for general whittling."

MY GRANDDAD'S KNIFE was the one he used to sharpen my arrows before I went off hunting imaginary lions in the tall grass behind the house, the same knife he used to peel an apple so that all the skin came off in one, long spiral, the knife I always wanted.

How old were you when you got your first knife? I was five. My grandfather gave me a small, two-blade folder similar to the one he carried everyday in his pants pocket. He kept his folder sharp as a razor and later taught me to do the same. He also taught me to cut away from

myself and to never cut with the edge towards another person.

Now I had my own knife. Now I could sharpen my own arrows. Now I was grown up, kind of, anyway. Big day. I bet you remember the day you got your first knife as well as I do mine. It was probably a pretty big day for you, too.

As I got older, there were other knives. In the fourth grade, I carved my initials into the wood paneling of my classroom. I cut them in good and deep, right in the middle of generations of initials carved by other kids. I was a Boy Scout and I used my Scout knife for the job. It just seemed like the right thing to do. I used that Scout knife to cut fishing poles, clean fish, shave kindling, and for general whittling. It had four blades. One of them was a can opener that I used to open cans of pork and beans on our weekend camp outs. One day I used it to pull the staples on Mr. Brauer's barbed wire fence that stood between our place and the Wildcat Creek.

I was never apprehended for pulling those staples, even though some of Mr. Brauer's hogs got out as a result of my misdemeanor. No such luck on the initials. Lucy Meyers ratted me out to the teacher the same day I carved those initials. It surprised me since she was the one who dared me to do it. I guess she was just that kind of kid.

I was called to Sister Edwina's office the next morning. She told me that Scouts were not vandals and that I should be ashamed of myself. She then confiscated my knife for the rest of the week and assigned me to write, "A Scout is not a vandal" one hundred times. At the end of the week, she returned my knife. The lesson had been learned, and in those days, in that place, it was understood that a pocketknife was a normal part of a kid's daily gear, along with rubber bands, marbles and a Tootsie Roll or two. Everyone knew that kids and knives just went together. How else could a kid play mumblety-peg?

Some time ago, one of my sons had a different kind of experience with a pocketknife at school. We had spent the weekend camping in the mountains near our home. On the first day, we cut fishing poles and caught a few tiny pan fish. We cooked them over a small fire while listening to coyotes sing in the early twilight. We slept on a bed of wild grasses under a shelter made with branches and leaves. The next day, we hunted for rabbits with bows and arrows we had made on a previous outing. That night, we ate fish again.

It was a great weekend and we got back late Sunday night with little time to get ready for school and work. As a result, my son didn't do a good job of cleaning out his book bag. He remembered to wipe down the modified Randall Model 1 he'd used for years, and he put it away in a chest. But he overlooked an Opinel folding knife in the bottom of his pack. The next day, while getting his books out for his first class, he noticed the knife at the bottom of his bag.

His school, like most schools today, does not allow students to have any kind of knife while on school grounds. My son, being concerned about doing the right thing, got permission to go to his counselor's office. Once there, he gave the knife to his counselor and told him the story of how the folder had come to be in his bag. The counselor called the school principal. The principal called my office to inform me that my son was being expelled from school and that criminal charges might be filed against him for possession of a deadly weapon.

It seems that the school had a "zero tolerance" policy on knives. Knives were weapons and could only be seen as weapons. This "educator" had to follow the rules. He acknowledged that my son had never been in any trouble at school. He acknowledged that my son had willingly went to his counselor to report his mistake, and that there was no question whatever of him having done anything wrong with his knife, except that he had the folder in his possession. He believed my son's story that he had forgotten the knife in his bag after a weekend camp out.

Possession As Oppression

But rules were rules and no student could have a weapon on school grounds. He also informed me that allowing kids to have knives was the height of parental irresponsibility because, aside from the possibility of accidents, the possession of such a weapon would inspire them to commit evil deeds. Upon enquiry, I found that his attitude was widespread among teachers and administrators in the school system.

Folks, something is dreadfully wrong here. The difference between my experience and my son's is greater than the 40 years that separate the two events—so great, it would seem, that the two of us had spent our childhoods in different countries. Well, maybe we did. I lived in a country where personal responsibility was taught. My son lives in a country where mindless obedience to the rules is required, where volition is assigned to inanimate objects, where knives are evil.

During an urban foraging demonstration, kids learned to cut bamboo using a Chris Reeve Mountaineer one-piece fixed blade.

I have read that during the late medieval period, the newly invented crossbow was thought to be an instrument of the devil since it allowed commoners to shoot through armor and strike a knight from his horse. This threatened the social order. Some crossbowmen were charged with attacking the church itself. Many of them pleaded innocent because, "The devil made me do it." The matter caused so much controversy that it was finally brought to one of the popes for adjudication.

It was decided that an inanimate object cannot be evil and cannot influence one's actions, because inanimate objects have no soul, no reason and no ability to persuade. Therefore, no responsibility could be assigned to inanimate objects. Reason, volition and responsibility could only reside in a being with consciousness: man or God. Therefore, the crossbow could not be at fault.

The fault and the responsibility could only lie with the individual. That decision pretty much settled the matter for about 500 years. Until now. The Enlightenment ratified and expanded this concept, and many others, providing the foundation for modern society. Now it seems that we are reverting to the Dark Ages.

A knife, like a crossbow, has no intention, no volition. It is an inanimate object. It can do nothing by itself. It can be tool or weapon according to the intention of the possessor. This would seem to be obvious to us all. But apparently it is not so obvious to some of our lawmakers and school administrators.

I have taught many kids the same lessons I learned when I was a kid, and have used knives as an instrument of that teaching. My sons, in particular, have each had their own knives since they were old enough to be able to assume responsibility for them. I have taught my kids (all my kids, not just my sons) practical wilderness skills, both with and without knives. Any of my kids can build a life-saving shelter and start a fire. Having done this both with and without a knife or matches, they are safer in the woods, and they further appreciate the value of a good knife.

They also learned that a knife is a primary tool and that, with it and the right knowledge and experience, one can build other basic tools. As I worked with the kids, we would talk about history and prehistory, the development of tools, steel, fire and writing. During these conversations, they learned how complex a civilization must be

Knives can still be just plain fun for kids. Recently, a three-year-old girl who lives near the author was trying to reach an orange that grew near the treetop. The author's youngest son cut a bamboo pole, tied his little Spyderco Cricket to the end of it, and cut an orange from the tree. The little girl's smile lit up the whole yard.

in order to produce such a simple, such a fine object as a steel knife. They learned to value the contributions of all those who had gone before them, the value of our civilization, their own value and their place in the world.

They also learned how powerful symbols are to humans. I have taught my boys to always have three things with them: a knife, a pen and a means of making fire. These are practical tools, but they are more. The knife, in addition to being a primary tool, is a symbol for the sword of the knight who protected the weak and defended civilization. The knife is, therefore, a reminder to behave honorably and to always do the right thing.

Knives that one of the author's kids has accumulated include, from left to right, a Frost Laminated Utility with buckskin cover on sheath; Al Mar Falcon; Spyderco Cricket; a Wayne Goddard custom knife; Fallkniven F-1; Chris Reeve Mountaineer; Benchmade Pardue; and a Victorinox multi-blade tool knife.

The gift of a knife symbolizes a certain rite of passage.

The pen is a symbol of learning, books and knowledge, the vast foundation and reservoir of civilization from which we all benefit. Therefore, the pen is a reminder of the debt we owe our society and the obligation to make a positive contribution. In ancient times, it was thought that fire came from the gods. Without fire, civilization would not have been possible. Fire is the symbol of light and reason. The knife, the pen, fire: powerful symbols they are all.

These symbols, perhaps more than the tools themselves, empower those who posses them. And maybe that's the problem. Maybe our school administrators, lawmakers and some parents just don't trust their kids, our kids. Maybe they don't want them to have the power that comes with a knife because they don't trust them.

It Cuts Two Ways

A knife can cut two ways. As a very educated friend of mine once said, "With a knife, you can cut your bread, and you can cut your neighbor." The intention lies in the person holding the blade, not the blade itself. You can teach values and responsibility in many ways. But all the ways involve, sooner or later, the empowerment of the individual. The drive towards individual empowerment has been at the center of western thought since the

Enlightenment, and was a central concept in the founding of our own country. You don't teach individual responsibility by substituting rules for reason, by withholding trust and responsibility.

If an individual proves himself irresponsible or of ill intent, then we must deal with that person's actions. If large groups of people act with ill intent or irresponsibly, then we have a social problem, one that cannot, and will not, be solved by prohibiting the use or possession of any particular object.

> *"Maybe our school administrators, lawmakers and some parents just don't trust their kids, our kids."*

Social problems are complex, and often no easy solution can be found. But a good starting place is with the raising of children. Parents, teachers, coaches and others in authority must do the work of teaching values and responsibility to their, our, children. This cannot be accomplished by withholding trust or responsibility.

It also can't be accomplished by simply giving a kid a knife. If you entrust a kid with a knife, teach

him the lessons to go with it. Teach him to never cut towards others. Teach him to take care of it like the valuable object it is. Teach him that a Scout is not a vandal. Give him some history, also, and some philosophy along with the practical and moral lessons. You might be surprised to see how quickly kids absorb history and applied philosophy when the lessons are accompanied by some practical applications, and how quickly they become responsible.

Some years ago, I was camping in the Los Padres Wilderness area with my sons. They were 14 and 10 years old at the time. While gathering firewood about a half mile from camp, they were confronted by a cougar. Cougars are protected; their population has outgrown the space we allow for them. As a result, attacks on dogs and small children have become common in this area.

The boys did exactly as they had been taught. The smaller one got behind the larger. Then they drew their belt knives, faced towards the cougar and slowly began to walk backwards, shouting all the time for help, and telling the cougar to go away. As soon as they got within my hearing, I ran to them and we drove the big cat off. Pretty brave kids. What they did took a lot more than a couple of knives. But the stuff that it did take came along with the knives.

I'm not saying that anyone should put his or her kids in harm's way. I did not intend to meet a cougar that day, but you never know what the world will bring to you. I'm not even saying you need to take kids camping. Everyone should work within his or her own comfort zone. But I am saying that it doesn't hurt to get kids' feet in the dirt and spend some time in the natural world. I'm also saying that a knife is not a bad thing in and of itself.

A couple of years ago, I taught three kids how to build a lifesaving shelter. This was in the far Northwest in the winter, as an offshore storm was coming in. One of the kids was a city girl who had never really stepped off the pavement. I

> ## "The gift of a knife symbolizes a certain rite of passage."

loaned her a Benchmade Axis folder for the exercise. When she started the task, she had no idea how to even hold a knife, let alone use it effectively. But she learned quickly. The work was hard, it was cold and wet, and she got a little scared as the sun set and the deep dark closed in around us. But she persevered. Never whined once.

That night, the temperature dropped to below freezing and there were long hours of wet snow

alternating with sleet and howling wind. We were warm and snug in our small shelter that the kids had built with folding knives, branches and sweat.

The next day, as we were leaving, she came to me to return the knife she had borrowed. She asked me how much such a knife would cost. When I told her the price of a new one, her face fell a little. She sighed and said, "Well, if I work and save, would you keep this one for me and sell it to me when I get the money? I want it as a reminder of all this."

She told me that she had learned in one short day and night that she did not have to be at anyone's mercy, that she could build her life as she did that shelter. She had just received a college scholarship and was afraid that she couldn't really do the work. She wanted to keep the knife to remind her that she could do what she put her mind to. Of course, she left with the knife in her pocket. I visited her at her school a few months ago. She is getting A's, and the knife sits on her desk next to her books.

Just Plain Fun Knives

Knives can still be just plain fun for kids. The other day, one of our neighbor kids was trying to reach an orange that grew near the treetop. My youngest son cut a bamboo pole, tied his little Spyderco Cricket to the end of it, and cut an orange from the tree. The three-

year-old girl's smile lit up the whole yard.

I have many good memories, some of which I have shared, of my childhood experiences with knives. No doubt many of you have similar experiences. So do my sons. But many of their friends have never had those experiences, because their parents have been conditioned, brainwashed or cowed.

I don't feel like being politically correct and mincing words on this topic. Their parents, teachers, coaches and the other authority figures in their lives have bought into the notion that knives are evil in and of themselves. In doing so,

> ## "Knives can still be just plain fun for kids."

they have abdicated the notion of individual responsibility for one's actions. They have accepted the archaic idea that an inanimate object can exert influence over a person's behavior. They are teaching kids the wrong lessons.

In our society today, these medieval-minded people seem to be in the majority. Today your kids probably cannot take a knife to school, or perhaps even carry one in their pocket. Many particular kinds of

From the age of 5 to 18 years old, one of the author's kids has collected knives. They are, from left to right, a Gerber Bolt Action; a Victornox multi-tool knife; a Frost Laminated Steel Utility with buckskin cover on sheath; a Spyderco Military; a Modified Randall Model 1; an Opinel; a Fallkniven H-1; and a Kershaw Liner Lock.

knives are illegal in certain jurisdictions. Most of the Boy Scout troops I have been involved with are not allowed to have Scout knives. If this continues, one day, you or your kids will not be able to have any kind of knife.

A letter from my lawyer got my son back in school, for a while anyway. That incident, and others, led me to take my son out of the public school system. He had learned a lesson from the experience, but not one that I wanted to reinforce. I did not want him to learn that he could not be trusted and that some object had power to influence his actions. Nor did I want him to live with the kind of hypocrisy supported by the system that teaches those lessons.

My grandfather taught me to never cut towards others, and to take care of valuable things. I also learned a lesson from Sister Edwina. I learned that a Scout is not a vandal, and that I could be trusted. Eventually, I went to see Mr. Brauer. I owned up to pulling down his fence and apologized for doing so. And, because my mother had taught me that talk is cheap, I fed his hogs every day for a week. I still can't stand hogs. My lessons, and my son's lessons, were 40 years apart, a world apart. Which lessons do you want your kids to learn? Which world do you want your kids to live in? ●

Two young adventurers limb a sapling with the Benchmade Axis.

Celluloid: The Clear Choice for Knife Handles

From the billiard rooms of millionaires' mansions to the handles of pocketknives, celluloid has a rich history

By Richard D. White

Photos by Richard White

THE MID-1800s WILL be remembered for the striking contrast between various classes of workers all over the world. The struggles of poor coal miners and railroad workers, many of them immigrants to the United States, were far removed from the lives of steel mill owners, railroad magnates and bankers. The rich split time between multi-room mansions and summer palaces. For them, extended hunting trips to exotic lands, like Africa, New Zealand and Australia were commonplace, and billiard tournaments in their respective dens were a preferred pastime.

With the surprising popularity of the game of billiards came a sudden scarcity of ivory used to produce the billiard balls. Without ivory, the billiard craze would certainly come to a screeching halt! Sensing this shortage, a contest of sorts was formulated, and substantial prize money was anteed up.

As is frequently the case in money-motivated contests or challenges revolving around inventions and discoveries, there were several chemists worldwide simultaneously experimenting with different chemicals, and all with one common goal—to produce a substance that exhibited the ideal properties for making billiard balls.

> **OFFICIAL NOTICE IS HEREBY GIVEN CONCERNING THE GRAND PRIZE OF $100,000 TO BE OFFERED**
>
> To the first person or persons able to produce a suitable substitute for real ELEPHANT IVORY used in the making of balls in the billiard industry. The substance must be able to withstand the force of direct, repeated blows directed to it by a panel of professional billiard players; without shattering, deforming, or cracking in any way. In addition, the billiard balls made from this material must duplicate the color, grain, and growth lines visible in billiard balls made from genuine ivory.
>
> —Mid-1800s contest bulletin

In the United States, in 1869, John Wesley Hyatt mixed several dangerous and potentially flammable chemicals together resulting in a substance he called "celluloid." Across the ocean, some 19 years earlier, an Englishman named Alexander Parkes had actually beaten the American chemist to the punch, becoming the first to synthesize the unique compound known stateside as "celluloid."

No matter who was making it, the process involved in formulating celluloid was quite harrowing and included soaking cotton fibers in nitric and sulfuric acids. When mixed with camphor and alcohol, the fibers turned into a plastic-like substance to which various pigments and colorings were added.

The mixture could be bent, molded, twisted and pressed into form, one factor that lent to the belief that celluloid was the perfect pocketknife handle material. In fact, celluloid was soon found to have thousands of uses. Unfortunately, making billiard balls would not prove to be one of them. Through trial and error, Hyatt discovered that celluloid billiard balls would literally explode once they hit each other because of the unstable nature of the substance.

Celluloid's ability to conform to a specific shape after being subjected to heat and pressure, and its ability to be stained into a multitude of colors turned out to be the material's greatest assets. For knife handles, celluloid was pressed into long sheets and combined with backing material in a variety of colors.

Soon, celluloid was being fashioned in a striking array of patterns and colors duplicating those found in nature, like feathers,

Celluloid's almost endless pattern possibilities are clearly shown on the handles of these pocketknives. The Kutmaster "glitter stripe" (bottom left) is directly below two "checkerboard" celluloid-handle knives made for the Blish-Mise-Silliman Hardware Co. The bottom checkerboard is yellow and green in color, while the top is red and white. Above the checkerboard knives is a Wards dogleg jackknife handled in mottled browns and yellows. At top left is a Christmas tree celluloid KA-BAR toothpick jack. On the bottom right is a black-and-white-striped Wallkill River Works whittler. Above it is a rare Commander brand mottled-celluloid, EZ-open jack, and at top right is a red-and-white-striped Kent jackknife.

One of the most collected celluloids is called "butter and molasses," an unusual celluloid that closely resembles its name. The large sheath knife, probably made by Colonial or Imperial, is outfitted with a beautiful butter-and-molasses celluloid handle. Below the sheath knife are two Western Boulder pocketknives, the right, a premium stockman, and the left, a whittler pattern, both also in butter-and-molasses celluloid.

cracked ice and swirls, as well as those that mimicked such goodies as red-and-white candy canes, butter or molasses.

Almost every domestic knife company used vast quantities of celluloid handles, and many of the businesses made a name for themselves in the process. Remington, which used tons of celluloid, coined its own name for the substance, calling it "Pyremite" (notice the "rem" in the center of the word, standing for the first three letters of the name "Remington").

Remington incorporated every known color of celluloid in its pocketknives, even using a red, white and blue American flag celluloid on many of its Boy Scout knives. Other knife manufacturers that used "flag celluloid" include Schrade Cutlery Co. and Imperial Knife Co.

Among the knife enterprises known to have extensively used celluloid handles were: Schrade and Imperial; Kent Cutlery Co.;

> *"Considering all the celluloid colors, serious collectors can put together a dazzling display of knives."*

Syracuse Cutlery Co.; Henry Sears and Sons; Hibbard/Spencer/Bartlett; Commander Cutlery; W. R. Case & Sons Cutlery Co.; Western States Cutlery; KA-BAR; Colonial; Wards; Wallkill River Works; Kutmaster; Wards; Hoffritz; Remington; Winchester; Pal Blade; Shapleigh Diamond Edge; Ulster Knife Co.; Utica Cutlery Co.; Keen Kutter; Robeson; Boker; and Cattaraugus Cutlery Co.

With so many knife companies building knives with celluloid handles, and considering the large variety of colors available, serious,

modern collectors are able to put together a dazzling display of brands and patterns. Some collectors, however, appear to take a different tact and settle in on a particular celluloid color, accumulating as many knives as possible bearing sides of a particular pattern and hue.

For these collectors, there seems to be two or three celluloids favored. The first is called "candystripe." Appearing like an actual candy-striped stick with alternating, wide red and white lines (some bound with a lighter orange), this celluloid has emerged as the top collectible pattern. Almost every knife manufacturer that used celluloid handles experimented with candystripe on some of its models, and a favorite pocketknife style for candystripe celluloid was the Texas toothpick, an elongated, single-blade folding knife. Boker, Imperial, Shapleigh, Remington and even Winchester unveiled toothpick patterns with candystripe.

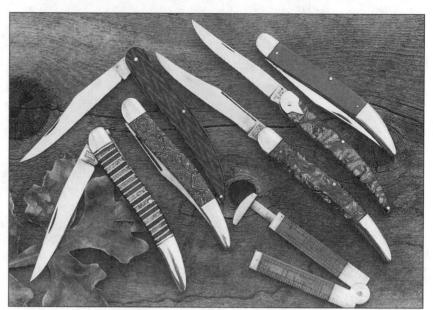

Texas toothpick pocketknives, because of their large size and fancy shape, are popular candidates for colorful celluloid handles. At bottom left is a Kutmaster folder with a glitter-stripe celluloid grip. Above it, an Imperial folder is handled in rare, mottled celluloid that looks like a microscopic section of a skin cell. Above the Imperial is an unknown brand with a red-and-black, zigzag-pattern handle. To the right is a mottled-celluloid-handle Imperial with reds and grays, a KA-BAR Christmas tree celluloid, and a solid-red-celluloid-handle Wards (top right).

Cutting Christmas Trees?

Although many favor candystripe, other pocketknife collectors swear that the finest celluloid color is found in "Christmas tree," a brilliant mixture of reds, yellows, blacks and greens, all swirled together in random patterns. For these collectors, nothing beats a huge Ka-Bar or Western States clasp knife with a Christmas tree celluloid grip.

Perhaps the most commonly used celluloid color was pale-yel-

> *"One that shimmers like copper granules, 'goldstone' remains a popular and collectible celluloid handle material."*

low or white celluloid containing random lines running deep through the material. This pattern, known as "cracked ice," looks exactly like its name implies. Because of its pale color, it was often used as a base for black-etched advertising knives.

Imperial, Western Boulder, Keen Kutter, Schrade, Wards and many others used cracked-ice celluloid, generally on small penknives, or on the largest folding knives—folding hunters. Inset with a shiny, nickel

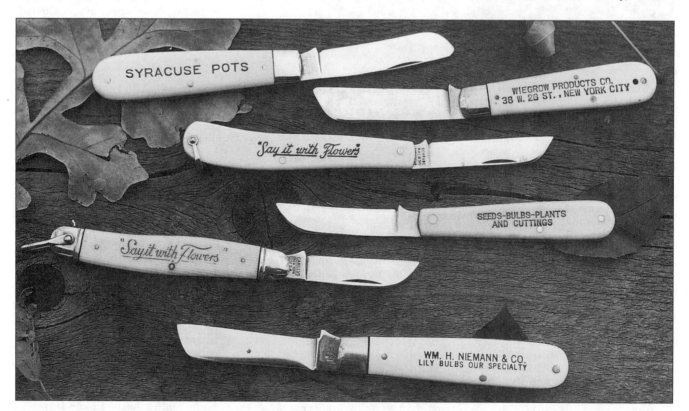

Florist knives, either displaying the traditional florist slogan "Say it With Flowers," or advertising their respective businesses and products, were almost always equipped with white-celluloid handles so that the black lettering would provide a striking contrast. Together, this grouping makes a unique and interesting display of special interest to florists.

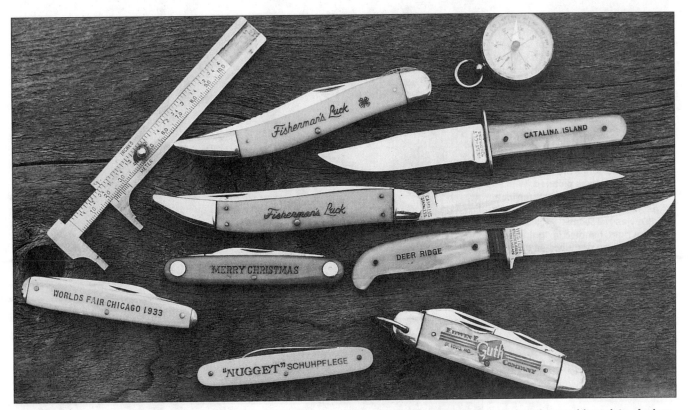

In addition to its use in florists' knives, light-colored celluloid, generally called "cracked ice," was employed on a wide variety of advertising and tourist knives. Included in this unique grouping are two Western Boulder sheath knives advertising "Catalina Island" and "Deer Ridge," as well as two Camillus fish knives engraved "Fisherman's Luck." Also pictured is a knife from the 1933 World's Fair, a German "Nugget" advertising knife, a Morley "Merry Christmas" knife and a four-blade Imperial advertising knife.

silver shield, cracked ice made for one stunning knife handle.

Collectors point to other descriptive celluloid names with fondness. One that shimmers like copper granules, "goldstone" remains a popular and collectible celluloid handle material. Perhaps the most intriguing celluloid is known in the cutlery business as "waterfall." This pale-tan celluloid was manufactured with a series of parallel, horizontal lines running the length of the plastic.

The waterfall pattern is identified by dark shadows that move through such a celluloid handle as the knife is rotated up and down, somewhat resembling the movement of water over a waterfall. According to knife collecting myth, early cutlery workers would cut small pieces of waterfall celluloid and wear them on strings like necklaces for good luck.

Recent attempts to reproduce waterfall celluloid have been less than satisfactory, the modern version lacking the movement found in early samples. Unfortunately, the original formulas for producing this fascinating handle material have been lost forever.

There were still other celluloids available to knife manufacturers, including one of the most celebrated celluloid designs used by Schrade, Western States Cutlery and Keen Kutter—butter and molasses. With a background of creamy, light tan (like butter), this celluloid had parallel bands of dark brown (molasses) edged with white running throughout the handle material. Butter and molasses knife grips were "tasty" specimens, indeed.

"Early cutlery workers cut small pieces of waterfall celluloid and wore them on strings like necklaces for good luck."

Another popular, but quite rare, celluloid color is "glitter stripe." Similar to candystripe with parallel stripes running throughout the handle, glitter stripe also parades transparent lines made of red, dark green, black, orange and light green, each surrounded by a thin section of white celluloid. Permanently attached to the back of glitter stripe is a backing sheet with millions of small bits of metallic glitter, and the silver glitter shines through the colored transparent strips giving a dramatic appearance to the knife itself.

Glitter stripe was employed by only a select number of knife manufacturers, the best known being W.R. Case & Sons of Bradford, Pennsylvania. Though not as well known as Case, Kutmaster appropriately donned many of its Texas toothpicks in dramatic glitterstripe grips. Toothpicks handled in glitter stripe give the pocketknife design a dramatic and definite "flashy" look.

The discussion of celluloid would not be complete without mentioning one of the most sought-after but bizarre-appearing patterns. Used primarily by the Kent Cutlery Co., a brand sold almost exclusively by F.W. Woolworths Department Stores, it is known as "end of the day." Again, according to legend, knife factory workers regularly swept the floors of the handle-assembly rooms at the end of the day.

Small pieces of celluloid that had been trimmed off of knife handles during a given period were swept up and collected. These pieces were placed into an oven where heat transformed the celluloid sweepings into a one-of-a-kind

Western Cutlery of Boulder, Colorado made a wide range of souvenir knives during its many years of production. The full-size sheath knives for Deer Ridge and Catalina Island flank three other knives. Below the Catalina Island souvenir knife is a "goldstone" celluloid penknife advertising "Seven Falls," a popular Colorado Springs tourist attraction. Perhaps some of the most interesting knife styles are the miniature sheath knives pictured. With an overall length of just over three inches, the bottom-left knife advertises "Davies Hardware," while the bottom right, handled in "goldstone" celluloid, was produced as a tourist knife for the "Royal George," located in Colorado. All of these knives were probably manufactured in the 1930s or '40s.

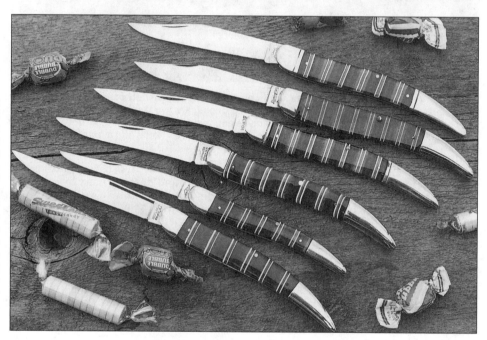

"Candystripe" celluloid has to rank as one of the most colorful and striking celluloid ever made. When used on the Texas toothpick knife style, the colorful candystripe is shown to its fullest advantage. Candystipe celluloid is generally dark red with parallel bands of pure white. In some cases, the red is actually an orange color, and at times contains stripes of lighter orange running along side of the white stripes. Included in this outstanding display are knives tang stamped (from bottom to top): Imperial, IKCO (Imperial Knife Company), Kutmaster, Wards, Remington and Utica Cutlery Co.

pattern of colorful celluloid. Knives donned in end-of-the-day celluloid are instantly recognizable and truly unique in their mottled mixture of colors.

In addition to these known celluloid patterns, there were dozens of others used by various knife companies. Some used solid colors, like red, black and yellow to indicate specific patterns. Fish knives, for example, were almost always made with pure, yellow celluloid so that they could be seen when dropped in water.

The Imperial Knife Co. used a good selection of celluloid colors and patterns, from swirls of pinks, browns, beiges, tans, blues and grays, to mottled patterns of green (almost looking like modern cam-

ouflaged uniforms), Imperial frequently duplicated natural hues.

Celluloid's Deterioration

Despite celluloid's beauty and uniqueness as a handle material on various forms of pocket and sheath knives, it has a dark side. Celluloid has a chemical instability that can potentially have disastrous results. That, coupled with the fact that early knife-production methods were inconsistent, led to the demise of celluloid use on knife handles for safety reasons.

The blades of some knives built in certain types of celluloid handles have been known to suddenly rust, especially the steel nearest knife handles. When examined closely, the careful observer notices the cel-

luloid itself begins to exhibit checkering, the first noticeable sign of celluloid decomposition.

What happens is that, as the celluloid ages, it gives off a gas, most probably a byproduct of the nitric acid used in the material's production. This gas can have a disastrous affect on not only the celluloid-handle knife, but on other blades in the same knife roll. If allowed to continue, this gas infects all knives like bacteria, rusting the blades and causing irrevocable damage.

The somewhat extensive research done on celluloid-handle knives has turned up some interesting information. In almost all cases, the knives that seem to suffer decomposition have all been outfitted with light-colored celluloid,

The use of "candystripe" celluloid was not limited to the handles of long, Texas toothpick knives. From the bottom left are a Shapleigh Hardware Co. premium stockman pocketknife; a Wyeth Hardware Co. premium stockman; an American Knife Co. serpentine jack; a Union Cutlery Co. jack; a Blish-Mize and Silliman cattle pattern; a KA-BAR slim serpentine jack; and three Texas toothpicks made by Kutmaster, Wards and Remington.

The handles of large, folding "coke bottle" pattern knives were frequently outfitted with celluloid handles, their large size providing a palette to show off various patterns and colors. This outstanding display includes a rare Colonial "linoleum" celluloid-handle knife (upper left). Below it are a beige, yellow and brown mottled Imperial coke bottle; a rare "dogshead" KA-BAR in cracked-ice celluloid; an Imperial with a Christmas-tree-celluloid grip; and a Keenwell Manufacturing Co. knife made by KA-BAR with a gorgeous, almost transparent, "onyx"-colored celluloid handle.

mainly yellow and clear celluloid. One theory is that these celluloids lack the binding and coloring pigments found in darker swirls and patterned celluloids, pigments that might have a stabilizing effect on the handle materials themselves.

Questions that arise from any discussion of celluloid and its potential deterioration include, "What do I do if I have a celluloid-handle pocketknife that is starting to exhibit a rusting blade or blades?" First of all, separate it immediately from other knives in a collection. Clean the blade steel carefully, applying a coat of preservative (light oil). If the steel continues to rust, and the handle material starts to harden and crack, removing the celluloid and letting a professional cutlery repairman replace the handle with another material may be a solution.

> ## *"Knives donned in end-of-the-day celluloid are instantly recognizable and truly unique in their mottled mixture of colors."*

Has this potential deterioration of the celluloid on pocketknives changed my opinion of purchasing and collecting celluloid knives? Not in the least. I still actively look for dramatic examples of glitter stripe, goldstone, cracked ice, candystripe, end of the day, butter and molasses,

and Christmas tree celluloids every chance I get. Knives dressed in these spectacular celluloid handles exhibit a dramatic beauty not found in any other object. As an example of the cutler's art, they are both finely tuned instruments and artistic expressions all in one package.

Because of the number of knife companies that used celluloids, the search for beautiful celluloid knives continues to this day. There are knife collectors who specialize in specific brands, patterns and colors, and the search for mint or near-mint examples has escalated to a frantic pace. The Internet auctions have only heightened the awareness of the value of these beautiful examples as they continue to appreciate in price. ●

5-Alarm Steel: Knives of the Firefighters

Sample some of the first blades firemen reach for when they hear "Code Red!"

By Joe Kertzman

LISTENING TO NEW YORK fireman Larry Guyett talk, you know he has responded to countless fire calls, entered charred buildings, fought back blazes and relied heavily on knives to cut him and others out of desperate situations. So what knives does he call to duty?

"I'm a knife guy and a fireman," he says. "I've got knives from Spyderco, Microtech and other manufacturers. I planned on bringing my Benchmade 710 into work tonight, but I've been carrying a Columbia River Knife & Tool M16-14. I usually pair it up with a Swiss Army knife [SAK]. I have a Victorinox Soldier right now. It's a little stouter than other SAKs.

"Here's the thing. When I came on the job 13 years ago, guys carried SAKs, stockmans and Buck 110s," he remarks. "There was a shift into tactical folders, but it was a price-sensitive shift. Not many firefighters can afford to carry hundred-dollar Benchmades. They're afraid to lose or break them."

The CRKT M16-14FD (Fire Department) is a locking-liner folder designed by Kit Carson with a 3.94-inch, black-titanium-nitride-coated AUS-8 tanto blade and a Carson Flipper. The Flipper is an extension at the base of the blade to speed opening. A red G-10

New York firefighter Larry Guyett swears by the Kit Carson-designed Columbia River Knife & Tool M16-14FD (Fire Department) as the ideal knife for the job. He is especially hooked on the Carson Flipper, an extension at the base of the blade that aids in opening. Guyett says the gloves he and other firemen wear are thick and heavy when wet, and stiff when dry. He prefers the Flipper to thumb studs for ease of operation wearing the gloves.

"It's like a tackle box that closes with hard latches," he details. "Someone had closed the lid on a roll of tape. I couldn't open the latches, and a crowd of people wanted me to do something. I jammed the tanto blade of the M16 behind one latch and, boom, popped it open. Then I jammed it behind the second latch and popped it."

> *"Our gloves are thick and heavy when wet, and stiff when dry. I can't feel a thumb stud wearing stiff gloves."*
> —Larry Guyett

Guyett wishes he could carry every tool appropriate for every emergency. Ideally, he would match the right tool for the right job, but he can't lug around that much equipment. Ethan Becker, president of Becker Knife & Tool, had similar sentiments expressed to him during conversations with S.W.A.T. team members, particularly from John Benner, the current head of the Tactical Defense Institute.

"John told me, in his opinion, exactly what the S.W.A.T. guys wanted," Becker says. "That's what I made—a pry bar with a sharp edge that you could use to beat on things. Like the S.W.A.T. guys, firemen can use it to open doors and windows."

Personal Entry Tool

"The TacTool is designed to be a 'personal entry tool.' If you use a battering ram to bust through a door, you drop it when you're done. You don't take it past the front door. The TacTool is something you keep on you once you're inside," Becker explains. The Becker Knife & Tool TacTool is a monster of a knife with a 7-inch, flat-ground 0170-6C high-carbon-steel blade. Rather than coming to a point, the tip of the blade is flat, like a sharpened chisel. A short, secondary edge juts down at a 45-degree angle, leading into a long, half-serrated main edge. The black, epoxy-powder-coated blade incorporates a sharpened rescue hook similar to a gut hook. A black, molded GV-6H handle anchors the knife. MSRP: $149.95.

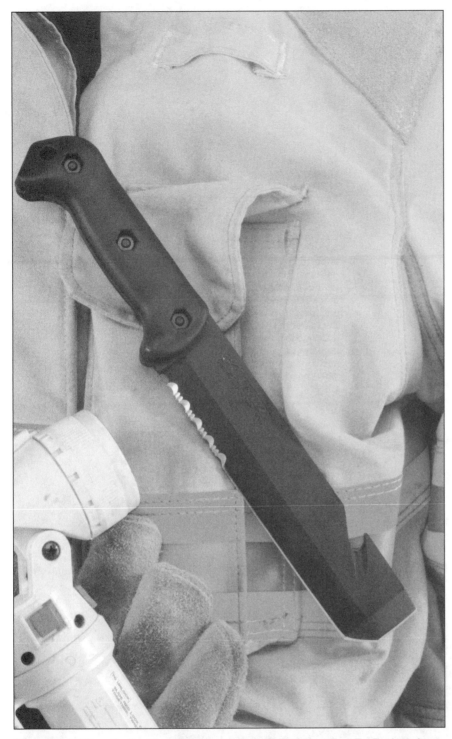

According to Ethan Becker, the front edge of the Becker Knife & Tool TacTool can be wedged between a door and its jam, or the 45-degree edge can be used like a sharpened hammer for hacking through a door. "EMTs use it because, among other things, that bend at the tip is ideal for beating through reinforced glass," he says, "and the hook on the blade is there for firemen who tend to reach out and pull things down, clearing glass and debris."

handle, stainless-steel liners and a LAWKS (Lake and Walker Knife Safety) complete the package. The manufacturer's suggested retail price (MSRP): $89.99.

"The thing I like about the M16-14 is the Carson Flipper. There's no better folding knife made that I can open wearing gloves," Guyett says. "Our gloves are thick and heavy when wet. As they dry out, they get stiff. I can't feel a thumb stud wearing stiff gloves."

In describing a recent emergency call, Guyett relates, "We responded to one call for a 'child struck' [struck by a car]. Traffic was backed up, and we were dealing with emotionally charged people. We parked about 200 feet from where the kid was, and I approached with a trauma box in hand.

"The front edge can be wedged between a door and its jam, or the 45-degree edge can be used like a sharpened hammer for hacking through a door," Becker allows. "EMTs use it because, among other things, that bend at the tip is ideal for beating through reinforced glass. The hook on the blade is there for firemen who tend to reach out and pull things down, clearing glass and debris."

Firefighting knives are readily available, yet, as Becker stresses, firemen and law enforcement officers are forced to be frugal. "They'll buy knives but usually their administrators won't pay for them," he says.

"I don't carry any specific brand," Chicago Fire Department battalion chief Rich Edgeworth says. "I carry knives for cutting seat belts, into upholstery and

> *"The hook on the blade is there for firemen who tend to reach out and pull things down."*
> —Ethan Becker

things of that nature, but they're not issued by the fire department. The one on my dresser is an inexpensive knife with a 3-inch, half-serrated blade that says 'Imperial Ireland Stainless' on it [an Imperial Schrade folder].

"I use it to cut rubber gaskets from around car windshields, stuff like that," Edgeworth remarks. "Sometimes you can't get to the gasket easily, so you have to bend the blade sideways a bit. The knives have to be sturdy, and not only for car rescues, but if someone is entangled in wires on a fire call, you have to cut the person loose."

People do get tangled in wires during household, industrial and office fires, Guyett concurs. "The computers we have today entail wires that are often channeled through walls and ceilings. You have heat and dryer ducts with small wires coiled inside to make them flexible, phone lines, fax lines and more. All of these things drop out of ceilings in fires," Guyett says. "I choose a folding knife I can reach, and one that opens easily with one gloved hand."

Edgeworth and others in his department also carry boot knives with 3-to-5-inch blades, usually

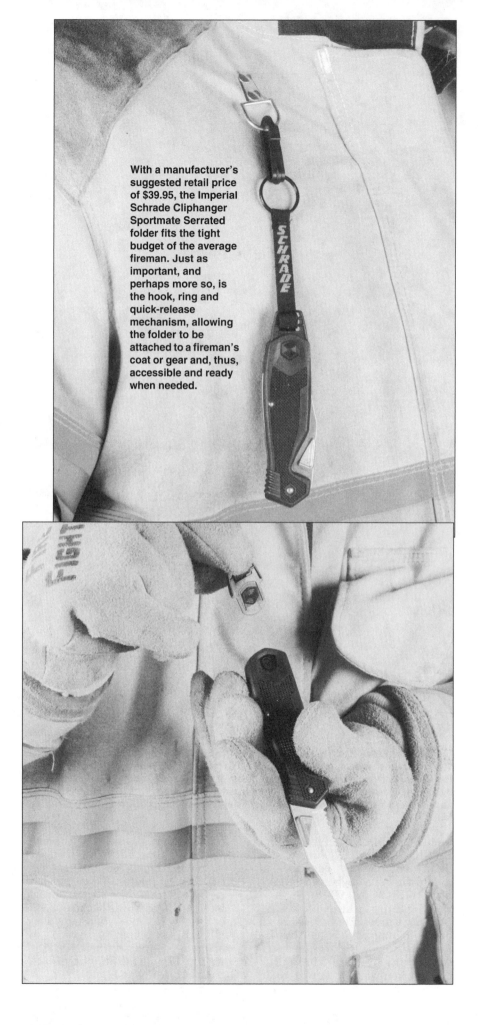

With a manufacturer's suggested retail price of $39.95, the Imperial Schrade Cliphanger Sportmate Serrated folder fits the tight budget of the average fireman. Just as important, and perhaps more so, is the hook, ring and quick-release mechanism, allowing the folder to be attached to a fireman's coat or gear and, thus, accessible and ready when needed.

dagger style, in leather sheaths or pouches. "If you get into a situation where you can't get at your pack, you can usually reach your boot," he says.

If Les Halpern of Phantom Knives had his way, all firemen would have a Rip Cord Rescue II at the ready, a knife, he notes, that can be carried in several positions, including attached to equipment and gear. The knife features a projectile-style (not automatic or gravity) opening mechanism and a chisel-ground and inwardly curved, retractable 154CM blade complete with sharp rescue hook and safety tip. It also sports an aluminum frame with lanyard, and an orange G-10 handle. MSRP: $219.99.

Popsicle-Stick Blade

"We came up with a Cordura® wrap-around sheath that attaches to the Blade-Tech 'Tek-Lok,' a hinged buckle for web gear or a service belt," Halpern explains. "With the knife enveloped in the sheath, firemen don't have to worry about it catching on anything. When the blade is retracted, it is attached to a connecting rod that looks like a Pop-

> *"Someone asked me what the melting temperature of G-10 was, and I said, 'higher than yours.'"*
> —Les Halpern

sicle stick. When you tug on the lanyard to remove the knife from its sheath, the rod simultaneously pulls out the blade.

"Firemen can wear the Rip Cord Rescue on respirator pack straps or attached to suspenders underneath their coats," he adds.

With the Rip Cord Rescue II, Phantom Knives makes a solid effort at shoring up the problem of a fireman fumbling to open a folder while he is wearing thick, stiff gloves. According to Halpern, the hook on the blade is ideal for disentangling people from chords and wires.

"We've cut up to 12-strand wire with the rescue hook, the kind of wire in residential or industrial electrical work," he says. "It will

cut boots or shoes off of people and works slick on shoe or boot laces and clothing.

"We did some research on cutting edges and found that the hawk-bill-style blade cuts rope and webbing best," Halpern adds. "It captures material inside the curve, and the safety tip is imperative up against people's bodies when cutting seat belts or clothing."

The bright-orange, textured G-10 handle serves an equally important purpose. "We used orange because we found that, if you drop a red-handle knife in the dark, it looks almost black and disappears. The most visible color we could get in G-10 is 'international orange.'" Halpern says. "Someone asked me what the melting temperature of G-10 was, and I said, 'higher than yours.'"

Guyett agrees that the handle melting isn't a primary concern. "I wear a rubber face piece and a plastic helmet," he says. "If the temperature is hot enough for my knife to melt, I won't survive. I think knife loss is more of a concern for firemen. I lost a Spyderco Rescue that was clipped to the pocket of my bunker coat. It hap-

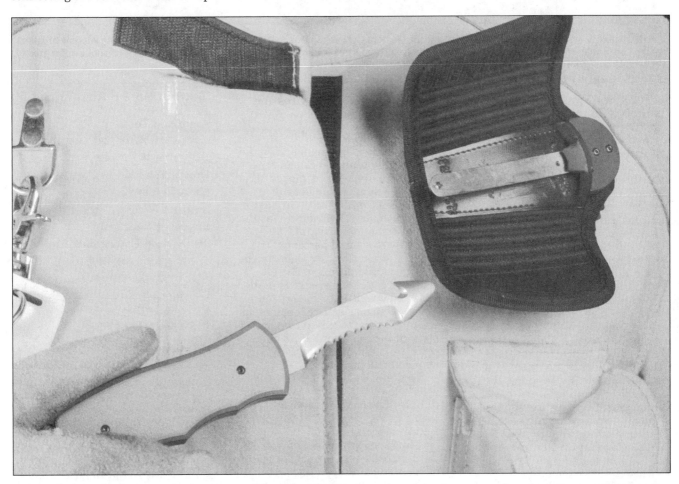

If Les Halpern of Phantom Knives had his way, all firemen would have a Rip Cord Rescue II at the ready, a knife, he notes, that can be carried in several positions, including attached to equipment and gear. The knife features a projectile-style (not automatic or gravity) opening mechanism and a chisel-ground and inwardly curved, retractable 154CM blade complete with sharp rescue hook and safety tip. It also sports an aluminum frame with lanyard, and an orange G-10 handle.

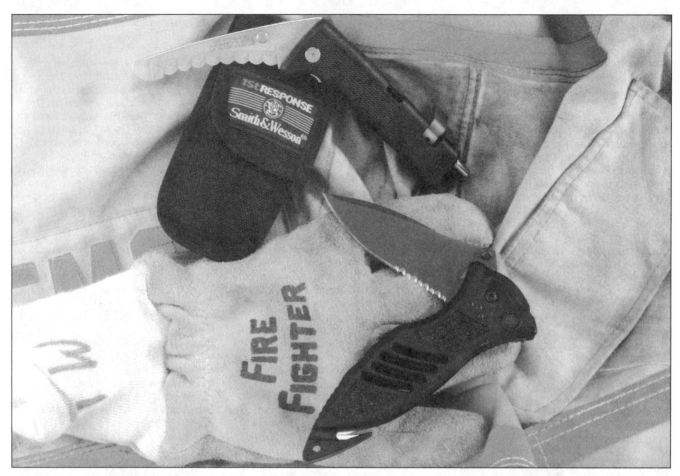

Both the Smith & Wesson First Response (top) and the Masters Of Defense Duane Dieter CQD folder are equipped with window breakers, but the similarities stop there. Handle and blade shapes and materials, locking mechanisms, lengths, thickness and prices differ greatly, but each is built with firefighting duties in mind.

pened when I was putting my air pack away in the truck, and it must have sprung the pocket clip."

Guyett believes that the recessed buttons on most automatics are too difficult to press wearing the thick gloves most firemen are issued. On the other hand, Jim Ray of Masters Of Defense defends automatics in certain situations. "In a lot of ways, an automatic is a good solution for emergency personnel. One of the big advantages of an auto, as far as I'm concerned, is that it can be locked closed and dropped down into a pocket or uniform pouch without the worry that it will come open," he says.

The Masters Of Defense Duane Dieter CQD Special Operations Tactical Folder is available in manual and automatic versions, the latter for certain military, law enforcement and fire personnel. Among its many features are a 3 3/4-inch, half-serrated or plain, black-titanium-carbonitride-coated 154CM blade and a plunge lock with secondary safety lock. The 6061-T6 aluminum handle has an integral, milled side hilt, a window breaker, a stainless pocket clip and a utility blade for cutting cords,

bands, tape, flex cuffs, wires and straps. MSRP: $299.98.

Support Blade

"The knife is large enough so the push-button plunge lock can be engaged easily wearing gloves," Ray says. "The support blade can rip right down clothing without having to worry about a live point near the skin of an accident victim."

Fires are a small percent of the calls the Rochester Fire Department responds to, according to Guyett, who says gas leaks, electrical problems and water problems are more common. "In an electrical emergency, you might have to take a switch plate off the wall. If it has 18 coats of paint around it, you might score it with a knife," he notes.

"In a fire, we have to cover the vent holes cut in the roof with plastic or tar paper. You cut the covering with a knife," he adds. "If you douse a burning mattress, the fire might look like it is out, but when you cut the mattress open, it's still burning inside. You cut it open and wet it down again, then cut it again. You could sink a burning mattress to the bottom of a lake and it would still be smoldering inside."

Several More 5-Alarm Knives*

American Tomahawk
   Vietnam Tactical Tomahawk
Benchmade Rescue Stryker
Emerson SARK
Ontario RTAK
Smith & Wesson First Response
Spyderco Rescue Jr.
Timberline Emergency
   Management Tool
TOPS Smoke Jumper
United Colt Firefighter
Victorinox Fireman
   Swiss Army Knife

*There are others.

Guyett's ideal fireman's knife is one he could carry in his pocket around the firehouse but attach to his air pack in an emergency. "I'd like to see it come with a Kydex® sheath that has some kind of ring I could clip to my air pack," he says. "If I respond to a call that requires me to suit up, I could take it out of my pocket and pop it into the sheath on the strap of the air pack." ●

Carry the Right Knife for the Job

There's more than one way to skin a rabbit, but using a machete or kukri isn't the smartest

By Hank Reinhardt

KNIVES AND SWORDS have been a passion of mine since I can remember. My dad was a meat cutter and knew quite well what a sharp blade could do. He tried to keep knives away from me, but after I reached 12 years old, he threw up his hands in despair. Like the proverbial kid who accidentally took out his own eye with an air rifle, my dad was convinced I was likely to cut off my arm with a knife. He proceeded to teach me how to use a knife properly—and how not to cut off my arm!

Dad was largely successful, as I have all four of my limbs.

One thing my dad managed to instill in me is to use the proper knife for the job. He was primarily talking about cleavers and butcher knives, but it applies to other knife tasks and, for that matter, to life in general.

All too often, people find that they have the wrong knife for the job at hand. Sometimes it's too much knife, sometimes too little. I have a great fondness for the kukri, but it really isn't suited for everything, so I think about what it is I *intend* to do with the knife, as well as what I might *have* to do with a blade.

Recently, I spent a weekend with a couple of friends in a cabin out in the boonies. Neither of these two guys is an out-doorsman, so each one foolishly looked to me to bring what we needed. When we got there, fire-wood was in abundance, but no kindling, no axe and no available wood within lazy walking distance. I had a small folder in my pocket and a Cold Steel SRK on my

> "It's awkward to skin a squirrel with a 12-inch bowie knife, and tedious to skin an elk with a caping knife."

belt. We did find an old hammer, thus we hammered the blade of the SRK through the firewood and split off enough to get the fire started.

The knife held up to the pounding and, my compliments to Cold Steel, the blade kept its edge quite well. But the knife was not intended for that purpose, and it would have been a lot easier if I had a large bowie, a

kukri or a small axe. It's awkward to skin a squirrel with a 12-inch bowie knife, and tedious to skin an elk with a caping knife.

What activity do you have planned? Is it a hunting trip, a casual camping trip, or an extensive hike along the Appalachian Trail? Interestingly enough, each of these presents its particular requirements and, to not be caught short, requires some prior thought.

Take hunting. The game you hunt will dictate in many ways what type of skinning knife you carry, and much depends on personal preference. I have friends who swear by blades with sharpened hook-like extensions known as "gut hooks." Others like drop-point blades, and some think that if a trailing point was good enough for their great granddaddy, it's good enough for them.

Recently, the author spent a weekend with a couple of friends in a cabin out in the boonies. When they got there, firewood was in abundance, but no kindling, no axe and no available wood. The author had a Cold Steel SRK on his belt. He hammered the blade of the SRK through the firewood and split off enough to get the fire started. The blade kept its edge quite well, but the knife was not intended for that purpose, and it would have been easier if he had a large bowie, a kukri or a small axe.

> **"You don't need a machete or a kukri in the arctic wilderness, and a 4-inch utility knife is damn-near worthless in the jungles of Brazil."**

Small Knife Skins Squirrel

The type of skinning knife you carry depends not only on your preference, but also on what you are hunting. Just as important, and maybe more so, is where you will be hunting. In your backyard hunting squirrels, a small knife, something with about a 3-to-4-inch blade, is about all you'll need.

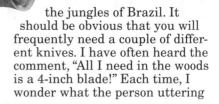

Northwest, or the cold tundra of Alaska and Canada? All of these are vastly different, and each will have varying requirements.

You don't need a machete or a kukri in the arctic wilderness, and a 4-inch utility knife is damn-near worthless in

But what about the desert Southwest, or the swamps in Florida, Louisiana and South Georgia, the rain forest of the Pacific

the jungles of Brazil. It should be obvious that you will frequently need a couple of different knives. I have often heard the comment, "All I need in the woods is a 4-inch blade!" Each time, I wonder what the person uttering

The Becker Knife & Tool Patrol Machete, available from Camillus Cutlery Co., is a reincarnation of a Filipino *Parang*, or jungle knife. Essentially, Parangs were weapons as well as tools, and each did its job quite well. In the series of photos, Ethan Becker of Becker Knife & Tool uses the Patrol Machete as a drawknife (top left), to make a maul, as well as to make other camp items by using the maul to drive the machete through a tree limb.

> *"What feels good in the sporting goods store may be heavy as the devil after three hours of trudging uphill. It was once said that you could follow the line of march of a Confederate army by the D-guard bowies lying on the road. This I can well appreciate."*

such nonsense would do if required to build an overnight shelter or cut through a thick branch.

On another level, I hear one person or another talk about having a good double-edged fighting knife, and that's all that's needed. While I like doubled-edged knives for weapons, I much prefer single-edged blades for "using" knives. I think they are more versatile, or able to perform more tasks.

Another important consideration is how far one will be from civilization. We all like to get as far away as possible, but knowing how far is half the battle. In an emergency, is it five miles, 50 miles, or even 500 miles to go for help? This becomes increasingly important when you journey to another continent. Find out what you can expect, and then try to prepare for the unexpected.

If it is unexpected, how can you prepare for it? Consider what you plan to do, then think of what you might need if everything falls apart.

Other than utility, there is another factor that the knife user must take into consideration: the weight of the knife. What feels good in the sporting goods store may be heavy as the devil after three hours of trudging uphill. It was once said that you could follow the march of a Confederate army by the D-guard bowies lying on the road. This I can well appreciate.

The first time I went on a long hike, I cussed everything I was carrying. After a time in the U.S. Army, I became aware at all times of the weight I was lugging around. When I was married and raising my kids, I tried pawning off the heavy stuff on my wife and daughters, but that didn't work either. The only thing left was to carefully consider the weight before we set out.

I can't tell you how to prepare for everything, and I don't even know how myself. I can only give you some idea of the knives, and what tasks they best perform. So let's look at some of the knives, and what they do best.

Machetes

Machetes are useful in light brush and jungle country, and are superb at clearing a path through high grasses and thick underbrush. Machetes are quite lightweight and, when properly used, are not nearly as tiring as you might think.

The machete should be kept razor sharp. In clearing brush, it should be swung lightly, letting the sharpness of the blade do the most work. When forced to do heavy work, like cutting some of the scuppernong vines that grow here in Georgia, you need a heavier blade. The force required to cut through some of these vines requires an axe or a kukri, as these vines are tough. This is a good example of using the right blade for the job. The vines can be cut with a machete. It's just that it requires more work to do so.

There are several excellent machetes on the market at present. Tramontina of Brazil makes a full line of inexpensive, but serviceable machetes. Camillus and Ontario

also make some good blades. One of the best is the Bolo machete from Cold Steel. This is patterned somewhat on the old U.S. Army bolo. Largely, the standard bolo is patterned after Filipino jungle knives that were encountered during the Philippine Insurrection in the late 19th century.

The jungle knives of the Filipinos are too numerous and varied to be described here. Essentially, they were weapons as well as tools, and each did its job quite well. In combat, as in doing heavy work, you need a slightly heavier blade than a machete. As I said earlier, it can be done, it's just more work. And as my wife and kids will tell you, I am a lazy man.

The Kukri

Next in line is the kukri. This is my personal favorite of the heavy work knives. The Gurkhas have made it famous as a weapon, but it is basically a work knife, and the "best of show," in my opinion. Sometimes, though, it is difficult

> *"In clearing brush, a machete should be swung lightly, letting the sharpness of the blade do the most work."*

for those not familiar with a kukri to use it to its full potential. You have to learn how to cut with it.

The trick is not to overexert yourself, or to use a great deal of force when you cut with the kukri. Instead, just before the blade strikes, you snap your wrist. This imparts a greater amount of momentum to the blade, but, since it is only done with the wrist, you don't get quite so tired. Once you learn, you can get a lot of output with little effort. It can be used to drive tent pegs, chop down small trees, cut firewood, turn over hamburgers on a grill and dig holes. It does not clear brush as well as a

machete. It is simply too short to do that effectively.

In the past 15 years or so, many kukri-shaped knives have come onto the market. With a good edge, I'm sure that each will cut well. I simply have not cut with all of them. Of the ones that I have used, my two favorites are at the opposite ends of the price spectrum. On the top end is the Cold Steel Gurkha Kukri. I have used it extensively, and it holds a good edge and cuts as well as any kukri I have handled.

Much less expensive is the Atlanta Cutlery Indian Army Kukri. Once sharpened, this cuts as well as any, and it's the perfect knife for throwing in the back of the car or pickup and forgetting about it. I can brag a little here, as I was instrumental in getting Bill Adams of Atlanta Cutlery to carry it. This was long before I started working with Bill, but I still pitched a fit. I really liked kukris, but at that time they were hard to come by, and few and far between.

In the past 15 years or so, many kukri-shaped knives have come onto the market. On the top end is the Cold Steel Gurkha Kukri, a knife the author has handled extensively and vouches for, saying it holds a good edge and cuts as well as any kukri.

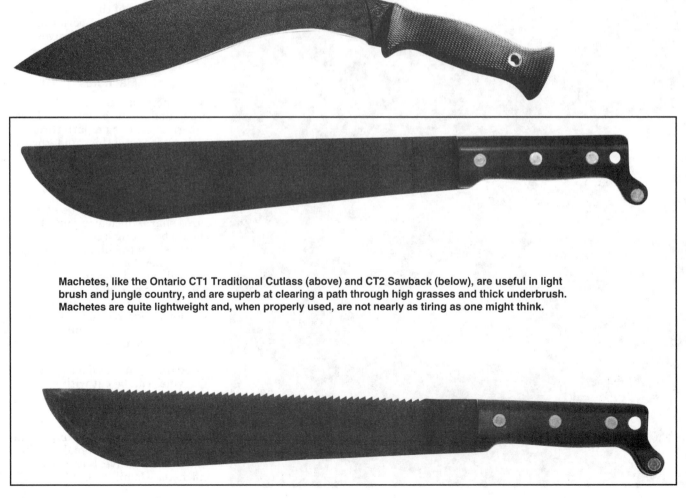

Machetes, like the Ontario CT1 Traditional Cutlass (above) and CT2 Sawback (below), are useful in light brush and jungle country, and are superb at clearing a path through high grasses and thick underbrush. Machetes are quite lightweight and, when properly used, are not nearly as tiring as one might think.

> ## *"A kukri can be used to drive tent pegs, chop down small trees, cut firewood, turn over hamburgers on a grill and dig holes."*

The Bowie Knife

The bowie is probably the most popular of the large knives in the country. It comes in many sizes, from small 4-inch blades to large 16-inch short swords. The most popular size range falls between 7-to-10 inches. The bowie gained well-deserved fame as a fighting knife, but it is splendid as an all-around utility knife, too. It can double as a camp knife, a chef's knife or a skinning knife. You can also eat with one if you're careful enough. If you're not, then you can get some nice scars.

One caution on bowies: there is a set belief system that the thicker the better. As a result, you'll encounter bowies with 3/8-inch-thick blades, and I ran across one that was a full 1/2-inch thick! Unless the blade is sharply ground, it can be too heavy.

Windlass Steelcrafts is bringing back some excellent reproductions of original bowie designs; C.A.S. Iberia imports some excellent bowies from Muela and Hanwei Knives; and the Cold Steel Trail Master series is plumb full of fine bowie knives.

Camp Knives

Camp knives are essentially bowies without back or double edges. They are a real necessity for any camper planning to stay in the wilderness for more than a couple of nights. Camp knives are considered to be the real working knives in the field. One advantage a camp knife has over a bowie is the lack of a back edge. This allows you to pound on it if needed, and can also allow you to grip the spine of the blade for detail cutting work. The maneuver is dangerous, and I don't recommend it. It should only be done in an emergency, and if you're smart, you carry another small knife on your belt for such chores.

Small Knives

I consider a small, general-purpose knife to be nearly as much of a necessity as I do a large camp, bowie or kukri. While I believe that a large knife is the most important, the small knife comes in a close second. SOG makes two knives that I favor, the X-42 Field Knife and the slightly smaller Field Pup. Both of these small knives are light, and easy to carry and use. The same can be said for the Pendleton Hunter from Cold Steel.

Skinning Knives

I bring up skinning knives last because everyone has a different idea of what best suits them, and I'm no different. A small deer can be skinned easily with a small knife. You can skin an elk with a small knife, but not so easily. A slightly larger knife would be better. If you plan to save the hide, a small caping knife is ideal for not puncturing the skin. Frequently a folder will suffice, but you do need a small blade for the fine work.

I would like to see some statistics on the types of skinning knives people prefer. Having been in the business for many years, I still can't tell you what knife is the most popular. I have a hunch (but that is all it is) that it's the drop-point skinner. The name "drop point" is derived from the way the point of the blade drops below the spine so, when skinning wild game with the edge up, the point is also up. This means you have less chance of cutting into the stomach when skinning. The drop point is also quite useful as a general-purpose knife.

A gut hook does the same thing, and a little better. Still, the hook tends to catch on things when performing other cutting chores. Alas, everything is a trade off.

The kukri is the author's personal favorite of the heavy work knives. The Atlanta Cutlery Military Issue Kukri Knives cut as well as any, and are the perfect knives for throwing in the back of the car or pickup and forgetting about until they are needed.

The bowie is probably the most popular knife in the country. It comes in many sizes, from small 4-inch blades to large 16-inch short swords. The most popular size range falls between 7-to-10 inches, like the Muela Tornado available from C.A.S. Iberia. It features a 7 1/8-inch stainless steel blade with partial serrations, a synthetic handle and a Nylon sheath.

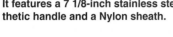

The trailing-point skinner has a long edge with a point that curves away from the back of the knife. This gives you a much longer stroke when skinning, which is effective. Trailing points are used by "professionals"—guys who skin out animals at slaughterhouses—and, being quite thin, trailing points are employed strictly for skinning. The trailing point can also be a good utility knife. However, if the blade is too curved, then you have to be careful when cutting hard stuff like wood. The blade can slip and "skate" off the wood.

Dear Old Dad

Frankly, I think my dad had a tendency to exaggerate, and I don't believe that you will cut off an arm or a leg if you're not careful to use the right knife for the right job. You can, I admit, get some cool looking scars like mine.

I will leave you with some remarks by a close friend of mine who once commented, "My wife and kids all say that I'm paranoid. But when something happens, and I solve the problem, they say I'm well prepared. After its over with, then I'm paranoid again."

I guess if you take the right knife for the job, you'll save both wife and limb!

●

Small, general-purpose knives are nearly as much of a necessity as large camp, bowie or kukri knives. SOG Specialty Knives makes two edged tools that the author favors, the X-42 Field Knife and the slightly smaller Field Pup. Both of these small knives are light, and easy to carry and use.

Cop a Compact Saw and Get Cutting

If all else fails, bare your teeth in the woods

By Dexter Ewing

FOR THE OUTDOORSMAN in you, having a good compact saw is a must. A saw comes in handy for campers in the sense of processing firewood and cleaning up the camp area. Meanwhile, wily hunters use a saw for cutting through big bones of the (hopefully) proportionately big game they bag. Saws are also useful for handyman chores and yard care tasks. Anyone who takes part in these activities could benefit from owning a quality compact saw.

The saws you will read about in this article fall into one of two categories: fixed blade and folding. The latter can be a single-blade dedicated saw, a part of a multi-blade configuration, such as the venerable Swiss Army Knife (SAK), or maybe even an implement in a multi-tool. Whatever saw you choose, make sure it is one that can be carried easily, which is especially important

It's hard to believe so many compact saws have hit the market, but it just goes to show the popularity and effectiveness of such outdoor tools. From bottom left is the Gerber Exchange-A-Blade Sport Saw, Outdoor Edge Griz-Saw, Corona RS7041 Razor Tooth Pruning Saw and Buck Knives Grip Saw.

for campers, hunters and hikers. Most fixed-blade saws come with belt sheaths, while folding saws are carried in pockets, as with the SAK's, or toted in belt sheaths.

The same rules of saw selection apply as they do with regular knives. Make sure the handle fits your hand comfortably. Given the nature of how a saw is used, you definitely want a secure and non-slip grip. In terms of blades, most of the compact saws on the market today have what is known as pull-cut teeth. This means the saw only cuts on the pull stroke for a smooth, back-and-forth sawing motion without binding.

> ## "Since it doesn't raise any hot spots on your hand, you can work longer and more effectively."

Another important thing to mention is teeth per inch (TPI). Within 1 inch of the length of the blade, there is a set amount of teeth. The lower the number per inch, the more aggressive the blade will be at cutting. For instance, a saw blade with 9 TPI is better suited to pruning tasks than one that has 17 TPI. Higher TPI blades are more useful for cutting jobs like carpentry work where a finer cut is desired. With these guidelines in mind, sit back and check out a random sampling of some of the compact saws that are available on the market.

The Buck Knives Grip Saw

Buck Knives' Grip Saw is one of many edged tools the company unveiled in 2002, the year Buck celebrated its 100th year of manufacturing knives. The Grip Saw features a 5-1/2-inch, 9 TPI steel blade and a highly ergonomic, molded-Kraton® handle. The handle design incorporates a finger hole where the user's index finger is inserted for better purchase, and a deep recess on the handle spine is strategically located where the thumb naturally rests in such a grip. The width of the handle is oversized, and the Kraton is a bit tactile, also adding purchase.

For durability, the tang of the saw blade runs the entire length of the handle. Each Grip Saw comes with a molded, high-impact-plastic slip sheath that covers the blade when not in use, and two strong magnets on the inside of the sheath opening ensure the blade locks in place. In the author's opinion, the only disadvantage of the Grip Saw's sheath is the lack of a belt clip or loop for ease of carry and access. Regardless, the saw is undoubtedly one of the most comfortable fixed blades of its type, thanks, in part, to the handle design.

Given the nature of how saws are employed, a crucial feature on any saw is the handle. It has to be comfortable enough for extended use without causing hand discomfort. As its name suggests, the Grip Saw is comfortable to hold. You can feel the security of the finger hole grip, which, in turn, gives you the confidence to put pressure on the blade to make the cut. In use, the Grip Saw is an efficient cutter. Since it doesn't raise any hot spots on your hand, you can work longer and more effectively. With the blade safely encased within the sheath, the Grip Saw is compact enough to toss in a backpack or carry in a back pocket. The manufacturer's suggested retail price (MSRP): $24.

Gerbe's Exchange-A-Blade Sport Saw

Gerber's Exchange-A-Blade Sport Saw is perhaps the nicest folding saw of the bunch here. The author has owned one for a few short years and used it many times to prune trees and cut out saplings. This is certainly a folding saw for serious use. It comes with a 9 TPI coarse-cut blade, making short work of pruning tasks, and a 17 TPI fine-tooth blade

that works well as a bone saw or for general carpentry chores.

Both blades measure 6-1/2 inches in length and are interchangeable in the handle. For user safety, each blade locks in the open and closed positions, and the lock is released with a firm push of a button located on the pivot of the handle. To switch blades, back out the pivot screw all the way (no tools required) and, while grasping the blade, depress the lock button. The blade will be liberated of the handle.

To insert the other blade, reverse the procedure and you're good to go! The handle of the Exchange-A-Blade Sport Saw is molded, high-

> ## "The author has owned one for a few short years and used it many times to prune trees and cut out saplings."

impact plastic, flaring at both ends to create integral guards and prevent forward or backward slipping. In addition, there are inlays of textured Kraton rubber that make this saw comfortable to use.

Speaking of use, the Exchange-A-Blade Sport Saw cuts like a dream. The rounded handle profile makes the Kraton inlays bulge out as to fill your grip nicely. Of the saws evaluated here, this one has the most aggressive teeth and, therefore, makes quick work of any pruning job. Each saw comes with a heavy-duty Cordura® belt sheath with Velcro flap closure. The secondary blade, safely encased in a clear plastic protective sleeve, rides

Bear MGC's Pocket Tool offers versatility with its multiple foldout implements, one of which is a pull-cut saw blade. The slim profile allows the Pocket Tool to be carried easily in—where else—the pocket.

in a separate pocket behind the saw itself. With two interchangeable blades, a great handle shape and a nice belt sheath, you'll be hard-pressed to find another folding saw that packs as much punch for its price. MSRP: $32.95

Corona Clipper Razor Tooth

Though not a knife manufacturer, one might recognize the Corona Clipper name. Based in Corona, California, the company manufactures high-quality consumer and professional-grade pruning tools, such as bypass loppers, hedge shears, pole pruning blades and handsaws, to name a few. In an article discussing compact saws, it would be amiss to omit an offering from Corona Clipper. The Model RS7041 Razor Tooth Pruning Saw is just one of many folding pruning saws in Corona Clippers' Professional Series.

The saw features a 7-inch, pull-cut, 8 TPI blade that has deep, aggressively ground teeth. The blade is set into a plastic handle with a molded, ribbed-rubber grip. The rear portion of the handle curves downward, forming a hook to ensure an even, powerful pull stroke for effective cutting action.

The handle features a blade lock similar to lock-back folding knives. Push down on one end of the lock-bar, and the opposite end rises, allowing the blade to be freely rotated to the closed position. The saw's blade lock is positive yet easy

"In action, this saw has a voracious, insatiable appetite for wood."

to release thanks to the raised portion of the lock-bar. As with other dedicated folding saws, the blade also locks closed for the user's safety. The Razor Tooth Pruning Saw's blade can be replaced when the need arises by backing out a large screw.

The aggressive teeth help make quick work of small-to-medium-sized pruning and sawing jobs. In action, this saw has a voracious, insatiable appetite for wood. The aggressive pull-cut teeth really do an effective job at making a fast but clean cut in the least amount of time. Certainly, it is something to expect from the pruning tool experts. One can locate the Corona Clipper Razor Tooth Pruning Saw at large hardware/home centers such as Home Depot, and also from specialty retailers or websites that sell tools for professional landscapers. The saw retails for $22.22.

Outdoor Edge Griz-Saw

Outdoor Edge has established itself as a major player in the hunting knife market. No doubt, the Griz-Saw has helped Outdoor Edge

achieve its reputation. It is a fixed-blade saw but that is where the similarities with other fixed blades ends. The Griz-Saw sports a T-shaped handle (similar to that of a push dagger) molded of textured Kraton rubber, a design that permits the user's hand to remain in-line with the wrist for a comfortable sawing motion.

The 9 TPI, 8-inch blade has pull-cut teeth, and the blade can be replaced by loosening one nut with a wrench (not included). Each Griz-Saw comes with a sturdy, molded-Zytel® sheath showcasing a split-ring and spring-loaded clip to attach the saw to a belt loop or backpack for convenient carry. The Griz-Saw securely locks into the sheath so it won't accidentally fall out, yet it is quickly extracted by using Outdoor Edge's patented one-hand release mechanism.

When put to use, the advantages of the Griz Saw's T-shaped handle become apparent. The Kraton cushions your grip, and it locks the saw into your hand. Another advantage of the unique handle shape is that, by allowing the handle to dangle from between your index and middle fingers, you can effectively use your saw hand to pick up the wood you just cut. In other words, you can grab objects without having to set the saw down, and then return to sawing. The blade cuts smoothly and, in conjunction with the handle shape, the author found the Griz Saw to

Victorinox Swiss Army knives have long been favorites among outdoorsmen who like the choices resulting from multiple implements useful around the campsite or on hikes. The main blade of the Rucksack features a lock for user safety and convenience.

A trusted name in pruning tools for the discriminating landscape professional, Corona Clipper offers the RS7041 Razor Tooth Pruning Saw. Its aggressive tooth blade makes quick work of sizeable limbs. This premium folding saw features a blade lock that secures the blade in either the open or closed positions.

be easy and a pleasure to use. The MSRP is $24.99.

Victorinox Rucksack

Victorinox's Swiss Army knives have long been favored companions for those who enjoy the great outdoors. They have proven themselves to be real handy with multiple blades that serve equally well at the campsite as at home. There are several models of Victorinox SAK's that incorporate a saw blade, one of them being the Rucksack.

The Rucksack is one of the larger SAK's, incorporating a main blade that locks open for safe cutting. The saw blade on the Rucksack cuts on the push and pull strokes. Given the relatively short 11 TPI saw blade, experiencing cutting action on the pull and push strokes makes sense to maximize its effectiveness.

In action, the saw tended to bind more than pull-cut blades, so it wasn't the smoothest saw of the bunch.

The author found that larger limbs (1-1/2 to 2 inches in diameter) took longer and more effort to saw than smaller ones (1 inch in diameter or less). For occasional sawing on small limbs while hik-

ing, the Rucksack would be perfect. Besides the saw blade and a main knife blade, the Rucksack also packs a can opener/small flathead screwdriver blade, a bottle opener/large flathead screwdriver blade, reamer, corkscrew, and a tweezers and toothpick imbedded into the handle scales. All this makes for a handy all-around tool, something in which the other folding saws cannot boast! The MSRP: $35.

Bear MGC Cutlery Pocket Tool

Bear MGC Cutlery's Pocket Tool was designed as a compact toolbox of sorts, incorporating several implements, such as flathead and Phillips screwdrivers, a knife blade, and yes, a saw blade. All the tools fold up into a stainless steel handle measuring a little over 3-1/2 inches in length, so the Pocket Tool can be carried in the pocket, purse, glove compartment or briefcase.

The saw blade is 2-1/2 inches, making the Pocket Tool's saw the smallest of the bunch. It boasts 10 TPI with the teeth arranged in a pull-cut style. Given the relative small size of the blade, one is not going to tackle any big sawing tasks. This particular saw is good for jobs in tight spaces where one of the above mentioned saws would

have a hard time fitting and maneuvering, and for smaller sawing jobs that don't require a lot of force or an aggressive-toothed saw blade.

An example of such task would be selective pruning where a bigger saw blade would inadvertently contact with other tree limbs. The Bear MGC Pocket Tool has the smallest handle of the bunch reviewed here. Given the lack of texture on the handle, it can be a bit difficult to hold with wet or sweaty hands. However, like the Victorinox Rucksack, the Pocket Tool also has other tools housed in the handle so its versatility can be maximized.

Accompanying the saw is a plain-edge blade, and flathead and Phillips screwdrivers. The Pocket Tool is carried in the same manner as a regular multi-blade pocket knife—in the bottom of the pocket—though it weighs a bit more than some of the multi-blades out there. The MSRP is $32.

To Sweep the Dust

There are many other good compact saws to consider if you are in the market for one. Most are either fixed blades or folders, and dedicated saws or multi-blade tools in which the saw blade is one of the implements. SOG Specialty Knives offers the Power Lock multi-tool that has a foldout saw blade. Gerber Legendary Blades' 650 Evolution multi-tool has a replaceable Rem-Grit saw blade. As opposed to traditional ground-in saw teeth, the Rem-Grit saw blade boasts a fused-carbide cutting edge, resulting in smooth yet aggressive cutting action.

Remington Knives offers a double-blade Rattlesnake folding lockback hunter, which features a broad, drop-point main blade and a saw blade for cutting through bone or wood. Camillus Cutlery Co. is the official producer of the Buckmasters series of hunting knives, endorsed by the famous hunting organization. The Buckmasters folding saw has an aggressive pull-cut blade set into an orange handle with rubber inlays for improved grip.

Browning offers the F.D.T. (Field Dressing Tool), a three-blade folding hunter that has a clip-point blade, gut hook and saw blade. W.R. Case & Sons' XX-Changer parades four interchangeable blades, one of which is a saw. Coast Cut-

"Once the dust settles and the wood is stacked for the night, it's nice to know there are so many compact saws on the market."

lery's Ultimate Pocket Tool is a multi-blade gem with a foldout saw blade, as well as other useful implements. Schrade's Old Timer Buzz Saw Trapper is a lean cutting tool with a main clip-point blade, as well as a saw blade.

The ever-popular Leatherman Super Tool 200 offers locking implements and a handy saw blade. Wenger's Mountaineer multi-blade is also a part of the famous Swiss-made pocketknife brands. Its large saw blade tackles sizable limbs to help make campfires.

So, once the dust settles and the wood is stacked for the night, it's nice to know there are so many compact saws on the market for outdoors enthusiasts who choose to be well equipped in their environs. Remember, push, pull, push, pull, and have fun out there. ●

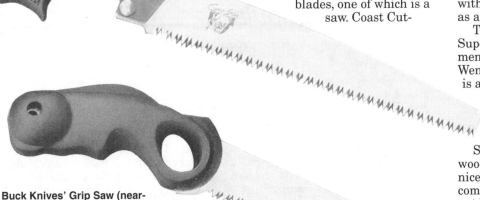

Buck Knives' Grip Saw (nearest) and Outdoor Edge's Griz Saw are fine examples of compact fixed-blade saws currently available. Both feature unique handle designs that promote user comfort.

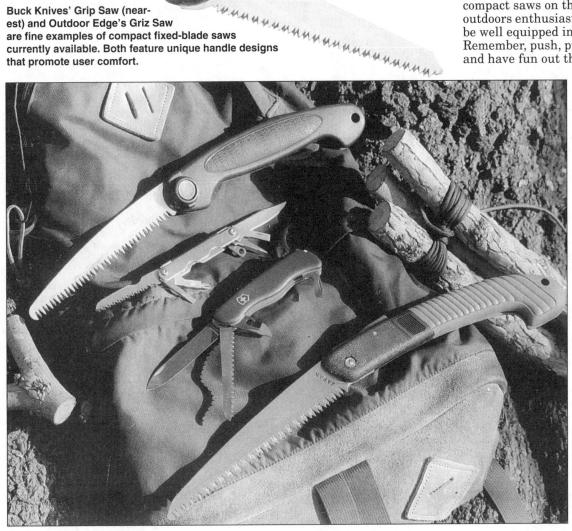

Ready for the knapsack or pack are (from top) Gerber Exchange-A-Blade Sport Saw, Bear MGC Pocket Tool, Victorinox Rucksack and Corona RS7041 Razor Tooth folding saw.

The Edge in Homeland Security

A review of the knife market reveals that tactical production knives have never been more popular

By Linda Moll Smith

About the author: *Linda Moll Smith is a health educator and journalist by trade, and on inactive status with the Texas State Guard. She says living in Texas accounts for why the bowie knife is her number one choice of blades.*

ANTHROPOLOGISTS THEORIZE THAT knives, primitively and painstakingly chipped out of rocks like basalt, flint, and granite, were the first tactical weapons of our hunter-and-gatherer forebears. The next step in weaponry design was the lashing of blades to branches or poles to make spears. Extension of reach was vital in fighting such fearsome beasts as saber-toothed tigers and woolly mammoths.

Centuries later, threats to mankind have evolved spectacularly beyond wild animals, yet carrying the essential edge—the tactical knife of one's choice for homeland security and defense—has remained essential for survival. As in caveman times, our modern versions of the tactical knife and cousin bayonet stand alone in efficiency. To put it bluntly, if close-quarters attack is your threat, a tactical knife should be at your side!

Another reason for the popularity of combat blades is their psychological appeal, also based on ancient archetypes. In terms of self-defense, our basic instinct is to oppose the enemy *mano a mano* (hand to hand). It's hard not to notice that most action movies are based on this construct. Even if the script calls for threats of nuclear

attack, the conflict plays out on a distinctly personal level, predictably ending with the protagonist and his evil nemesis engaged in heated hand-to-hand combat.

As psychologists who analyze these aspects of human nature are fond of pointing out, except for strangulation, dispatching an

enemy with a knife is the single most intimate form of defense.

Essentially, defense of hearth and homeland is an individual responsibility. That fact was emphasized two years ago, as our nation struggled to recover from the devastation and shock of the 9-11 terrorist attacks. While we wait to see what

changes the passage of the controversial Homeland Security Bill may bring, we will examine how tactical knife manufacturers and users, including armed forces units, have responded in the meantime.

In general, a review of the knife market reveals that tactical production knives have never been more popular. In fact, it would be easy for the casual buyer or knife neophyte to become overwhelmed by the variety of knife styles, blade sizes and steel standards available. Rather than attempt to catalogue all these choices, we will outline some representative models.

Begin the Beguine With the KA-BAR

A logical beginning to any discussion of tactical knives is the KA-BAR. Basic equipment for the U.S. Marine Corps (USMC) during World War II, this classic clip-point fixed blade has since vaulted to the top of the list for civilians as well. Much of the KA-BAR's popularity can be traced to combat lore retold by The Few and The Proud themselves, and also from commercialization of the KA-BAR and facsimiles that have become part of our cultural heritage.

"The tactical knife of one's choice for homeland security and defense has remained essential for survival."

Remember the TV heroes of the '80s, the A-Team? Howling Mad Murdock (Dwight Schultz), Face (Dirk Benedict) and Col. Decker (Lance LeGault) fought bad guys for 100 episodes between 1984 and 1987. If memory serves, these renegade commandoes were outfitted with KA-BAR look-alikes. Even earlier, in the 1960s, G.I. Joe was equipped with an oversized KA-BAR in both comic book and doll incarnations. And who can forget Arnold Schwarzenegger grabbing what looks like a KA-BAR out of a glass case at the pawnshop he visits before launching his island raid in 1985's "Commando."

Over a million of the original KA-BAR fighting knives were produced for the USMC by the Union Cutlery Co., with other armed services

branches adopting the knife as standard issue. Because demand exceeded supply, similar knives, licensed under other company trademarks, were also produced, although all were universally known as "KA-BARs." By 1952, KA-BAR had become such a household name, the Union Cutlery name was changed to KA-BAR Cutlery, Inc.

Although production of the original KA-BAR ceased immediately after World War II, similar versions were used by fighting men in the Korean, Vietnam and Desert Storm conflicts. Despite the underlying assumption that KA-BAR's are for killing, none of the veterans I interviewed for this article actually had to defend his life with his KA-BAR. One, a highly decorated veteran who survived injury and peril in two major conflicts, declared, "No, I never had to kill the enemy with a knife, and thank God. I probably would have thrown up afterwards if I had!"

Instead, veterans and civilians alike praised the KA-BAR for its versatility in everyday tasks, such as repairing equipment, opening ration cans, sharpening tent stakes, cutting fishing line and general woodsman use.

A testament to the KA-BAR's continuing reliability is the number of outlets that offer it for sale. Over 1,000 outlets worldwide feature KA-BAR's, and these include both exclusive dealers and non-exclusive mail-order catalog houses.

The traditional KA-BAR appears on the KA-BAR website (www.ka-bar.com) as the USMC Fighting/Utility Knife #1217. It features a 7-inch, epoxy-powder-coated 1095 blade wed with an oval-shaped, stacked-leather handle to create an 11-7/8-inch package housed in a USMC leather snap-top sheath. For around $60, it is an inexpensive and utilitarian piece of history to own.

Knifemaker Dan Harrison of Edom, Texas has kept his original KA-BAR from the time it was assigned to him at Camp Pendleton during the Korean War era. It's been a constant companion through his years of coaching a Marine Corps women's rifle team, his study with a world-champion fencing master, and situations as a police officer where he had to disarm knife-carrying suspects, all of which he describes as "not very exciting." Compared to what, Dan?

KA-BAR introduced a "new-school" D2 Combat Knife #1464 (or Spear Point #1461) in 2002. With a 6-inch, laser-cut, D-2 steel blade and a contoured-Micarta® handle,

The author poses (left) with Bill Hardwick, who retired as a Sgt. First Class after 23 years in the U.S. Army, specializing as a military policeman. Hardwick, who served in both Korea and Vietnam, holds a Timberline Zambezi fixed blade. A Greg Lightfoot design, the Zambezi stands at attention from the tip of its stout, half-serrated, 6-inch black blade to its olive drab handle. (*Overton and Smith photo*)

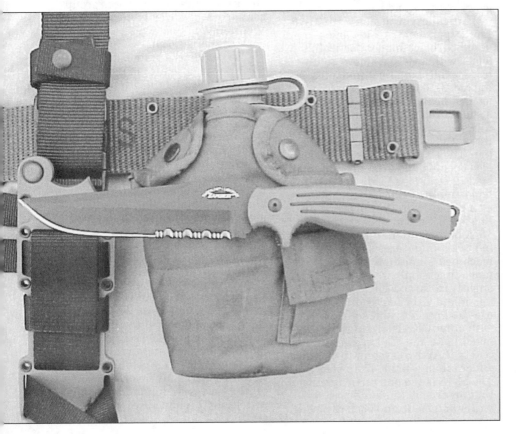

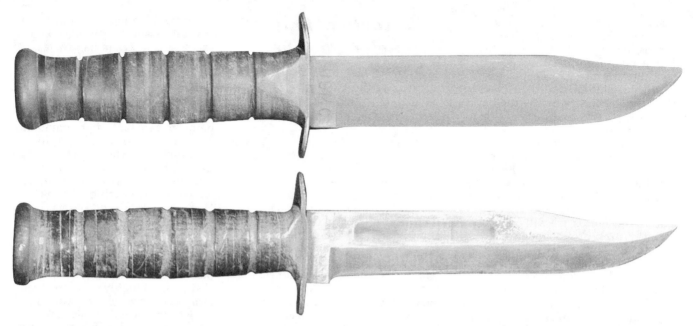

The top knife is a KA-BAR repro, about 5 years old, and the bottom knife, blade worn by use, is one owned by knifemaker Dan Harrison of Edom, Texas. It is Dan's original USMC blade issued to him at Camp Pendleton, in 1953, and he still carries it! (Harrison photo)

it is both handsome and intimidating for around $150. A $90 pick is the Warthog #1463, which, true to its name, boasts a stubby snout profile and a deep-rooting 3-5/8-inch blade combined with a contoured-Zytel® handle and ballistic-nylon Eagle sheath. Not to be overlooked is the 'piglet,' or folding Warthog, easier to carry than its boar-like brother but sporting an equally lethal blade, it is less than $50.

CRKT Arms Professionals with Able Blades

A subset of tactical knives can be identified with domestic police, fire and public safety officers. Although these groups are exempt from state and federal regulations that prohibit the general public from carrying switchblades and double-sided blades, none of the several police, sheriff or public safety officers interviewed for this article routinely carry a tactical knife for use as a weapon.

They agreed that they leave fighting knife use to SWAT teams and prefer Mace or pepper sprays, batons, flashlights or back-up revolvers carried in boot, ankle or small-of-the-back (SOB) holsters. The most popular blade among these officers was not a tactical knife, but a multi-tool (more about them later).

However, some knife production companies are marketing tactical knife lines aimed specifically at domestic peacekeepers and firemen. One of these is Columbia River Knife & Tool (CRKT), which touts its M-16 line as especially designed

"Much of the KA-BAR's popularity can be traced to combat lore retold by The Few and The Proud themselves."

"For Those Who Serve" in law enforcement, fire fighting, emergency services and the military.

Particularly winsome is the M-16 Fire Department, a Kit Carson-designed, black-bladed tactical folder with a G-10 frame, a stainless-steel locking liner and a blazing red G-10 handle to guard against heat conduction. The blade, a slight drop-point spear, is crafted in a slim silhouette of AUS-8 stainless with triple-point partial serration. The Carson Flipper extension aids opening and acts an additional blade guard. This blade fits the hand and the job for around $80.

A big $100 brother to the M-16 line is Kit Carson's latest, the M-18. A bit brawnier, this striking lightweight features CNC-machined-aluminum handles, a multi-functional swedged and slightly re-curved spear-point blade and inlaid G-10 handle scales in eye-catching red, blue or black. As with other CRKT offerings, the patented Lake and Walker Knife Safety (LAWKS) system turns this folder into a reliable fixed blade. The M-18 is the one tactical knife that my friend, knife industry writer and blade and book reviewer,

Mac Overton, chose to give to his nephew, Devon Foust, when Foust was called up for active duty in the Army National Guard last year.

SOG Bowies Stick to the Point

Knives by SOG deserve special mention as tactical weapons. SOG was founded on a tradition of the original Vietnam-era, fixed-blade bowie knife and, indeed, is named after the Studies and Observation Group, an elite joint services group that operated covertly during the Vietnam War. See www.sogknives.com.

The company's trademark S1 SOG Bowie, a replica of the original knife used by the 5th Special Forces group of Vietnam, is truly the classical beauty of all tactical knives. Its universally appealing 6-1/4-inch SK5 Carbon Steel blue blade with faceted tip is an exquisite example of a combat knife. A second, even more elegant replica, the Recon Bowie's 7-inch, gun-blued SK-5 blade fairly reverberates with the courageous spirit of the Alamo. Like the S1, it is equipped with leather-washer handle, brass guard and tip, and leather lanyard and sheath.

At around $275 and $225 respectively, each is worth every penny to the collectors who covet them (not to mention the invaluable significance the originals hold for the Vietnam veterans who still have theirs!). When I claimed the Recon Bowie as my favorite among all the knives highlighted in this article, my 17- and 19-year-old sons exclaimed, "But Mom, it's so simple!" Which is exactly the point.

SOG's famously rugged tactical knife line includes, among others, the S43 Tsunami (a tanto point, of course), the M14 Mini Pentagon (a viciously clever little boot dagger), the wicked X-42 Recondo (a tactical bad boy) and the Northwest Ranger S24 (an all-round knife with a 5-inch blade that would also serve well the hunters and outdoorsmen among us).

Cold Steel Goes for the Gusto

Cold Steel (www.cold-steel.com) offers the tactical weapons collector an entire glossy catalog of high-performance choices that span knife blade shapes, sizes and types. Sharing equal billing are clip-point folders less than 2 inches in length, an impressive Recon 1 folder line and full-12-inch, curved Kukris that would make any Gurkha, ancient or modern, proud.

A couple examples of Cold Steel's fixed blades are the SRK and the San Mai III Stainless Steel Trail Master. The SRK (Survival Rescue Knife) is designed to withstand the abuses of battleground rigors. It is a strong, hard-bellied, versatile knife with a Carbon V black-epoxy-coated, 6-inch, 3/16-inch-thick blade, hand honed to a hair-splitting edge. It features a single, quillon guard and a black-Kraton® handle with thong hole. For less than a Ben Franklin, the SRK is a tactical blade bargain, friendly to the palm and pocketbook!

Compare it to the big and brawny, don't-talk-back Trail Master. The San Mai III Stainless Steel version requires minimum maintenance and elicits a maximum of awe with its incredible 9-1/2-inch, clip-point blade, which Cold Steel shows on video severing 4 inches of free-hanging rope. Equipped with a Kraton handle and a Cordura® sheath, the husky 17-1/2-ounce Trail Master is one living-large tactical weapon to heft. The going price from Cold Steel of the Carbon V Steel version in the latest powder-coated style is about $180.

A handmade knife by Dan Harrison, the Scorpion showcases a stinger of a tactical blade and a quick-draw pancake sheath. (Smith and Overton photo)

Even at a list price of $433.99, the San Mai model is also a personal favorite of at least two tactical knife aficionados I know. If you are itching to use your tactical knife to its intended end, take note: Cold Steel president Lynn Thompson has expanded the company's training division by releasing a new six-video knife fighting training set, "The Warrior's Edge." Techniques are based on western fencing and boxing, and Filipino martial arts, as well as Thompson's own experiential methods. For serious tactical fighters who want to refresh or refine footwork, timing and defensive moves, this $200 set is a gift from the war gods themselves.

More Specialists of Fighting Ilk

What was it I noticed being wielded in heated combat as Jet Li fought to defend Bridget Fonda in 2001's "Kiss of the Dragon?" I thought I glimpsed, in the hand of the one of the evil "Twins," an Emerson folding Karambit. This new copy of an ancient Indonesian

Alternatives to tactical fixed blades are the KA-BAR Wharthog (top) and a KA-BAR Precision Folder designed by Dan Harrison of Edom, Texas. (*Smith and Overton photo*)

knife designed for self-protection sports an absolutely evil-looking blade curved like a tiger's claw or raptor's talon, intimidating in the extreme, and a knife I suspect the average caveman would appreciate! See www.emersonknives.com.

What's a Swamp Rat? The answer is a slick-as-a-rodent new production line of "less expensive" knives from Busse Combat Knife Co. (www.bussecombat.com). The Battle Rat, at $148.95, is the flagship of the line, patterned after the infamous Busse Combat Battle Mistress. Ultra survivor knives plus entertaining copy equal a must-see visit to www.swamprat-knifeworks.com.

For any of you planning a drop behind enemy lines, I have the perfect tactical weapon for you! It's the Zambezi by Timberline (www.timberlineknives.com). A Greg Lightfoot design, the Zambezi stands at attention from the tip of its stout,

"When I claimed the SOG Recon Bowie as my favorite among all the knives highlighted in this article, my 17- and 19-year-old sons exclaimed, 'But Mom, it's so simple!' Which is exactly the point."

half-serrated, 6-inch black blade to its olive drab handle. This soldier is housed in a parachute-jumper's synthetic button-release sheath. (My three sons actually agreed on the Zambezi as their top pick!)

Hardcore tools for hardcore individuals is how Strider Knives (www.striderknives.com) bills its field knives, chosen for harsh condition use by the former military personnel who operate the company. Look for the double-edged fixed blade JW models with cord-wrapped handles, or the distinctive tiger-striped blades of the EB series in spear or tanto points.

Sexy Scandinavians have infiltrated the U.S. Marines and U.S. Navy! Since 2000, the black versions of the FD1 and S1 survival knives, produced by the Swedish manufacturer Fallkniven, have been supplied to our troops. Sorry, no blondes, but they are still worth a gander at www.fallkniven.se or www.fallkniven.com (also the official knife of the Swedish Air Force).

Which Blades Win When Cutting Up with Combat Buddies?

After this review of tactical knives, we have to ask, "So which knives do the men in fatigues actually use in this day of ever-more-alert homeland defense?" The answer(s) surprised me. I provide as disclaimer that it's difficult, even with enlisted pals, to discover what Special Forces Ops—the likely hand-to-hand combatants—use. With that proviso, here's what I was told:

One to-remain-unnamed Navy Seal points to aforementioned Texas knifemaker Dan Harrison's new Scorpion as, "the best tactical knife I've ever had." The specs: a sleek 4-1/2-inch spear-point fixed blade bears no guard and is cunningly chic, with curved linen-Micarta handle, but tough with D-2 high-vanadium steel. The pancake

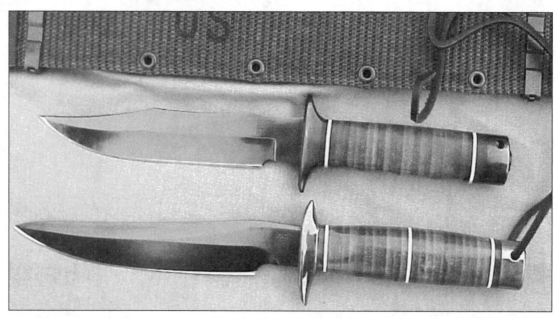

Surprisingly named as most popular among peacekeepers interviewed are multi-tools—represented here by a Leatherman WAVE (left) and Victorinox SwissTool. (*Overton and Smith photo*)

When author Linda Moll Smith claimed the Classic SOG Bowie, shown with its sibling RECON bowie, as her favorite, her 17- and 19-year-old sons exclaimed, "But Mom, it's so simple!" Which is exactly her point. (*Overton and Smith photo*)

"I'm still on the lookout for the one essential knife I would not enter combat without."
–Staff Sgt. Brian Olson, survival instructor at the U.S. Air Force Survival School

quick-draw leather sheath lies flat to the leg, belt or arm, allowing the Scorpion to speedily slide out for stinging. Harrison is also working on a prototype entry tool for possible U.S. Marshal/SWAT use. E-mail Harrison at dwhclh@msn.com.

SFC Bryan A. Lasater, of Headquarters, 19th Brigade, Texas State Guard, shares the opinion of a number of combat troops or public safety officers I interviewed who cite a multi-tool as their favorite tactical-bladed adjunct.

Lasater, who served in the U.S. Air Force from 1995-2000 as a security policeman, and has served as a military policeman in the Texas State Guard since 2000, notes that Texas State Guard troops (the civilian complement of the Army National Guard) are not allowed to carry combat knives on their uniforms. As a result, he prefers to tote a Leatherman Super Tool. He described it as "heavy-duty, reliable, lightweight and extremely compact," listing its components as: pliers, wire cutter, ruler, saw, flathead and Phillips screwdrivers, can/bottle opener, three knife blades and file.

Other multi-tools mentioned as favorites included the SOG Paratool with angled pliers head and black-oxide finish (around $60), and the Victorinox (known for its Swiss Army knives and watches) SwissTool.

Also a multi-tool fan is Staff Sgt. Brian Olson, survival instructor at the U.S. Air Force Survival School. He helps train about 4,000 students a year, mostly fliers who may find themselves stranded in a hostile landing zone. He explains, "We are in the woods teaching 50 weeks out of 52, regardless of conditions. Training, in general, covers sustenance, signaling, personal protection, evasion, evasion living and navigation, to name a few.

"Students are provided a fixed-blade knife and a folding-blade knife as basic issue," Olson expounds. "The brands change as time goes, and the training is generally geared toward learning how to use any knife to meet survival needs. Those at the SERE (Survival, Evasion, Resistance & Escape) school are not trained in hand-to-hand combat with knives, nor do we receive much coaching in bayonet use—that falls to Army Rangers.

"Students are allowed to bring any other knife (aside from their issued blades) that they want to try out, within reason. Multi-tool knives are quite popular. As an instructor, I am issued a multi-tool and I find them very handy," Olson says. "What's my favorite knife? I couldn't really say. I generally use those issued to me. I'm still on the lookout for the one essential knife I would not enter combat without."

Aside from a multi-tool, he's still on the lookout for the one essential tactical knife? What say we airdrop the Staff Sgt. and his men a care package bundled with multiple copies of this publication, stat! ●

Cold Steel's SRK (top) and Trailmaster bowies are designed to withstand the abuses of battleground rigors. (Overton and Smith photo)

The Kit Carson M-18 from Columbia River Knife & Tool is a brawny, striking, lightweight tactical folder featuring a CNC-machined-aluminum handle, a multi-functional, swedged and slightly re-curved spear-point blade and an inlaid G-10 handle in eye-catching red, blue or black.

So Speaks the Artist Behind Angel Sword

A true sword craftsman looks past the edge and into the steel

By Edward Crews

Angel Sword's Daniel Watson performs differential quenching on a knife blade to harden the edge while retaining toughness along the spine.

DANIEL WATSON STILL owns the first sword he ever acquired—a 300-year-old Chinese *Jian* (the English translation for a double-edged Chinese straight sword, somewhat popularized by the tai chi martial arts). The sword was a present from his father who obtained it during World War II service in the Pacific Theater. Although he was only 9 years old at the time, Watson clearly remembers the elation he felt when he first lifted the weapon, gripped it in his hands and felt its heft and balance.

> **"I want to take a sword that's considered an archetype and push it further than anyone ever thought it could be."**
> —Daniel Watson

The Jian stimulated an enduring fascination with swords. The weapon also led Watson to master metalworking and forging, and to put these skills to use fashioning swords, knives and daggers. Sword making also gives Watson an outlet for his imagination.

I want to be thought of as an artist, he said. "I want to take a sword that's considered an archetype and push it further than anyone ever thought it could be."

Watson has been testing the limits of creativity and craftsmanship in sword making for almost a quarter of a century. In 1979, he established Angel Sword, a company dedicated to making swords, knives and daggers. Implicit in all Watson does is a respect for the traditional sword maker's means and methods—hammer, anvil, fire and sweat.

Today, Angel Sword operates from a site in Driftwood, Texas, a rural community near Austin. Like a colonial craftsman, the proud proprietor lives above the main workshop. The entire complex also accommodates bluing tanks, compressors, offices, a showroom and a storage area.

Watson describes Angel Sword as a custom shop with individual laborers working in a collaborative effort. This arrangement allows the company to produce a significant and varied volume of high-quality edged tools and weapons. Annual output typically amounts to 400 swords and 600 knives or daggers, and these are all custom pieces! An Angel Sword or knife often parades exotic woods, custom alloys and gemstones. They also cover a huge gamut of blade styles: rapiers, sabers, katanas, Jians, long swords, short swords, falchions, scimitars and many others.

While the styles may range, Watson stresses that the company does not make replicas. Instead, each piece is a custom creation that may be informed by various traditions, but is ultimately unique. Every piece must also meet ancient standards of combat reliability.

"Our approach is to find the heart and functionality of real, battleworthy weapons. Then, we make them into works of art," Watson said years ago in a newspaper interview. But, the philosophy still holds true.

> ### *"I eventually learned etching, woodworking, carving and casting from different sources. No one person knew all I needed to know."*
> —Daniel Watson

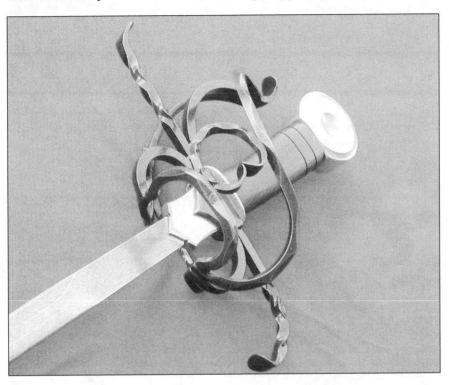

The 40-3/4-inch rapier features a distal-tapered blade of Angel Sword's own Techno-wootz damascus, a technologically advanced steel that Daniel Watson believes recreates the crystalline properties of the legendary wootz of ancient Indo-Persia.

Demand for these goods is steady. And, that helps explain why his shop operates six days a week to meet the demand of a clientele that stretches across the United States. Angel Sword employs eight people working under Watson's watchful eye.

"The employees perform many tasks—grinding, polishing, assembling, and paying attention to fit and finish," said Tom Gerrow, marketing director for Angel Sword. "But, Daniel is around all the time. He does the forging. He provides the artistic dimension. He gives the final okay. Very little happens here without his guidance."

Watson's attention to detail has been evident since his first sword came to fruition in 1979, while living and teaching martial arts in Cuernvaca, Morelos in Mexico. He also worked as an artist, selling watercolors in Mexico City galleries.

Swords From Spikes

During the late 1970s, in Cuernvaca, Watson more or less appren-

The Avatar knife from Angel Sword showcases an 8-3/8-inch Techno-wootz blade, a stainless-steel guard and a walnut handle with matching wooden scabbard.

ticed under a local man who produced machetes. This artisan had actually made swords from railroad spikes for military use during the Mexican Revolution. Watson sold his early edged weapons through his martial arts school. The ready acceptance of his creations prompted him to develop his sideline into a full-time business. In 1983, he returned to the United States and opened a shop in Driftwood.

While the Mexican craftsman gave Watson some initial instruction, his mastery of the sword smith's art has taken him to many teachers.

"I eventually learned etching, woodworking, carving and casting from different sources," Watson said. "No one person knew all I needed to know."

Besides finding tutors, Watson read extensively and conducted hands-on research with swords, daggers and knives. He practiced different sword production techniques and edged-weapons fighting styles. He built a huge library. (Anybody interested in benefiting from his research should visit the company website www.angelsword.com, and go to the "Readings" section. The bibliography is huge, ranging from the 19th Century classic "The Book of the Sword," by Victorian adventurer Richard Burton, to "The Modern Blacksmith," by Alexander Weygers.)

> ## *"I'll take one sword and make it all bright and shiny. And, I'll make another evil and dark."*
> —Daniel Watson

Along the way, Watson also collected dozens of antiques, including a Renaissance rapier and a 10th Century Norman sword. Through intense study of the originals, a process that sometimes includes disassembly, Watson learns about manufacturing, balance, and the combat limits and strengths of each piece. He also draws on his knowledge of martial arts. All this informs his creations.

Watson also relies on customer feedback. "Our customers have become a testing facility," he said.

Finally, but most importantly, Watson would argue, his creations are formulated by his complex views on art and craftsmanship.

After forging, Angel Sword journeyman smiths grind the blades into their final shape.

The Angel Sword Jian is a double-edged Chinese straight sword that weighs 2 pounds, 5 ounces and sports a 31-7/8-inch S-7 blade, a rosewood handle with a brass inlay of a dragon, and a brass guard and pommel.

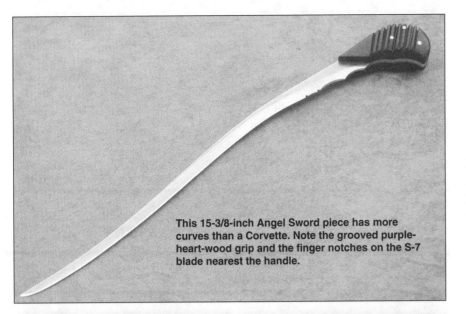

This 15-3/8-inch Angel Sword piece has more curves than a Corvette. Note the grooved purple-heart-wood grip and the finger notches on the S-7 blade nearest the handle.

It's fun to gaze at the detail photo of two blades from an Avatar La Belle Rapier and Katzbalger, both Angel Sword creations, showing Techno-wootz damascus patterning.

Prices vary, depending on the time and materials put into each piece. Knives and daggers range anywhere from $295-$5,000, with most pieces falling between $495 and $2,000. Swords fall into the $1,500-$10,000 price range, the bulk selling for between $3,000 and $7,000.

Avatar knives and daggers are $195-$2,000, typically between $295 and $1,500; and Avatar swords range from $2,000-$10,000, most coming in at $2,000-$6,000.

Bright Knights, the most popular line of the company's swords, knives and daggers, are more modestly priced, ranging from $79-$1,000, typically in the $125-$400 price point. Bright Knights swords reach $595-$5,000, and the bulk are available for $795-$1,500.

As the prices suggest, each line aims at different would-be customers. Bright Knights, for example, was developed to offer an affordable, entry-level product that still met Angel Sword's high standards. The line is rich in variety and detail. Exotic hardwoods like cocobolo, cardinal wood and African purple-heart share the limelight with other materials, including horn, brass, bone and bronze. At one time, the company also produced a Buccaneer line of knives and daggers. A few remain but the line has been discontinued.

"Production methods vary based on the product line," Gerrow said. "Angel Swords and Avatars are made using a traditional Catalan forge with a hand bellows and charcoal fire. The Bright Knights begin with stock removal and are finished by hand. While we start off with a variety of commercial steels, it's important to note that the steel you end up with after forging isn't the same steel you started with. Forging changes the nature of the steel, often dramatically."

Angel Sword's artisans are particularly pleased with the options provided them by modern metal technology. This is especially true when it comes to the Avatar line.

"Avatar damascus blades feature our Techno-wootz damascus, a technologically advanced blade steel that [we believe] recreates the crystalline properties of the leg-

These are explored fully on the company's second website www.swordarts.com. A third site—www.swordmagick.com—explores "the paths of magic together through the symbolism and power of the sword."

In an essay, Watson writes, "Skilled craftsmanship is necessary for art. But there is a lot of skilled craftsmanship that is not art. When I go to a museum or an art gallery, I watch myself for a certain emotional response, not just asking myself if it is beautiful or well done. But, how do I respond to it emotionally? Do I say, 'Wow, that hits me?' Art has to move us emotionally and, for that to happen, the artist has to put emotions into the piece. Otherwise, it's still just craftsmanship."

With each sword or knife, Watson seeks to go beyond craftsmanship. He wants to achieve a work of art that inspires a powerful connection in customers.

"My approach is to have vision of a piece, to pursue that vision and to make something that will sing when you touch it," Watson said.

What Evil Lurks Beyond the Sword?

"I'll take one sword and make it all bright and shiny. And, I'll make another evil and dark. People will look at them and see one as noble and one as bad. I also want an emotional response," Watson said.

This goal is evident in three complete lines of knives, daggers, swords and other custom blades.

> ## "If we were just concerned about craftsmanship, then we could make thousands of items, all exactly alike."
> —Daniel Watson

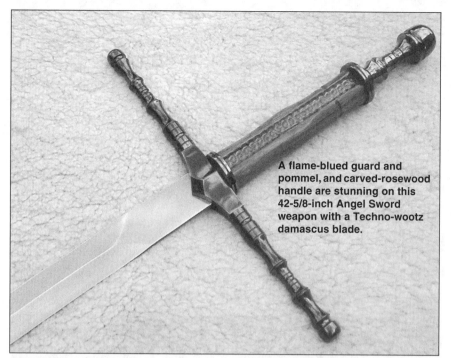

A flame-blued guard and pommel, and carved-rosewood handle are stunning on this 42-5/8-inch Angel Sword weapon with a Techno-wootz damascus blade.

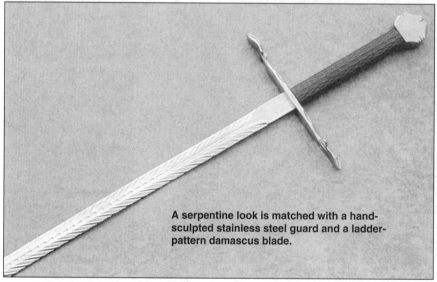

A serpentine look is matched with a hand-sculpted stainless steel guard and a ladder-pattern damascus blade.

endary wootz steel of ancient Indo-Persia," Gerrow said. "The crystal-line structure of the steel in Avatar damascus blades results in beautiful surface patterns that Daniel can manipulate to produce a variety of stunning effects."

Besides having these established lines, Watson continues to do custom work based on clients' ideas. However, commissions are rare, and Watson tries to satisfy customers' desires with existing designs. If a commission seems appropriate, Watson questions a buyer closely about what he wants.

"I start by asking about what period and type of sword a customer wants," Watson said. "Then I show them what we have. I get a customer to pick up a sword and see how it feels to him. I try to narrow down what he wants regarding size, weight and his hand size. If I can find something close to what a buyer is looking for, then I try to interest him in something we already have. If that won't work, though, then I'll develop a custom piece."

Some Collect, and Others Admire

Both Watson and Gerrow stress that there is no one type of Angel Sword customer. They come from many backgrounds. Some are men, some are women, some collect, and others admire. Still others use Angel Sword pieces for cutting practice. Customers are extremely loyal, with Angel Sword's repeat business accounting for roughly 60 percent of total sales.

"The majority of Angel sword blades are sold at Renaissance fairs, but not all of our customers are Medieval and Renaissance enthusiasts. They make up just one segment. Martial arts practitioners are another. Angel Sword Jians are quite popular with tai chi artists, while more European designs appeal to folks in the Association for Renaissance Martial Arts. Additionally, Daniel has a number of fans who collect his work, and some of these folks fly across the country to the fairs just to visit

with him and check out the latest swords," Gerrow said.

Over the years, Watson has found that some of the nation's largest Renaissance festivals are his best markets. He regularly attends the Scarborough Faire in Waxahachie, Texas, the New York Renaissance Faire in Sterling, and the Texas Renaissance Festival in Plantersville.

Many customers begin collecting Bright Knights items, and they usually move up into the other lines as they come to appreciate the effort that goes into Angel Swords' products. Watson has a long-standing policy of helping customers through his trade-up policy.

"If you buy one of our products, then you can use it for years and trade it in on another item with no depreciation in the original value," Watson said.

In line with the trade-up policy, Watson also offers a lifetime guarantee on all goods. Each is guaranteed against what Watson terms "reasonable misuse."

Customer feedback provides an explanation for this loyalty. Buyers like the custom, one-of-a-kind aspect of each item. They also like the fact that Angel Sword products hold their edges well.

Watson believes a major reason for his products appeal is their feel. That is the same quality that attracted him as a boy to his father's Jian.

"Each of our items must have balance, the right feel and comfort," he said. "The tactile quality is important. A weapon's looks come second to its feel. Because you can only appreciate these qualities when you pick up one of our products, we really don't believe that

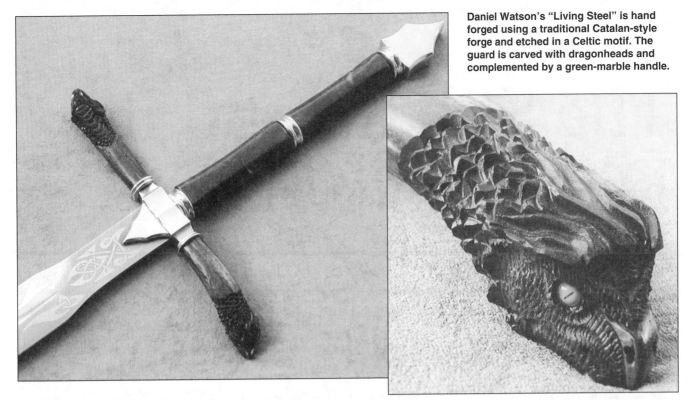

Daniel Watson's "Living Steel" is hand forged using a traditional Catalan-style forge and etched in a Celtic motif. The guard is carved with dragonheads and complemented by a green-marble handle.

Angel Sword has many fans at renaissance fairs, where visitors enjoy getting a hands-on feel for the blades.

the Internet site or a catalog can do justice to our goods. Most people need to put one of our swords in their hands and get its 'tactile essence.'"

Gerrow confirmed the importance of the weapons' heft: "The balance and feel of Angel swords is another big differentiator. One of the things we like to do is get the swords into peoples' hands so they can feel how well they are balanced. The focus on balance is probably a result of Daniel's experience as a martial artist. For instance, we have a two-handed sword that is just over 64 inches long and weighs 6 pounds, 10 ounces. But it has a balance point that is 3-3/4 inches in front of the guard. This makes wielding it feel fluid and graceful even though it's more than 5 feet long."

Looking ahead, Watson says he will continue doing what he does now—that is pursuing fine craftsmanship that sparks powerful, heartfelt response in buyers.

"If we were just concerned about craftsmanship, then we could make thousands of items, all exactly alike," Watson said. "But, when you aim for an emotional response, this is something different from craftsmanship or even art. If one of my swords or daggers doesn't touch people at a certain level, then I'm not doing the right thing. I want to

see somebody pick up a sword and get a sparkle in his or her eyes. That's why I like going to the fairs and meeting with people. When I see an enthusiastic reaction, that's when I get back some of the fire needed to create more pieces." ●

For more information, contact Angel Sword, attn: Daniel Watson, 350 Jennifer Ln., Driftwood, TX 78619 (512) 847-9679 a.sword@ccsi.com, www.angelsword.com.

The Stiletto and its Distinctive Snick

Often associated with subversive characters, the stiletto traces its roots to courtiers and aristocracy

By Greg Bean

STILETTO—THE WORD conjures up images of spiked heels on sexy shoes, switchblades, the mafia and street gangs from the 1950s. The slender stiletto, with its distinctive snick, was both exciting and threatening, eventually becoming a symbol for teenage gangs and violence. Notwithstanding the 1958 Switchblade Act, the stiletto, with button in handle to automatically extract the blade, is still a beloved collectors item for knife aficionados and has spurred numerous organizations, websites and newsletters devoted to it.

The stiletto's history is 500 years older than New York street gangs, and runs from "Romeo and

> *"Ladies and gentlemen wore them, commoners carried them, and political operatives concealed them."*

Juliet" to "West Side Story" and "The Spy Who Came in From the Cold." Its association with assassination brings to mind shadowy doorways, hidden passageways and subversive characters wearing cloaks concealing deadly needles.

Slender and elegant, the Italian Renaissance stiletto was often a part of the couture of the courtiers and aristocracy, both men and women. At that time, the stiletto was a universal and very Italian personal effect,

The Arms and Armor Italian stiletto is a circa-1480 reproduction of a Venetian piece with a grip cast in steel using an investment casting method. The blade is forged by hand in a traditional manner.

whether for fashion or function. Ladies and gentlemen wore them, commoners carried them, and political operatives concealed them.

Early stilettos sported triangular- or rectangular-style blades, 6- to-16 inches long. While grips might have been plain and made from common materials, they were more likely to be exotic and decorative. They were often made from a single piece of steel, a tour de force at which the Italians excelled. Purely for thrusts and punctures, the light weapon was of little use in a normal fight. It only worked up close, preferably from behind.

One version of the stiletto was actually a practical tool, at least to artillery operatives. The Bombardiers stiletto, dated to mid-17th-century Venice, had a set of scales on its blade designed to correlate cannon bore with the cannonball's weight. The bore was on one side, the weight of the shot on another. The Bombardier stiletto became a status symbol for the military and was worn by many outside of the artillery ranks.

Civilian styles, often with inaccurate scales, followed.

The stiletto was not the sole instrument of assassination anymore than the brush was the only artist's tool, but it had a distinctly Italian flavor that was recognized throughout Europe. Writers from the Renaissance to modern times have associated the stiletto, as well as a hot-blooded nature, with the Italians.

A sampling from writers through the centuries describing the stiletto follows:

"The Venetians were always highly sensitive about factional honor and many were ready to defend against perceived insults from other factions using weapons that every artisan routinely carried about the city – the handy stilettos."

"In Italy, there used to be the tradition – in cases when the stiletto was insufficient for revenge – to brawl with a curious percussive tool. A thick, 60-to-90-centimeter-long staff carried three 30-centimeter sticks, weighted down with lead

and iron rings, fixed like flails, which served for attack and defense as kept in swinging motion."

"A 19th-century political rabble-rouser, Mazzini and his Young Italy secret political society was described as the party of the dagger, of the stiletto."

"Scorning all treacherous feud and deadly strife, the dark stiletto and the murderous knife..."

"In Italy and Sicily there was a preference towards the ultra quick stiletto."

"Images of swarthy banditti from Italy's hardscrabble south armed with stilettos and carrying on vendettas were spread among the intolerant American public by anecdote and in the press."

Assassination and the Stiletto

As the intrigues of the Renaissance aided the birth of the modern nation state, the 20th-century nations of WWII experienced a rebirth of political intrigue, assassination and the stiletto.

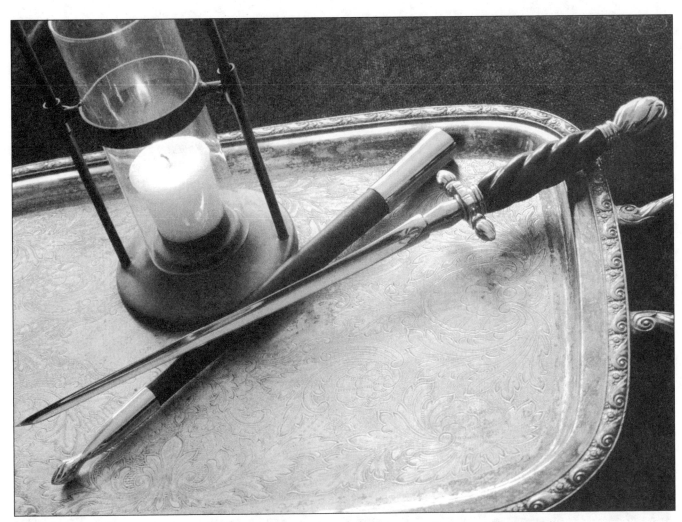

The C.A.S. Iberia Renaissance stiletto could be worn as a fashion statement in an age that served lethal statecraft as casually as a steward serves wine. The buffalo-horn grip and leather scabbard, with its metal throat and tip, displays the fine finishing expected of the Italian aristocracy.

When Nazi Germany made its first decisive move against the western Allied nations, the British were squeezed out of Europe through the portal of Dunkirk, a stinging revelation of how inadequate their land-based forces were. Winston Churchill, resurrected from political obscurity, called for "specially trained troops of the hunter class, who can deliver a reign of terror down on these (enemy occupied) coasts." He named these hunters "Commandos," a respectful tribute to a skillful enemy from the Boer War.

With Britain alone, isolated and expecting a German invasion at any moment, the Commandos were first expected to serve in a guerilla role, with hit and run, disruptive tactics. The invasion never materialized and the Commandos became the shock troops of a new amphibious assault force designed to take out key installations in Nazi-occupied territory.

Training for the Commandos, coordinated by Adm. Sir Roger Keyes, emphasized the skills needed for amphibious raids behind enemy lines. Their training included field craft, navigation and compass reading, surveillance, explosives training, cliff climbing, leaping ashore from landing craft in high seas, and close-quarters combat.

Enter the stiletto, in this case more true to its textbook definition as a small dagger having a slender, tapering blade. The close-quarters combat training of the Commandos became legendary, taught by two officers whose imminence in military hand-to-hand combat is still recognized. Capts. William Fairbairn and Eric Sykes learned their craft as policemen in the British-controlled city of Shanghai, a crossroads where they encountered every martial arts system in the Orient. Out of need, they developed a highly practical dirty tricks system of their own. They trained the Commandos in unarmed combat, firearms use and knife fighting.

Part of the legacy of Fairbairn and Sykes is the killing dagger they developed for the Commandos. The slender double-edged blade, small guard and cylindrical handle of the Fairbairn-Sykes dagger are instantly recognizable to both knife aficionados and scholars of WW II history. Worn in either a boot sheath or a forearm sheath, the hidden F-S dagger contributed to the image of the stealthy, silent Commando.

The Commando dagger became a symbol of British resistance to the Nazi war machine, and the Brits were not shy about publicizing its intended use. Manuals and photos released to the press show a Commando silencing a sentry with a hand over his mouth, the head pulled back to open the neck for a lethal thrust. The celebrity of the Commandos and their daggers was intended to boost the public morale.

Commando Stiletto

British Commando training, a 12-week course at the "Commando Castle" in Achnacarry, Scotland, became the model for all Allied Special Forces. French, Norwegian, Dutch, Belgian, Polish and German Jewish fighters were trained here.

A switchblade stiletto adds a touch of Italian exotica to any knife collection.

Achnacarry, guided by the American's Maj. Gen. Truscott and Maj. Gen. Hartle, was the birthplace of the U.S. Rangers.

Out of the elite Commandos and the Long Range Desert Patrol, the latter a desert surveillance unit, another Special Forces group grew, the Special Air Services, or SAS. Founded by Commando David Sterling, the SAS was a smaller, more highly trained and conditioned force, typically five-man teams instead of the 50-man units of the Commandos. Their initial missions were failures, being expected to act as front line troops instead of behind-the-lines saboteurs. Soon enough, they were put to effective use, such as destroying German aircraft while still on the ground, timed to coincide with an Allied air mission.

While most of the British military stood down following the end of the Third Reich, the SAS continued with a covert deadly mission. The SAS ferreted out and assassinated Nazi war criminals too minor

"The CIA term for an operation that succeeds and leaves no loose ends or trails is the same one often used to describe a stiletto – 'elegant.'"

to stand trial at Nuremberg, but still deserving and still dangerous to the British eye. They were especially eager to meet with the Nazis responsible for the deaths of SAS operatives.

This mission of the SAS remained dark until the 1998 publishing of the book "Official Assassin" by SAS member Peter Mason, who claimed he'd executed 16 Germans. Mason later met Ian Fleming, the writer of the James Bond series. At Mason's suggestion for greater realism, Bond was outfitted with silenced weapons.

After the James Bond success, Fleming sent Mason a thank you gift of the timeless spy's tool, a dagger. Some things never change.

Another of Churchill's inventions was a system of saboteurs and spies integrated into the everyday life of the German-controlled territories. With the executive order for "a proper system of espionage and intelligence along the whole coasts, to harass the enemy from behind the lines," the Special Operations Executive (SOE) was born. The agents gathered and passed information, maintained escape lines, trained and armed De Gaulle's resistance organization, and committed what acts of sabotage and assassination they could.

Fairbairn and Sykes, building on their success with the Commandos, trained the men and women of the SOE in weapons, explosives, unarmed combat and, their specialty, silent killing. Equipped with these skills and enough spy gadgets to fill a movie prop house, the SOE were to blend into the occu-

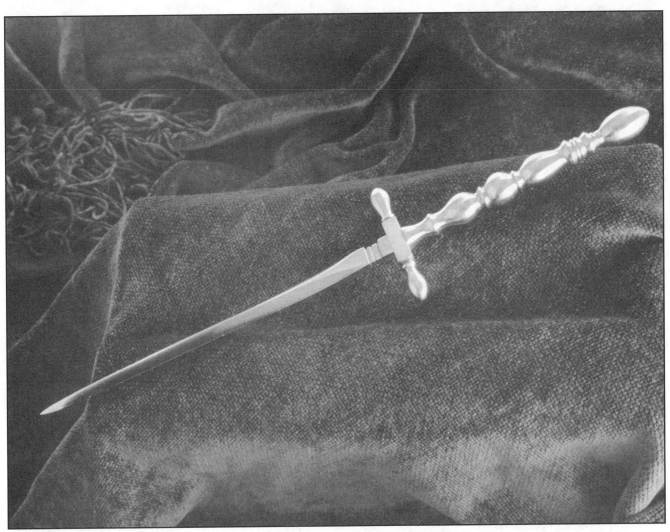

The Museum Replicas contribution to stilettos showcases the blade-making skills the Italians made as synonymous as their methods of political advancement.

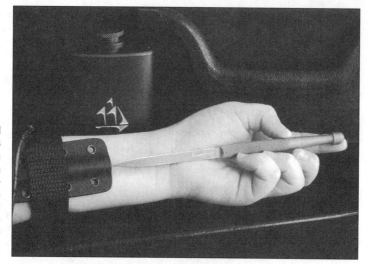

The Crawford Knives OSS dagger, which is hidden up a sleeve, contrasts with its showy and fashionable Renaissance counterpart.

The well-equipped saboteur might wear a WWII sleeve dagger, Crawford Knives style.

Stiletto Sources

A Minneapolis-based company, Arms and Armor is a licensed reproducer of the Wallace Collection in London, one of the largest collections of arms, armor and weapons. The Arms and Armor catalog includes Renaissance daggers, rapiers and bucklers. In business for 20 years, all knives are made stateside.

The company's circa-1480 Italian stiletto is from Bresci, an area of Venice known for its steel-cutting expertise. The grip, molded from the Wallace Collection original, is cast in steel using an investment casting method. The blade is forged by hand in a traditional manner by owner Christopher Poor and production manager, Craig Johnson.

Either can be reached by phoning 800-745-7345, or through their website www.armor.com.

C.A.S. Iberia, a historical weapon supplier, imports from around the world and manufactures its own Hanwei line. Owner Barry Ross travels to international museums and armories where original weaponry is to be found. From the Tower of London to private collections anywhere, Ross searches the world for weaponry that epitomizes an era, and then recreates these pieces.

From the Hanwei forge of Paul Chen, C.A.S. offers an Italian Renaissance stiletto that features a buffalo-horn grip and a leather scabbard reinforced with a steel throat and tip, a look that could have graced the finest-dressed of both men and women. Other period offerings include daggers, rapiers and, for the proper lady assassin, a women's stiletto/scissors.

Crawford Handmade Knives, a father-and-son business, is located in West Memphis, Ark. Pat started making knives in 1973 and Wes just grew up in the trade. They primarily produce tactical folders but have a few popular pieces outside of that venue. Their bench-made knives start as steel blanks and are shaped through stock removal, during which they are cut from steel, ground, drilled, milled and ultimately heat-treated, buffed and polished. They work from a standard set of patterns but make the

pied territories and, in Churchill's words, "set Europe ablaze."

Following the lead of the British, U.S. Maj. Gen. William J. Donovan created an American counterpart to the SOE, the Office of Strategic Services, or OSS.

Exploding Rats and Their Own Stiletto

Their tools of the trade included lighters that fire bullets, code equipment, disguised radio transmitters, lock picks, silenced guns, miniature cameras, wire garrotes, explosives disguised as lumps of coal, exploding rats and their own stiletto.

Looking like a minimalist Renaissance stiletto, the OSS sleeve dagger was, "specifically designed to be concealed on arm or leg, especially during body search."

Political assassination had entered the modern era as the OSS evolved into today's CIA. In a poetic twist, the CIA term for an operation that succeeds and leaves no loose ends or trails is the same one often used to describe a stiletto – "elegant."

Assassination by the CIA was outlawed in 1976 by President Ford, and then strengthened and affirmed by Presidents Carter and Reagan, a reaction to numerous failed and embarrassing attempts to assassinate foreign leaders, including Fidel Castro.

The CIA's November 2002 assassination of an al-Qaeda leader in Yemen indicates President Ford's executive order may be under review. Since the 9/11 attacks and the start of the war on terrorism, the CIA is again on war footing. Dark alleys and stilettos are back in style.

"Other period offerings include daggers, rapiers and, for the proper lady assassin, a women's stiletto/scissors."

knives by hand, usually making three or four at a time.

Their OSS sleeve dagger, which they call the Devil Dart, is built from 440C stainless steel and includes a nylon and Velcro sleeve sheath, and a Kydex® neck sheath and chain.

They can be reached at 870-732-2452, or through their website at www.crawfordknives.com.

ESA-SWORDS, located just outside of Columbus in central Ohio, is an authorized seller of Wilkinson Sword Ltd., and only markets authentic Wilkinson Sword products. The relationship with Wilkinson Sword started in the early 1990s when the owner of ESA-SWORDS, Ken Pfarr, became a customer while attached to the Royal Hong Kong Police Force. ESA-SWORDS has become a central point of purchase for Wilkinson Sword to sell its Commando Knives to customers in the far corners of the world.

Wilkinson Sword was the first maker of the Fairbairn-Sykes dagger. With three patterns, the Mark I, Mark II and Mark III, this is one of the most popular and reproduced knives. Now made from a variety of metals and finishes, each is offered with a display case and a sleeve or boot scabbard. Though reproduced by many makers, ESA-Swords in the only American supplier of the Wilkinson Sword versions.

ESA-Swords can be reached by dialing 937-644-2170, or through its website at www.esa-swords.com.

The Knife Guy is an Internet-based business (www.theswitch-blade.com) that sells switchblades exclusively. Owner Rick Wichman offers knives in styles from classic stilettos to contemporary tactical knives. With an 11-year background as a gunsmith doing restoration and customizing work, Rick was familiar with knife and gun shows, which is how his knife business started. Now strictly Internet based, federal law allows The Knife Guy to sell and ship automatic knives, but it is up to the buyer to know and be in compliance with local laws.

The Knife Guy's inventory includes limited-pro-duction pieces by custom makers, traditional knife manufacturers, small shops and major gun companies. Automatic blade-opening mechanisms include lever locks, swing guards, scale releases, OTF (out the front) and hidden-release designs. The knives are manufactured in Czechoslovakia, Germany and the United States, and the stilettos are from Maniago, Italy, a city famous for their manufacture.

Museum Replicas, a supplier of historical weaponry, clothing and artifacts, together with its sister company Atlanta Cutlery, are owned by Windlass Steelcraft. Windlass, from India, produces edged weapons for military forces in seven countries, and manufactures about 90 percent of the product Museum Replicas offers. All prototypes are created in its Atlanta, Georgia location, where the final fitting and assembly for its weapons and clothing lines are performed.

The Museum Replicas Italian stiletto is a traditional stiletto with grip and blade made from a single piece of steel. The triangular blade and rounded grip showcase the steel-cutting art for which the Renaissance Italian knife industry was famous. The company sells clothing, for both men and women, to complete the well-tailored assassin. Atlanta Cutlery, a sport, camping and military knife company, offers a Fairbairn-Sykes commando dagger and an OSS stiletto, calling it the Three Angle Knife. ●

Wilkinson Sword was the first maker of the Fairbairn-Sykes dagger. With three patterns, the Mark I, Mark II and Mark III, this is one of the most popular and reproduced knife patterns. Now made from a variety of metals and finishes, they are as likely to be bought in display cases as with sleeve or boot scabbards. Though reproduced by many makers, ESA-Swords is the only American supplier of the Wilkinson Sword versions.

REAL-WORLD POLICE AND MILITARY KNIVES

Practicality and regulations shape soldier and sergeant steel—then it's battle tested!

By Jim Williamson

IT'S UNCERTAIN JUST who coined the term "tactical" but it's so widely used (and abused!) today that it's applied to almost anything intended for military or police SWAT use. It's a generic buzzword that sounds dramatic, but means little. In the knife field, it seems to encompass almost any model for official use or for civilian self-defense, as opposed to ordinary knives for pocket carry, hunting or fishing.

The types overlap to some degree, and some writers have given the impression that a tactical knife is the sort that Rambo would carry in the movies. One tends to expect blades of 10 inches or so, with saw teeth along the spines. Hollow handles abound. Chisel points and Oriental styling appeal to some buyers. Waiting to be explored is a more realistic sort of tactical knife, a form more likely to pass muster in real-world police and military scenarios.

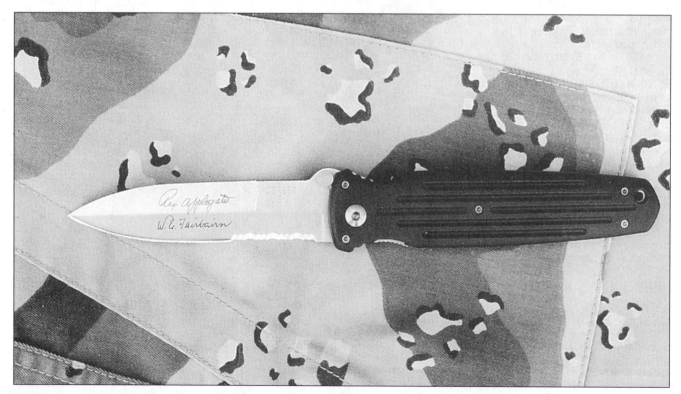

One of the author's favorite real-world military knives—the Gerber Applegate-Fairbairn—also happens to be popular with U.S. troops in Afghanistan. It provides good utility value in what is probably the best "folding fighter" of the genre. (*Williamson photo*)

Muela of Spain makes this excellent tactical fixed blade, somewhat similar to the SOG knife used by U.S. Navy SEALS, but less expensive. Those interested can contact Matthews Cutlery, 4401-E Sentry Dr., Tucker, GA 30084 (770) 939-6915. (*Williamson photo*)

> *"Some writers have given the impression that a tactical knife is the sort that Rambo would carry in the movies."*

Both practicality and regulations shape the form and size acceptable in such applications. What's acceptable varies widely with each police force or military unit. Some officers in rural areas may well be able to carry stag-handle beauties that would, at best, earn a raised eyebrow from a big city supervisor. The need for discretion is such that we won't look at many fancy knives here, but even some of the better black, tactical knives have an air of elegance and style.

At the outset, let's look at how such knives are used. One traditional military use has been for elimination of enemy sentries. That's a task usually handled today by suppressed (silenced) firearms, although it can't be altogether ignored. A pilot evading searchers behind enemy lines is normally going to do his best to avoid contact.

Most airmen don't think in terms of edged weapons. They should. However, the relatively low likelihood of needing the knife as a weapon is only one factor in choosing to carry one.

This custom-made and designed Starfighter tactical folder by Robert Terzuola is the epitome of the modern tactical folder, and has probably inspired several similar knives in its time. For more information, contact Terzuola, 3933 Agua Fria, Santa Fe, NM 87501 (505) 473-1002. (*Weyer photo*)

A cop most likely to need a defensive knife might be an off-duty officer who lost his gun in a struggle with a robbery suspect, or who emptied a five-shot snub .38, only to wind up having to grapple with an assailant. At such a moment, one of the vaunted boot knives or tactical folders is worth its weight in gold.

The same is true for the undercover cop who needs an edged tool that won't blow his cover if found. Fortunately, there are so many high-tech folders on today's market that a law enforcement officer carrying one is less suspicious to most crooks than he once was. A common hunting knife should also be good in this role.

The sole occasion when I had to work undercover without a gun (as a military cop), I chose a Buck 105 Pathfinder hunting knife. I didn't have to use it (thank goodness!), but feel sure that it would have sufficed. Frankly, it was selected mainly because it's what I owned for sporting purposes.

Most police use knives as tools rather than as weapons. Uses range from relying on the screwdriver blades in a Swiss Army knife to tighten loose screws on a gun or the rearview mirror of a patrol car, to food preparation in a hotel room or apartment where a surveillance team is conducting a stakeout.

Police divers may need a sharp blade for the same reasons that a civilian diver would. Someone may

"As a kid, I heard about a police officer who used his pocket-knife to lop the head off a snapping turtle that grabbed a wading boy by the foot."

"In one case, a doctor performed a tracheotomy aboard an airplane, something no longer possible given the ban on knives in planes."

become entangled in kelp or other water plants, rope or fishing line. Probing for evidence in a muddy bottom happens. More adventurously, an aggressive fish or alligator may have to be discouraged.

Policemen working on boats, whether divers or not, need to cut rope and may need to pry. Bales that contain narcotics or other prohibited substances have to be cut open for examination, especially by customs agents and Coast Guardsmen.

A Slicing Turtle?

A knife may be required to slice tape, string or burlap wrapping. As a kid, I heard about a local officer having to use his pocketknife to cut off the head of a snapping turtle that grabbed a wading boy by the foot. The unrelenting jaws couldn't be pried open until the turtle's head had been detached.

Officers at the scene of an accident or airplane crash may need to free passengers from seat belts or to cut away clothing in order to dress wounds. Clothing or sheets can be cut into strips to immobilize broken limbs, or for emergency bandages.

A choking individual may need a tracheotomy, and the folks that work for Victorinox, the Swiss Army knife people, have letters in their files noting that the company's knives were used for precisely this purpose! In one case, a doctor performed the surgery aboard an airplane, something no longer possible given the ban on knives in planes.

There are other uses for knives in police work, and many in the military. Concentrating on pocketknives, which are actually the most likely to see use, the Swiss Army knives by Victorinox or Wenger are ideal. Lighter than Boy Scout models, they offer additional functions, as well. The best for police/military use may be the basic Soldier or the Spartan, both from Victorinox. The company offers several minor variants on the Soldier theme, with red handle scales. One includes a saw, a useful item. These knives are excellent bargains for what one gets.

The longer models with red- or black-nylon scales fare best in the pocket of a patrol jacket. They're just a bit too big to be fully comfortable in most

officers' trousers pockets. Some police and military officers prefer folding knives with locking blades and larger tools. They work especially well for rural patrol or when tracking fugitives in wilderness areas.

The traditional Buck 110 lockback folder is the archetype of the modern tactical folder. The Buck 110 and similar knives from Puma and Schrade have seen the most use on police belts. At one time, Puma advertised that its Game Warden with a second saw blade was issued to the Royal Canadian Mounted Police, probably for bush patrols.

Fallkniven's A1 is a superb military/survival knife. The blade is high-carbon VG-10 stainless steel, and the handle is Thermorun®, a durable synthetic. (*Williamson photo*)

The Gerber Harsey Air Ranger I is an overall classic design employing a drop-point blade and checkered-aluminum handle. The design is open along the back of the handle, which might appeal to some more than others. This feature does make cleaning the knife easy in dusty or sandy areas. (*Williamson photo*)

Many cops take a liking to folding knives with pocket clips, attaching them to either their pants or inside a patrol jacket. Others wear them in boots. Spyderco is likely the most common make, and a pioneer in this field. The company has a huge law enforcement following.

One reason for this is that many models are available with lightweight Zytel® handles. Another factor for the popularity of Spyderco folders is the reasonable cost, and a third reason is surely that so many cops see their buddies carrying them. Knowing little about knives, if they see something that carries prestige within their peer circles, that's what they buy, especially if they know it works. Spyderco was among the first, and maybe the premier initiator of one-handed-opening folders with partially serrated blades and pocket clips.

The Gerber Applegate-Fairbairn comes in three sizes, including a new mini, and is probably my favorite. To my delight, a Gerber rep tells me that it's exceptionally popular with our troops in Afghanistan. It provides good utility value in what is probably the best "folding fighter" of the genre. The medium Covert model is best suited for city wear, and is light enough to carry in a coat.

The original Gerber Combat Folder goes well in a belt pouch. Its blade measures 4-1/2 inches, a good length for its purpose. The grooved handle completely contains the blade until pivoted open via a thumb stud, and the overall workmanship is excellent. The black handles are glass-filled nylon, and feel better to the touch than some modern materials. This is a fine selection in all three sizes.

Gerber also offers several other folders. The ones I prefer are the Spectre and the Harsey Air Ranger. The latter has checkered-aluminum handle scales and a drop-point blade. The Spectre showcases black G-10 scales and a dark, nitride-coated 3-1/2-inch blade. Handle liners are titanium for lighter weight. This is a classy, fairly new model that's worth buying. The drop-point blade may make it more acceptable in certain social circumstances than is the Applegate-Fairbairn's modified-dagger blade.

> ## "Most police use knives as tools rather than as weapons."

Celebrated Classic Cutters

The Benchmade 710 and smaller 705 are my pick of the line. They're already classics that combine G-10 synthetic scales, ATS-34 drop-point blades and Benchmade's celebrated Axis blade lock. Smooth operators, these are popular field-tested knives. The unique lock attracts many who don't like locking liners.

Camillus is a traditional maker of fine cutlery, including its CUDA series. I've used the large and medium CUDA for about three years with great satisfaction, although I had a little trouble adapting to an open handle frame. That looks and feels odd at first, and the Harsey Air Ranger from Gerber is also in this vein. The open back, or spine, of the knife does allow easy cleaning in an extremely dusty or sandy environment. Handles scales are G-10, and the CUDA line has several blade options.

The SOG SEAL 2000 passed truly grueling government trials before being adopted for issue to naval special warfare teams. The blade has a powder-based coating to protect it, but is stainless. (*Williamson photo*)

The blades of CUDA folders open easily via thumb discs that slide along arched grooves on the handle. With practice, this action becomes fast and smooth. It's about as close to a switchblade as we'll probably ever see. Once extracted, the blade is propped open by a conventional locking liner.

Masters of Defense (MOD) and Kershaw offer attractive tactical folder choices. A particular MOD example is one designed by retired SEAL "Patches" Watson. Very sturdy and well made, it's a fine example of this sort of knife, with the saw teeth carried further forward on the blade than is usually the case. There's still about an inch of "plain" blade for starting cuts that don't require teeth.

The Kershaw I have is dubbed the Black Out, presumably for its uniformly sable color. The blade opens via a mechanism developed by custom maker Ken Onion. With the blade partially opened through the usual pressure on the thumb stud, the assisted-opening effect flips it out the rest of the way under spring pressure. Yet, it isn't a switchblade. So far, I haven't had the knife open unexpectedly, and haven't heard of it happening. The price on this one is often well under $100, but I think buyers usually select it for the features and style as much as for relatively modest cost. Kershaw has other models that may please a particular buyer.

As popular as folders are, there remains substantial interest in tactical sheath knives. Some call these "fixed blades." They are certainly welcome when there's a need for strength. No folder will withstand as much heavy-duty use, even abuse, as will a good fixed blade knife.

Unfortunately, many military men can't carry sheath knives in today's political climate. If they can, local commanders tend to look with disfavor on larger examples. Many magazine articles on subjects like this tend to forget that, and recommend knives more likely to be found on a movie set than on a real soldier or SWAT cop.

The best chance for carrying larger knives is in special operations units or airborne forces. Probably rural policemen have more options than do most urban officers. Nonetheless, there is still some use of such knives by those officers assigned to paramilitary duties, or who join posses to pursue fugitives into wild areas.

Those who can't get away with wearing a knife with a 7- or 8-inch blade can often manage to pack a 5-inch model. That's enough for most needs, and the knife will remain a stronger, handier tool than a folder. Let's look at some good knives that will do the job and hopefully not push the tolerance envelope too badly. Keep in mind that what's banned in one place may be allowed in another.

Starting with smaller fixed blades, one of the best is Fallkniven's S1. Its blade is a shade over 5 inches and single-edged, so it will comply with regulations banning double-edged blades. The handle is Kraton® or Thermorun®, the catalog having listed both in various editions. Black blades are a popular option, and are required for U.S. aircrew use, for which this knife is specifically designed. The manufacturer claims the U.S. Air Force has joined the U.S. Navy and Marine Corps in approving the S1.

The VG-10 high-carbon stainless steel is among the best available, and sheaths are offered in Cordura®, Kydex® or leather. The butt of the knife has a lined hole for a thong, and the handle is said to be highly resistant to insect repellent, and most oils and solvents. The convex edge grind is razor sharp, but withstands being pounded through wooden sticks for building fires or making an emergency shelter. The S1 fits the sheath on U.S. survival vests, an important factor in its official capacity.

Fly Blades

Another choice long popular with aviators is Randall's Model 5 with a 5-inch blade. Longer blades are offered, the 5-inch one being chosen if it needs to fit a pilot's vest sheath. Stainless or O-1 carbon steel are the options, with stainless being 440B or 440C. Randall's craftsmen forge the blades, somewhat changing the steel's characteristics. For survival or military/SWAT use, the black-Micarta® handle seems the best choice, but Randall offers many other materials. Keep in mind that stag and ivory-Micarta are more apt to draw attention than black handles will. Leather handles are standard, but Micarta is worth the extra money for a knife that may be used in all sorts of weather and temperatures.

There are certainly other good knives about this size, but these are widely used by men who take their knives in harm's way. Should a stag handle be acceptable, Puma's Outdoor model is another good selection. It's a classic sportsman's design that will perform well in the far places of

Randall's famed Model 14, shown here in many variations, is perhaps the most widely recognized sheath knife in the special operations community. (*Weyer photo*)

The Benchmade Model 910 has saw teeth, useful for cutting seat belts. The grooved and checkered handle scales are high-tech G-10, and the unique Axis lock is among the best for folding knives. (*Williamson photo*)

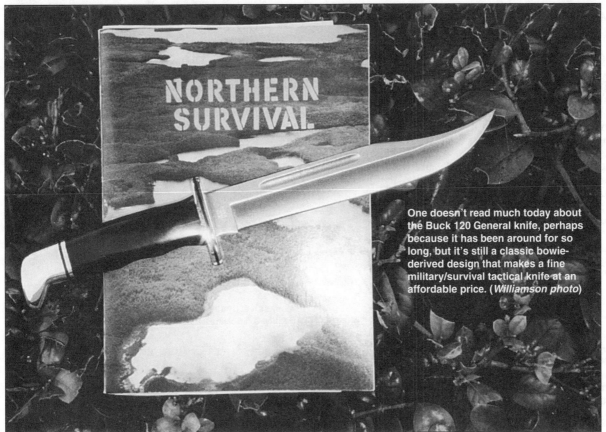

One doesn't read much today about the Buck 120 General knife, perhaps because it has been around for so long, but it's still a classic bowie-derived design that makes a fine military/survival tactical knife at an affordable price. (*Williamson photo*)

the world. All three knives possess the requisite attributes of being sharp and sturdy, and they feel good in the hand.

Large sheath knives, with (roughly) 7-inch blades, are strong enough to pry in an emergency. Most employ high-carbon, stainless blades and synthetic handles that will stand up to the elements and hard use. A hole in the butt for a wrist thong is highly desirable.

Randall's Model 14 is a military classic. It sports a 7-1/2-inch blade, a black-Micarta handle, complete with thong, and an excellent sheath. Divers may prefer the slightly slimmer Model 16.

SOG's SEAL 2000 is a superb military/SWAT item with a pedigree of having passed grueling Navy tests. The sheath is protective and durable. Muela of Spain has a similar edged beauty, the Tornado, at an attractive price.

Fallkniven's A1 features a 6-inch VG-10 blade and Thermorun (or Kraton) handle. It's basically a larger, stouter form of the splendid S1 Forest Knife, a real value!

Finally, don't forget the Buck Models 119 and 120, which provide both value and ready availability. These have been appreciated by our troops for a couple of generations. The new ones are the best yet. Buck's Nighthawk is a modern, effective design.

I hit the highlights, and any knife mentioned will serve you well. Take care of it, and it will take care of you. ●

The Cuttingly Beautiful Clip Point

The author bares all about a blade shape—his favorite—the clip point

By Mac Overton

OH, COME ON now. It's just a blade shape, not a matter of life and death, assert the naysayers. A curve here and another there, and you form a clip point. Big hairy deal! There are many useful knife-blade shapes, most of which have been in use for millennia.

But there's more to the cut than meets the eye.

Some blade shapes are good for specific purposes, like pruning blades with their hawk-bill-like inward curves. Others are generalists, such as the spear point or drop point. These provide great service in many instances, but are lacking in finesse when it comes to jobs requiring a needle-sharp point, such as digging out splinters.

Two of my favorite blade shapes are the sheepsfoot and the Wharncliffe, both of

which have completely straight edges, similar to straight razors in profile. They differ in that, on the Wharncliffe, the back, or spine, of the blade curves down sharply to a fine point. The sheepsfoot blade, on the other hand, descends less

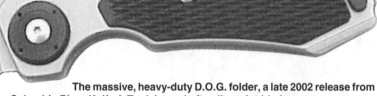

The massive, heavy-duty D.O.G. folder, a late 2002 release from Columbia River Knife & Tool, has a hefty clip-point blade.

Two sizes of Kershaw's traditional-style trappers, top and middle, exhibit useful clip-point blades with re-curved edges, while A.G. Russell's FeatherLite sports what is sometimes called a "folding bowie blade."

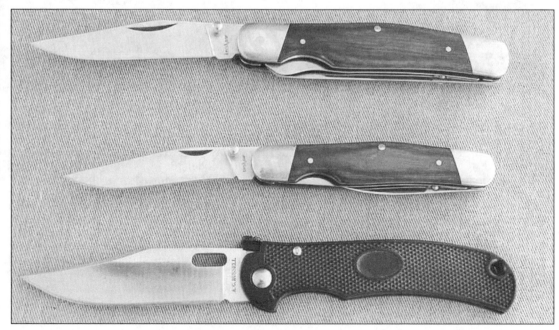

> ***"The clip can be short and steep, or long and gentle."***
> —*Ken Warner in his 1976 book "The Practical Book of Knives"*

abruptly and terminates at more of a blunt point.

But in my experience, the best and most useful all-around blade is the clip blade, in all its various forms.

"In all its various forms?" you may ask.

In the "Introduction to Folding Knives" section of the knife resource book and price guide "Levine's Guide to Knives and Their Values," published by Krause, there is one "Clip Pocket Blade" in a picture portraying the Schrade Company Pocketknife Blades, 1926. It resembles the main blade on today's Schrade Old Timer 8OT or the Schrade Uncle Henry 8875UH full-size stock knives.

In the same book, under the header "E.C. Simmons, 1930," are shown two shapes of clip blades, including the saber clip. Pictured in an old Remington catalog (probably from the 1920s or 1930s) are seven different sizes and shapes of clip blades.

Yes, the clip blade is found in many, many variations, all fitting the definition: an edge, usually curved slightly upward from tang to tip, and a blade spine slanting down to meet the edge in a concave curve.

Knife expert Ken Warner, in his 1976 book "The Practical Book of Knives," noted, "Clip blades vary widely. All include a curved edge

with the back slanting down to it in a concave clip. The clip can be short and steep, or long and gentle. A long one is sometimes called a California clip. There is also a straight clip, which means there's no curve in the line of the clip."

The California clip he referred to is usually the main blade on trapper knives, and the only blade style on 2-bladed muskrat-pattern folders. It is also usually found as the main blade on mid-size serpentine stock knives, like the fine Schrade 897UH (3-1/2 inches closed), one of my personal favorites.

Incision With Precision

Knifemaker Dan Harrison, who has designed knives for Kershaw, Ka-Bar, Bear MGC and others, said that, "The clip point is the best all-around blade shape there is. The keen point makes incisions better than other styles. It allows you to do delicate precision work, and lets you do it more accurately than the broader points [of some other blade types] that require dragging so much metal through [a cutting medium.]"

He cited the example of "old bowie knives," which, of course, had clip-point blades. "The frontiersman could fight with a bowie knife, or clean game with it," said Harrison. "You had a broader part of the blade further back from the point," adding to the knife's strength and versatility.

Harrison said that the popularity of drop-point blades, rather than clip points, among custom knifemakers stems from the fact that, "They are the easiest knives in the world to grind."

Knife writer Durwood Hollis, in his 2001 Krause-published book, "The Complete Guide to Hunting Knives," described it this way: "The

> ***"I think the popularity of the clip blade can be traced to the popularity of the premium stock knife."***
> —*Wally Gardiner*

clip-point pattern is characterized by the back of the blade point being 'clipped' away to join the cutting edge. Because they fit so compactly into knife frames, clip-point blades are often found in folding models."

Hollis added that the clip-point blade style is also common on many fixed-blade models. Indeed, the famous Marble's Ideal and other knives derived from the Ideal, like the Ka-Bar of World War II fame, exhibit how well the clip-point blade can function on a full-sized, fixed-blade knife.

"The blade 'clipping' can take several forms," Hollis said, "including the abrupt spey pattern." I feel, nevertheless, that the spey blade is too abrupt to fit my definition of a clip-point blade. Hollis described the long, slim, extremely fine-pointed clip blades usually found on muskrat folders as "Turkish clips."

"One of the more popular clip-point patterns is the saber clip," Hollis related. He determined that the concave shape of the back gives it the "appearance of a miniature saber or cutlass."

The California clip, with its elongated clip, is sometimes referred to in old catalogs as a "Turkish clip," for some unknown reason. I've even seen some relatively old catalogs in which it was referred to as a "scimitar blade." It seems like it may have been listed

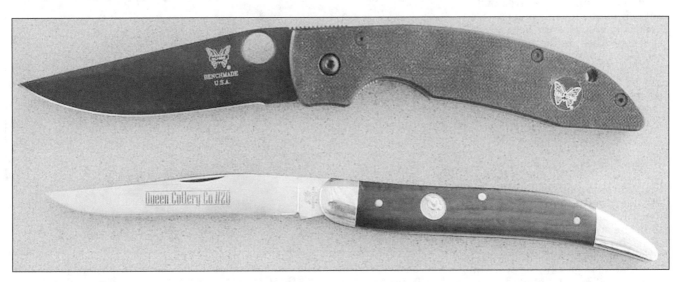

The large Benchmade folder (top) and Queen Model 20 "toothpick" demonstrate how clip points complement long, slim profiles.

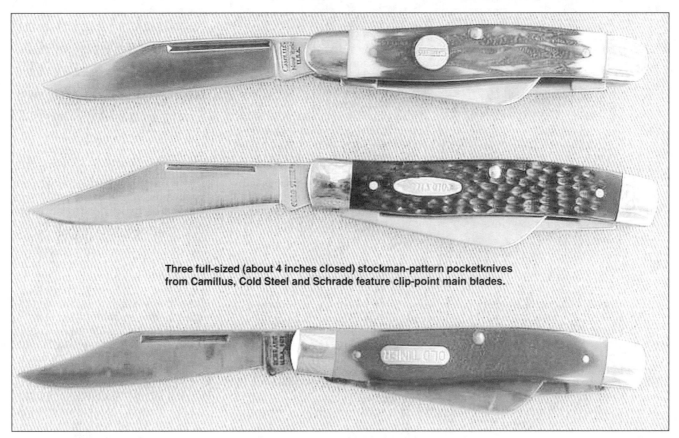

Three full-sized (about 4 inches closed) stockman-pattern pocketknives from Camillus, Cold Steel and Schrade feature clip-point main blades.

that way in a 1940s Maher and Grosh Catalog. (Maher and Grosh was an early knife mail-order house that, I think, went out of business sometime in the 1970s.)

Wally Gardiner, president of the cutlery giant Imperial Schrade, has his own ideas about the apparent enchantment with the clip blade.

"I think the popularity of the clip blade can be traced to the popularity of the premium stock knife," Gardiner said. "This pattern was introduced before the turn of the century [1890] as a more dressy, less bulky, upscale version of the cattle knife. Cattle knives had many master blade shapes, while premium stock knives had only clip-style master blades. Premium stock knives became everyone's best seller and still represent a large part of our business."

The best Schrade examples of premium stock knives today are the Uncle Henry 885UH and the 8OT.

Clip and Point

Ken Warner said, "People like the clip-point for an embarrassingly obvious reason—the clip puts the point where they apparently want it, and it permits a finer point than the spear- or drop-point patterns. It probably doesn't hurt that a majority of the 300- or 400-million American jackknives ever built had at least one clip blade."

Several recent Columbia River Knife & Tool (CRKT) knives feature clip blades.

CRKT co-owner Rod Bremer said, "The clip point is a classic in the knife business, like John Deere is to farming tractors. The shape may not be the best shape for any specific use, but it's difficult to find a better all-around blade. Whether skinning small game or coring an apple, it's tough to beat a hollow-ground clip point for an all-purpose edged tool."

I'm not alone in my adoration of the clip blade. It has been called "the most popular blade shape in America," and it probably is the most popular shape for sporting knives.

Two Spyderco folders (top) parade high-tech, modified clip points, and were the inspiration for knifemaker A.T. Barr's One-Eyed jack model (bottom).

Ka-Bar's Folding Warthog (top) combines a stout clip blade with plenty of belly for skinning. The Col. Littleton lockback (middle) has the Bear MGC-style upturn to the blade. Custom maker Alan Ray puts an abbreviated clip on the main blade of his small trapper.

Consider that it is the blade shape used in the Buck 110 and Schrade LB7 Folding Hunters, as well as other similar knives from many makers. It is almost always the shape of the main blade on stock knives available from virtually all old-line American companies, including Camillus, Schrade, Buck, Queen, Ka-Bar and others. Bear MGC, while not an old-line company, still offers numerous models made in traditional patterns, and most of them feature the clip blade!

Like many shapes, it has been in use for hundreds, if not thousands, of years.

I saw a picture a few years ago of a German or Viking rendition of a scrama-sax (a long, heavy knife used by the ancient Franks in war and in hunting), which was said to be roughly 600-700 years old. The blade was about 14 inches long. The edge was virtually straight for most of its length before curving slightly just behind the point. The back of the blade came down in a "clip" to the point.

The scrama-sax is, essentially, a short sword. I consider it an ancestor of the bowie knife. While no one knows with 100 percent certainty what the knife used by Col. James

Bowie at the Alamo looked like, many depictions and modern replicas show it with a pronounced clip.

And at a knife- and sword-maker's booth at a renaissance fair, I held an authentic Viking sword that experts determined, from the type of laminations in its construction, was made between 1,000 and 1,100 years ago. It was appraised at $100,000. It had a clip point.

What makes the clip-point blade, in all its variations, so useful and versatile on sporting and general-purpose knives?

The blade provides a straight, or nearly straight, section of cutting edge, useful for whittling, wood carving, and cutting rope, cardboard, twine or other fibrous material.

Then, there is the point, which on better specimens can be almost needlelike. It is good for puncturing, sticking or poking, as well as smaller, but essential jobs, like impromptu surgery on a splinter.

Turned-Up Edge

The edge's way of turning upward toward the point gives enough curve to facilitate skinning and other game-handling chores. Cutting downward against a sur-

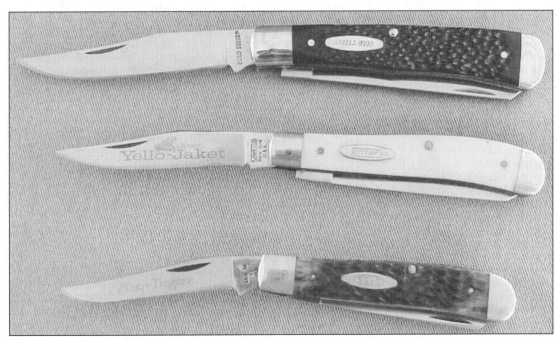

These three trapper pocketknives from Cold Steel (top), Camillus (Yello-Jaket) and Case (Mini-Trapper) all show that there is plenty of room for interpretation in the California clip main blade.

Four fixed-blade knives are dressed up in clip points for the hunt. At top is the Cold Steel Trailmaster, and others, in descending order, include a Blackjack, the SOG Field Pup, and a John Greco/Lile collaborative fixed-blade knife.

"I grew up in a farming community in southeast Missouri, and any boy who didn't have a knife was suspected of not having much else going for him, either."

face is easier than with, say, a Wharncliffe blade, in which only the point contacts the work surface.

The clip blade has been my favorite cutting instrument since I was first entrusted with knives at the age of 6 or 7, so thinking about clip-blade knives engenders sufficient nostalgia.

My first knife was a little Camillus three-blader, a tiny stock pattern. In those days, the late 1950s and early 1960s, we didn't have the paranoia we do today that prohibits carrying of knives in school. That little knife was often carried daily to the classroom, and was even borrowed by the teacher a few times. I grew up in a farming community in southeast Missouri, and any boy who didn't have a knife was suspected of not having much else going for him, either.

My grandfather gave me my first "real" knife (more than toy size) on a cold, December Friday afternoon. School had dismissed early because of snow, but before the snow came

down, Grandfather had been to one of those small-town grocery stores that carried a dozen or so such knives on cards behind the cash register. It was a hollow-metal-handled Barlow pattern made by Imperial, and I still have it. It is 3-1/4 inches closed with loose and rickety handle halves, and the plastic grips are cracked. The simple, carbon steel (probably 1095C) main blade has a clip point, and is stained dark from cleaning untold numbers of fish, squirrels, rabbit, ducks and other small game.

I carried it until I was about 13 years old, when I had saved up the grand sum of $3 and ordered a light, trapper pattern from Maher and Grosh.

It was a Schrade Walden 293, which was later discontinued in favor of the Uncle Henry 285UH and a similar Old Timer model in carbon steel.

The long, slim California clip blade made it a great knife for deer,

as well as the smaller game and fish the little Imperial had handled.

And, while it was small enough to ride in a jeans pocket every day, it was big enough to handle just about anything you were likely to encounter in southeast Missouri, and therefore became my daily carry knife.

Later, I replaced it with an 885UH, which in those days had carbon-steel blades. Stainless models would come along later.

My first deer was field dressed with my grandfather's 6-inch, bowie-inspired Marble's Ideal hunting knife, which had, you guessed it, a clip point.

When dress slacks instead of jeans became part of my regular work uniform, I bought and carried Schrade's 897UH. This slim stock knife had an elongated California clip as its main blade, and was one of the first production knives from anybody to feature "super stainless steel." I think 440C was used then, in the late 1970s, and Schrade switched to specially heat-treated 440A, giving even better cutting results.

Bladed Buddy

For maybe 25 years, this knife or its Old Timer equivalent, Model 98OT, was my constant companion, no matter what other knives I had on my person.

A Camillus Yello-Jaket small trapper, with its clip master blade, was my bladed buddy on many happy outings. There were many, many others, including a Queen Trapper and a Queen Texas Toothpick, that met my cutting needs at various times. Thinking about them brings back memories, and the main thing the knives of my youth have in common is a clip-point blade.

Yes, it is just a blade shape, and not a matter of life and death, but in cutting matters, the clip point is as good or better a blade shape than many that have come before or after it. ●

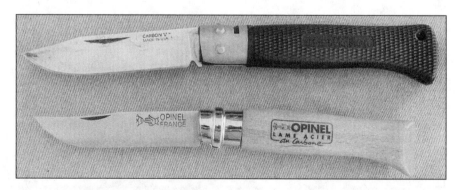

The famed French Opinel folder (bottom) with its rotary lock, and the Cold Steel TwistMaster, which it inspired, both have useful clip-point blades. Stains on the Cold Steel are from dressing deer, a task for which it proved adept.

Exit Dull—

ENTER EXTREME SPORTS KNIVES!

By Durwood Hollis

IN THE WORLD of outdoor recreation, some sports are practiced at the extreme level. Hiking generally doesn't involve personal perils, but mountaineering has an elevated level of risk, and free climbing (with little in the way of safety equipment) is sure to present an even more serious threat to one's existence.

In the same vein, boating, snorkeling and similar water sports are fairly safe. However, river running, kayaking and diving could be considered extreme versions of the same activities. If your outdoor sport of choice fits into this category, then selecting a personal cutting implement will be an important decision. A look at what the market has to offer in

▶The Benchmade H2O (Model 110H20) has several features that have endeared it to those who take water sports to the "extreme."

the extreme sport knives arena might just be of assistance in making that choice.

Benchmade Knife Co.

If you're an extreme water sports zealot, one who doesn't fret class five rapids, then the Benchmade H2O (Model 100SH20) fixed blade is a wet-world asset. The full-tang H1 stainless steel blade makes for a virtually non-corrosive cutting edge. Bull-nosed in shape, and partially serrated, the blade qualities are ideal for on-the-water performance.

The bull-nose form, without a pointed tip, prevents the puncturing of inflatable rafts or human skin if the knife is dropped while the boat is being tossed around in the waves. The hollow-ground edge is half-serrated for cutting rope and clothing, and the handle scales are sculpted to form-fit the hand.

A molded-Kydex®-thermoplastic sheath and a sheath-mounted, lash-tab clip make for a variety of carry options. Light, strong and able to handle all of the realities of aquatic environs, this knife is extreme to the max.

▲Designed by a leading sea-kayaker, the Buck Tiburon (Model 185) is an edged tool that can handle a broad range of aquatic cutting needs.

Buck Knives

Buck Knives called upon the experience of top sea kayaker Ed Gillet to develop a knife that meets the demands of extreme water sports enthusiasts. The result of that collaboration is the singularly outstanding Model 185 Tiburon fixed blade.

A single piece of 17-7PH stainless steel—an ultra-stain-resistant metal—this multi-purpose edged tool is the right choice for extreme aquatic applications. The blade itself showcases a 4-inch, partially serrated cutting edge and comes to a chisel point. A notch on the blade spine is designed for cutting lines and straps, and wrench openings. A tool adaptor slot and a carabineer/lanyard hole are integral parts of the lightweight handle.

The ambidextrous, molded-thermoplastic sheath sports a belt, clothing or gear clip. Shooting the rapids has never been safer than with the easy-to-use-and-maintain Tiburon, an excellent choice for kayaking, rafting, boating and diving.

Cold Steel

The element of danger is an accepted part of most extreme sports. When adventuresome sportsmen and sports ladies need a sharp edge, there's usually no time to fumble around with a knife. Cold Steel planned for such emergencies with the Land & Sea Rescue folder, a model that can be called into the game at a moment's notice.

The AUS-8A stainless steel blade is fashioned in a useful sheepsfoot pattern. The flat-ground blade edge features some rather aggressive serrations along most of its length, with only a short, plain-edge section near the tip. A thumb stud and back-spring lock release make for speedy one-hand blade opening and closing.

The molded Zytel® handle is deeply checkered and contoured for a non-slip surface, and a steel pocket clip is another feature that makes this knife an ever-ready steel sidekick. This is a small and powerful knife that can cut with the fury of a chainsaw. That, alone, should pique the interest of extreme sports fans.

Columbia River Knife & Tool

In collaboration with custom knifemaker Jim Hammond, Columbia River Knife & Tool has produced what could well be the ultimate dive and whitewater knife. The Hammond A.B.C. fixed blade (Model 2604/2605) showcases several design features that will

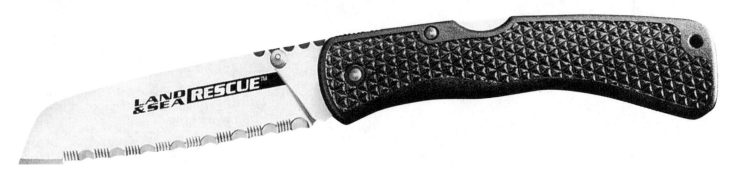

Cold Steel's Land & Sea Rescue knife is a small folder, but its one-hand blade rotation, non-slip handle surface and steel pocket clip make it ready for action.

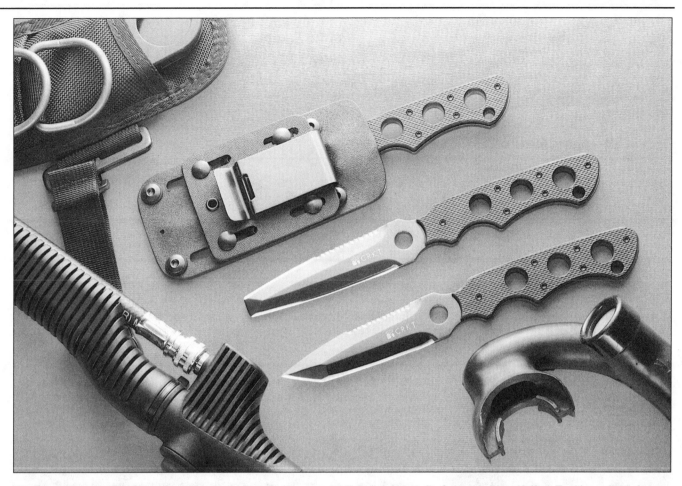

Touted as "the ultimate dive and whitewater knife," the Hammond A.B.C. fixed blade by Columbia River Knife & Tool is available in two versions-blunt-point and drop-point.

interest scuba divers and those who are addicted to running river rapids. The steel used in this edged tool is AUS-8 stainless. Two blade versions—the Aqua blunt point dive configuration and Operator's drop-point Tanto—are available.

The knife is just a tad over 8 inches long and features a 3-1/4-inch main cutting edge. A short section of Triple-Point serrations are located on the blade spine for cutting through cord, line and underwater entanglements. The Hammond A.B.C. showcases a full-

length, skeletonized tang for optimum tool integrity, and the entire piece has been black-titanium-nitride coated for enhanced corrosion resistance. The molded- Zytel handle is literally bolted to the tang with steel Torx® fasteners.

▼The tiny White Water La Griffe claw knife from Emerson Knives can slice through cordage and rope with amazing speed.

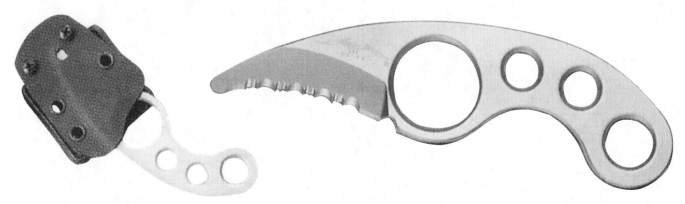

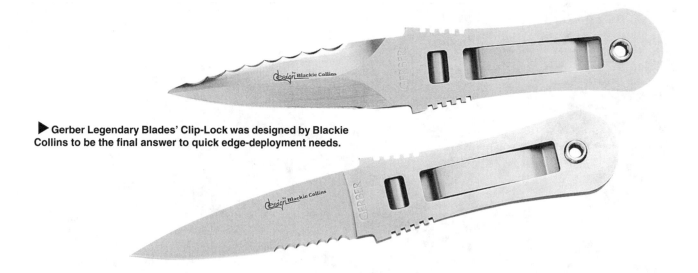

▶ Gerber Legendary Blades' Clip-Lock was designed by Blackie Collins to be the final answer to quick edge-deployment needs.

Carrying convenience is accomplished by means of dual-attachment panels and a stainless steel clothing clip. The sheath is designed so that there are eight carry modes and a wide range of attachment orientations. This is an extremely versatile knife that can be an indispensable companion for those who take their water work to the extreme.

Emerson Knives, Inc.

While most Emerson Knives products are designed for personal defense, the little White Water La Griffe is right at home in the hands of kayakers, river rafters and other extreme sports devotees. Designed by noted French knifemaker Fredric Perrin, this tiny terror is a claw-shaped cutter made from 154CM stainless steel with a silver

Strong, simple and a delight to carry, the new Schrade Spitfire LTD has a locking ATS-34 stainless blade, a carbon fiber handle and a detachable carrying lanyard. (*Imperial Schrade/Images Group photo*)

satin finish. The curved edge is serrated for slicing through cordage and rope, and the tip of the blade is round and blunt for safety.

Blade and handle are a single, curved, continuous piece of steel without handle scales and made even lighter by a series of round holes machined through the piece. The largest of these holes, located at the midpoint of the knife, is designed for index finger insertion. A molded sheath secures the knife in the tip-up position and is easily accessed by either hand. Even though the White Water La Griffe was created specifically for aquatic cutting needs, it can certainly fill a much wider role in any extreme sports venue.

▼With a design heritage descending directly from the famous Ka-Bar fixed-blade knife that served our military troops in battle, the Warthog Folder is both tough and versatile.

Gerber Legendary Blades

When your extreme sport demands quick edge deployment, then nothing tops Gerber's Clip-Lock fixed-blade knife (Models 5301/5302). Designed by Blackie Collins to be the ready answer for cutting needs, the knife blade and tang are one piece of rust-resistant stainless steel. Two versions—single- and double-edged—are available for many applications.

In its thermoplastic sheath, an innovative clip presses firmly against the handle so the knife is held securely in place. The clip is pressed down to release the knife and bring it into play. A thin profile and ready access are features that make the Clip-Lock a fine-edged tool for extreme sports fans.

Imperial Schrade

When the need for a sharp edge is manifest, you certainly don't require a knife with all of the proverbial bells and whistles. Strong, lightweight and easy to carry, the new Imperial Schrade Spitfire LTD (Model SPF1LTD) is more than just a gimmick. The ATS-34 stainless steel blade is

◄ The Kershaw Sea Hunter is available in two blade styles—pointed and blunt—and, best of all, the blades are interchanged with relative ease.

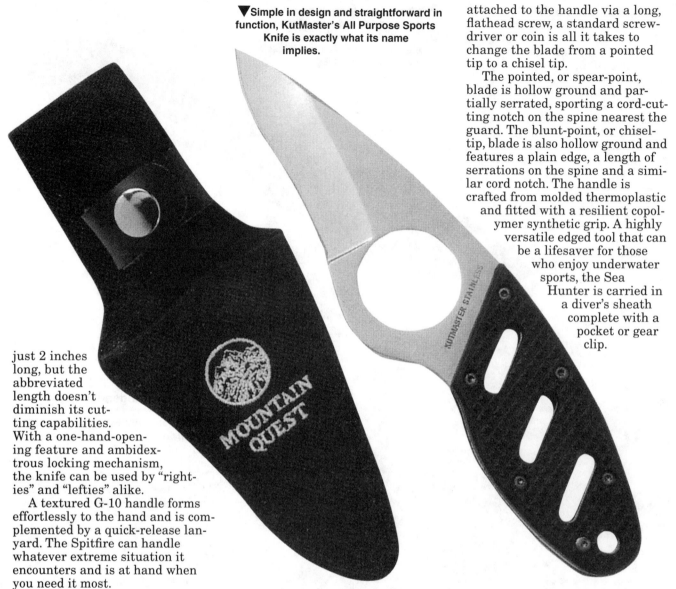

▼Simple in design and straightforward in function, KutMaster's All Purpose Sports Knife is exactly what its name implies.

attached to the handle via a long, flathead screw, a standard screwdriver or coin is all it takes to change the blade from a pointed tip to a chisel tip.

The pointed, or spear-point, blade is hollow ground and partially serrated, sporting a cord-cutting notch on the spine nearest the guard. The blunt-point, or chisel-tip, blade is also hollow ground and features a plain edge, a length of serrations on the spine and a similar cord notch. The handle is crafted from molded thermoplastic and fitted with a resilient copolymer synthetic grip. A highly versatile edged tool that can be a lifesaver for those who enjoy underwater sports, the Sea Hunter is carried in a diver's sheath complete with a pocket or gear clip.

just 2 inches long, but the abbreviated length doesn't diminish its cutting capabilities. With a one-hand-opening feature and ambidextrous locking mechanism, the knife can be used by "righties" and "lefties" alike.

A textured G-10 handle forms effortlessly to the hand and is complemented by a quick-release lanyard. The Spitfire can handle whatever extreme situation it encounters and is at hand when you need it most.

Ka-Bar Knives, Inc.

In participating in one of the extreme sports, you never know when or how your knife of choice will be called into play. For this reason, I believe the Ka-Bar Warthog Folder (Models 3070/3071) is an ideal choice for these kinds of activities. With a design heritage descending directly from the famous Ka-Bar fixed-blade knife that served our military troops in battle, this little lock-blade folder is tough and versatile.

The AUS-8 stainless steel blade has a broad, drop-point shape, available with either a plain or partially serrated cutting edge. A thumb rest on the blade spine near the handle is a feature that provides increased functional control. The blade can be brought into play with one hand by means of a

reversible thumb stud, and a locking liner secures it in the open position.

The handle is molded Zytel with three linear grooves to facilitate a secure grip. An attachment clip is mounted on the handle so the knife can be carried in the tip-down position. When all is said and done, the Warthog Folder is tough enough to use as a cutting, digging and prying tool. What more could an extreme sports fan ask for?

Kershaw Knives

Located in the Pacific Northwest, Kershaw shows a strong interest in water sports with its Sea Hunter (Models 1008/1008BL-P) diver's sheath knife. The Sea Hunter's 420J2 stainless steel blade comes in two, interchangeable shapes with pointed and chisel tips. With a blade tang

KutMaster

In its Mountain Quest line, KutMaster unleashes the All Purpose Sports Knife (Model MQ640CP). This edged tool's extreme-sports strong points are clearly manifest. To begin with, the 400 stainless steel blade has a full-length tang for strength. The blade pattern is a slight drop point and features an index finger insertion hole to enhance edge control.

The hollow-ground cutting edge is slightly re-curved in shape and hand honed for maximum sharpness. Molded, high-impact thermoplastic handle scales stand up to the nastiest outdoor elements. A nylon sheath with a snap strap holds the knife securely. Simple in design and straightforward in function, the All Purpose Sports Knife is exactly what its name implies.

While it's part of the Masters of Defense personal defense knife line, the Scorpion fixed blade has plenty of features for extreme sports work.

The Meyerco Buddy System neck knife is an affordable edged tool that has serious extreme sports applications.

point-pattern blades, with the Buddy System II model offering a broader and bolder shape. The knife locks safely into a molded sheath, complete with attached neck cord, until it is released via a spring-loaded button.

Outdoor Edge Cutlery

When you need a sharp edge, immediate access is of paramount importance. This is certainly one of the strengths of the Outdoor Edge Wedge (Model WG-1) and Wedge II (Model WG-2) fixed-blade knives. Flat-ground, drop-point-pattern 6M stainless steel blades lead into teardrop-shaped, molded-Delrin® handles with ridges along the handle rims for non-slip grip.

Size is the difference between the Wedge, with a 2-3/8-inch blade, and the Wedge II blade, which stretches a full 3 inches. The Finger Touch Lock Release sheaths sport swivel clips and cord loops, assets that provide a variety of attachment options. The perfect quick-access knives, the Wedge and Wedge II meet the cutting needs of any extreme sports fanatic.

SOG Specialty Knives

When outdoor activities shift to the extreme, then the advantage is often decided by the slimmest of edges. Understanding just how important this really is, the folks at SOG have created the new Outline (Model S090) fixed-blade knife. Crafted entirely from AUS-6 stainless steel, with a full-length skeletonized tang, this knife is both slim and functional.

The hollow-ground blade is designed with a modified tanto point and features an aggressive serrated cutting edge. The blade tang is skeletonized and has no handle scales. Interestingly, this tang opening can double as a bottle

Masters of Defense, LLC

Masters of Defense has come up with a fixed blade that possesses many extreme-sports-knife features. The Scorpion parades a 2-1/2-inch 154CM high-carbon stainless steel blade with a plain edge and partial serrations on the spine, pushing the envelope for overall cutting performance. The handle is an extension of the skeletonized blade tang, and the entire knife has been finished with diamond-black DLC for increased resistance to corrosion.

A molded-Prilon thermoplastic sheath allows it to be strung around the neck or carried on the belt. The design emphasis of this knife is squarely placed on low weight, accessibility and broad

utility. As such, it should prove to be a valued companion to extreme sports devotees.

Meyerco

It doesn't take an entire week's paycheck to acquire a knife that meets your extreme sports needs. The folks at Meyerco have recently unveiled an affordable fixed-blade knife duo—the Buddy System and Buddy System II (Models MCBUDH and MAGGBUD). Designed by Blackie Collins, these small fixed-blade wonders can be carried conveniently around the neck.

With 440 stainless steel blades and Fiberesin handles, either model is ideal for outdoor recreation, especially extremes sports. The knives have flat-ground, drop-cap remover. A Kydex® sheath safely secures the blade. Carried by means of the sheath-attached neck lanyard, or clipped at the edge of a pocket or boot, this knife is the definitive utilitarian edged tool.

Spyderco Knives

The Spyderco Dodo Model (C80) has a sensible-size blade mated to a rather large handle. A shorter blade doesn't draw unwanted attention to the knife user, and the oversize handle can provide greater cutting leverage, both to the advantage of the extreme sports enthusiast.

The blade is CPM S30V, a premium stainless steel, and features a hollow-ground cutting edge with an arched belly (for greater cutting power) and a down-sloped tip (for fine, detailed work). A unique Ball Bearing Lock mechanism secures the folding blade open in use. The lock is remarkably strong and inhibits blade wobble or movement. The blade release is accessible on either side of the G-10 handle, making this a truly ambidextrous tool.

A flexible wire clip can be affixed to either side of the handle, which allows a wide range of carrying options. The name of this knife comes from the resemblance of the blade to the bill of the dull-witted Dodo bird (originally found on the island of Mauritius in the Indian Ocean, but now extinct), yet there is nothing "dull" or unintelligent about this knife design.

Victorinox

Most would agree that parachuting is an extreme sport. Just the thought of jumping out of a perfectly sound aircraft with my life dependent on a silk chute makes me uncomfortable. I have noted, however, that sport jumpers do carry pocket folders. Chute rigging and cord can get tangled, so having a knife along for the ride makes sense. No better choices are available for this sport than the Victorinox Parachutist (Model 54864), or the equally functional Jumpmaster (Model 53846).

Both knives feature a number of stainless steel implements—a large locking main blade; a belt-cutting blade; Phillips screwdriver; a reamer; can opener/small screw-

When you're in need of an "edge," then look no farther than the SOG Outline (Model S090). With its skeletonized handle, modified Tanto point and serrated cutting edge, this knife is the right choice for serious cutting needs.

New this year is the Outdoor Wedge II neck knife, featuring a flat-ground, drop-point-pattern 6M stainless steel blade and a teardrop-shaped, molded- Delrin® handle with ridges along the handle rims for a non-slip grip.

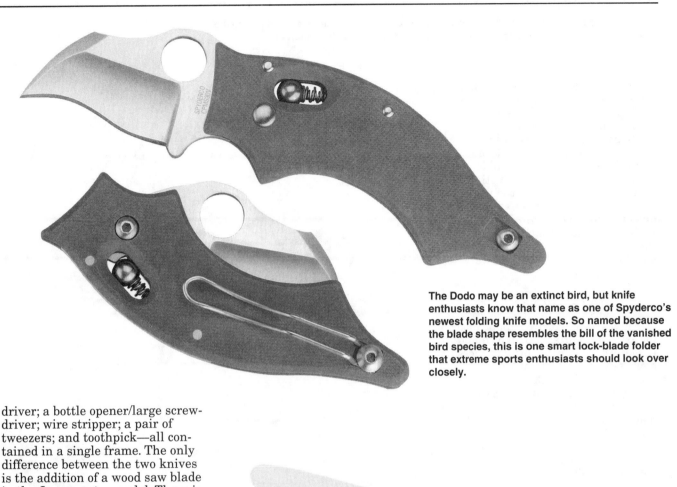

The Dodo may be an extinct bird, but knife enthusiasts know that name as one of Spyderco's newest folding knife models. So named because the blade shape resembles the bill of the vanished bird species, this is one smart lock-blade folder that extreme sports enthusiasts should look over closely.

driver; a bottle opener/large screwdriver; wire stripper; a pair of tweezers; and toothpick—all contained in a single frame. The only difference between the two knives is the addition of a wood saw blade in the Jumpmaster model. There is a Swiss Army Knife model for nearly every sport and activity, and now, even sport parachutists can own their own special version.

Wenger

For the extreme mountain bikers, Wenger delivers the Pocket Mountain Bike (Model 16855) folder. Hidden in the knife frame are a number of bike-friendly implements, including a chain rivet setter; removable Allen wrench; removable spoke adjustment tool; hex key for nuts;

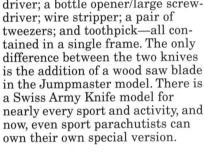

Those who practice sport parachute jumping (an extreme activity if there ever was one) will appreciate the features of the Victorinox Parachutist Swiss Army Knife Folder.

Similar to the Parachutist, the Victorinox Jumpmaster knife model adds a wood saw to the package, bringing it into the realm of a multi-tool for extreme outdoor sports use.

screwdrivers for slotted or Phillips screws; and a cap lifter/wire stripper blade. A large spear-point main blade completes the Swiss Army Knife package. With this all of these implements and functional applications in hand, most bike problems can be managed with little trouble. Throughout the world, such Wenger knives have saved the day over and over again. The Pocket Mountain Bike is a pattern the extremist sports person should keep in mind when knife selection is made.

The Last Word

Knives with features applicable for extreme sports use can be found in many cutlery lines. Most are less aggressive than tactical knife designs, yet they lack little in performance. Such edged tools should be just as tough as any battle blade. The final decision rests with those who participate in those intensely demanding activities. When up against all odds, only the best of the best will do.   ●

Mountain bikers and other hard-driving cycle riders will realize the advantages that are built into the Wenger Pocket Mountain Bike Swiss Army Knife.

Death to the Sword?
Not on Your Life!

Swords, loppers, choppers, tactical and fighting knives thrived at the 2003 Sword and S.H.O.T. Show

By Hank Reinhardt

BACK IN 1985, when Bill Adams and I started Museum Replicas, several people informed us that we would never be able to make it fly. They said that there were only a few people who were interested in swords, and certainly not enough to support a full-size mail order operation.

After returning home from attending two recent industry shows—the 2003 S.H.O.T. (Shooting Hunting Outdoor Trade) Show and the 2003 Sword Show, held concurrently in Orlando—I wondered what those same people would say 18 years later. There were seven large wholesale operations displaying their edged product lines, all of them selling swords, and all are doing quite well with it.

Museum Replicas was started, not just as a business, rather as a labor of love. Bill and I were both into swords and knives, and although time has aged us both, it hasn't lessened our love of the two. At the 2003 shows, it was a great deal of fun to see all of the new stuff and watch the progress being made in the field.

Lynn Thompson at Cold Steel has been around awhile, and has always produced fine knives. As of late, he has entered into the sword field and is fashioning the same quality in swords that he has proven capable of achieving with knives. Although I had seen pictures of some of his swords, this was the first chance I had to handle them.

Lynn builds a version of the 1917 U.S. Naval Cutlass and it is a superb copy of the original. I've owned an original, and the Cold Steel version is just as good, if not better. Cold Steel also markets a 1917 Cutlass Saber. This is identical to the Naval Cutlass, but with a longer blade made into a saber. It isn't orig-

▶Cold Steel builds a version of the 1917 U.S. Naval Cutlass, and the author says it is as good as, if not better than, the original.

▲With a 33-inch blade and a total weight of just over 3 pounds, the Cold Steel Hand-and-a-Half medieval sword is most impressive.

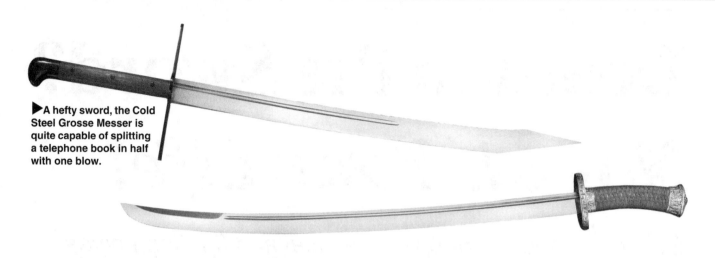

▶A hefty sword, the Cold Steel Grosse Messer is quite capable of splitting a telephone book in half with one blow.

▲New to the Cold Steel line is a Chinese Saber, a light but effective cut-and-thrust sword favored by cavalry and foot soldier alike.

▶The Asian martial arts segment of the industry can rejoice in the new C.A.S. Iberia kung fu sword, which can be ordered sharp, or dull for practice fighting.

inal, but it is a sweet sword. While on the subject of replica military swords, Cold Steel also fashions one of my favorite sabers, the 1796 Light Cavalry saber, the original of which was used with telling effect in the Napoleonic Wars.

Cut Through the Yellow Pages

Cold Steel also unveils a new Hand-and-a-Half medieval sword that is most impressive. The blade is 33 inches long, with an overall length of 42-1/2 inches. Weight is slightly over 3 pounds. Cross section is a flattened diamond, and although not a copy of a specific sword, is fairly accurate for the late-Middle Ages. Along with it, Lynn has a Grosse Messer. This is a big knife that was popular in Germany and Northern Europe. A hefty sword, it is quite capable of splitting a telephone book in half with one blow.

Asian martial arts are well represented also. Cold Steel is the only company, to my knowledge, offering a double-edged katana, and it's a beauty. There are two sets of *katanas*, *wakizashis* and *tantos*. The Imperial Series is quite ornate and highly polished, while the

Warrior Series is not quite so fancy, but just as effective in cutting.

Nor has China been forgotten. New to the Cold Steel line is a Chinese Saber, a light but effective cut-and-thrust sword favored by cavalry and foot soldier alike. There are two Gim swords, the first a one-handed weapon with a 30-inch straight, double-edged blade, and the other, a two-handed version sporting a 35-inch blade. These are both attractive weapons.

Two other Cold Steel swords that I particularly liked were the Scottish Baskethilts. One is the typical broadsword, double-edged, with a central fuller and two smaller ones, and the other is a backsword, a singled-edged blade with a long fuller. Both are good looking.

After I left the Cold Steel booth, I wandered over to C.A.S. Iberia to see what Barry Ross and Paul Chen had to offer. I expected a lot from them, and I wasn't disappointed.

Kung Fu Fighters

Paul Chen made quite a splash when he entered into the sword market. He offers some of the finest katanas available anywhere, and the prices are reasonable. In coordination with C.A.S. Iberia, Paul's workmanship, which was excellent to start, has continued to improve, and the scope of offerings has also increased.

The Asian martial arts segment of the industry can rejoice in two new kung fu swords. One of these is quite light, and completely dull. It is designed for practice and for

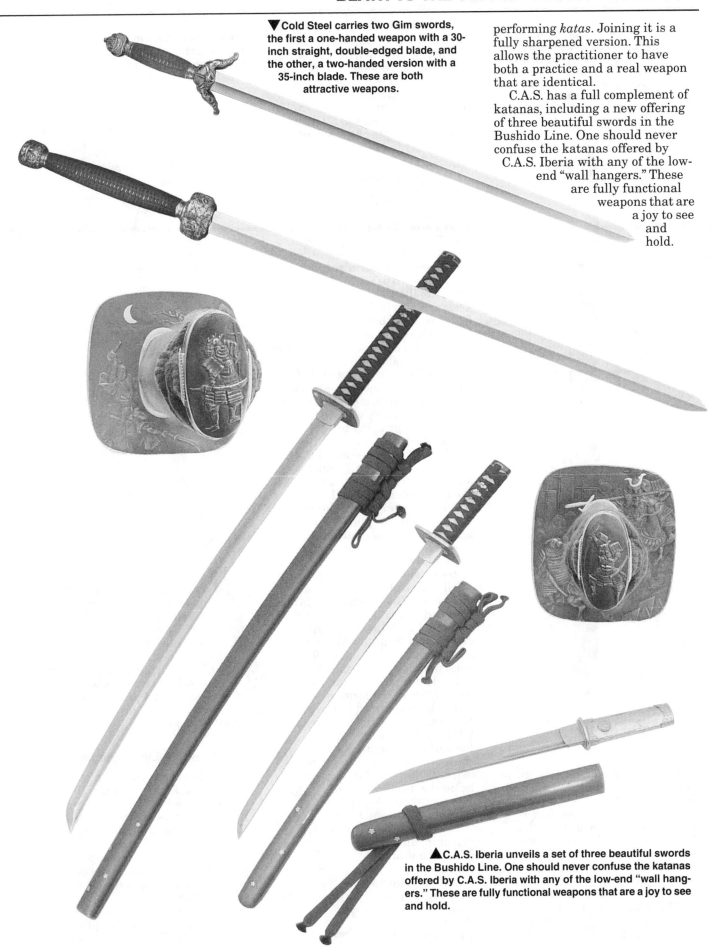

▼Cold Steel carries two Gim swords, the first a one-handed weapon with a 30-inch straight, double-edged blade, and the other, a two-handed version with a 35-inch blade. These are both attractive weapons.

performing *katas*. Joining it is a fully sharpened version. This allows the practitioner to have both a practice and a real weapon that are identical.

C.A.S. has a full complement of katanas, including a new offering of three beautiful swords in the Bushido Line. One should never confuse the katanas offered by C.A.S. Iberia with any of the low-end "wall hangers." These are fully functional weapons that are a joy to see and hold.

▲C.A.S. Iberia unveils a set of three beautiful swords in the Bushido Line. One should never confuse the katanas offered by C.A.S. Iberia with any of the low-end "wall hangers." These are fully functional weapons that are a joy to see and hold.

▼To complement a random-pattern-damascus blade, the grip of the C.A.S. Iberia Han Sword is a beauty, with silver-inlaid scroll pattern in the rosewood. This is truly an example of the sword maker's art.

by the intricate cross-section of the sword. The Han Wan sword sports a single, deep fuller, but the sides of the fuller are somewhat raised to make slight ridges. The point is also reinforced. The grip is a beauty, with a silver-inlaid scroll pattern in the rosewood. This is truly an example of the sword maker's art.

Tai Chi "Chopppers"

Available for the Tai Chi practitioner is a highly flexible sword with a straight blade in C.A.S. Iberia's Practical series, a group of swords designed for the user and allowing him or her a good blade with which to practice.

C.A.S. Iberia has two weapons designed purely for infantry, one Chinese, the other European. The Chinese weapon is the Pudao. This is a wide-bladed sword mounted on a red-wrapped shaft. The blade is 26 inches long, with a width of a whopping 3-3/4 inches and an overall length of almost 6 feet. This is a surprisingly quick weapon, and it would be frightening to have to face it in battle.

The European section of C.A.S. Iberia's work is equally impressive, starting with two Scottish swords, the Lowlander and the Highlander. The Highlander is a traditional claymore with a spherical pommel and down-sloping quatrefoil guards. It is an accurate copy of the original, as is the Lowlander, the latter of which is a big sword with a full length of 69 inches, and a 48-inch blade. The Lowlander's grip is wrapped in a cross pattern and decorated with tacks. The steel cross guard is quite wide and curves downward, making for a most impressive sword.

Real showpieces manifest themselves in the forms of a C.A.S. Iberia pierced-hilt rapier and companion dagger. Pierced-hilt rapiers were popular in the early 17th century, and the motifs are many and varied, with vines and flowers being the most common. What most people don't realize is that, aside from the beauty and the workmanship, the pierced hilt had a practical value, as well.

Not only did such a hilt lighten the overall weight of the sword, it had a pierced cup that

▶A wide-bladed sword mounted on a red-wrapped shaft, the C.A.S. Iberia Pudao stretches nearly 6 feet.

could catch an opponent's blade. If a thrust came straight in toward the cup, it could slip off and land on an arm or even the body. Sometimes a lip was added to the cup, but piercing worked just as well. C.A.S. Iberia's rapier and dagger set would be at home in the streets or the courts of Renaissance Europe.

Geared Up Like a Gladiator

Another beautiful and effective piece is the Roman Dagger. This is a copy of the Pugio that accompanied the Roman soldier from England to the Mid-East, and from Germany to North Africa. It is both a utility dagger and a last-ditch weapon, and the C.A.S. Iberia version would work as well, if not better, than the original.

The Marshall sword has been quite popular, and deservedly so. Named after William Marshall,

The Chinese martial arts are well represented in C.A.S. Iberia's line. The company offers a stunning Yanling Sword, developed during the Song Dynasty, with a damascus blade. The grip is stingray skin covered with cord, and the scabbard is adorned with polished ray skin.

Another damascus offering is the Han Sword. This is a straight-bladed sword, and the random damascus pattern is complemented

▼The C.A.S. Iberia Lowlander Scottish Sword features a grip wrapped in a cross pattern and decorated with tacks. The steel cross guard is quite wide and curves downward, making for a most impressive sword.

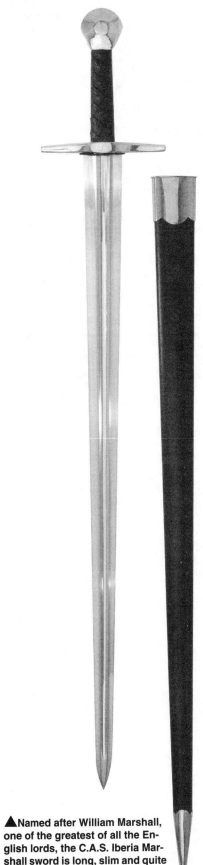

▲Named after William Marshall, one of the greatest of all the English lords, the C.A.S. Iberia Marshall sword is long, slim and quite deadly. It is considered by many to be the most beautiful of all the medieval swords still in existence.

Although Spanish companies have been producing swords for many years, it was Museum Replicas that started the interest in functional, accurately copied swords. Now owned by Windlass Steelcrafts, Museum Replicas has grown and expanded under capable hands.

One sword that I take pride in is the English Tuck. This is a highly accurate copy of one of the originals in my collection, and is every bit as effective as the original. The tuck is considered by many to be an early form of rapier. It was used when armor was becoming increasingly effective, and the long, stiff blade was used to punch through openings in armor, or to punch through mail. The tuck is a simple sword without a fancy guard, a thrusting instrument.

Another excellent replica is the Higgins Sword, named after a museum. This is an exact copy of a medieval sword in the John Woodman Higgens Armoury.

Museum Replicas has recently signed an agreement to reproduce some of the weapons in the armory, and the Higgins is the

one of the greatest of all the English lords, the sword is an exact copy of #A458 in the Wallace Collection. Long, slim and quite deadly, it is considered by many to be the most beautiful of all the medieval swords still in existence.

I have one, and have also been lucky enough to see and handle the original years ago. This is another sword that has a complex cross section. The blade features a deep, central fuller and a slight, hollow grind, so that the combination produces a sword with two ridges. The two-ridge configuration provides a great deal of rigidity to the blade, however my own experimental cutting shows that this does not affect the shearing power of the sword.

The fantasy field has not been ignored. C.A.S. Iberia's Dark Sentinel is a beautiful sword, and it handles like a dream. The long, curved blade has a deadly point, and the back has a false edge that lessens the load of the blade, making it light enough for one-hand use, but with a long grip that allows for both hands if desired. The studded handle gives a good grip. Not an expensive sword, it is certainly an effective one.

The newest C.A.S. Iberia sword is the Banshee. This is a beautiful, simple and oh-so-deadly all-around tool and weapon. The blade is slim, broadening towards the point, single-edged and about 18 inches long. The grip is also slim and leather wrapped. The first thing you think about when holding this sword is just how fast it is. Fast, yet the blade is thick and strong enough to take a beating. It's a real beauty.

first, exhibiting a wide-bladed, cut-and-thrust design that is most impressive and effective.

A Slice of Senility

I have yet to cut with the Higgins sword, but have used similar ones. Having handled it, I can tell that it will work quite well, and it won't be long before I'll be shearing, chopping and behaving with

▼One sword the author takes pride in is the Museum Replicas English Tuck, a highly accurate copy of one of the originals in his collection. The tuck is considered by many to be an early form of rapier.

all the dignity of a 69-year-old nut. Oh well, it's fun.

Museum Replicas' new Schiavona sword is modeled after one originally carried by the Slavonic mercenaries working for the Doge of Venice. There are many in collections in Scotland, where the sword was accepted and served alongside the classic *baskethilt*. This version has a beautifully blued blade, with a black baskethilt and brass pommel.

There are two impressive choppers in the Museum Replicas line, one taken from the Maciejowski Bible. It is a large, two-hand weapon, but there are no original pieces known to exist. The blade is made purely for cutting and crushing armor, and would do a splendid job of it. The companion piece is basically fantasy, but based on the vague sketches from the same source. Fantasy weapons are not ignored by Museum Replicas, especially considering the Eye of Balor, an expertly crafted piece by Bruce Brookhardt. This is a large, single-edged weapon that is quite impressive and hasn't abandoned efficiency for looks.

United Cutlery has produced a full line of swords and artifacts from the "Lord of the Rings" trilogy of movies. These are beautiful and well-made copies of the ones used in the flicks. All of them have false edges, and it is expected that, as the final movie is released, there will be additional swords that have not yet been seen. Although no official announcements have been made, I doubt if they will pass up making any of the weapons shown in the movie. Certainly there is a market for many of the elfin and "Orcish" blades.

Trippin' to the 2003 S.H.O.T. Show

In Year 2003, the S.H.O.T. Show was held in Atlanta and, believe me,

▲Fantasy weapons are not ignored by Museum Replicas, especially considering the Eye of Balor, an expertly crafted piece by Bruce Brookhardt. This is a large, single-edged weapon that is quite impressive, and hasn't abandoned efficiency for looks.

▼The Cadillac of the Camillus Knives line is the Jerry Fisk Bowie, a beautiful, large knife, with a blade that stretches 11 inches and a fiddleback-maple handle.

the weather was much different from the usual S.H.O.T. Show atmosphere. This was pleasant. The show, as usual, was huge, and for someone who likes guns and knives, it was a wonderland.

Knives were very much in evidence, with some new blades that

Replicas of old bowies are perfect for re-enactors as well as collectors who can't afford the originals. From Atlanta Cutlery, such pieces would include the Sheffield Style (shown), the Mexican and two Dueling Bowies.

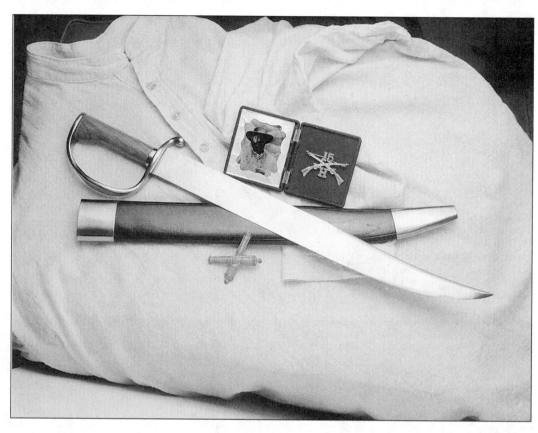

The South is well represented in the bowie category. Atlanta Cutlery sends a Southern D-Guard Bowie (shown), a Texas Bowie and an Arkansas Toothpick to market.

were especially nice. Regretfully, you would need a volume to describe all of the knives presented. I doubt if I saw all of them, but the ones I did view were quite impressive.

Bowies Burgeoned

Bowies are without a doubt the most popular American knife. They come in all sizes and styles. Camillus Knives has some that are quite impressive. The Cadillac of the line is the Jerry Fisk Bowie. This is a beautiful, large knife, with a blade that stretches 11 inches and a fiddleback-maple handle. The Fisk Bowie is sent to market in a limited edition of only 750, which I think is a shame, as it is a real beauty. The blade is carbon steel.

If the Fisk Bowie is the Cadillac, certainly Camillus's Becker Combat Bowie is the four-wheel-drive Humvee. As tough as a Humvee, the Becker Combat Bowie will take on the most difficult jobs without any complaint or sign of wear. The blade is close to 1/4-inch thick and, though plain, it is brutal.

Atlanta Cutlery offers replicas of old bowies, and these are perfect for re-enactors as well as collectors who can't afford the originals. At present, there are several models from which to choose, all made from high-carbon steel and reasonably priced. These are the Sheffield Style, the Mexican, two Dueling Bowies offered as a set or as singles, some Southern D-Guard Bowies, the Texas Bowie and even an Arkansas Toothpick. All of these

knives are quite attractive and affordable. If you like old-style knives with up-to-date workmanship and steel, check out these beauties.

Cold Steel's Trailmaster has long been recognized as one of the top knives in the bowie field. With a Kraton® handle and Carbon V blade, it is capable of the toughest chores and requires little maintenance. The Trailmaster Bowie is also offered in a San Mai Damascus blade.

Cold Steel has come up with a new and attractive bowie, the Laredo. It is somewhat longer than the Trailmaster, sporting a 10-1/2-inch, flat-ground blade with a fully sharpened 4-1/2-inch back edge. The coffin-shaped grip is fashioned from exotic hardwood, and the

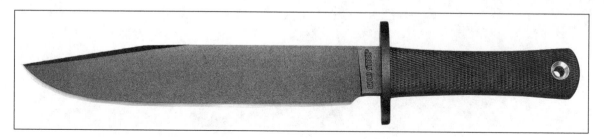

▲Cold Steel's Trailmaster has long been recognized as one of the top knives in the bowie field. With a Kraton® handle and Carbon V blade, it is capable of the toughest chores and requires little maintenance.

knife features a traditional heavy leather sheath. This is an impressive bowie, and although good looking, it is also made for use.

Muela has been making fine knives in Spain for a number of years, and modern bowies fit right into its line of fine knives. The Navajo is a medium-size knife parading a Kraton handle and a 7-inch blade with a false back edge. The Jabali has olivewood scales with a 8-1/4-inch blade that is hollow ground, providing for a knife that is lightening fast and lightweight for its size.

The Ti-Lite and the Tanto

There were many tactical knives displayed at the S.H.O.T. Show, and a detailed description of each would take up most of this book. Two, in particular, just begged for comment from a guy who found them particularly attractive and effective.

Hanwei debuts a beautiful tanto, a knife that combines the style of the old Japanese models with modern elements, characteristics that come together on one spectacular piece. Hanwei's tanto has a stingray-skin grip and

▼ The Ti-Lite tactical folder from Cold Steel is not only a tough, good-looking knife, but also retro, looking a lot like the Italian switchblades popular in the 1950s.

a distal-tapered, 7-inch blade hardened to 60RC on the Rockwell Hardness scale. The sheath is steel with a vise-clip mounting that lets you carry the blade either handle-up or handle-down. It is a simple yet elegant knife.

Cold Steel has a new tactical folder that is not only good looking and tough, but something of a retro knife, looking a lot like the Italian switchblades that were popular in the 1950s. Yet, no Italian switchblade was ever this strong or had a blade this sharp. The Ti-Lite showcases a forged-titanium handle and an AUS-8A stainless steel blade. I played with this a good bit, and it is smooth as silk and strong.

Of Lopping and Chopping

Atlanta Cutlery brought out the first commercially produced Kukris in 1979. After all this time, the kukri, in all its forms, remains popular. Atlanta Cutlery continues to offer the Indian Army Kukri, a tough, inexpensive knife that is nearly impossible to destroy. But if you do lose it or manage to damage it, your compensation is that it was reasonably priced from the onset.

Cold Steel offers four kukris: the LTC, the Gurkha, the Light Gurkha and the Mini Light Gurkha. All of the above have 12-inch blades, except the Mini, which sports 9-1/2 inches of sharpened steel. All have Kraton handles and Carbon V blades. I've cut with each and every one of them and find all to be excellent knives, comfortable for heavy work.

The Navajo (bottom) from Atlanta Cutlery is a medium-size knife parading a Kraton handle and a 7-inch blade with a false back edge. The company's Jabali model has olivewood scales with a 8 1/4-inch blade that is hollow ground, providing for a knife that is lightening fast and lightweight for its size.

▲Cold Steel markets a Two Hand Machete, a blade that is shaped much like a Ram Dao with a broad cutting head. The Two Hand Machete is fashioned from spring steel, and is designed for heavy chopping work.

◄The Patrol Machete, another Camillus/Becker Knife & Tool offering, is a hefty knife, with a 14-inch blade that swells to the point, giving more weight to a cut.

Cold Steel markets a Two Hand Machete, a blade that is shaped much like a Ram Dao with a broad cutting head. The Two Hand Machete is fashioned from spring steel and is designed for heavy chopping work. Although much lighter than an axe, it will do almost the same work, cutting weeds and brush without any problems. It fills a niche that has been vacant until now.

In addition, Cold Steel also has a good, heavy knife of the Filipino barong variety. The barong has long been known as a superb jungle knife, gaining a good reputation as a weapon during the conflict in the Philippines in the last century. This is a large knife, with a blade about 18-to-19 inches in length, and a traditional wooden grip.

Becker Knife & Tool unveils two excellent choppers in the BK1 Brute and the BK6 Patrol Machete. The Brute is well named, with an overall length of 15 inches and a 9-inch blade that is a full 1/4-inch thick. This gives substantial weight and cutting authority to the blade, which is also small enough to be used for regular chores. The Patrol Machete is a hefty knife, with a 14-inch blade that swells to the point, giving more weight to a cut. As with all of the Becker blades, these have hard, plastic handles that are tough and serviceable.

There are many fine blades out there, and I'm sorry I am not able to write about all of them. Heck, I'm sorry that I can't afford to buy one of each. The trouble with being a knife and sword nut is that you can never have too many. You can have too many girlfriends, too much money and too much weight, but you can never have too many knives or swords. •

►The Becker Knife & Tool Brute from Camillus Knives is well named, with an overall length of 15 inches and a 9-inch blade that is a full 1/4-inch thick.

Step Up to a Sporting Folder

By Durwood Hollis

IN PERSUIT OF fun and recreation in the great outdoors, the need for a handy knife is paramount. While some people prefer carrying fixed-blade patterns, the vast majority of outdoor enthusiasts lean heavily toward lock-blade folding knives. Certainly, backpackers, campers, anglers and hunters fit into this category.

Those who are involved in these activities want all the right stuff in their edged tools. The features most sought after include one-hand blade access, a dependable blade locking system, an ergonomic handle with a superior gripping surface, and overall low maintenance. All of these characteristics and more can be found in this year's lineup of sporting folders.

Al Mar Knives

Since 1979, Al Mar has been making knives at a quality level that rivals many handmade edged products. The Model ND-2 Nomad locking folder is one serious knife that has several sporting applications. Designed by American Bladesmith Society master smith Kirk Rexroat, it features a 3-inch drop-point-pattern blade crafted from VG-10 stainless steel.

A grooved swelling on the blade spine nearest the tang increases thumb purchase, and a slightly recessed finger choil has been engineered into the blade for offsetting pressure with the forefinger. Further promoting a good grip is a molded and textured G-10 handle.

The Nomad blade is opened via a thumb stud and complemented nicely by a tempered-stainless-

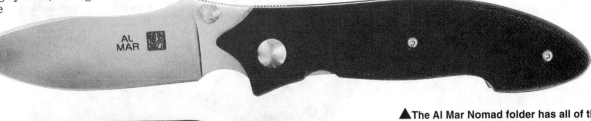

▲The Al Mar Nomad folder has all of the features—ready blade access, a bank-vault-tight locking system and low maintenance—sporting knife users relish.

steel locking liner, the latter of which turns the Nomad folder into a fixed blade once the cutting edge is deployed. It is a big knife that fits perfectly into the palm of the hand. No matter what the sporting assignment—fishing, hunting or just simply outdoor trekking—this fine folder is the right choice.

Bear MGC Cutlery

New this year, the large Bear MGC Model 401 One-hand Opener has much to offer. The hollow-ground, drop-point pattern, high-carbon stainless steel blade has an oval cutout that ensures thumb

▶Affordable and well designed, the Bear MGC Cutlery large One-hand Opener (Model 401) has what it takes to deal effectively with most sporting knife applications.

▶Of several lock-blade folders in the Benchmade Griptilian series, two particular models are right at home with sporting chores. Each features a 440C stainless steel blade, one in a modified sheepsfoot pattern (Model 550), and the second (Model 551) showcasing a modified-drop-point blade, both with hollow-ground edges.

engagement for easy one-hand opening. The blade locking mechanism retains the blade in the open position until the mid-frame lock release is depressed.

The handle frame is molded from glass-reinforced Zytel® thermoplastic, offering lightweight and rugged service. Resilient Kraton® inserts on both handle scales enhance hand purchase. The Model 401 folder is available in a wide range of handle colors to please every taste. It is a well-designed knife that carries a price tag most outdoor sports enthusiasts can well afford.

▲While specifically designed for field-dressing big-game animals, the Browning Extreme F.D.T (Model 690) certainly has wider sporting knife applications.

Benchmade Knife Co.

In collaboration with custom knifemaker Mel Pardue, Benchmade Knife Co. has manufactured one of the strongest blade-locking systems — the AXIS lock — in the sporting knife market. Of several lock-blade folders in the Benchmade Griptilian series, two particular models are right at home with sporting chores. Each features a 440C stainless steel blade, one in a modified sheepsfoot pattern (Model 550), and the second (Model 551) showcasing a modified-drop-point blade, both with hollow-ground edges.

The sheepsfoot blade employs an oval hole, strategically situated on the spine nearest the handle, to effect blade rotation. The Model 551 drop-point utilizes a similarly placed thumb stud for the same purpose. Both models showcase the patented AXIS blade locking system for ultimate overall knife strength and safe use.

Blades of the Griptilians rotate from the handle frames by means of tension-adjustable, oversized main pivot pins. The handle scales are deeply checkered and swelled in the palm areas to afford uncompromising grips. Any and all discriminating outdoors sports enthusiasts will immediately recognize the Griptilian models as being at the top of their class.

▲The Buck Folding Alpha Hunter, with its modernistic lines, is definitely a departure from the ordinary sporting folder look. Nonetheless, it has all of right features to make it a standout in its class.

Browning

Most of the knives in Browning's extensive line could be classified as sporting in nature, yet the new single-blade Model 690 Extreme F.D.T. is a great all-around lock-blade folder. While the Extreme F.D.T. is purpose designed for field-dressing game, it has broader functional sporting applications.

The 3-1/2-inch 440C-stainless-steel blade is crafted in an abrupt drop-point pattern. Combine this with a blade-mounted thumb stud and titanium locking liner, and it's a one-hand-opening folder that competes with the best of the durable, steel-frame knives of its kind. In fact, the frame of the F.D.T. is coated in Mossy Oak® Break-Up camouflage that will please most bow hunters. A frame-mounted pocket clip ensures ready access, so the knife is right at home in camp, on the trail or in your favorite tree stand.

Buck Knives

The West Coast cutlery manufacturer has always had a strong suit in sporting folders. A year or so ago, Buck Knives introduced a new knife that has the potential to become the big-game folder of the new millennium. The Folding Alpha Hunter (Models 276, 277, 278 and 279, all varying slightly), with its sculpted lines and inset handle scales, is a definite departure from the ordinary.

The knife features a 3-1/2-inch drop-point blade deeply hollow ground to a fine edge. Your choice of blade steel options — 420HC or ATS-34 — is available, and the blade comes with or without an integral gut hook. The Folding Alpha Hunter incorporates the immensely popular locking-liner system and one-hand blade opening and closing capabilities. A thumb stud is mounted just forward of the main pivot pin to assist blade manipulation.

The handle scales, which are set inside of the margin of the stainless steel frame, come in resin-impregnated rosewood, walnut or a slightly resilient rubber. Depending on the handle material choice, either a Cordura® nylon or leather belt case is supplied with the knife. Whether or not this knife is as successful as the Buck 110 Folding Hunter remains to be seen, however, with all of its innovative features, I wouldn't be surprised to see it happen.

Cold Steel

Active people who prefer the outdoors to the couch and television will appreciate Cold Steel's series of Trail Guide lock-blade folders. Available with a choice of clip- or drop-point-pattern blades, in medium (2-5/8 inch) or large (3-3/4 inch) lengths, each has been flat ground to a precision edge. Breathtakingly sharp, these blades are made from Carbon V® steel and have been designed to maximize cutting energy.

Each of the blades is equipped with an ambidextrous thumbhole for easy, one-hand opening. The blade lock release is situated at the rear of the handle where it doesn't interfere with a secure grip. The Valox glass-impregnated nylon handle is virtually unbreakable and features deep checkering and a sculpted profile for a comfortable, non-slip grip.

A strong pocket clip mounted on the handle rounds out the Trail Guide, promising the knife will be ready and available at all times. This is definitely a no-nonsense folder that can deal with anything one might encounter after leaving the couch and television for the call of the wild.

Columbia River Knife &Tool

Columbia River Knife & Tool makes so many fine knives that could easily fit into the category of "step-up" folding hunters, it is difficult to pick just one. The new Model 6674 Serengeti Hunter immediately caught my eye. At first glance, the knife resembles a hefty folding skinner, but upon closer inspection you'll find that one removable handle scale is actually a fixed-blade hawksbill caper knife, the other a detail skinner. It's effectively three knives in one.

Designed by custom knifemaker Mike Franklin, the Serengeti Hunter is able to handle virtually every field-dressing and trophy-preparation chore imaginable. The hollow-ground blade is crafted from AUS-6 stainless steel and set into a satin-finished 420J2 stain-

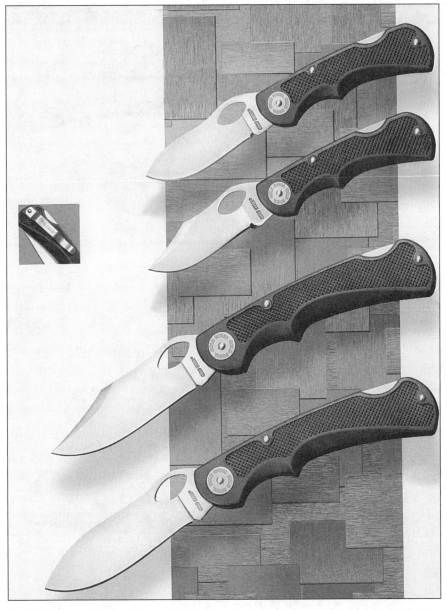

Available in two different sizes, with either a clip- or drop-point pattern blade, the Cold Steel Trail Guide lock-blade folder is more than able to handle a wide range of sporting applications.

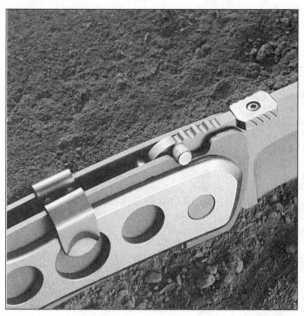

▲ ▶The new Columbia River Knife & Tool Serengeti Hunter (Model 6674) is really three-knives-in one. In addition to the folding lock-blade skinning knife, a small caper and a detail skinner are part of the package. A unique sporting knife design, this keen cutter has incredible versatility.

less frame. The patented Lake and Walker Knife Safety (LAWKS®) securely locks the blade bank-vault tight in the open position.

A machined thumb disk and Teflon® bearing allow for easy blade opening with either hand. The two, small, piggyback knives are also crafted from AUS-6 and feature single-edge grinds. These tiny wonders are locked on either side of the knife frame by saddle clips, with the cutting edges safely flush up against the frame. The little caper has a 1-3/4-inch serrated blade that is just the ticket for working around antler and horn bases. Likewise, the detail skinner sports a 2-inch, curved blade that's great for working the hide free from wild game. An extremely versatile and well-integrated game care system, the Serengeti Hunter is hard to beat.

Gerber Legendary Blades

The demands placed on sporting knives haven't changed over the years, but the knives designed for those activities have become lighter, stronger, ergonomic, more specialized and easier to carry. The latest sporting folder from

▲The Gerber GAMEPRO® (Model 8460) is certainly an innovative adaptation of a proven knife design, and the one-hand-opening feature and locking liner are highly desirable in a sporting folder.

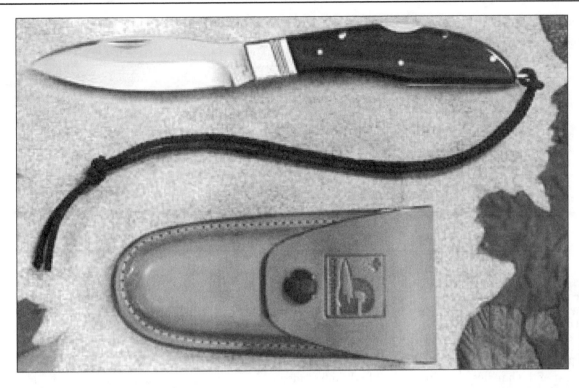

At long last, Grohmann's classical D.H. Russell fixed-blade knife design is available in a lock-blade folder.

Gerber is proof that the trend continues.

Designed by custom knifemaker Rick Hinderer, the Gerber GAME-PRO® (Model 8460) is a modern adaptation of a proven folding knife design. The broad, drop-point-pattern, surgical-stainless-steel blade is accompanied by an ergonomically designed handle made from the same rust-resistant material.

To ensure a positive gripping surface, a resilient, synthetic insert has been inlaid into the handle. The blade's thumb stud facilitates one-hand opening, and a locking-liner mechanism secures the edged tool in the open position. I am extremely pleased to see that the folks at Gerber are continuing to produce some outstanding folders for those of us who enjoy outdoor sports.

Grohmann Knives

Based on the classic D.H. Russell fixed-blade hunter/skinner, the freshest creation from Canadian knife manufacturer Grohmann Knives is a folding version of the original edged tool. The Model R300 D.H. Russell Lockblade has a unique elliptical-shaped, high-carbon stainless steel blade that reaches just a tad under 4 inches long. Nickel silver is employed for the bolsters, rivets, liners and pins, all complemented by a rich rosewood handle shaped to lie nicely in the palm of the hand.

A hand-stitched, top-grain-leather belt sheath is supplied with each knife. Built for effective skinning, this folder has enough taper to the point to be useful in all primary big-game field-care assignments. The D.H. Russell belt-knife line of fixed blades has been recognized around the world as a superior group of blades. It's gratifying that at long last the same elliptical blade pattern is available in a folding configuration.

Imperial Schrade

One of America's largest knife manufacturers, Imperial Schrade continues to bring out novel and innovative edged tools. Schrade's latest sporting folders come in the form of the X-Timer series (Models 60TX, 60TXG, 60TXB, and 60TXBU) that offers a whole handful of hot cutlery features.

▶The latest sporting folder from Imperial Schrade is the X-Timer. Not only is the blackened, drop-point-pattern blade the right shape for most sporting needs, the aluminum handle scales are deeply checkered for a sure grip.

▶Designed by custom knifemaker Bob Dozier, the Folding Hunter (Model 4062) and Folding Skinner (Model 4063) are part of Ka-bar's Precision Hunters knife series.

The modified drop-point-pattern, 3-3/4-inch blades on these knives are black-epoxy coated for low reflectivity. Furthermore, each blade is hollow-ground, with thumbholes for spread-hand opening. Spring locks positioned at the rear of the handles securely prop open the blades.

The handle scales are machined aircraft-grade aluminum in a variety of anodized colors (blue, green, gray and silver). The handles are deeply checkered for outstanding hand-to-knife marriage. Definitely high-tech folders, the Schrade X-Timers are top-quality throughout and can conquer any challenge in camp, or out in the field.

Ka-Bar Knives, Inc.

A pair of practical sporting folders designed by custom maker Bob Dozier can be found in the Ka-bar line this year. The Folding Hunter

(Model 4062) features a spear-point blade and the Folding Skinner (Model 4063) has an abrupt drop-point-pattern blade. Both models parade AUS-8 stainless steel blades with reversible thumb studs for one-hand maneuvering.

Rugged, thermoplastic handles, which feature deep checkering, are also part of the package. Functional pocket clips are reversible, or can be relocated on either side of the handles. The Folding Hunter and Folding Skinner benefit from practical design, resulting in affordable tools for big game hunters.

Kershaw Knives

It seems as if there's no end to the ingenious variations of lock-blade folders knifemaker Ken Onion can devise in his continuing collabora-

tions with Kershaw Knives. Certainly, the Boa (Models 1580 and 1580ST) folder is a prime example of this man's design genius.

Featuring the Onion Speed-Safe blade opening system, this knife almost unfolds all by itself—almost. Of course, it takes manual manipulation of the thumb on the steel stud protruding from the blade to activate the Speed-Safe. Speaking of "safe," for added security, a lock on the spine prevents the blade from accidentally opening while it's carried in the pocket.

The S60V stainless drop-point blade is coated with black titanium nitride for protection from the elements outside. The 6061-T6 aircraft-grade-aluminum grip features a lightly textured finish. A removable and reversible pocket clip eliminates the need for a belt sheath. The Onion Boa is definitely "technology with an edge."

▲The Ken Onion custom-designed Boa folder (Models 1580 and 1580ST) from Kershaw features the patented Speed-Safe assisted blade-opening system. In many sporting applications, the need for a ready edge is of prime importance, and the blade deployment system on this folder has few equals in instantaneous opening.

▶In collaboration with master bladesmith Bob Loveless, Lone Wolf Knives is now offering the famous Loveless fixed-blade designs in locking folders. Marked by exceptional design and outstanding fit and finish, these folders are priced so that almost anyone can afford a Loveless knife.

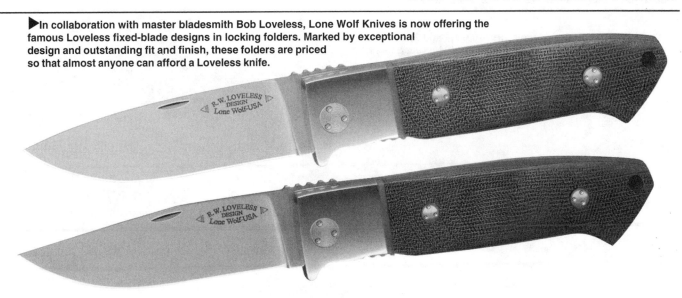

KutMaster

The KutMaster Model MQG100 Diamond Grid Lockback is unleashed with a 400-series stainless steel blade complete with a one-hand blade-opening hole near its steely spine. A mid-frame lock secures the edged steel in the open position, and the handle of the Diamond Grid Lockback is molded from lightweight Zytel, a glass-reinforced thermoplastic paired up with a non-slip Kraton rubber insert for enhanced grip surface. On the backside of the handle, a stainless carrying clip allows for confident belt or pocket containment. This folder is slim, lightweight and well suited for sporting applications.

Lone Wolf Knives

Last year, Lone Wolf Knives entered the knife industry as the "new kid on the block." The company's introduction of two classic R.W. Loveless fixed-blade designs was seriously impressive. New for 2003, those same blade patterns— traditional drop-point and utility clip-point — are now available as locking folders. And, the famous Loveless semi-skinner has joined the pair to make it a trio of outstanding sporting folders.

The 3-1/4-inch blades are crafted from LV-02 high-carbon stainless steel. Likewise, the bolsters, frame liners, main pin and rivets are also stainless. Handle scales are green canvas Micarta®, a Loveless favorite. A lanyard hole is positioned at the end of the handle for easy attachment to a length of leather or nylon parachute cord. Additionally, a top-grain-leather belt pouch, a padded zippered storage case and a cleaning cloth are part of the overall knife package.

Each of these new folders is marked with the Loveless logo, indicating that it is an authorized original design by the master himself. Any of this trio of exceptional folders has peerless fit and finish, along with an almost unlimited performance envelope. What more could you want in the best-of-the-best sporting folders?

Meyerco

New for this year, in Meyerco's Blackie Collins-designed Rubber-Grip Folder series, is a clip-pattern, lock-blade folder that features an integral gut hook on the blade spine near the tip (Model MACAMP36GH). The hollow-ground 440-stainless-steel blade is 3-5/8 inches in length. Edged steel opens entirely with one hand by mean of an opening in the back of the blade near the main pin. A back spring locking mechanism secures the blade in the open position.

The Rubber-Grip Folder is named for what Meyerco terms a ProGrip ergonomically designed handle molded from synthetic rubber. This handle material gives a comfortable and easy-to-hold grip because, when the job gets tough, sometimes it's hard to hold onto your knife. The handle on this folder eliminates any worry about safe knife use. All of the frills have been eliminated, but what remains makes the knife a winner!

Custom knifemaker Blackie Collins is responsible for the design of Meyerco's Rubber-Grip Folders. New for this year is a large frame-locking folder that incorporates a gut hook into the clip-pattern blade. Of course, the resilient synthetic rubber handle scales are the ultimate in knife-grip comfort.

▼ The Puma Oval Series (Models 28-1010, 1011 and 28-2010, 28-2011) has futuristic lines that give it a rich look. However, this is serious sporting folder that features all the right stuff.

Puma

Based in Solingen, Germany and distributed by Coast Cutlery, the European cutlery manufacturer named "Puma" has always been involved in the development of fine sporting knives. In 2003, the Puma Oval series (Models 28-1010, 28-1011, 28-2010 and 28-2011) showcases clean and futuristic lines. The 440 stainless steel blades are available in drop-point patterns just right for most sporting chores.

Stainless steel handle frames come with a choice of stag or wood inlays. Functional locking liners prop open blade in use, and pocket clips allow the Oval knives to be toted with ease. In recent years, and under new leadership, the folks at Puma have stepped fully into the 21st century with their innovative knife designs, yet the same Old World craftsmanship continues to remain and is well manifest in the edge products.

Queen Cutlery

Those of you who are fans of D-2 high-carbon, high-chromium steel will like what Queen Cutlery is offering in its Cocobolo, Carved Stag and Winterbottom folding knives. While there are and will always be plenty of Queen pocketknife models to choose from, many of which have serious sporting applications, I prefer the two-blade Folding Hunter (Models 39COBO, 39CSB and 39WB). This is a traditional folding knife that's been around for many years.

While there isn't a blade locking system on the Folding Hunter, nonetheless, if used properly, there shouldn't be a worry about accidental blade collapse. The large folder features a primary clip-pattern, hollow-ground main blade and a straight-back, flat-ground companion blade.

The knife frame employs a nickel-silver bolster, brass liners and your choice of rich cocobolo-wood, carved bone (which resembles stag) or Winterbottom Delrin® plastic handle scales. I carried a knife similar to one of these all through my adolescent years in every outdoor assignment, from gutting a limit of trout to field dressing a buck, and it never failed me. That's a lot to say about any knife design!

Remington

During the first half of the last century, this famed firearms manufacturer was one of the leading domestic producers of quality cutlery. Since the early 1980s, Remington has reintroduced several of their original models, as well as many new cutlery designs. Some of the best new sporting folders can be found in their Rattlesnake One-Hander® line.

My own favorite in this series is the Camo Rattlesnake Drop-Point/ Saw folder that pairs a one-hand-

▼The Remington Camo Rattlesnake Drop-Point/Saw lock-blade folder easily opens with one hand, it locks up tight and combines a drop-point main blade with an efficient bone saw.

►Custom designed with innovative features that will endear it to big-game hunters, the new Spyderco Impala (Model C73) is one of the best of this year's new sporting folders.

opening, drop-point main blade with a bone saw. Each blade locks independently, with paired lock releases positioned mid-handle for added safety. Providing ease of main blade access, a hole in the spine allows for thumb engagement. The handle scales are camouflage coated for those who want to disappear in the woods. This knife is ideal for big-game field care.

Spyderco

When I first handled the new Spyderco Model C73 Impala, I knew my dream knife was a reality. Designed by South African custom knifemaker Ed Scott, this folder has all the features a big game hunter should have. The blade is made from VG-10 stainless steel, and the 3 3/4-inch edge is superior to any other blade steel I've used.

The drop-point blade is available in two versions — snub nosed and gut hook. The first version is thick at the tip, and textured with furrows on top of the blade spine and again just above the blade-opening hole. The furrowing gives the index finger enhanced control over the edge when doing trophy work.

The other blade variant has a gut hook on the blade spine, just behind the tip. The radius of the gut hook is double-beveled and sharpened on both sides. When it comes to making all of the necessary incisions in the hide preparatory to skinning, nothing does it better than a well-designed gut-hook blade.

There are a number of small grooves in the steel that offer enhanced cutting command. Of course, the trademark Spyderco round hole in the blade facilitates one-hand opening, and a locking liner within the frame secures the blade in the open position. The ergonomic handle scales are made from G-10 (epoxy resin filled with woven glass fiber), which can stand up to almost any environmental invective. A pocket-attachment clip is positioned on the handle for a lower carrying profile. This sporting folder stands at the top of its class for true functional design and peerless craftsmanship.

Tigersharp Technologies

If you're a fan of lightweight knives, then the Tigersharp Xenon (Model TS415) folder is right up your alley. At the heart of this locking folder is a 420-J2 stainless-steel blade housing with replaceable steel edges. That's right, when your Xenon knife exhibits signs of edge deterioration, simply remove the worn edge insert and replace it with a new one.

Edge inserts are crafted from GIN5 stainless steel and hardened to 61 RC on the Rockwell hardness scale for extended cutting life. In a matter of 30 seconds, you can swap a dull blade insert for a fresh, sharp one.

Teflon inserts allow for smooth cutting edge insertion so that blade exchange isn't troublesome. Precision engineering ensures that debris doesn't accumulate in the blade slot. The knife handle is molded from lightweight Zytel

▼By using replaceable blade-edge inserts, the TigerSharp Xenon (Model TS415) completely eliminates knife-sharpening concerns.

thermoplastic, and it features tactile rubber inlays for a superior grip. Able to handle any field assignment, the Xenon folder makes knife sharpening a thing of the past.

W.R. Case & Sons Cutlery Co.

W.R. Case & Sons Cutlery Co. introduces a mid-size Mid-Folding Hunter Knife (Model 1205) available in three handle materials — jade, stag and chestnut bone. The Mid-Folding Hunter is a quality knife from beginning to end. Case's Tru-Sharp surgical-stainless-steel

blade parades a steeply clipped and rather elongated shape.

A thumb stud and locking liner allow for easy blade access and one-hand opening. Of course, that famous movement of the blade tang across the spring and snappy opening ("walk and talk") is part of every Case folder.

Personally, I like the blade shape for many sporting chores, not the least of which is gutting a limit of trout. However, this folder is just as capable at field dressing

▶Brand new from Case, the Mid-Folding Hunter Knife (Model 1205) is available in three handle styles, which include jade, stag and chestnut bone.

small and large game. Case Cutlery has made sporting knives and pocket folders for more than 100 years, and it's important that the company is keeping abreast of modern technology, continuing to respond to the needs of cutlery consumers.

William Henry Knives

Among the many models produced by William Henry Knives, the Carbon Fiber Series makes up my favorite sporting folders. The largest model, the Spearpoint Folder (Model

▼The Spearpoint Folder from William Henry Knives is a rugged knife that can handle tough cutting chores with ease. With carbon-fiber handle scales, a 154CM stainless steel blade and a titanium locking liner, this sporting folder is on the leading edge of cutlery development.

T12-CF) is an excellent example of the William Henry commitment to superior design, construction and durability in folding knives.

This knife combines a hollow-ground, 3-1/4-inch 154CM stainless blade, a titanium locking liner and a solid carbon fiber handle. The one-hand-opening blade travels on Teflon® bushings for unimpeded action.

Designed to fit in the palm of the hand, each handle scale is ergonomically rounded, satin finished and attached to the knife frame by means of stainless Torx screws. A titanium pocket clip is mounted on the reverse side of the frame and keeps the knife attached to the pocket regardless of activity.

Designed and built to serve as a "companion tool," the folder is made for hard work and years of service.

The Final Cut

Sporting pursuits demand the highest level of knife performance. Both cutlery design and knife readiness must be considered when selecting a knife for your sport of choice. The successful completion of any cutting assignment is highly dependent on the knife selection, so a wise choice will keep you in the game no matter what transpires! ●

Cutting In— Tactical

By Dexter Ewing

THE 25TH ANNUAL S.H.O.T. (Shooting Hunting Outdoor Trade) Show was held February 13-16, 2003, at the sprawling Orange County Convention Center in Orlando, Fla. For knife industry professionals, this is the annual coming-out party for what's new, including everything related to guns, knives, and other hunting, camping and general outdoor gear.

No doubt, every major knife company takes this opportunity to showcase its new models for the coming year. The author was right in the thick of it all, in order to bring you, the inquisitive reader, a complete rundown of the freshest in tactical knives for 2003. For those who might think that tactical knives are

◀ The Mel Pardue-designed 5000 Auto Axis Lock folder is the first of Benchmade's automatic knives to employ the exclusive Axis Lock, resulting in a beefy folding knife for those tough cutting jobs.

Benchmade's booth was a happening place at the 2003 S.H.O.T. Show. There, visitors could chat with the custom knifemakers who are a part of the company's design team. Such would include Mel Pardue, Warren Osborne, Bill McHenry and Jason Williams. (*Hoffman photo*)

on their way out, please read this and decide for yourselves!

Al Mar Knives

American Bladesmith Society (ABS) master smith Kirk Rexroat lands a knife deal with Al Mar Knives, yielding a stylish, collaborative tactical folder called the "Nomad." It features a 3-inch, VG-10, spear-point blade and a textured G-10 handle. Now that's a tactical!

A saw-tooth spine option has been added to Al Mar's SERE Operator fixed blade, and the company is also making the switch from 154CM to S30V blade steel for all the SERE Operators, effective immediately.

Knives Stay in Step

▶Tim Wegner of Blade Tech Industries is now producing his folding hunter design, formerly made by Spyderco, but with a few refinements over the previous production version. His latest model features dual, nested steel liners, a CPM S30V blade, a teardrop-shaped blade-opening hole, an eccentric pivot, and a choice of tip-up or tip-down, and left-hand or right-hand pocket clip positioning. It is pretty much the ultimate folding hunter for the serious outdoorsman.

Benchmade Knife Co.

Benchmade unveils yet another handle color for its popular Griptilian series of Axis Lock folders—olive-drab—a militaristic hue available on both the regular and mini sizes of this knife. The Oregon knife company will also be reviving its Steve Schwarzer-designed Kuma Zume push dagger, but plans to redesign the knife to bring it up to modern standards.

Debuting at the S.H.O.T. Show was the 42SS Bali-Song, a 303-cast-stainless-steel-handle version of the 42 Bali-Song. For the knife collectors out there, the 42-01 Bali-Song now comes with a S30V Weehawk style blade and a T6-6061 aluminum handle with G-10 inlays. "Automatically yours" is the Model 5000 Auto Axis Lock, the first auto-opening folder from Benchmade that incorporates its popular Axis Lock mechanism. Based on a Mel Pardue design, the Axis Lock acts as the release for the blade instead of a button, and it also provides rock-solid lockup.

Blade Tech Industries

Blade Tech owner Tim Wegner releases the Blade Tech Pro

The ATF (Advanced Tactical Folder) is Boker's latest development in designing and creating serious, high-end tactical folders. Starting with a spear-point blade of CPM S60V steel, and setting it into a T6-6061 anodized-aluminum handle, Boker adds an easy-opening, hard-use folder to its line.

Hunter, a refined version of the now-discontinued Spyderco C48 Wegner model. Wegner has updated this great folder design with dual, nested steel liners, an S30V blade, an ambidextrous pocket clip, and tip-up or tip-down knife carry options. A large "V-hole" in the blade provides ease of opening, even when wearing gloves. Everything that makes the Pro Hunter the ultimate folding hunter also makes it a great tactical folder. Carbon fiber and G-10 handle versions are available.

Boker U.S.A.

Boker is licensed to use the AK-47 name in producing a couple tactical folders inspired by the legend-ary assault rifle. The AK-47 knife has a 440-C clip-point blade in the design of an AK-47 bayonet, and an aluminum handle with raised G-10 inlays. The AK-47 LTD is the collector version with a dual-finished 440C blade (mirror bevels with satin flats) and raised-snakewood handle inlays.

The ATF is Boker's newest in serious tactical folders. It features a spear-point S60V blade with integral hand guards and an aluminum handle. The folder opens easily with just a flick of one of the handle guards. The H&K P2000 series of lock-back folders are fine tactical knives in their own right, showcasing molded-Zytel® handles and X-15 T.N steel blades.

Buck Knives

This year, Buck Knives and custom knifemaker Tom Mayo are teaming up to produce the company's newest collaborative folder, the TNT. This knife features a 3-1/8-inch drop-point S30V blade, bead-blasted titanium handle slabs with lightening-shaped holes, and a sturdy integral lock mechanism. This is sure to be a hot seller, as Mayo's handmade version is wildly popular with the custom tactical folder crowd.

Camillus Knives

Continuing to make waves and noise over its knife collaborations

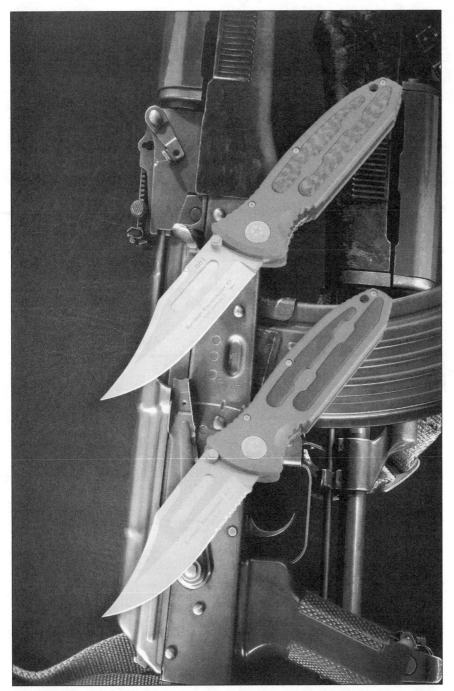

Boker now has the exclusive rights to produce knives with the AK-47 name. As a result of this special arrangement, the knife company has released the AK-47 and AK-47 LTD folders. The bayonets that were used with the legendary AK-47 assault rifle inspired the blade designs, and Boker uses only premium materials for these pieces, including T6-6061 aluminum handles, 440C blades and G-10 inlays. For a limited time, a collector version of the AK-47 knives is also available, with a dual-finished 440C blade and snakewood handle inlays.

with Darrel Ralph, Camillus introduces the Aftermath mega folder. A 5-1/2-inch D-2 blade mates with a titanium, integral-locking handle carved in a red-hot flame pattern. Ralph and Camillus also unleash the Dominator tactical folder, which parades a 3.65-inch S30V blade, a flipper for ease of opening, a titanium handle and an integral lock. Both the Aftermath and Dominator have Camillus' patent-pending Robo-Power assisted-opening mechanism, aiding in fast and easy blade deployment.

Bolstering its Becker Knife & Tool line of heavy-duty fixed blades, Camillus premieres the BK10 Crewman Utility knife, just what the doctor ordered in a stout, yet agile fixed blade for camping or pilot-survival use.

Columbia River Knife & Tool

Of all the knife companies at the 2003 S.H.O.T. Show, Columbia River Knife & Tool probably had the biggest knife rollout of all. With about 23 brand-new models, mostly encompassing custom-collaborative knives, their booth was abuzz with interest from the public on the new models.

Greg Lightfoot's stout M1 tactical folder is a hollow-ground tanto featuring a one-hand-opening flipper mechanism and textured-Zytel handle scales. Jim Hammond's beefy Cascade lock-back folder showcases a heavily textured Kraton® handle with a clip-point blade and ambidextrous thumb studs. The First Strike, designed by Steve Corkum, is the company's initial foray into traditional Japanese fixed blades, showcasing a cord-wrapped handle and stingray-leather grip underlay.

Bud Nealy's Pesh-Kabz Folder takes his famous fixed blade design to a more compact folding version with an AUS-6M blade and a molded-Zytel handle. The blade has his signature hollow

▶Hawaiian knifemaker Tom Mayo's TNT integral-lock folder is one of the hottest selling custom knives on the market. Recognizing this fact, Buck Knives is collaborating with Mayo to produce a high-end production version of the famous folder. Buck's interpretation showcases a 3-1/2-inch CPM S30V blade and a titanium integral lock frame, resulting in a comfortable-to-carry, yet hard-working folder.

As usual, Camillus displayed its impressive and extensive product line at the 2003 S.H.O.T. Show. Show goers were treated to new Camillus pieces such as the Darrel Ralph-designed Aftermath and Dominator models, and the second installment of the company's OVB line—a Jerry Fisk Southwest Bowie. (*Hoffman photo*)

grind with a reinforced tip. Pat and Wes Crawford's Fixed Falcon embodies a compact fixed blade for either belt or neck carry, and is a dead ringer for the knifemaking duo's custom version.

The company's highly successful collaboration with Kit Carson has yielded yet another addition to the popular M18 series called the "M18K." It parades an all-black appearance and choice of either black or olive-drab G-10 inlays. Michael Walker's BladeLock 2 is a stylish "gent's tactical" that is shod with the maker's own BladeLock mechanism to secure the blade in the open and closed positions. The lock is operated via a user-friendly thumb stud. Columbia River Knife & Tool has other new knives too numerous to list!

▲Camillus calls this behemoth knife the "Aftermath." Designed by custom knifemaker Darrel Ralph, the Aftermath qualifies as a bona-fide mega folder with its 5-1/2-inch D-2 steel blade, titanium frame and integral locking bar. (*Hoffman photo*)

Combat Elite, Inc.

Knifemakers Darrel Ralph and Ryan Wilson have partnered up to produce the finest mid-tech tactical knives on the market. The Tactical Elite is their large, 4-inch-blade, frame-lock folder. The most recent addition to this line is the green and black color scheme. The titanium frame is coated with green Armor Tuff® coating with black G-10 raised inlays. Along those same lines, their Tactical Auto Stiletto automatic folder is also available with the green Armor Tuff coating.

Cutters Knife & Tool

A new company, Cutter Knife & Tool used the 2003 S.H.O.T. Show to not only debut the Walter Brend Model 2 folder, but also introduce the first frame-lock Karambit folder designed by knifemaker Reese Weiland. Dubbed the Bengal, the Weiland folder has a 2.36-inch 154CM blade and a choice of three finishes. This looks to be an interesting piece!

Emerson Knives

The leader in hard-use tactical knives furthered its reputation with multiple new product offerings at the S.H.O.T. Show. The CQC10 is the latest custom Ernest Emerson handmade design to trickle into production, and it will be an exclusive for Heckler & Koch

gun company, and only available through the H&K website.

The Emerson Knives Super CQC7 is a "Hoss" of a tactical folder with a 4-inch, chisel-ground tanto blade and Wave blade opener. Next up is the Combat Karambit, an exciting new design that is currently stirring up a lot of interest with Karambit fans. It will be the first folding production Karambit. The Super SOCFK is another folder that has been pumped-up in size. Like the Super CQC7, the Super SOCFK's blade is 4 inches and also has the Wave opening feature.

The Fusion is Emerson Knives' first collaboration with custom maker Allen Elishewitz. This stylish tactical folder has titanium liners with G-10 overlays and a 154CM blade.

Gerber Legendary Blades

The Paraframe series of Taiwan-made, frame-lock folders are available in three sizes featuring skeletonized steel scales and AUS-8 clip-point blades. Bill Harsey's X-Frame folder is a small, stylish, locking-liner folder with skeletonized-aluminum handle scales.

The Alliance is Gerber's first automatic folder, which was designed in conjunction with Ernest Emerson. A 154CM black-coated blade is paired with a T6-6061 aluminum, hard-coat-anodized handle with integral guard. The Alliance features a unique safety that can be released simultaneously as the blade is fired.

Camillus debuts the Dominator assisted-opening folder, another Darrel Ralph design featuring a patent-pending, Robo-Power, assisted-opening mechanism and a premium CPM S30V blade. (*Hoffman photo*)

At the Columbia River Knife & Tool booth, one was treated to the company's many new 2003 models, as well as chatting with CRKT's collaborating knifemakers like Jim Hammond, Ed Halligan, Kit Carson, Greg Lightfoot, Allen Elishewitz, Bud Nealy, and Pat and Wes Crawford. (*Hoffman photo*)

▶The BladeLock 2 is the second Michael Walker design from Columbia River Knife & Tool—a stylish knife featuring an AUS-6M *wharncliffe*-style blade and a contoured handle. The blade locks open and closed, and is released via a thumb stud.

▲ ▶Designed by Steve Corkum, the First Strike is Columbia River Knife & Tool's first foray into traditional Japanese fixed blades. It features a razor-sharp AUS-6M blade, a cord-wrapped stingray-leather handle and a molded sheath.

Columbia River Knife & Tool's Fixed Falcon is a compact and cstylish fixed blade for tveeryday carry. The AUS-6M clip-point blade is wide and long enough to handle most cutting chores, while the molded and textured thermoplastic handle provides a secure grip in all conditions.

Joe Pardue Knives

Custom knifemaker Joe Pardue has decided to commercially manufacture his Toggle Folder design, complete with a 3-1/2-inch 440A blade, an extended toggle to facilitate easy blade opening, stainless liners and a Zytel handle.

Ka-Bar Knives

The all-black Dozier Thorn tactical folder made its debut alongside three Ka-Bar/Tecnocut locking-liner folders imported from Italy—two models with wood handles and bolsters, and a titanium integral-lock folder with an anodized handle. Also new is the Ka-Bar/Maserin Tom Anderson-designed folder.

Kershaw Knives

Kershaw offers a folding knife designed by action film star Steven Seagal and custom knifemaker Ken Onion. The folder sports a 3-5/8-inch AUS-8 blade and an anodized-aluminum handle with stingray-leather inlays. Also look for one, possibly two, new Onion folders to debut at the 2003 Blade Show in Atlanta.

Lone Wolf Knives

Lone Wolf introduces a massive, heavy-duty Bill Harsey Tactical Folder equipped with a 4-3/4-inch

▲▼Columbia River Knife & Tool is now manufacturing all-black versions of its popular M18 folder designed by Kit Carson.

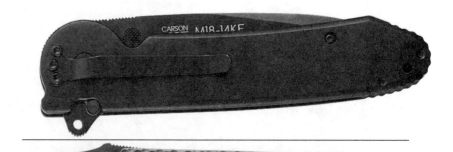

▲▼Greg Lightfoot successfully engineered the Columbia River Knife & Tool M1 to be a beefy and stout tactical folder.

▶The Pesh Kabz
is the only folding production
version of Bud Nealy's famous fixed blade. The Columbia
River Knife & Tool version features the same blade grinds that
lend a strong, reinforced blade tip design. The textured-Zytel® handle allows for a non-slip grip, and the flipper protrusion on the
blade tang permits for fast and easy opening at a moment's notice. A stylized pocket clip rounds out
this package.

CPM S30V clip-point blade, a safety lock and a black-Micarta® handle. Also on display are two Brian Tighe designs—the Tighe Stick with a radical S30V tanto blade and a machined-titanium handle, and The Tighe Tactical in a carbon fiber handle.

Masters Of Defense

Masters Of Defense announces two knife collaborations. Jeff Harkins has teamed up with the company for a production version of his Triton OTF automatic knife, sporting a double-edged 154CM steel blade and a symmetrical aluminum handle. From the mind of Allen Elishewitz, look for the Masters Of Defense Phoenix, a straight knife with a blade that can be extended or retracted depending on the length needed.

The ATFK is a Masters Of Defense knife available strictly through Special Mission Knives (www.specialmissionknives.com). This folder utilizes an aggressive spear-point blade mated with a Masters Of Defense Trident handle.

For knife collectors, Masters Of Defense offers the CQD collector set—any of the company's CQD folders or fixed blades presented in hardwood presentation cases.

Microtech

Breathing new life into its Mini SOCOM folder, Microtech updates the classic design with an integral lock and hollow-ground S30V blade. By employing integral lock construction, the weight of the Mini SOCOM has been significantly reduced.

The QD Scarab OTF is currently the flagship of Microtech's auto-opening folding knife line. The handle and trigger are rigged so the knife can be used wearing tactical gloves. The Scarab also comes with a carbide glass breaker on the butt of the handle.

At the 2003 S.H.O.T. Show, the UMS knife model made its official debut. Based on the Microtech LUDT auto opener, the UMS integrates tape inlays for a sure grip, and a hollow-ground CPM S30V blade. Microtech generated a lot of interest at the show with the debut of its Bob Terzuola ATCF collaboration. This is a bolster-release, double-action (manual and automatic opening) folder built with premium

materials—a 4-inch S30V blade, titanium bolsters and a carbon fiber handle. This particular knife will be available only through cutlery distributor CFI Arms.

SOG Specialty Knives

A camouflage coating has been applied to SOG's Zytel-handled Flash assisted-opening folders, and two small fast-deploying folding knives were added to make up the Twitch series. In the fixed blade department, the SEAL Revolver represents a new approach to fixed blades. As its name implies, the SEAL Revolver pivots for one of two blade options. By rotating the edged steel on a pivot pin, a fighter-style AUS-8 clip-point blade is employed on one end, or a pull-cut saw blade is put into action on the other end. Depending on which configuration is locked in and ready for use, the other blade disappears into the knife handle.

The Columbia River Knife & Tool Rollock is manufactured under license from Benchmark, which made the original Rolox knife, and the design of the current production version is by Allen Elishewitz.

The Kershaw Knives' booth provided a relaxing atmosphere for introducing the company's new products. (*Hoffman photo*)

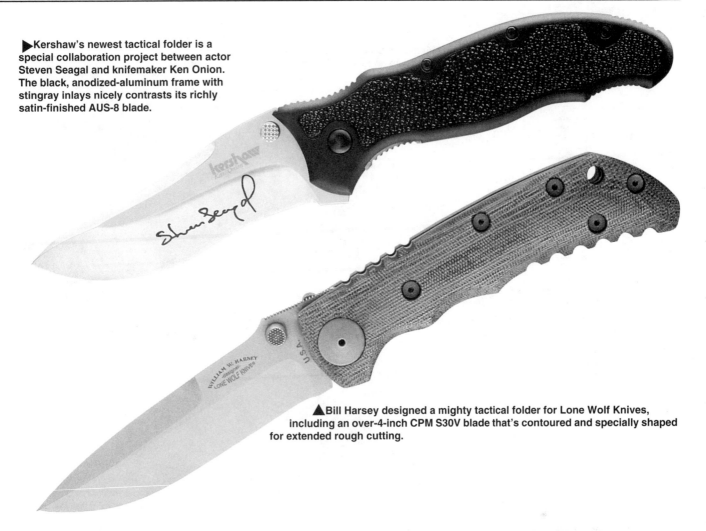

▶Kershaw's newest tactical folder is a special collaboration project between actor Steven Seagal and knifemaker Ken Onion. The black, anodized-aluminum frame with stingray inlays nicely contrasts its richly satin-finished AUS-8 blade.

▲Bill Harsey designed a mighty tactical folder for Lone Wolf Knives, including an over-4-inch CPM S30V blade that's contoured and specially shaped for extended rough cutting.

Spyderco, Inc.

Spyderco always seems to have groundbreaking knife projects underway at any given moment, and the latest is no exception. Spyderco teams up with knifemaker Mike Snody and knife writer/combat instructor Michael Janich to bring forth the Ronin FB09 with a VG-10 blade and Micarta handle.

Shifting into rescue mode, the C82 D'Allara Rescue makes use of the company's exclusive Ball Lock mechanism, a S30V sheepsfoot blade, and a textured and contoured-Zytel handle. The C79 Assist is perhaps the most advanced rescue knife Spyderco has made, and potentially the most advanced anywhere! It displays a blunt-nosed VG-10 blade, a reinforced tip for prying, a retractable carbide glass breaker and a Zytel handle with a built-in whistle.

The ATR (At The Ready) is a beefy tactical folder incorporating an S30V spear-point blade and a titanium handle with an integral Compression Lock. The unusual-looking C80 Dodo is a compact knife with a big bite due to its re-curved cutting edge. A short, 2-1/2-inch blade is paired with an ergonomic G-10 handle. The blade locks open via the Ball Lock.

Spyderco's C63 Chinook II, a design by master-at-arms James Keating, is a lighter, more-refined version of the original Chinook, yet retaining the same basic profile and design lines. Finally, all-black versions of the FB04 Fred Perrin, FB05 Temperance and FB08 SPOT neck knife made their debuts at the 2003 S.H.O.T. Show. A ceramic-based coating is applied for a mix of both low-profile appearance and corrosion protection. Spyderco also announced that its C36 Military model is soon to be switched to S30V steel to improve an already hard-working, top-selling folder.

Sure Fire/Strider Knives

Strider Knives and Sure Fire, LLC, leading producers of tactical flashlights and weapons lights, have teamed up to bring out a limited edition knife-and-light set available only from SureFire. The knife is Strider's exclusive Model SF, a clip-point S30V fixed blade with double integral guards and a durable and gripping paracord-wrapped handle. The accompanying flashlight is SureFire's M2 Centurion model integrating a shock-isolated lamp assembly and a click-on, lockout tail cap (aka "Charlie Tailcap"). This special tail cap has never before been offered as standard equipment on any SureFire light. Both the knife and light bear the same serial number.

Taylor Cutlery

Taylor Cutlery introduces two Smith & Wesson folder lines, including the S&W Extreme Ops folders that sport 440C tanto- or clip-point blades and G-10 handle scales. The S&W Border Guard was designed by knifemaker Darrel Ralph to incorporate a spear-point

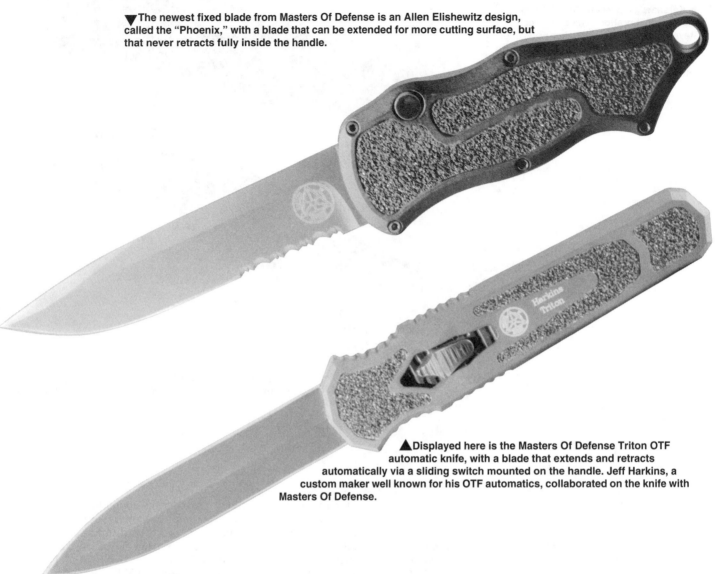

▼The newest fixed blade from Masters Of Defense is an Allen Elishewitz design, called the "Phoenix," with a blade that can be extended for more cutting surface, but that never retracts fully inside the handle.

▲Displayed here is the Masters Of Defense Triton OTF automatic knife, with a blade that extends and retracts automatically via a sliding switch mounted on the handle. Jeff Harkins, a custom maker well known for his OTF automatics, collaborated on the knife with Masters Of Defense.

blade with flippers for quick and easy one-hand opening.

Timberline Knives

Timberline Knives and custom knifemaker Greg Lightfoot team up once again, this time on the Zambezi Back Up, a rugged tactical folder meant as the folding companion to the standard Zambezi fixed blade, and on the Pistol Grip, which sports a highly ergonomic handle. Both Lightfoot models have AUS-8 blades and Zytel handle scales.

Slated for delivery in late March 2003 is the Tim Herman Wall Street Tactical. This slender and sleek tactical folder is for the suit-and-tie types and features gold-plated thumb pins to aid in easy blade opening. The Herman Money

Clip is a diminutive folder that has a mirror-polished blade and frame, with 24-karat-gold inlays and screws, also designed by Herman. Butch Vallotton's Kick Start is set to rev up for a June delivery and has an assisted-opening mechanism for rapid deployment. Alaskan knifemaker Russ Kommer's Bush Pilot Axe is made of 1/4-inch stock of 440C with Kraton® rubber scales and a ballistic nylon belt sheath.

United Cutlery

Knifemaker Fred Carter has designed two new folders for United. The first is the Uzi tactical folder, built rugged like its firearm namesake, and the next is the M4-K folder with a 440A blade, aluminum frame with grip tape inlays,

and a unique drop-pin locking mechanism. The M4-K Fighter is a fixed-blade companion to the folder and showcases a form-fitting Bolt-aron sheath.

United is the distributor for Eickhorn knives, and debuts the Eickhorn Elishewitz knives designed in conjunction with custom knifemaker Allen Elishewitz. Stylish, custom-designed folders, the Eickhorn Elishewitz knives sport 420 steel blades with G-10 handles and choices of three overlays—carbon fiber, *matrona* wood or anodized aluminum.

Every year, production knives are getting better and better in terms of selection, design and the evolution of materials used to manufacture tactical knives. If you were observant, there are a few

◀ Spyderco calls this one the "Dodo," and it's definitely a unique looking folder. In fact, there's no other bird quite like it.

◀ One of the newest Spyderco collaboration pieces, the Michael Janich/Mike Snody FB09 Ronin is patterned after one of the most desired custom fixed blades around. The *wharncliffe*-style blade offers an acute tip for precise cutting tasks, and the tapered-Micarta® handle makes for a comfortable grip.

trends emerging for 2003. This year, we will be seeing a dramatic increase in the use of high-end blade steels like CPM S30V. Karambits are definitely in and, as we have seen, several manufacturers generated a lot of interest with the prototypes they displayed, with more to come later down the road.

The mid-priced range keeps opening up exponentially with an impressive selection of the bang-for-the-buck-type knives that have won over so many knife users on a daily basis. Custom collaborations between companies and handmade knifemakers continue to be the backbone of high-end production knives and are what drives the market to explore new designs, materials and manufacturing processes. Yes, there is no time like the present to be a knife enthusiast! ●

The Multi-Tasking Multi-Tools

By Joe Kertzman

LOOK AT THE belt of any construction worker. Do you see the shirt bulging out at the hip of the warehouse worker? Have you noticed a little black pouch attached to the tool belt of the maintenance man? What on earth is the factory owner carrying on his waist? What do those guys store there? Start looking and you'll be surprised at just how many people, whether blue-collar workers or white-collar professionals, wear multi-tools, in sheaths, attached to their belts.

Regardless of anti-knife sentiment in the world, and despite 9/11 terrorists who just so happened to have chosen utility knives rather than straight razors or ice picks, people continue to realize a need for tools, edged and otherwise. When duct tape needs cutting, when a box needs opening, when a rose needs pruning, when a string needs severing, when a package needs perforating, a knife is a logical choice. Likewise, when a bolt needs tightening, a screw needs turning or a spark plug needs gapping, certain other tools work best for each individual situation.

The nice thing is that, not too terribly long ago, a couple of knife and tool companies — namely Leatherman and Buck, and there were others before, during and after them — popularized the multi-tool. The multi-tool is useful. The design works. Folding into a handle or handle halves are several tools, usually including a knife blade because it's the tool

employed most often. The multi-tool is a self-containing, compact unit. It's a little toolbox that fits into your pocket, so to speak.

Speaking to the great ingenuity of this country of ours, the knife companies took this novel idea and ran with it. They literally and figuratively hit the ground running! They've changed, added to, improved and evolved the design of the multi-tool in many ways. They've grown the market for the darn thing tenfold, no, make that 20- or 30-fold, many, many times over, to be blunt.

Early multi-tools incorporated knife blades, files, cap lifters, can openers, screwdrivers, leather punches, pliers and saws. Along came wrenches, then socket wrenches with socket heads, and bit holders with interchangeable bit heads. To make them more dramatic or easier to find when dropped, colorful handles were added. Next came translucent handles, which were, and are, also every color of the rainbow, and combined with lights, they shimmer and sparkle and look beautiful.

Tools in multi-tools grew to include those specifically designed to tighten in-line roller skate wheels, ski and snowboard bindings, and mountain-bike frames. If there is a job that needs doing, there's probably a multi-tool that will do it.

Don't take this wrong. A multi-tool will never replace the tools in the workshop. Multi-tool wrenches won't work on large pipes, the

screwdrivers won't turn the worst of corroded screws, and the files aren't meant for taking off bolt heads. These are easily carried toolboxes for small-to-medium-sized jobs in a pinch. They save a few steps to the toolbox. They work on most jobs around the house that don't call for hours of planning and labor.

Other big advantages include multi-tasking, affordability and fun factor. These marvelous little mechanical gadgets are a blast to play with, admire, open and close, experiment with and just plain use. Each knife company makes its own version. There's something that will appeal to everyone. Through the forum of *Sporting Knives 2004*, it is possible to see all of the multi-tools at the same time and learn about their specifications — how they're built, with what materials, in what sizes and weights — and discover what makes them tick.

So, without further ado, it's time to present the magical little multi-tasking multi-tools.

Bear MGC Cutlery

Multi-tools have been a part of the Bear MGC game plan since 1996, when the company took home the BLADE Magazine Most Innovative Design Award for the Pattern 53, 2-1/2-inch Mini Bear Jaws multi-tool. The Mini Bear Jaws is a folding pliers with strong steel jaws, a knife blade, cap lifter, screwdriver, file, ruler and more. Add black, blue, green and red handle choices, a key ring attachment, and an under-$40 suggested retail price, and Bear has a winner on its hands.

Other multi-tools followed, and in 1999, Victorinox, a big-league player in multi-tools and the "maker of the original Swiss Army knife," purchased Bear MGC. The year 2000 saw a complete revamping of the original

▶An odd but useful bird in the multi-tool genre is the 157SM Bear Jaws Sportsman Bird knife. This 5-inch multi-tool comes with a shears, a bone saw, hook, rulers, knife blade and a quality ballistic sheath that can be worn horizontally or vertically on a belt.

▼Electric in its design is the Pattern 155EL 4-inch Bear Jaws Electrician, which performs 19 functions, many of which electricians will find useful.

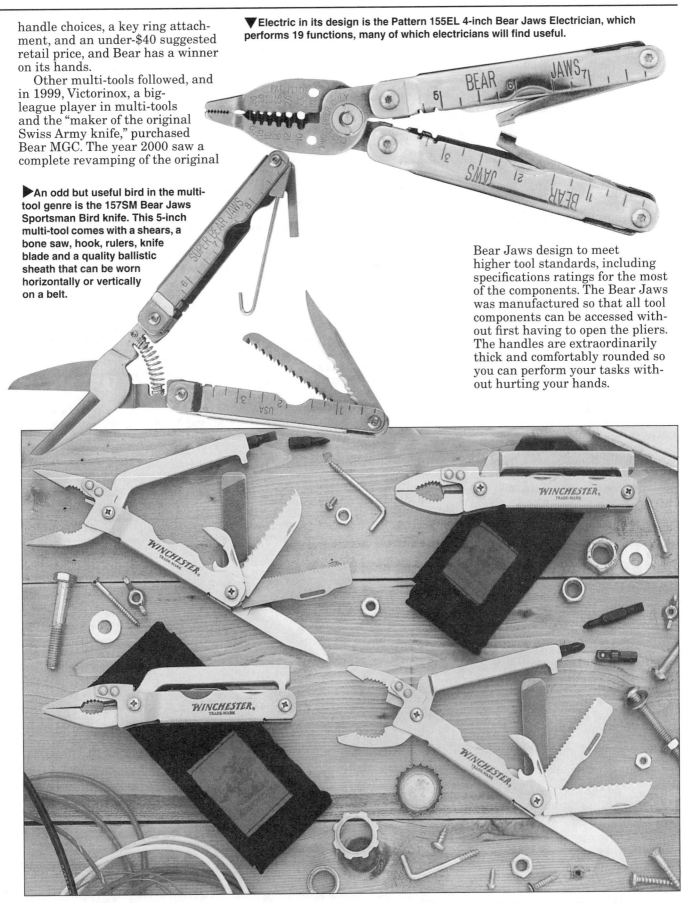

Bear Jaws design to meet higher tool standards, including specifications ratings for the most of the components. The Bear Jaws was manufactured so that all tool components can be accessed without first having to open the pliers. The handles are extraordinarily thick and comfortably rounded so you can perform your tasks without hurting your hands.

The Regular-jaw and Needle Nose Winchester Pliers & More multi-tools showcase pliers; can and bottle openers; files; rulers; screwdrivers with four interchangeable, magnetic locking bits; wire cutters; clip-point skinning blades; cross-cut saws; and serrated blades. The master clip-point blades parade the Winchester tang stamps.

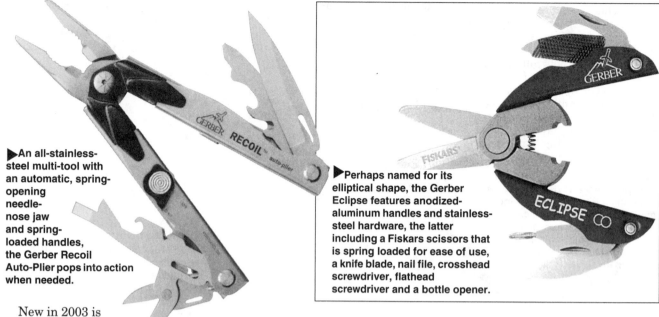

▶An all-stainless-steel multi-tool with an automatic, spring-opening needle-nose jaw and spring-loaded handles, the Gerber Recoil Auto-Plier pops into action when needed.

▶Perhaps named for its elliptical shape, the Gerber Eclipse features anodized-aluminum handles and stainless-steel hardware, the latter including a Fiskars scissors that is spring loaded for ease of use, a knife blade, nail file, crosshead screwdriver, flathead screwdriver and a bottle opener.

New in 2003 is the Pattern 155EL 4-inch Bear Jaws Electrician, which performs 19 functions, many of which electricians will find useful. All components within the grips of the 155EL lock in place for safety, and within the jaws of the pliers are six sizes of wire strippers.

Another Bear specialty multi-tool is the 157SM Bear Jaws Sportsman Bird knife. This 5-inch multi-tool comes with a shears, a bone saw, hook, rulers, knife blade and a quality ballistic sheath that can be worn horizontally or vertically on a belt.

Blue Grass Cutlery

It's funny how tools and tradition go hand-in-hand. What is more traditional than sweat equity? Then again, what is more traditional than a Winchester rifle and a few rounds to go with it? Winchester is a registered trademark of the Olin Corp., and Blue Grass Cutlery is licensed to make Winchester knives. Some knives feature a Winchester shield on jigged-bone-like Delrin® handles. Some Blue Grass Cutlery Winchester knives showcase shot-gun-shell-shaped handles, and others exhibit traditional celluloid, stag, pearl, cast-and-engraved bronze, and bone grips.

Blue Grass Cutlery also presents Winchester multi-tools, marketing them as "pliers and more." The Regular-jaw and Needle Nose Winchester Pliers & More multi-tools showcase pliers; can and bottle openers; files; rulers; screwdrivers with four, interchangeable, magnetic, locking bits; wire cutters; clip-point skinning blades; cross-cut saws; and serrated blades. The mas-

The Schrade i-Quip is part computer, part multi-tool, part survival kit and all business when it comes to safe and successful outdoor challenges and adventures.

Socket wrenches, bit drivers and bits are relatively new innovations in the multi-tool industry, and the Schrade Tough Tool ST5E employs all three. It is 100 percent stainless steel with 18 functions in all, including tools like a vise, wire cutter, saw and a knife blade.

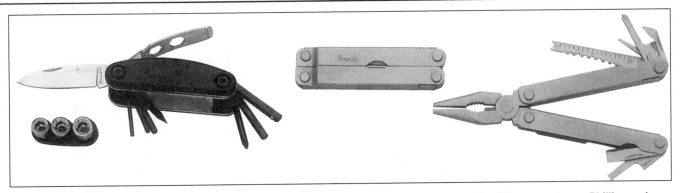

Joy Enterprises named one of its multi-tools "Nostalgia" (far left). Encased in one handle are five Allen wrenches, a Phillips and flathead screwdriver, a socket wrench and three sockets, two spanner wrenches and a knife blade. And you can pocket that! The All Purpose Multi-Tool (right) is another handy gadget from Joy Enterprises, this one employing nine implements, one of which is a combination saw blade/ruler.

ter clip-point blade parades the Winchester tang stamp.

Gerber Legendary Blades

"The call of the wild hasn't changed," those at Gerber say. "The gear has. It's lighter, it's stronger and has become more specialized, ergonomic and portable. For as long as you've been escaping the lure of couches, remote controls and micro-meals, we've been right there beside you."

Clearly, Gerber's mission statement calls for making tools for the great outdoors, whether on the job, on the run doing errands, working around the house, tinkering in the barn, shop or garage, or in the woods answering that call of the wild.

The Gerber Recoil Auto-Plier is an all-stainless-steel multi-tool with an automatic, spring-opening needle-nose jaws and spring-loaded handles. The large-sized tools include a Fiskars scissors, a one-hand-opening knife blade, wire stripper, twine cutter, crosshead screwdriver, bottle opener, flathead screwdriver and can opener. All components lock, and the tool can be carried in a ballistic-nylon sheath.

Gerber's new Total Eclipse could be classified as a mini multi-tool that attaches to a key chain. The compact tool features anodized-aluminum handles and stainless-steel hardware, the latter including a Fiskars scissors that is spring loaded for ease of use, a knife blade, nail file, crosshead screwdriver, flathead screwdriver and a bottle opener.

Imperial Schrade

After 95 years of making knives, Schrade would probably be the first to admit that edged tools rarely get

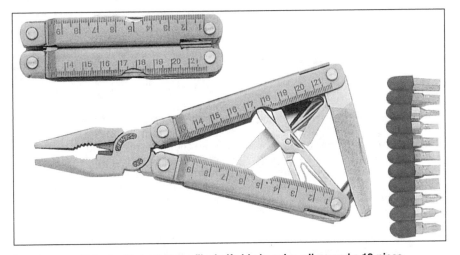

Imagine a multi-tool with a scissors, file, knife blade, ruler, pliers and a 12-piece screwdriver set with interchangeable heads. That's just what is included in the Joy 88036 multi-tool, and it features so many implements, the tool requires a carrying pouch.

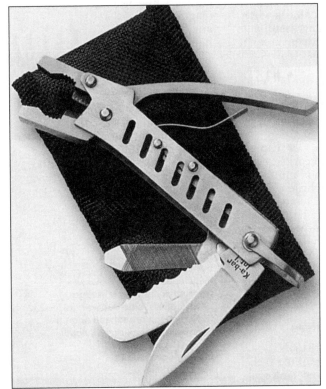

◄ Ka-Bar's Multi-Tool could be considered the ideal design for soldiers, as are many of the knives carrying the Ka-Bar logo. The Multi-Tool showcases sturdy pliers jaws with large wire cutter blades, a saw blade, knife blade, combination saw/screwdriver and lanyard loop. The Multi-Tool is delivered in a nylon belt pouch with Velcro flap closure.

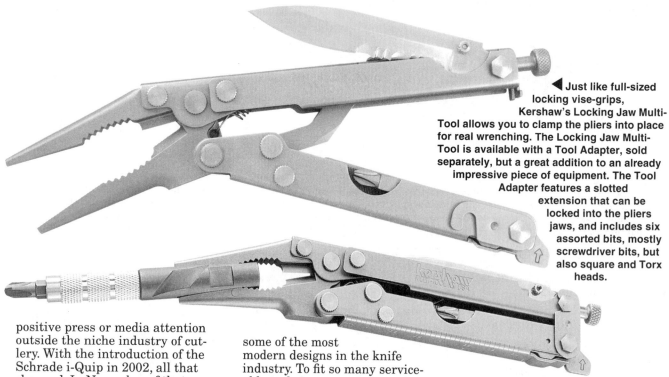

Just like full-sized locking vise-grips, Kershaw's Locking Jaw Multi-Tool allows you to clamp the pliers into place for real wrenching. The Locking Jaw Multi-Tool is available with a Tool Adapter, sold separately, but a great addition to an already impressive piece of equipment. The Tool Adapter features a slotted extension that can be locked into the pliers jaws, and includes six assorted bits, mostly screwdriver bits, but also square and Torx heads.

positive press or media attention outside the niche industry of cutlery. With the introduction of the Schrade i-Quip in 2002, all that changed. In November of that year, *Time magazine* called the i-Quip one of the "coolest inventions" of 2002. *The Wall Street Journal* claimed the i-Quip "makes climbing and backpacking much easier and safer sports." The i-Quip also garnered the *Popular Mechanics* 2002 Design & Engineering Award.

Seldom does an edged tool or, in this case, multi-tool, redefine the marketplace. The Schrade i-Quip is part computer, part multi-tool, part survival kit and all business when it comes to safe and successful outdoor challenges and adventures. In addition to man's oldest tool — a knife blade — features include an altimeter; barometer; digital compass; clock with stopwatch, alarm and backlight; LED flashlight; signal mirror; survival whistle; lighter compartment; belt clip; screwdrivers; scissors; saw; cap lifter; can opener; and corkscrew.

Expanding the line of multi-tools in 2003 is the Schrade Tough Tool ST5E, which boasts an adjustable pliers head, a slip-joint jaw and an exclusive three-in-one drive tool — a socket driver that also employs screwdriver bits. It is 100 percent stainless steel with 18 functions in all. Other tools include a vise, wire cutter, saw and blade.

Joy Enterprises

In some ways, multi-tools encompass forward-thinking technology, advanced engineering and some of the most modern designs in the knife industry. To fit so many serviceable tools in one compact unit, especially with a palm-swelling handle, a razor-sharp blade and powerful pliers jaws, is nothing short of remarkable.

In another way, the multi-tool could be considered a throwback to a simpler time when handcrafting was a way of life. Do you remember the big, beefy Scout and Swiss Army knives of the past? Some of them employed scissors and compasses, while others even featured magnifying glasses and flints for starting fires.

Perhaps it is in an attempt to recapture some of the ingenuity of the past that Joy Enterprises named one of its multi-tools "Nostalgia." Encased in one handle are five Allen wrenches, a Phillips and flathead screwdriver, a socket wrench and three sockets, two spanner wrenches

and a knife blade. And you can pocket that!

The All Purpose Multi-Tool is another handy gadget from Joy Enterprises, this one employing nine implements, one of which is a combination saw blade/ruler. Other tools include screwdrivers, a can

KutMaster's Sportsman's/Archer Multi-Tool has the usual assortment of blades and implements, but also includes a nock installation pliers for bows; a taper nock removable wedge; an awl; pliers; side cutters; guthook blade; a broadhead and tip-removal tool; locking hex head; and a wrench with 12 interchangeable bits in a bit holder.

opener, punches and pliers. The piece is 4-1/4 inches closed and comes with a carrying pouch.

In another attempt to recapture some design ideas of the past, but furthering the technology involved in doing so, is the Joy 88318 Gift Set. Packaged together in an aluminum canister is a five-implement pocketknife — complete with corkscrew, can opener blades and screwdrivers — and a multi-tool with pliers and eight other handy implements.

Imagine a multi-tool with a scissors, file, knife blade, ruler, pliers and a 12-piece screwdriver set with interchangeable heads. That's just what is included in the Joy 88036 multi-tool, and it features so many implements, the tool requires a carrying pouch.

Ka-Bar Knives

Ka-Bar's relationship with the Armed Forces is not only documented and well known in the United States, but worldwide. Some of the most storied, historical and collected military knives extant are edged tools and weapons from Ka-Bar. Stacked-leather-washer handles and black U.S.M.C. blades are mainstays in the Ka-Bar line.

With the relationships between the United States and Iraq and North Korea deteriorating today, and with the high levels of alert thrust upon the American people, Ka-Bar military knives are more valuable than ever if we want to make the world a safer place to live.

In an article titled "The Edge in Homeland Security" in this edition of "Sporting Knives," author Linda Moll Smith interviewed several present and ex-military members, many of whom, surprisingly, singled out multi-tools as some of the most important soldier knives. Maybe it isn't so surprising that soldiers, like civilians, need tools to go along with their edges.

Aptly named the "Multi-Tool," the only such offering under the Ka-Bar umbrella showcases sturdy pliers jaws with large wire cutter blades, a saw blade, knife blade, combination saw/screwdriver and lanyard loop. The Multi-Tool is delivered in a nylon belt pouch with Velcro flap closure.

Kershaw Knives

The Kershaw Locking Jaw Multi-Tool has to be one of the most thought-out and well made of its kind. Just like full-sized locking vise-grips, the Locking Jaw Multi-Tool allows you to clamp the pliers into place for real wrenching. The degree of pressure of the pliers' jaws is adjusted via a vise-grip-type finger screw on the butt of the handle.

Employing some of the same technology incorporated into its modern folding knives, the blade of the Multi-Tool is propped open via a locking liner. The partially serrated blade and five other sturdy implements, and they are beefy, are 440C stainless steel. Complementing the pliers and blade are a hacksaw, a slot screwdriver, a combination can opener/cap lifter, a two-sided file, a Phillips screwdriver and a ruler.

The Locking Jaw Multi-Tool is available with a Tool Adapter, sold separately, but a great addition to an already impressive piece of equipment. The Tool Adapter features a slotted extension that can be locked into the pliers jaws, and includes six assorted bits, mostly screwdriver bits, but also square and Torx heads.

KutMaster

The Mountain Quest line of knives and tools from KutMaster is aimed at outdoor activities in an era when people have many and varied interests. Take the 5807CP 30-Function Sportsman's/Archer Multi-Tool. This puppy has the usual assortment of blades and implements, but also includes a nock installation pliers for bows; a taper nock removable wedge; an awl; pliers; side cutters; gut-hook blade; a broadhead and tip-removal

With the KutMaster 5030CP 17-Function Multi-Tool, opened and extended implement blades are locked into place by closing the handle halves. By opening one of seven implement blades and closing the handle halves, the Locking L Safety Device is activated and secures the thus extended blade into place.

▶ **Leatherman's Juice S2 comes with a choice of a "flame-orange" or "storm-gray" handle, and is loaded with tools, including a needle-nose pliers; straight blade; wire cutters; extra-small screwdriver; bottle/can opener; lanyard attachment; and corkscrew.**

tool; locking hex head; and a wrench with 12 interchangeable bits in a bit holder. All fold into a 4-1/2-inch frame, and the tool fits in a nylon pouch with bit compartment.

With the 5030CP 17-Function Multi-Tool, opened and extended implement blades are locked into place by closing the handle halves. By opening one of seven implement blades and closing the handle halves, the Locking L Safety Device is activated and secures the thus extended blade into place. Tools employed by the Model 5030CP are a pliers; wire cutter; coarse and fine files; a serrated sheepsfoot blade; a ruler; saw blade; clip-point blade; can/bottle opener; screwdriver bits and bit adapter; and a lanyard hole.

Another multi-tool working off the Locking L Safety Device is the 17-Function MultiMaster with many of the same implement blades, but incorporating needle-nose pliers instead of a regular pliers head.

Leatherman Tool Group

Incorporated in 1983, Leatherman remains owned and operated by its founder, Tim Leatherman. The Leatherman name and multi-tools are one-in-the-same, it seems, and many would credit Tim for having invented the multi-tool, or at least the modern version of compact hand tools.

Tim's story is worth retelling. In 1975, he was traveling through Europe with little money and a car that was difficult to keep running. His Scout knife couldn't handle the necessary mechanical jobs, and Tim wished he had a set of compact tools, including full-size pliers. Back home in Oregon, he put his engineering skills to work and, after seven years, the original Leatherman Tool was a reality.

Leatherman celebrates its 20th anniversary with a commemorative multi-tool. At the 2003 S.H.O.T. (Shooting Hunting Outdoor Trade) Show, Leatherman premiered the 20th Anniversary Limited Edition Wave. It sports a black-and-stain-

less finish on a handle frame emblazed with a "20 Year" logo. Incorporated in the design are long, slender pliers jaws for reaching in deep recesses; hard-wire cutters; a saw; knife blade; a file; screwdrivers; cap lifter/can opener; and a scissors.

The Leatherman Juice models parade anodized-aluminum handles in bold colors. The Squirt S4 is a key-chain-size multi-tool available in "glacier-blue," "inferno-red" and "storm-gray" handles, and features tools ranging from scissors to tweezers, and screwdrivers to a file.

The Juice S2 comes with a choice of a "flame-orange" or "storm-gray" handle, and is loaded with tools, including a needle-nose pliers; straight blade; wire cutters; extra-small screwdriver; bottle/can opener; lanyard attachment; and corkscrew.

In all, Leatherman produces nearly two-dozen handheld tools. The company is one of the most successful garage start-up success stories in the history of garage start-ups, and definitely one of the most interesting names in tool manufacturing. Over the years, Leatherman has grown from a small garage to its current 93,000-square-foot headquarters, proving that multi-tools are necessary and popular equipment.

◀ **The Leatherman Squirt S4 is a key-chain-size multi-tool available in "glacier-blue," "inferno-red" and "storm-gray" handles, and features tools ranging from scissors to tweezers, and screwdrivers to a file.**

Ideal for bow hunters, rifle hunters and muzzleloaders, the Outdoor Edge Sportsman's Multi-Tool embodies such features as a nock point crimping tool and a gut-hook blade.

Take a walk with the Outdoor Edge Trek Tool, which employs a spring-loaded pliers with wire cutter; a partially serrated blade; double-sided file; saw; chisel/scraper; can/bottle opener; a punch; and magnetic drive bit adapter with 12 bits.

Outdoor Edge Cutlery Corp.

Two multi-tools from Outdoor edge — the Sportman's Multi-Tool and Trek Tool — show the versatility of the inherent compact design. The Sportsman's Multi-Tool is ideal for bow hunters, rifle hunters and muzzleloaders, as it features a pliers head with nock point crimping tool; a wire cutter; clip-point knife blade; gut-hook blade; wood bone saw; a broadhead wrench; chisel; can/bottle opener; punch; lanyard attachment; ruler and magnetic drive-bit adapter with 12 bits.

The Trek Tool has an unmistakable swirl-brush handle treatment and employs a spring-loaded pliers with wire cutter; a partially serrated blade; double-sided file; saw; chisel/scraper; can/bottle opener; a punch; and magnetic drive bit adapter with 12 bits.

SOG Specialty Knives

According to Spencer Frazer, president and chief designer of SOG Specialty Knives, the company makes the only multi-tools in the world with one-handed, flip-open and gear-driven compound leverage for double pliers power. SOG is also the inventor of the push-button SwitchPlier, with a pliers head that projects out of the handle like a spring-loaded knife or switchblade.

Push a button and "Pow!" the pliers-head of the SWPL76 Switch-Plier springs to action faster than you can say, "Fix it." Nestled within aircraft-aluminum handle halves are five locking tool components, namely a can opener/small screwdriver; a half-serrated knife blade; a bottle opener/medium screwdriver; a three-sided file/ large screwdriver; and a Phillips screwdriver.

Some of SOG's more mini multi-tools feature titanium-nitride coatings for scratch and wear resistance. The coating also looks cool. One such tool that comes with the titanium-nitride-coating option is the CrossGrip CG55, a small, gear-driven, compound-leverage pliers tool with a pliers/ gripper/wire cutter; a straight blade; a nail file; medium screwdriver; Phillips screwdriver; bottle opener/small screwdriver; tweezers; ruler; lanyard ring; and vinyl carrying pouch.

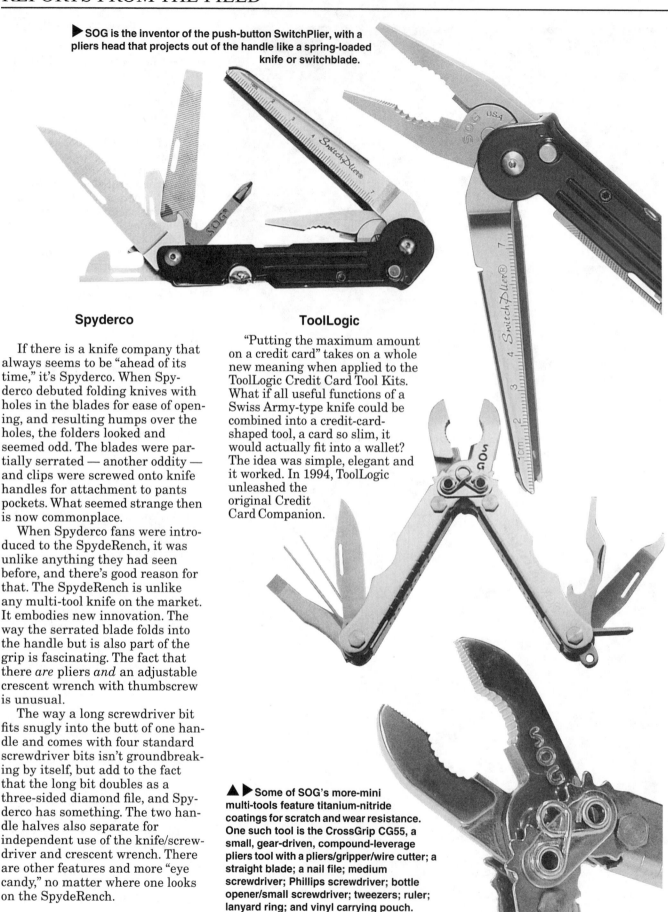

▶ SOG is the inventor of the push-button SwitchPlier, with a pliers head that projects out of the handle like a spring-loaded knife or switchblade.

Spyderco

If there is a knife company that always seems to be "ahead of its time," it's Spyderco. When Spyderco debuted folding knives with holes in the blades for ease of opening, and resulting humps over the holes, the folders looked and seemed odd. The blades were partially serrated — another oddity — and clips were screwed onto knife handles for attachment to pants pockets. What seemed strange then is now commonplace.

When Spyderco fans were introduced to the SpydeRench, it was unlike anything they had seen before, and there's good reason for that. The SpydeRench is unlike any multi-tool knife on the market. It embodies new innovation. The way the serrated blade folds into the handle but is also part of the grip is fascinating. The fact that there *are* pliers *and* an adjustable crescent wrench with thumbscrew is unusual.

The way a long screwdriver bit fits snugly into the butt of one handle and comes with four standard screwdriver bits isn't groundbreaking by itself, but add to the fact that the long bit doubles as a three-sided diamond file, and Spyderco has something. The two handle halves also separate for independent use of the knife/screwdriver and crescent wrench. There are other features and more "eye candy," no matter where one looks on the SpydeRench.

ToolLogic

"Putting the maximum amount on a credit card" takes on a whole new meaning when applied to the ToolLogic Credit Card Tool Kits. What if all useful functions of a Swiss Army-type knife could be combined into a credit-card-shaped tool, a card so slim, it would actually fit into a wallet? The idea was simple, elegant and it worked. In 1994, ToolLogic unleashed the original Credit Card Companion.

▲ ▶ Some of SOG's more-mini multi-tools feature titanium-nitride coatings for scratch and wear resistance. One such tool is the CrossGrip CG55, a small, gear-driven, compound-leverage pliers tool with a pliers/gripper/wire cutter; a straight blade; a nail file; medium screwdriver; Phillips screwdriver; bottle opener/small screwdriver; tweezers; ruler; lanyard ring; and vinyl carrying pouch.

▼The two handle halves of the Spyderco SpydeRench separate for independent use of the knife/screwdriver and crescent wrench. Features abound on the multi-tool that is truly ahead of its time.

◀ToolLogic offers an entire line of compact multi-tool credit cards, some designed for everyday carry, and others made specifically for golfing, entertaining or business uses.

Stanley Tools and United Cutlery team on the 8-Function Automatic Multi Tool and the 12-Function Compound Leverage Multi Tool, which both pack numerous tools into compact, handheld units.

People responded to the innovative design and the practicality of having a formidable set of tools in a slim, credit card shape.

ToolLogic eventually released an entire line of compact multi-tool credit cards, some designed for everyday carry, and others made specifically for golfing, entertaining or business uses. For their size, the tools pack a lot of punch. Every tool has one thing in common — a knife blade — and some employ lights for seeing while working in dark areas. Other tools include compasses; tweezers; scissors; power lenses; can/bottle openers; screwdrivers; staple removers; awls; nail files; toothpicks; rulers; and lanyard holes.

United Cutlery

As if it wasn't enough that United Cutlery is the official maker and distributor of Colt Knives; Harley-Davidson Motorcycles Knives; Columbia Sportswear Co. pieces; Outdoor Life fillet knives, axes, folders and saws; Ford knives; and Eickhorn Solingen Knives, now the company has landed the Stanley line of folding knives, multi-tools, wood carvers and sharpeners.

The Model SL0040MTNC 8-Function Automatic Multi Tool features spring-loaded pliers with push-button opening mechanism, a stainless steel knife blade, a cast-metal handle, a wire cutter, file and screwdrivers.

Second in line is the 12-Function Compound Leverage Multi Tool. This one packs a needle-nose pliers, wire cutter, half-serrated

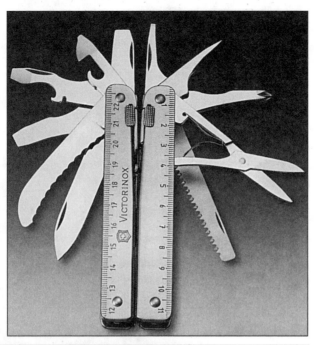

Victorinox carries a multi-tool for every lifestyle. In the hard-core multi-tool category are such tool knives as the SwissTool RS. Of the 26 functions the RS tool performs, some of the more unusual implementations include seat-belt cutting, wire cutting, chiseling, scraping, strong-crate opening, wire bending, wire stripping and wood sawing.

The Victorinox SwissTool CS Plus is a 36-function toolbox in a leather belt pouch. Torx wrenches meet Phillips screwdrivers "head on" within the boundaries of the CS Plus, and wire bending, stripping, scraping and crimping is all in a day's work.

Victorinox carries a multi-tool for every lifestyle. In the hard-core multi-tool category are such tool knives as the SwissTool RS. Of the 26 functions the RS tool performs, some of the more unusual implementations include seat-belt cutting, wire cutting, chiseling, scraping, strong-crate opening, wire bending, wire stripping and wood sawing.

The SwissTool CS Plus is a 36-function toolbox in a leather belt pouch. Torx wrenches meet Phillips screwdrivers "head on" within the boundaries of the CS Plus, and wire bending, stripping, scraping and crimping is all in a day's work. A metal file, metal saw, wood saw, reamer and chisel/scraper can handle the rough work, while screwdrivers, bottle openers, a knife blade, corkscrew and lanyard hole are more adept at the everyday chores.

Wenger

Wenger traces its roots back to supplying the Swiss Army with knives. Wenger prides itself in knife technology, and more specifically, furthering the evolution of knives into precision multi-tools. It becomes clear as multi-tools emerge into the limelight that, clearly, they are an evolution of knives. The knife and blade came first. The multi-tool was spawned from it, but not spawned as in new birth, rather as if an extension of a knife, forming a new incarnation with more purpose, expanded use, implementation and function.

If you have a multi-tool, you might as well call it the Tool Chest Plus, this one in a red handle. More tools unfold from within the frame of a 3-1/4-inch Swiss Army knife than James Bond could use in a year. Those include a large blade; double-cut wood saw; adjustable pliers with wire-crimping tool and wire cutter; fish-scaling blade, hook disgorger and line guide; mineral crystal magnifier with precision screwdriver; metal file; metal saw; straight-edge ruler; spring-less scissors; and universal wrench.

Singularly spectacular is the Wenger Serrated Master with a 100 percent serrated, large, locking blade, a double-cut wood saw, adjustable pliers, scissors, screwdrivers and more.

blade, screwdrivers, metric ruler, awl and bottle opener into one stainless-steel package.

Victorinox

Many companies could hold claim to having invented the original multi-tool, but none have more impressive an argument than Victorinox. Switzerland in 1884 found Karl Elsener, who started a cutlery factory in the small village of Ibach. There, in Ibach, Elsener landed a deal with the Swiss Army for servicemen to carry the "Soldier's" pocketknife. He also built a light, more elegant "Officer's Knife" that would later become known as the "Original Swiss Army Knife."

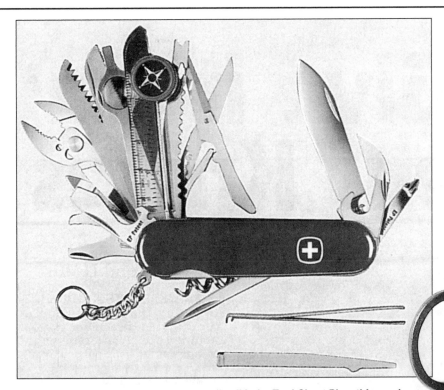

If you have a multi-tool, you might as well call it the Tool Chest Plus, this one by Wenger in a red handle. More tools unfold from within the frame of a 3-1/4-inch Swiss Army knife than James Bond could use in a year.

Xikar announces the MTSC, a scissors, nail file, bottle opener, knife blade and screwdriver with a key-chain attachment for easy access.

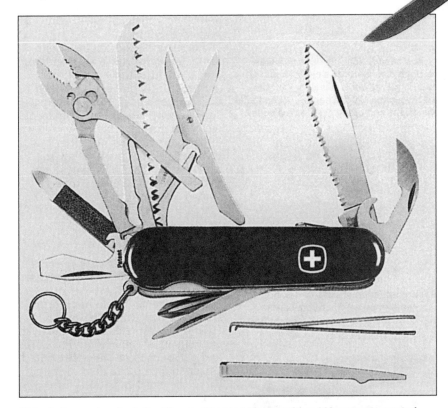

Singularly spectacular is the Wenger Serrated Master with a 100 percent serrated, large, locking blade, a double-cut wood saw, adjustable pliers, scissors, screwdrivers and more.

Xikar

Cigar cutters from Xikar caught the attention of many a knife-industry professional and enthusiast early on in the company's history. Then, Xikar proved it was a player in gentlemen's knives and tools by debuting some of the slimmest, most lightweight, quality gentlemen's folding pocketknives the industry had ever encountered.

Keeping up a tradition of excellence, Xikar announces the MTSC, a scissors, nail file, bottle opener, knife blade and screwdriver with a key-chain attachment for easy access. Xikar also markets the XI MTX Multi-Tool, a lightweight, compact multi-tool that incorporates a folding cigar scissors, a cigar poker, knife blade, screwdriver and bottle opener. The cigar scissors can cut up to a 54-ring-gauge cigar. ●

Let's Give it up for Gear Knives

▲The Al Mar Havana Clipper is the cigar smoker's best friend. Not only does this little pocket folder have an excellent main cutting blade, but it also features a cigar clipper engineered into one side of the black-linen-Micarta® handle. It works like this: with the blade unfolded, or open, a cigar tip is inserted into a hole in the Micarta handle. When the blade is consequently folded into the handle, it lops off the end of the cigar as it closes.

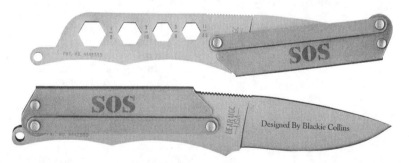

▲The Bear MGC SOS is a drop-point fixed blade incorporating four sizes of hex-bolt-head openings machined through the blade tang. Depending on whether you want to loosen hex bolts or cut something, a protective sheath rotates to cover either the cutting edge or the hex openings.

▲ For big game hunters, Bear Cutlery also makes a Cushion Grip Lockback folder that pairs a gut-hook/bone-saw blade with a clip-point main blade.

By Durwood Hollis

IN WEBSTER'S NEW World Dictionary, Third College Edition, one of the listed definitions for the word "gear" is "... apparatus or equipment for some particular task." Therefore, a "gear knife" would be a cutting tool that includes one or more additional blades designed for a specific assignment. Since folding knives lend to the inclusion of more than one blade, typically most "gear knives" are folders.

For example, an angler's gear knife, in addition to a main cutting blade, might employ a hook dis-gorger/scaling blade. Likewise, a bird hunter's gear knife could possess a choke tube wrench blade, as well as a gut-hook blade. A review of what the market now offers in this cutlery venue will allow the reader to see just how specialized tool blades have become integrated into knife design.

Al Mar Knives

An Oregon-based cutlery company, Al Mar Knives has earned an impressive reputation with its edged products. While not a brand-spanking-new knife, the Model HCBM1 Havana Clipper is the best friend a cigar smoker can have, and, following suit, the abbreviated chisel-shaped blade does everything the average pocketknife owner would ask of it. The best part is the cigar clipper engineered into one side of the black-linen-Micarta® handle.

It works like this: with the blade unfolded, or open, a cigar tip is inserted into a hole in the Micarta handle. When the blade is consequently folded into the handle, it

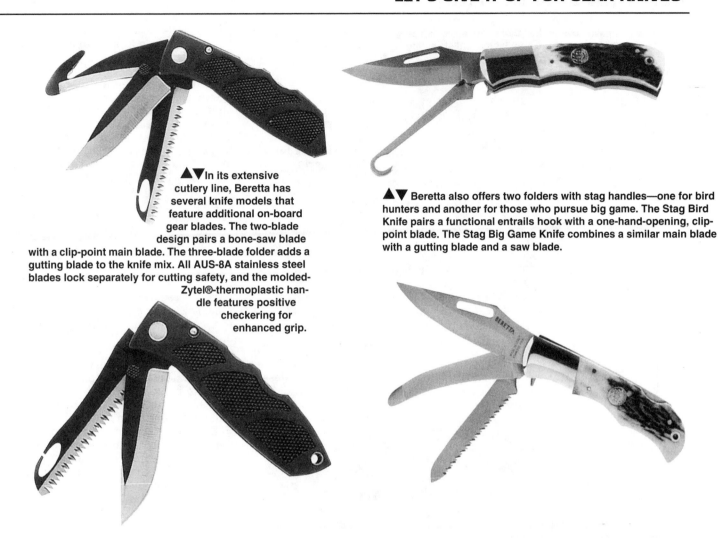

▲▼In its extensive cutlery line, Beretta has several knife models that feature additional on-board gear blades. The two-blade design pairs a bone-saw blade with a clip-point main blade. The three-blade folder adds a gutting blade to the knife mix. All AUS-8A stainless steel blades lock separately for cutting safety, and the molded-Zytel®-thermoplastic handle features positive checkering for enhanced grip.

▲▼ Beretta also offers two folders with stag handles—one for bird hunters and another for those who pursue big game. The Stag Bird Knife pairs a functional entrails hook with a one-hand-opening, clip-point blade. The Stag Big Game Knife combines a similar main blade with a gutting blade and a saw blade.

lops off the end of the cigar as it closes. A pocket clip on the outside of the opposing handle slab holds dollar bills or secures the knife to a pants pocket. All steel components, including a thumb stud, pivot pin, frame and handle pins, are AUS-8 stainless steel. The Havana Clipper is the perfect choice for cigar lovers, and it doubles as a useful pocketknife in any application.

Bear MGC Cutlery

Bear MGC Cutlery delivers a couple knife models with integrated gear applications. The fixed-blade Model 108 SOS designed by Blackie Collins incorporates four sizes of hex-bolt-head openings machined through the drop-point-blade tang. Depending on whether you want to loosen hex bolts or cut something, a protective sheath rotates to cover either the cutting edge or the hex openings. Made entirely from high-carbon stainless steel, there's never any worry about upkeep with the SOS gear knife.

For big game hunters, Bear Cutlery also makes a Cushion Grip Lockback folder (Model 460GH) that pairs a gut-hook/bone-saw blade with a clip-point main blade. Both blades are high-carbon stainless steel and lock tightly when put to use. The Kraton® handle scales have raised texture and provide good hand purchase. When it comes to big game field care, having an additional gear blade makes sense.

Beretta U.S.A. Corp.

The European firearms manufacturer also offers a line of quality fixed-blade and folding knives. Among the four models in Beretta's Fieldlight series are two game-care cutting tools. The two-blade design (Model 79182-1) pairs a bone-saw blade with a clip-point main blade. The three-blade folder (Model 79183-8) adds a gutting blade to the knife mix. All AUS-8A stainless steel blades lock separately for cutting

▲ ▶ When it comes to gear knives for big game hunters, the Browning Extreme F.D.T. (Field Dressing Tool) knives feature a number of different blade options.

▼ Browning hasn't overlooked those who enjoy camping. The Model 425 Camp Knife is a folder that enlists eating utensils (spoon and fork), a can/bottle opener and a drop-point main blade in the same handle frame.

▲ Incorporating a gut-hook/saw blade, the Buck Crosslock Hunter is designed to make wild game gutting, skinning and meat care easier. (Hollis photo)

▲▼ The tiny Buck Metro and larger Approach have pronounced lanyard openings to facilitate carabineer attachment. For those who enjoy climbing, trekking, and mountaineering, these knives are welcome assets.

safety, and the molded-Zytel®-thermoplastic handle features positive checkering for enhanced grip.

Beretta also offers two folders with stag handles—one for bird hunters and another for those who pursue big game. The Stag Bird Knife (Model 79636-9) pairs a functional entrails hook with a one-hand-opening, clip-point blade. The Stag Big Game Knife (Model 79637-6) combines a similar main blade with a gutting blade and a saw blade. All blades are 440C stainless steel for low maintenance and high performance.

Hunters have learned to appreciate specialized gear blades that make the difference when it comes to efficient game care in the field.

Browning

When it comes to hunting, fishing and outdoor living, the folks at Browning are cutlery professionals who make it their business to know gear knives. New for 2003 are two multi-blade Extreme F.D.T. (Field Dressing Tool) knives, Models 691 and 692, that

parade 440-C stainless steel blades, titanium locking liners and Mossy-Oak®-camouflage-finished handles.

Model 691 marries a one-hand-opening, drop-point (with gut hook on its spine) main blade with a quick-cutting bone saw. Model 692 takes this theme one step further by pairing a contoured drop-point main blade with a gutting blade and a saw blade. A Ballistic Cloth belt sheath is included with each knife for copasetic carry. These are great game care tools and welcome additions to the Browning cutlery lineup.

While Browning has always considered hunting knives its main focus, those who enjoy camping haven't been overlooked. The Model 425 Camp Knife is a folder that enlists eating utensils (spoon and fork), a can/bottle opener and a drop-point main blade in the same handle frame. Speaking of the knife frame, it can be separated into two individual components—fork and can/bottle opener in one, and spoon and main cutting blade in the other—for simultaneous use. All of the tools and utensils, as well as the knife frame, are stainless steel for ease of maintenance. Carried in its belt sheath, the Model 425 Camp Knife gear knife is bound for the campground.

Buck Knives

Buck has several offerings that blend easily into the gear-knife realm. For hunters, the two-blade Crosslock Hunter Camo folder (Model 180D3) showcases a gutting/skinning blade with a saw back and a drop-point main blade paired in the same frame. The setup allows a successful hunter to quickly slit the hide with the gut hook, and the saw edge on the reverse side of the blade is useful for cutting through rib cage cartilage and the pelvic girdle. If there ever was a gear knife for big game hunters, this is it.

Three new models in the Buck Knives line were designed in collaboration with world-renowned mountaineer Peter Whittaker. What makes the models suitable gear-knife candidates are not only the multi-use configurations, but also the carry systems.

The Metro (Model 759) is a tiny folder that fills more than one role. In addition to the abbreviated drop-point blade, a portion of the

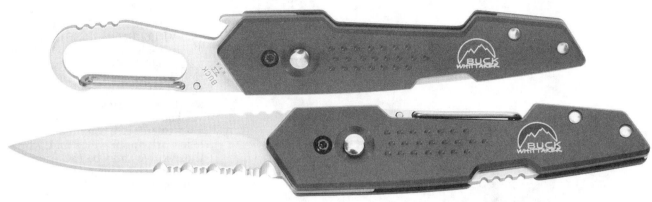

▲ When the lightweight, locking aluminum handle of the Buck Revolution-XT is rotated to cover the cutting edge of the blade, the exposed blade tang provides a clip for attachment to a pack, a belt loop or anywhere else handy.

knife frame serves as a bottle and can opener. An extremely functional tool, this Lilliputian cutter saves fingernails and prevents frustration when thirst demands satisfaction. Likewise, both the Approach (Model 751) and its little brother the new Short Approach (Model 752) folders feature large lanyard openings to accommodate full-size carabineers. Since carabineers are often used in mountaineering, backpacking and climbing, the oversize openings allow for attachment to packs, climbing harnesses or belt loops.

Finally, the new Buck Revolution-XT (Model 437) is a hybrid fixed-blade knife featuring a handle that doubles as the blade sheath. This design provides the benefits of a compact folding knife with the strength of a fixed blade. When the lightweight, locking aluminum handle is rotated to cover the cutting edge of the blade, the exposed blade tang provides a clip for attachment to a pack, a belt loop or anywhere else handy. The Revolution also has the customary bottle opener notch at the base of the tang. Once again, Buck Knives creates a cutting tool that's both handy and functional.

Camillus Knives

Camillus is one of the nation's oldest cutlery manufacturers and, to be expected, it offers a wide range of both fixed-blade and folding knives. The Camillus Model 1760 Camp Knife is available in several versions, including four-blade and five-blade configurations. In all models, a main spear-point blade is teamed with several useful camping gear blades. In short, the Camp Knife is little more and nothing less than an

American version of the basic folder issued to Swiss Army troops.

Those who are blue water adventurers will appreciate the pairing of a sheepsfoot blade with a knot-untying spike in all three versions of Camillus's Marlin Spike Knife (Models 695, 696, and 697). If you've had to deal with water-soaked knots, then you'll understand just how valuable the marlinspike is on a pocket folder. Of course, stainless steel components lessen knife maintenance.

Those who work as tradesmen will find the two-blade Electrician Knife (Model 278) and the similarly configured Workhorse Knife (Model 326BP) to their liking. Both of these gear knives pair flathead screwdrivers with main cutting blades (either clip- or drop-point patterns, depending on the model). And, like many of Camillus's edged offerings, both blades are high-carbon stainless steel.

◀ The Camillus Model 1760 Camp Knife is available in several versions, including four-blade and five-blade configurations. In all models, a main spear-point blade is teamed with several useful camping gear blades.

▲ Those who are blue water adventurers will appreciate Camillus's Marlin Spike Knife, pairing of a sheepsfoot blade with a knot-untying spike.

Case Cutlery

When it comes to gear knives, one needs look no further than the extensive Case Cutlery catalog. New for this year in the Case Jade Knife series is none other than the Bartender's Knife (Model 1198/64130-SS). The tavern owner's favorite edged buddy combines a drop-point-pattern main blade, a small spear-

▲ For the workhorse in you, the Camillus Workhorse includes a flathead screwdriver and high-carbon stainless steel knife blade. Have at it!

▲ New for this year in the Case Jade Knife series is none other than the Bartender's Knife, combining a drop-point-pattern main blade, a small spear-point blade, a curved wine-label-cutting blade and a corkscrew.

point blade, a curved wine-label-cutting blade and a corkscrew. Of course, all Case Tru-Sharp® stainless steel blades hold their edges, yet the one feature that sets this knife pattern apart is a vivid green-jigged-bone handle, resembling mineral jade in its natural state. Those who keep bar, professionally or in their homes, never had it so good.

Case was one of the earliest manufacturers of pocketknives that include eating utensils within the framework of their designs. Typically, this design combination includes a slender clip-point main blade with a fork/cap lifter blade. Case now introduces a three-blade Hobo (Model 052/6354HB SS) that adds a spoon blade to the traditional knife/fork pair. Those who make their home on the road can well appreciate what this particular knife brings to the table.

Another pocket folder in the Amber Bone series is the Mini Trapper with Golf Tool (Model 051/6207G SS). If knocking the ball around the greens is

your passion, you'll find this little folder a great asset to your game. There's a small amber-bone-handled Pen Knife with Scissors (Model 258/6233RSC SS) that adds another dimension to the usual penknife configuration.

All three of these models feature stainless steel blades so that environmental invectives won't be a problem. Of course, amber bone handle scales and nickel-silver bolsters are also part of the package.

Case Cutlery hasn't neglected the blue-collar crowd. In its Utility Working Knife series, four gear knives stand out above the rest.

The Electrician's Knife (Model 127/62031LHR

SWS), the Marlin Spike (Model 125/62146RL SS), Camper's Knife (Model 114/640045R SS) and the Camper's Knife with Pliers (Model 124/65045R SS) are all fully functional in design. Each knife features stainless steel blades, jigged synthetic handles and nickel-silver bolsters. The various blade assortments are combined for specific work applications and, while these knives may be rather utilitarian, each one is no less a dependable tool on the job.

Gerber Legendary Blades

A respected maker of outstanding edged products, Gerber's innovative Model 6967 Urban Companion is a prime example of forward-thinking design. The lock-blade folder exhibits a drop-point main blade complementing a handy little pair of scissors. The blade itself sports a partially serrated edge for cutting fibrous, gritty or woven materials, as well as an exposed thumb stub for opening ease. Best of all, the stainless steel blade and scissors are low maintenance and high performance. A Gator TEX® handle insert provides positive hand purchase in all situations. Lightweight and well thought out, this is one keen cutter!

Imperial Schrade

Known for pocketknives, hunters, outdoor knives and utilitarian pieces, Schrade also offers a good selection of gear knives, not the least of which is the tiny Simon (Models SS1, SS1AB, SS15, SS16 and SS17) folder. With a one-hand-opening blade, just 2-1/4 inches

▲ Available with a knife and fork, or a knife, fork and spoon, the ever-popular Case Hobo folding knife can make a road trip more enjoyable.

▲The Case Camper's Knife with Pliers is a fully functional knife featuring stainless steel implements, jigged synthetic handles and nickel-silver bolsters.

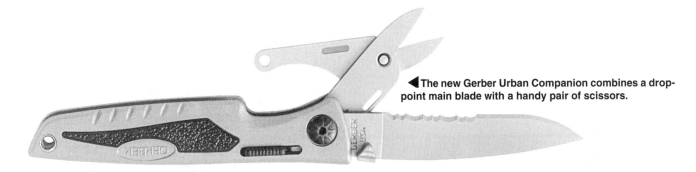

◀ The new Gerber Urban Companion combines a drop-point main blade with a handy pair of scissors.

long, and a stainless steel handle with an aluminum blade guard, this knife is a no-nonsense approach to the cutting challenges of modern society. When closed, the unique carabineer-type clip will allow fast and easy attachment to a key ring, a belt loop or almost anywhere it can gain purchase.

The Clip-Hanger (Models CH1, CH3S, CH4S, CH4FE, CH7S, CH8S, CH8FE, CH14S, CH18S and CH18FE) folder has been around for a number of years, nonetheless, it is still one of the best cutlery choices for those on the go. Each model is equipped with a patented quick-release personal attachment system mechanism. Available in drop-point or clip-point blades, in several lengths and with plain or serrated edges, choices are what make this knife so desirable. Superior workmanship and the finest stainless and injection-molded-thermoplastic materials complete the total Clip-Hanger package.

The i-Quip (Model IQ180) is a gear knife that is as much "gear" as it is "knife." This creation is part computer, part survival kit and all business when it comes to dealing with the challenges of the everyday life. In addition to a main drop-point cutting blade, the tool assortment consists of both Phillips and flathead screwdrivers; scissors; saw blade; a can opener; corkscrew; and a cap lifter. Other features include an altimeter; barometer; digital compass; stopwatch/alarm with backlight; LED flashlight; signal mirror; whistle; and belt clip. Definitely a departure from the usual, the i-Quip redefines a marketplace. No matter where you find yourself—backyard or backwoods, cities or suburbs—this cutting implement is like no other!

Ka-Bar Knives, Inc.

Ka-Bar's Hobo (Model 1300/1301) is an easily disassembled

utensil kit that has been around for so long that it might be taken for granted. However, this knife has the gear blades necessary to make it an all-in-one dining experience. The all-stainless-steel knife features a clip-point main blade, as well as both a fork and a spoon. All

three utensils disconnect from one another and, just as quickly, they are reassembled for belt-pouch containment and carry. Just the thing for dining outdoors, this gear knife can also handle fin, fur and feathered game field dressing chores with equal aplomb.

The tiny Schrade Simon folder, with a one-hand-opening blade, just 2-1/4 inches long, and a stainless steel handle with an aluminum blade guard, is a no-nonsense approach to the cutting challenges of modern society.

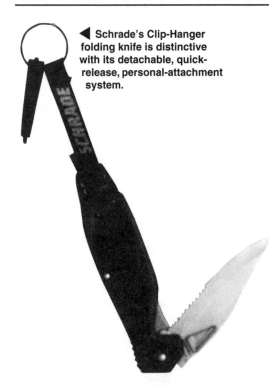

◀ Schrade's Clip-Hanger folding knife is distinctive with its detachable, quick-release, personal-attachment system.

As much "gear" as it is "knife," the Schrade i-Quip combines a drop-point cutting blade with everything from a digital compass, altimeter and barometer, to screwdrivers, scissors and a saw. (Hollis photo)

Kershaw Knives

An Oregon-based knife company, Kershaw can proudly boast of "technology with an edge," a mission statement that is certainly accurate with its recent introduction of the Model 1004 National Geographic Carabineer Tool knife. Designed to provide expedition-quality function and integrity, the new gear knife features a one-hand-opening AUS-6A stainless steel blade with a locking liner, a bottle opener, a pair of screwdrivers (slot and Phillips style) and an aircraft-aluminum, carabineer-style frame. This little wonder clips quickly and easily onto a backpack, camera case or belt loop.

The spring-loaded locking latch holds the clipped knife in place, even under the most rigorous activities.

For the wine-and-cheese crowd, Kershaw is proud to offer a Sommelier's Tool (Model 2170). Crafted from AUS-6A stainless steel, the curved wine-wrapper blade, corkscrew and cap lifter are resistant to environmental invectives. The satin-finished handle is also stainless steel and features a warm rosewood inlay. In the restaurant or even at home, with this gear knife in your pocket, dealing with hard-to-open wine bottles is no longer a problem.

Shotgun users will appreciate the Kershaw Shotgun Shell Knife (Model 12GAD). Made the same

Long a staple in the Ka-bar product line, the Hobo is one of the original on-the-road-eating utensil kits.

▲ For the wine-and-cheese crowd, Kershaw is proud to offer a Sommelier's Tool. Crafted from AUS-6A stainless steel, the curved wine-wrapper blade, corkscrew and cap lifter are resistant to environmental invectives.

Kutmaster

Kutmaster makes no-nonsense knives for many different applications. Two folders in the K-Series Special Purpose Knife line are designed for electrical work. The Electrician's Knife models differ only by the number of blades, with the Model 2558 two-blade folder featuring a spear-point main blade and a self-locking combination screwdriver/insulation cutter/wire-scraper companion blade. The

◄▼ The KutMaster Electrician's Knife, (Models 2558/3558) is available in two- or three-blade versions. Each model provides the basic tools necessary to work with electrical wiring and appliances.

three-blade Model 3558 adds an insulation stripping/pruning blade. Both knives have high-carbon stainless steel blades with solid bolsters and unbreakable Delrin® handles. Built to withstand the rigors of day-after-day use, either knife will provide a lifetime of durable service.

Queen Cutlery

For nearly three-quarters of a century, Queen Cutlery has been engineering knives for unlimited applications. In its Winterbottom Series, the Fish Knife (Model 46WB) is the classic angler's folder. The elongated-clip-pattern main blade is paired with a slender hook

size and shape as a 12-gauge shotgun shell, this handy folder easily slips into a shooting vest shell loop. In addition to the clip-pattern main blade, a screwdriver/file blade is also incorporated into the knife frame. The handle itself is rosewood and the bolsters are high-polished brass. Always handy, this little knife is heaven sent for bird and small game care chores.

extractor/scaling blade/bottle opener blade for functional diversity. Both satin-finished blades are made from D2 carbon steel, which takes and holds a fantastic edge. And the handle scales are Winterbottom-patterned Delrin plastic for a positive gripping surface. With this one pocketknife an angler can gut and scale a boatload of fish, as well as pop the caps off a few favorite beverages, and that's saying a lot for any knife!

SOG Specialty Knives, Inc.

SOG debuts a fixed blade and a folder that qualify as "gear knives." The new Model REV-7 SEAL Revolver puts an unusual twist on a rugged fixed-blade knife. Utilizing technology developed by designer Robbie Roberson, the edged tool is instantly converted from a knife blade to a survival saw. Just depress the locking lever and rotate the blade 180 degrees to make the transformation. The saw and the blade are AUS-8 stainless steel, and the deeply and heavily checkered handle is molded from glass-reinforced Zytel thermoplastic. When it comes to making do in

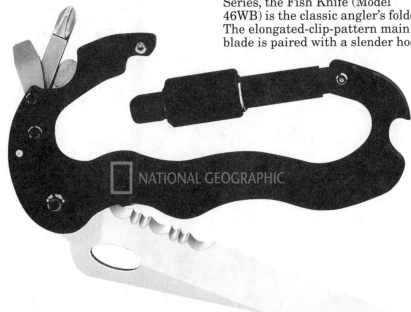

NATIONAL GEOGRAPHIC

▲ The Kershaw National Geographic Carabineer Tool Knife can clip onto your backpack, camera case, belt tool or other handy locations.

▶Utilizing technology developed by designer Robbie Roberson, the SOG REV-7 Revolver is instantly converted from a knife blade to a survival saw. Just depress the locking lever and rotate the blade 180 degrees to make the transformation.

tough situations, it doesn't get any better than the SEAL Revolver.

Wine connoisseurs will quickly realize the distinct capabilities of the SOG Model CRK77 Vino. The little folder has three functional gear blades, which include a spiral auger for cork removal, a cap lifter and a serrated foil knife blade. All three of these stainless edged assets are contained in a streamlined aluminum handle. A finely crafted tool, this is a gear knife that will warm the hearts of professional waiters and wine drinkers alike.

ToolLogic

This creative cutlery firm has brought to market an idea that is long overdue—a folding knife with an integral LED flashlight. The stainless steel

▲ Wine lovers will be quick to see the functional applications of the SOG Vino folder, complete with corkscrew, cap lifter and foil blade.

drop-point-pattern blade features a partially serrated edge for use on a wide range of cutting mediums. An oval opening hole milled through the edged steel provides purchase for the thumb so the knife can be opened with one hand, and a locking liner holds the blade open for in-use safety and security.

The brilliant white LED flashlight rises above the back of the knife handle and is aimed for low-light illumination of the cutting medium. A stainless steel pocket and belt clip, lanyard hole and emergency whistle are other features of the knife. Two blade lengths are available, making the folder useful in almost any situation. Other models are available with the same knife-handle platform, but substituting a whistle or a fire starter in place of the flashlight. The edged tool series offers a host of useful and potentially lifesaving features in a lightweight folding knife configuration.

United Cutlery

In its Colt knife line, United Cutlery includes a Folding/Utility Knife (Model CT0101) that features a carbide glass-cutting blade tip combined with a seat belt cutter located at the end of the aluminum handle. There are four blade patterns in this series, each 440 stainless steel with bead-blasted finishes. No matter which blade

shape is chosen, each features a partially serrated cutting edge. Any member of this lightweight, rescue-type pocketknife grouping has an oversize blade-release and locking mechanism for use with gloves. A stainless steel pocket clip is just the ticket for carrying ease.

When it comes to the specialized needs of law enforcement or rescue personnel, the onboard gear assets of the locking folder can make a difference in a dynamic situation.

Victorinox

The Swiss Army Knife concept is the original gear knife design. The current Victorinox catalog lists nearly 100 models that contain a wide assortment of gear blades. Some of the more unusual features that have been integrated into this manufacturer's folding knife lineup are whistles; LED mini lights; money clips; thermometers; altimeters; ball point pens; watch faces; magnifying glasses; divot repair tools; tee punches; and a host of other cutting and tool blades for every imaginable application.

Since the 1891 introduction of the multi-blade Soldier pocketknife, Victorinox has prided itself on being "an icon of precision, quality, functionality, versatility and outstanding value." Certainly, this has become a truism in the world of cutlery design.

▲ ToolLogic has brought to market an idea that is long overdue—a folding knife with an integral LED flashlight.

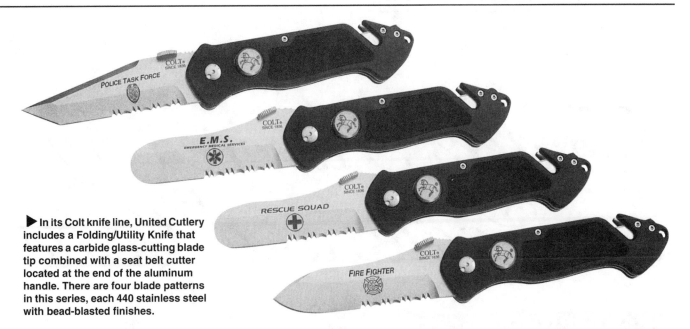

► In its Colt knife line, United Cutlery includes a Folding/Utility Knife that features a carbide glass-cutting blade tip combined with a seat belt cutter located at the end of the aluminum handle. There are four blade patterns in this series, each 440 stainless steel with bead-blasted finishes.

Wenger

Proud to be the "Genuine Swiss Army Knife" manufacturer, the folks at Wenger have a wonderfully diverse product line with nearly every model qualifying as a gear knife. In addition to the main cutting blades of each knife model, any one of dozens of gear-blade implements can be added to the handle frame. It may be as simple as the inclusion of a nail file, and handle-mounted toothpick and tweezers on the tiny Model 16924 Crusader pocketknife, or as elaborate as the 14 implements and 17 functions of the Survivor (Model 16989) folder.

Stainless steel blades that hold an edge, and molded-thermoplastic handles able to withstand almost anything, these are product distinctions that make any Wenger pocket or gear knife the right choice. With more gear blade assets than you can imagine, this Swiss Army Knives cutlery producer has obviously thought of everything!

The Bottom Line

My father taught me long ago that, "With the right gear, you can solve any problem." No matter whether it's a broken fingernail, or an outright life-or-death emergency, there's a gear knife that can make the difference between a successful outcome and the alternative! ●

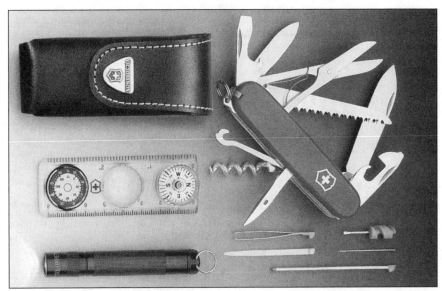

▲ Fresh from Victorinox is the Huntsman Plus, a gear knife extraordinaire, incorporating a blade; ballpoint pen; straight pin; mini-screwdriver; compass; magnifying glass; ruler; thermometer; flashlight; and leather belt pouch.

► "More gear for the buck" might be one way to look at the Wenger Survivor, boasting 14 implements and 17 functions. (Hollis photo)

Folders Favored by the Ladies and Gents

By Butch Winter

ONE OF THE latest trends in knives has its beginnings in a time not too long ago when every man carried a knife, every man, and some women. If he was a farmer or outdoorsmen, he usually carried a rather large, rugged knife, one that could be and probably was abused and, in time, used up. Knives of this sort had to be rather simple and, since they weren't really intended to last very long, inexpensive.

But there were other folks who didn't require large, rugged knives. These people didn't expect to have to cut anything substantial. They weren't going to be depending on their pocketknives to dress game, cut rope, scrape plows or open large crates.

These men and women spent much of their time indoors, working in offices, stores, banks and other such places. The most trying chore a pocketknife carried by them might be asked to do was open a small box, cut twine, trim a fingernail, open an envelope or perhaps peel an apple or cut some other type of fruit.

Since these pocketknives weren't expected to undertake many arduous chores, they tended to last longer, and some never needed to be replaced. Indeed, this type of pocketknife became a part of a person's everyday wardrobe and was treated as such, not as a mere tool to be used up and replaced, but a treasured object to be cared for and, in some cases, passed from one generation to another.

This type of pocketknife might have possessed handles of ivory, stag or even precious metal. Most weren't very large. Their job description didn't require bulk, and large knives tended to make a trouser or vest pocket bulge in an unsightly manner. These were sleek, light, unobtrusive, and in some cases elegant pocketknives—just the sort of folder a lady or gentleman might want.

Call it a change of time, the search for the sublime, or just a different avenue to express an artistic urge, but the "gentleman's folder" is back. And it's back with a vengeance!

Al Mar Knives

Al Mar Knives, perhaps best known for knives that stand the test of time, has always had the lady and gentleman in mind. From

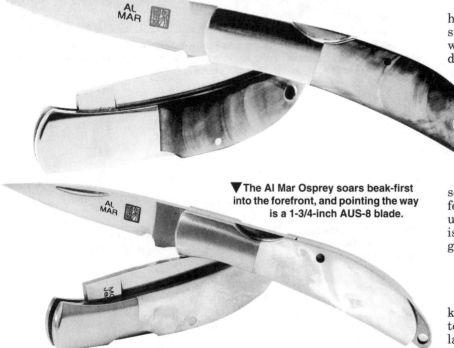

▼Targeted toward the ladies and gentlemen, the Al Mar Hawk comes in such dressy handle materials as mother-of-pearl, black pearl, black linen Micarta®, honey jigged bone and cocobolo wood.

▼The Al Mar Osprey soars beak-first into the forefront, and pointing the way is a 1-3/4-inch AUS-8 blade.

▶With a 2-1/2-inch blade, nickel silver bolsters and a choice of a zebrawood, cocobolo, oak, red-bone, stag, mother-of-pearl or genuine Indian stag bone handle, the Bear 40 Pattern covers all the bases for folders designed with ladies and gentlemen in mind.

the beginning, Al Mar has carried knives in its line for the well dressed, the dignified, the professional and the discerning. Today, there is the Classic line of small, neat folders designed for that somebody who wants a knife to complement his or her finest attire.

The Hawk sports a 2-1/2-inch, spear-point AUS-8 stainless steel blade. The overall length is 5-3/4 inches, and it weighs a mere 1-1/2 ounces, unusually light for a knife this size. Hawk handle materials would be mother-of-pearl, black pearl, black linen Micarta®, honey jigged bone and cocobolo.

Little brother to the Hawk is the Osprey, featuring a 1-3/4-inch AUS-8 blade and an overall length of 3.95 inches. The modified-*wharncliffe* blade of this front-lock design tapers to a perfect point. The slim, trim Osprey weighs only 1/2 ounce and showcases handle scales of mother-of-pearl, black linen Micarta or honey jigged bone. All Hawk and Osprey classics come in leather slip pouches that can be carried in purses or pants pockets to protect the knives from scratches by car keys or loose change.

Bear Cutlery

Bear's extensive line of Mini-Executive patterns covers about all the bases for folders designed with ladies and gentlemen in mind. The 40 Pattern dons a 2-1/2-inch stainless steel blade, nickel-silver bolsters and a choice of a zebrawood, cocobolo, oak, red-bone, stag, mother-of-pearl or genuine Indian stag bone handle. The Mini-Executive is outfitted with a positive lock and a hollow-ground blade. A variation of the 40 Pattern is available with a stainless steel or Zytel® handle and without bolsters.

The 25 Pattern, on the other hand, is delivered with either a stainless steel handle, or a choice of a black, a translucent-amethyst, translucent-blue or translucent-ruby Zytel grip. Each Mini-Executive pattern can be teamed with a mini-flashlight in a gift tin.

▶The Bear 25 Pattern is delivered with either a stainless steel handle, or a choice of a black, a translucent-amethyst, translucent-blue or translucent-ruby Zytel® grip. Each Mini-Executive pattern can be teamed with a mini-flashlight in a gift tin.

Benchmade Knife Co.

Benchmade's new Model 310 Benchmite is a product of the fertile imaginations of custom knifemakers Bill McHenry and Jason Williams. By squeezing the outside of the Benchmite's handle, the locking pin is released, allowing the blade to be opened. The handle is squeezed again to close the blade. Featuring a blue-anodized and *skeletonized* titanium handle, and a 154CM stainless blade, the Benchmite stretches 4-3/4 inches and weighs only 1 ounce.

▲Featuring a blue-anodized and *skeletonized* titanium handle, and a 154CM stainless blade, the Benchmade Benchmite stretches 4-3/4 inches and weighs only 1 ounce.

▶A sintered-titanium blade makes Boker's Titanium Zeta a folder technically inclined people will love.

▶The Buck ADRENALINE-Ti gets the adrenaline pumping, or at least the eyes bulging, while looking at its blue/purple-anodized-titanium locking liner exposed through an open, die-cast-aluminum handle frame.

▼A knife with a handle shaped like a tuxedo tie isn't exactly targeted toward a rough and tumble crowd, but the Camillus Tuxedo two-blade penknife can still cut it in the wilds using a 1-1/2-inch spear blade and a 1-1/4-inch pen blade.

◀A modern gentleman's folder from Camillus is the Medium Silversword Lockback. This neat little knife has a 2-inch, stainless steel, hollow-ground, drop-point blade with a brushed stainless steel handle.

Boker U.S.A.

Boker's entry into the gentleman's folder field is something entirely new, and the company came into it with a knife that technically inclined people will love. It's called the "Titanium Zeta," the world's first folding knife with a sintered-titanium blade.

The blade material is actually a sintered-titanium powder made up of hard metal carbides, a composition that weighs 40 percent less than steel. Sintered titanium reportedly stays sharp longer than steel, will not rust and retains flexibility. Unlike many other state-of-the-art materials, sintered titanium can be honed using conventional methods.

The semi-drop-point blade stretches 2-1/2 inches and incorporates a thumb stud for easy opening. Boker's revolutionary Titanium Zeta employs a Delrin® handle with a locking liner and weighs just 1.3 ounces. The folding pocketknife is a mere 3 inches closed.

Buck Knives

Buck calls its gentleman's knife the "ADRENALINE-Ti," a moniker stemming from its super-strong, lightweight, blue/purple-anodized-titanium locking liner exposed through the open, die-cast-aluminum handle frame. The ADRENA-LINE-Ti features a 3-inch, black-oxide-coated ATS-34 blade in a modified-drop-point pattern. The blade is double tempered to reach 60-61 RC on the Rockwell hardness scale, then finished using Buck's exclusive Edge 2x technology.

The extra-smooth pivoting action makes the ADRENALINE-Ti easy to open and close with one hand. At 4-1/4 inches closed and 2.4 ounces, it packs a lot of punch in a small package. The stainless steel pocket clip is a handy carrying device.

Camillus Knives

Camillus has been around for over 120 years and has a full line of traditionally styled knives that have been carried by gentlemen for generations. Available from Camillus are models such as the Tuxedo two-blade penknife, featuring a spear blade 1-1/2 inches long teamed with a 1-1/4-inch pen blade. It employs high-carbon stainless steel for each blade and nickel silver bolsters.

A more modern gentleman's folder from Camillus is the Medium Silversword Lockback. This neat little knife has a 2-inch, stainless steel, hollow-ground, drop-point blade with a brushed stainless steel handle.

Case

W.R. Case & Sons Cutlery Co. is one of the most famous knife concerns in the United States, if not the world. Case has always had the lady and gentleman in mind with small, elegant knives included in each of its many cutlery lines. Small knives with mother-of-pearl, stag or other natural handle materials have been available from Case for generations.

▼Each blade in a series of Case Executive Lockbacks is just short of 2 inches long each, and total knife weight is kept down to 1-to-2.3 ounces.

The Executive Lockback series of small folders incorporates completely modern designing, including stainless steel blades and either brushed-stainless-steel or Zytel handles to resist corrosion. Blades are just short of 2 inches long, and total knife weight is kept down to 1-to-2.3 ounces each. Pocket clips are included for convenient toting.

Cold Steel

Cold Steel's Voyager series of folders spans the spectrum of compact-to-large knives. The small Voyager suits those who prefer a lock-back blade in a Zytel handle, a knife that features the latest technology in a lightweight package. The Voyager Medium sports a 3-inch clip-point or tanto AUS-8 blade, complete with a thumb stud for one-hand opening and accompanied by a mid-handle lock system. Each of these models comes with a choice of a plain or half-serrated edge. Overall length of the Medium Voyager is 6-7/8 inches (open), yet it weighs only 1.8 ounces, truly a substantial knife in an unobtrusive package.

Columbia River Knife & Tool

Columbia River Knife & Tool has an extensive line of knives that will fit most any need. New this year is something old—the Rollock, a throwback design from 1975. The blade of the Rollock rolls, for lack of a better word, into and out of the handle when opened and closed.

Allen Elishewitz designed the modern version, and the Rollock is aimed at the lady or gentleman who wants something just a little differ-

ent. It parades a 420J2 stainless steel frame, a 2-1/4-inch, straight or half-serrated AUS-6M blade and a translucent polycarbonate handle available in four colors for a unique and attractive look. Overall length closed is 3-1/2 inches, and it weighs 2.3 ounces.

Ed Halligan's minimalist K.I.S.S. (Keep It Super Simple) frame-lock knives are just right for pocket carry or as money clip blades. The series has been expanded by the addition of the P.E.C.K. and S.S.T. models. The P.E.C.K. (Precision Engineered Compact Knife) weighs less than 1 ounce and is only 2.7 inches closed. The S.S.T. (Short Stubby Thing) is comparably sized, featuring a 2-1/4-inch blade and an overall length of 2.81 inches. Weight is 1.8 ounces.

Emerson Knives, Inc.

A company most knife enthusiasts would not expect to be included in a roundup of small, lightweight folders is Emerson, better known for tactical and combat

knives. The Emerson Hard Wear line of economically priced, small folders is designed for the gentleman or gentle lady who wants just a little more performance out of his or her pocketknife.

Emerson's Hard Wear folders come in three versions, the Reliant, Endeavor and Traveler, all the same size, weight and length (3.4-inch blade and 7.9 inches open). They differ only in blade shape. The Reliant showcases the trademark Emerson tanto-style blade, half-serrated. The Endeavor's blade is a semi-drop point, also half serrated, while the Traveler sports a more aggressive, drop-point, half-serrated blade. Each model employs a mid-lock and a thumb-hole on the blade for easy opening.

Grohmann

Grohmann, a name most often associated with hunting knives and, particularly, Russell belt knives, also carries a couple of blades that fit right into the gentle-

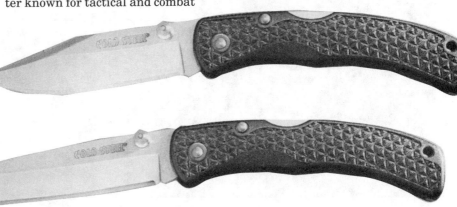

▲Cold Steel's Voyager Medium sports a 3-inch clip-point or tanto AUS-8 blade, complete with a thumb stud for one-hand opening and accompanied by a mid-handle lock system.

A throwback from 1975, the Allen Elishewitz-designed Columbia River Knife & Tool Rollock is aimed at the lady or gentleman who wants something just a little different.

Ka-Bar Knives, Inc.

Ka-Bar is an old-line company that has arrived in the 21st century with a new International line of collaborative knives in conjunction with Maserin of Italy. These knives span the gamut in elegantly designed folders. The KM252 Money Clip, for instance, is just as its name suggests, a money clip knife with a frame-locking system. It weighs 1 ounce and includes a 2-1/4-inch, drop-point 440A stainless steel blade.

At 4 ounces, the KM270 Clip Point is a bit larger and integrates a 4-inch, drop-point, 440A stainless blade, a stainless steel handle and a side lock.

Katz Knives

"Elegant and refined" is the way Katz describes its line of gentleman's knives. These are available in seven models with handles of black pearl, mother-of-pearl, white Micarta, cocobolo and genuine stag.

The blades are ATS-34 steel, each 2-1/2 inches long. Overall length of each piece is 5-3/4 inches (open), and the weight is a mere 1.6 ounces. Standard scrimshaw on the Micarta handles portrays either a bald eagle or a black bear, and custom scrimshaw is available on request. Each knife is delivered in an attractive presentation box.

manly category. These are the Grohmann Pocket Knife and the Featherweight Lockblade.

The Grohmann Pocket Knife is a slim, one-blade folder with nickel silver bolsters, brass liners and brass pins. It has a 3-inch, stainless blade, stainless back spring and rosewood handle. Overall length is 6-3/4 inches. Though the same size, the Featherweight Lockblade, true to its name, weighs only 1.4 ounces. It exhibits a black-Zytel handle, a 3-inch stainless steel blade and a standard back-lock mechanism.

Imperial Schrade

Schrade calls its new technology "Schrade's Q-3," which stands for "*quick* and *quiet* operation with world-class *quality*." The Schrade Black Ice is an elegant gentleman's folder with a tapered point. The locking stainless blade is pierced for one-hand opening and stretches 3-1/2 inches. The handle involves a transparent polycarbonate, a strong, durable, weather-resistant resin originally developed for bulletproof windows. It is also lightweight, with the entire knife weighing in at 2.4 ounces.

Ed Halligan took a minimalist approach in designing the Columbia River Knife & Tool P.E.C.K., just the right type of knife to carry in a pocket or in place of a money clip.

It might be a Short Stubby Thing, but the Columbia River Knife & Tool S.S.T. packs plenty of bite in its 2-1/4-inch blade.

Kellam Knives Co.

Kellam, noted for knives of Scandinavian origin, introduces the Big Jouni Folder, a knife designed and reportedly carried by company president Jouni Kellokoski. The Big Jouni Folder enlists a 3.2-inch, AUS-8 stainless blade, a side lock and a thumb-stud opener. It showcases a cocobolo-and-ivory-Micarta handle, and there is an adjustable pivot pin that allows the user to fine-tune the folding blade's action to his or her personal satisfaction. This is an elegant knife that any lady or gentleman will want to put in the old pocket or pocketbook.

▼▲Emerson's Hard Wear folders come in three versions, the Reliant, Endeavor and Traveler, all the same size, weight and length (3.4-inch blade and 7.9 inches open). They differ only in blade shape.

Kershaw Knives

Kershaw and custom knifemaker Ken Onion have proven to be a "dream team" of sorts in the knife industry, and the dynamic duo's new creations—the Leek and Chive—are small, elegant and colorful pocketknives for ladies and gents to fondle, use and ogle. The Rainbow Leek, with a scratch-resistant, rainbow-titanium-oxide

It looks like its name suggests—Black Ice—and it's an elegant gentleman's folder with a tapered point.

coating covering the entire knife, was the 2002 Blade Magazine Overall Knife of the Year® award winner. Its remarkable rainbow-like hues of the titanium oxide are created using electric currents in different intensities and durations. The Rainbow Leek features a 3-inch 440A stainless steel blade. Closed, it is 4 inches long and weighs only 3.1 ounces, perfect for the pocket or purse.

The Rainbow Chive has the same type of handle as the Leek, but with a 1-15/16-inch 420HC stainless steel blade. The closed length of the Chive is only 2-7/8 inches, and it weighs 1.9 ounces. The blades of both knives are secured in the open position by means of a frame lock. The Rainbow Chive comes in a gift tin, while the Rainbow Leek fits into a soft zipper case. Either knife is

►Ka-Bar's new International line of collaborative knives in conjunction with Maserin of Italy spans the gamut in elegantly designed folders. The KM252 Money Clip (top) is just as its name suggests, a money clip knife with a frame-locking system. The KM270 Clip Point is a bit larger and integrates a 4-inch, drop-point, 440A stainless blade, a stainless steel handle and a side lock.

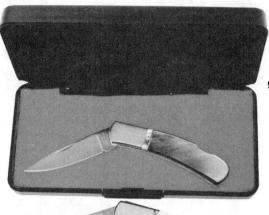

◀ "Elegant and refined" is the way Katz describes its line of gentleman's knives. These are available in seven models with handles of black pearl, mother-of-pearl, white Micarta, cocobolo and genuine stag.

◀ Kellam's Big Jouni Folder enlists a 3.2-inch, AUS-8 stainless blade, a side lock, a thumb-stud opener, and a cocobolo-and-ivory-Micarta handle.

This little knife is 5-1/4 inches overall, weighs only 1.2 ounces and comes in a Lone Wolf gift box.

available without the "rainbow" treatment, the Leek with a bead-blasted, stainless steel finish, and the Chive with a highly polished finish.

Lone Wolf Knives

Lone Wolf Knives is the new kid on the block and, as such, is going all out to prove it has something special to offer the knife lover. Lone Wolf's new gentleman's folder is a bit of something new and a dab of something old. The Paul Pocket Knife is named after folder designer Paul Poehlmann, whose claim to fame in the knife industry is an unusual axial locking mechanism that secures a folding blade both open and closed.

The Engraved-Stainless Paul Pocket Knife is lightweight and thin, and constructed entirely of high quality stainless steel. The stainless handle is engraved in a rich, floral pattern. The drop point blade reaches a full 2 inches and is of 420 stainless. Overall length of the Engraved-Stainless Paul Pocket Knife is 5.12 inches open, and the weight is a mere 1-1/2 ounces. Included is a leather pocket sheath and cleaning cloth.

Also new from Lone Wolf is the Paul Perfecto gentleman's folder, an entirely new design. The Perfecto features a 2-1/4-inch, 420 stainless steel wharncliffe-pattern blade. It has, of course, the unique Paul axial locking system and stainless steel handles with ivory- or wine-colored Micarta scales.

Outdoor Edge

Designed by custom knifemaker Darrel Ralph, Outdoor Edge's Impulse combines the ultimate of form and function for today's urban lifestyles. Handles are fashioned from die-cast aluminum, fully contoured for maximum comfort. Kraton® inter-frames lend extra security and grip

control, and geometric slots in the blade improve balance, reduce weight and allow for easy one-hand opening. The Impulse has a locking liner and a pocket clip for sheath-free carry.

With a 3-inch, 12C27 stainless steel blade, offered in either a plain or serrated edge, the Impulse is 6-7/8 inches overall and weighs 2.7 ounces.

Queen Cutlery

One of the oldest cutlery companies in the nation, Queen is well known for its extensive inventory of folding knives. In the Schatt & Morgan premium line of pocketknives are several that might be found in gentlemen's pockets, but one in particular stands out.

The Office Knife is a recreation of a well-known pattern of the past. The new version is a 3-1/4-inch, equal-end, two-blade senator-pattern pocketknife sporting a genuine wooly mammoth ivory handle.

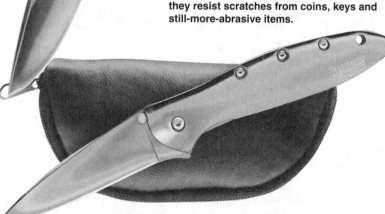

◀▼ Strikingly beautiful are the Kershaw Rainbow Chive (top) and Leek, but they are also extremely durable. With rainbow-titanium-oxide coating covering both knives, they resist scratches from coins, keys and still-more-abrasive items.

The Paul Perfecto gentleman's folder from Lone Wolf Knives is an entirely new design featuring a 2-1/4-inch, 420 stainless blade working off the Paul axial locking system, and a stainless steel handle with ivory- or wine-colored Micarta scales.

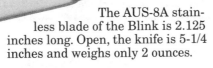

The name "Official Knife" is laser cut in the handle, and the "Schatt & Morgan" logo is etched into the 420 HC stainless blade.

The Office Knife is part of a limited run of 600 pieces in the Premier Collector Series, which also features a two-blade Barlow-pattern pocket folder; a two-blade physicians knife; a three-blade whittler; a single-blade lock-back Mountain Man folding hunter; and a Wildcat driller two-blade Sleeveboard.

SOG Specialty Knives

SOG calls it the "Blink," a new executive lock-back folder with assisted-opening technology. Once the operator starts the blade in motion, the assisted opener of the Blink literally "springs" to action, swinging the blade open and locking it tightly in place. The handle is 6061-T6 aircraft aluminum, hard anodized with graphite coloring and featuring a reversible, low-carry pocket or money clip.

▶ Designed by custom knifemaker Darrel Ralph, Outdoor Edge's Impulse combines the ultimate of form and function for today's urban lifestyles.

The AUS-8A stainless blade of the Blink is 2.125 inches long. Open, the knife is 5-1/4 inches and weighs only 2 ounces.

Spyderco

Spyderco's latest edition of a gentleman's folder is the Kiwi, which sports a classically shaped, 2-inch, wharncliffe blade of VG-10

stainless steel. In addition to the proprietary opening hole in the blade, the Kiwi is designed with two slip-resistant thumb and forefinger notches, aiding in precision cutting. The handle showcases amber-colored, jigged-bone scales set into brushed stainless steel bolsters. Although the Spyderco name is almost synonymous with serrated edges, the Kiwi comes in a plain edge only.

▶The Queen Cutlery Office Knife is a recreation of a well-known pattern of the past. The new version is a 3-1/4-inch, equal-end, two-blade senator-pattern pocketknife sporting a genuine wooly mammoth ivory handle.

▶SOG calls it the "Blink," a new executive lock-back folder with assisted-opening technology.

Although the Kiwi looks similar to the tropical bird it is named after, there is a certain, elegant quality about the knife. At home in the office or at the club, the Kiwi is a knife for the lady or gentleman that will perform far beyond its size. Best of all, it weighs only 1.8 ounces.

▲ Spyderco's latest edition of a gentleman's folder is the Kiwi, which sports a classically shaped, 2-inch, wharncliffe blade of VG-10 stainless steel, and an amber-colored, jigged-bone handle.

Tigersharp Technologies

Tigersharp, already an award-winning, innovative outfit that markets knives with replaceable cutting edges, hits the gentleman's knife market running. The Tigersharp Classic incorporates hi-tech handle materials, including titanium, carbon fiber and cocobolo, and the grip is available in a standard titanium, black, purple/gold or blue-polychromatic finish.

▲ Tigersharp folding knives are known for their replaceable blades, eliminating the need for sharpening the blades in the field or in the office.

There's a new blade bevel design that provides a better cutting edge on the 2-1/2-inch GIN5 steel blade, which is hardened to 61Rc on the Rockwell Hardness scale. The blade replacement system allows the installation of a new cutting edge in only 30 seconds. Serrated blades are available as an option, and the Classic frame lock weighs only 1 ounce and features an overall length of 5-3/4 inches.

Timberline Knives

Tim Herman designed the Money Clip gentleman's folder for Timberline Knives. The piece employs a 420J2 stainless steel frame that also acts to lock the blade open. This neat, elegant folder has a 24-karat-gold inlay design on the stainless steel handle. The 1.9-inch blade is AUS-6A stainless steel, mirror polished and offered in a half-serrated or plain edge. A money or pocket clip gives the knife its name. Overall length when open is 4.2 inches.

William Henry Fine Knives

William Henry rules the roost as far as high-end folding knives are concerned. William Henry folders feature integral-titanium frames inlaid with pearl, ironwood, precious gems and other organic material.

Bolsters are made from mokumé forged by Mike Sakmar, while

The neat, elegant Money Clip gentleman's folder from Timberline Knives is designed by Tim Herman and incorporates a 24-karat-gold inlay design on the stainless steel handle.

blades are ground from Mike Norris stainless damascus. There are innovations in blade actions, such as button locks and detents to help ensure the blade closes into the handle, not onto the fingers. Then, there is the tiny switchblade model, legal because it is less than 2 inches long, weighing less than 1 ounce and featuring a damascus blade.

There you have it—the latest in lady's and gentleman's knives from the finest knife companies in the world. There's something here for a man of all seasons, whether he works in the city, wants the fanciest knife available and expects only lightweight cutting, or he finds himself changing from jeans to slacks and wants something a little lighter than the heavy blade he normally carries.

It's all here. All one must do is choose a gent's knife or two, purchase and play.

Fixed Blades Rule the Outdoors

By Butch Winter

THE STRAIGHT KNIFE is man's oldest edged tool and, even today, the simplistic form of brute blade and hefty handle remains the most versatile and useful of all work implements. The knife, as we know it, evolved as early man learned he could improve the leverage of a chipped flake of stone by adding a handle to it.

Over the ages, camping, hunting and sporting knives have been made from all sorts of material: stone, bone, wood, copper, bronze, iron, steel and, recently, space-age materials like Talonite, Stellite, titanium, ceramic, Liquidmetal and meteorite.

The essential task of a hunting or sporting knife has both evolved and remained the same. Such an edged tool is employed to dress and dismember game; clear brush; notch an arrow; fillet a fish; mark a trail; wedge into a rock crevice to steady a mountain climber; open a package; prepare food; separate a blown mountain bike tire from its rim; perform first aid; build shelter; and shave camp stakes.

Knife designs have changed and improved with the passing of time. A sporting fixed blade these days may range from a simple piece of steel and supporting handle to a complex knife with a coated, stain-resistant blade, a contoured and slip-resistant handle, an integral guard, a thong hole, hammer butt, saw back and multi-carry sheath system. In short, there's a fixed blade out there these days for every sportsman or sports lady no matter how difficult the

▲▼The Bear Cutlery Feathermate is one of those bare-bone hunt and camp knives the author loves so much, this one featuring a 4-inch, hollow-ground, stainless steel blade and a choice of a contoured cocobolo, Zytel® or India stag bone handle.

►Fresh from Bear Cutlery is the Large Switch-A-Blade hunting knife that can easily be switched from a drop-point hunter to a skinner, and finally to a gut hook merely by changing blades.

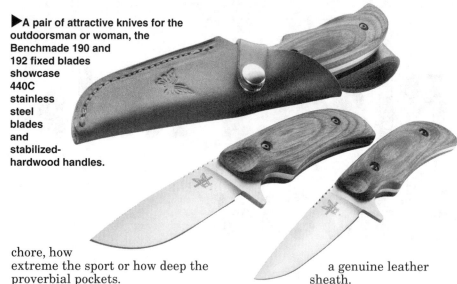

▶A pair of attractive knives for the outdoorsman or woman, the Benchmade 190 and 192 fixed blades showcase 440C stainless steel blades and stabilized-hardwood handles.

chore, how extreme the sport or how deep the proverbial pockets.

Bear Cutlery

New from Bear Cutlery is the Feathermate knife designed by Blackie Collins. The Feathermate is one of those bare-bone hunt and camp knives I love so much, this one featuring a 4-inch, hollow-ground, stainless steel blade and a choice of a contoured cocobolo, Zytel® or India stag bone handle. The Feathermate is furnished with

a genuine leather sheath.

Also fresh from Bear is the Large Switch-A-Blade hunting knife that can easily be switched from a drop-point hunter to a skinner, and finally to a gut hook merely by changing blades. The Large Switch-A-Blade comes with three replaceable 4-inch, hollow-ground, high-carbon stainless blades, each inserted as needed into a 4-1/2-inch, contoured-thermoplastic handle. The knife is outfitted with a high-quality leather sheath.

Benchmade Knife Co.

The newly released models 190 and 192 fixed blades from Benchmade are a pair of attractive knives for the outdoorsman or woman. A drop-point hunter and bird-and-trout knife, respectively, both showcase 440C stainless steel blades and stabilized-hardwood handles.

While blade thickness of the hunter is .125 inches, the blade of the bird and trout is quite a bit thinner, at .08 inches, for more precise cutting work. Both knives are outfitted with full-grain leather sheaths.

Boker USA, Inc.

Boker is taking a "back-to-the-future" stance this year by introducing, or re-introducing, some basic European knife patterns. Anyone who has been around knives for any length of time will recognize the Model 5721HH. This little hunter features a 4-1/2-inch, 440A stainless steel, spear-point blade with a genuine stag handle. Full-tang construction leads to excellent balance, and the 5721HH is just right for the hunter or outdoors person who prefers tradi-

▶This little hunting knife from Boker oozes of European styling, including its traditional stag handle and slim spear-point blade.

▶A combination of German steel and South American stag, three Boker fixed blades feature full tangs running through hot-drop-forged stainless handle frames right up to their pommels, the latter of which are high-polished aluminum and complemented by brass guards.

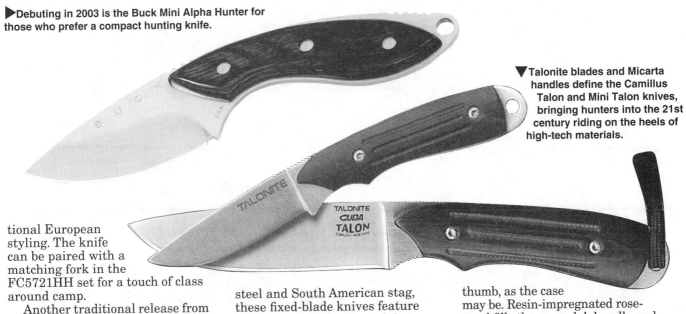

▶Debuting in 2003 is the Buck Mini Alpha Hunter for those who prefer a compact hunting knife.

▼Talonite blades and Micarta handles define the Camillus Talon and Mini Talon knives, bringing hunters into the 21st century riding on the heels of high-tech materials.

tional European styling. The knife can be paired with a matching fork in the FC5721HH set for a touch of class around camp.

Another traditional release from Boker comes in the slightly varied form of three models, the 560, 561 and 562. A combination of German steel and South American stag, these fixed-blade knives feature full tangs running through hot-drop-forged stainless handle frames right up to their pommels, the latter of which are high-polished aluminum and complemented by brass guards. The 560 and 561 showcase 4-1/2-inch blades, and the 562 features 5 inches of sharpened steel. A belt sheath is included with each knife.

Buck Knives

The Buck Alpha Hunters have become some of the most popular hunting knives from a traditional and proud company. Debuting in 2003 is the Mini Alpha Hunter for those who prefer a compact hunting knife.

The Mini Alpha Hunter is a small, full-tang fixed blade with a slightly curved 2-inch modified drop point. Ridges on the spine of the ATS-34 blade allow cutting leverage with the forefinger or thumb, as the case may be. Resin-impregnated rosewood fills the open-slab handle and is ergonomically shaped to meld perfectly into someone's open palm. Overall length is 6-1/4 inches, and it weighs 3.6 ounces.

The blade has been finished with Buck's Edge2X sharpening system, reportedly making it keener out of the box, better able to hold an edge and easier to sharpen. A leather sheath completes the knife package.

Camillus Cutlery Co.

Camillus is an old-line company that has established a name as a maker of fine blades. The knife company leads the way into the future with the use of manmade, space-age materials, especially in its employment of Talonite blades. Talonite is a cobalt-based blade material noted for its edge-holding ability.

Camillus' Talon and Mini Talon integrate such Talonite blades and are as up-to-date as tomorrow, ready for action in any outdoor activity, no matter the extreme. The Talon sports a 3.7-inch drop-point blade, a Micarta handle and a Concealex Tek-Lok sheath. The Mini Talon is identical but with a 2-1/4-inch blade.

Case

W.R. Case & Sons Cutlery Co. is another well known, and perhaps the most recognized American knife manufacturer. This year, Case debuts several models pur-

This year, Case debuts several models purpose-built for the outdoorsman and hunter, the most interesting of which is a line of three Ridgeback models-the Ridgeback Caper, Ridgeback Drop Point and Ridgeback Hunter.

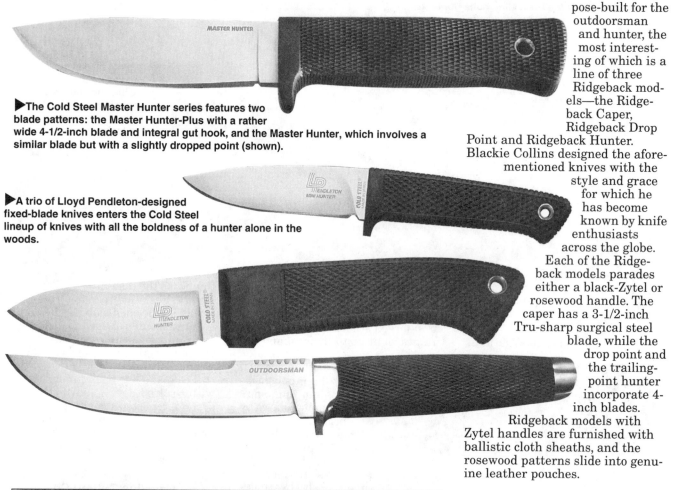

▶The Cold Steel Master Hunter series features two blade patterns: the Master Hunter-Plus with a rather wide 4-1/2-inch blade and integral gut hook, and the Master Hunter, which involves a similar blade but with a slightly dropped point (shown).

▶A trio of Lloyd Pendleton-designed fixed-blade knives enters the Cold Steel lineup of knives with all the boldness of a hunter alone in the woods.

pose-built for the outdoorsman and hunter, the most interesting of which is a line of three Ridgeback models—the Ridgeback Caper, Ridgeback Drop Point and Ridgeback Hunter. Blackie Collins designed the aforementioned knives with the style and grace for which he has become known by knife enthusiasts across the globe. Each of the Ridgeback models parades either a black-Zytel or rosewood handle. The caper has a 3-1/2-inch Tru-sharp surgical steel blade, while the drop point and the trailing-point hunter incorporate 4-inch blades. Ridgeback models with Zytel handles are furnished with ballistic cloth sheaths, and the rosewood patterns slide into genuine leather pouches.

Cold Steel, Inc.

Cold Steel's Master Hunters and Pendleton Hunters are tried-and-true knives that have stood the test of time. The Master Hunter series features two blade patterns: the Master Hunter-Plus with a rather wide 4-1/2-inch blade and integral gut hook, and the Master Hunter, which involves a similar blade but with a slightly dropped point. While the Master Hunter-Plus is sent to market in Cold Steel's proprietary Carbon V steel, the standard Master Hunter is available in either Carbon V or AUS-8A stainless steel. All blades are teamed with checkered-Kraton® handles.

From the mind of custom knifemaker Lloyd Pendleton are the Cold Steel Pendleton Hunters, available in two blade styles—the Mini-Hunter with a 3-inch, hollow-ground, drop-point AUS-8A stainless steel blade, and the Pendleton Hunter with a 3-1/2-inch AUS-8A blade. The Pendleton Hunter has a bit more sweep to its blade and is more of an all-around design. Both Pendleton Hunters feature checkered-Kraton handles and, outfitted

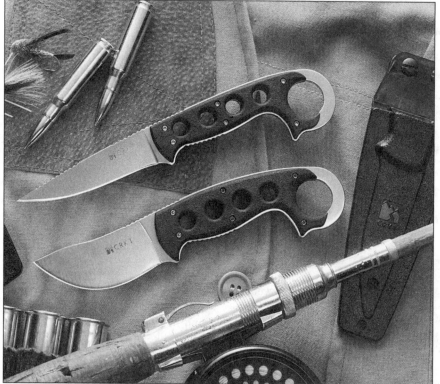

Russ Kommer, an Alaskan game guide and knifemaker, engineered the Columbia River Knife & Tool Alaska Caracajou and Cobuk knives, each with completely different blade designs, but sharing the same handle pattern.

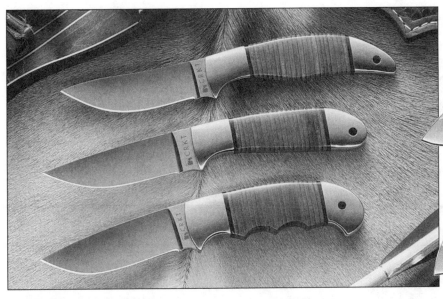

Brand new from Columbia River Knife & Tool is the Kommer Alaska Pro Hunter series of knives, each one featuring a stacked-leather-washer handle, full-tang construction, stainless steel bolsters and a 3.12-inch AUS-8A blade.

with Secure-Ex (Kydex®) sheaths instead of leather, the hunting knives are state-of-the-art bladed wonders.

Columbia River Knife & Tool

Columbia River Knife & Tool surrounds itself with an extensive stable of custom knifemakers, each chosen as an expert in his particular field of edged-tool design. Russ Kommer, an Alaskan game guide and knifemaker, engineered the Alaska Caracajou and Cobuk knives, each with completely different blade designs, but sharing the same handle pattern. The design of the grip separates itself from the competition, incorporating a skeletonized tang and Zytel scales pierced with holes to keep the weight down.

At the end of the blade tang is a hole big enough for a finger to fit through and help secure the knife, but also to allow the knife to swing down and hang from a pinkie if hands are needed for chores other than cutting. Finger grooves along the back of the handle aid grip in slippery conditions.

The Caracajou has a 2.88-inch, spear-point blade of AUS-6M stainless steel designed for cleaning fish and birds, caping and other precision tasks. The Cobuk sports a 2-3/4-inch slightly dropped-point skinning blade with a full belly profile, also of AUS-6A steel. Both knives feature polycarbonate sheaths.

►With a belief in giving customers the best from which to choose, Ka-Bar Knives introduces (from top) the Drop Point, Game Hook and Skinner, all with 2-1/8-inch blades, and the Large Drop Point and Large Skinner, employing 3-1/8-inch blades.

Brand new from Columbia River Knife & Tool is the Kommer Alaska Pro Hunter series of knives, each one featuring a stacked-leather-washer handle, full-tang construction, stainless steel bolsters and a 3.12-inch AUS-8A blade. Although the blades all reach the same length, there are subtle differences among them. The Brooks Range Pro Hunter is a semi-skinner with a dropped point and a big-bellied edge. The Chugach Range Pro Hunter integrates a modified drop point, and the Wrangell Range Pro Hunter comes with a classic drop-point design. All blades are hollow ground, and each knife is delivered in a leather shoulder harness decorated in a basket-weave motif.

◄The Ka-Bar Large Game Hook and the Classic feature 3-5/16-inch and 3-9/16-inch blades, respectively. Both are hollow-ground 440A stainless steel complemented by Kraton G handles. Leather sheaths and wrist cords are standard with each knife.

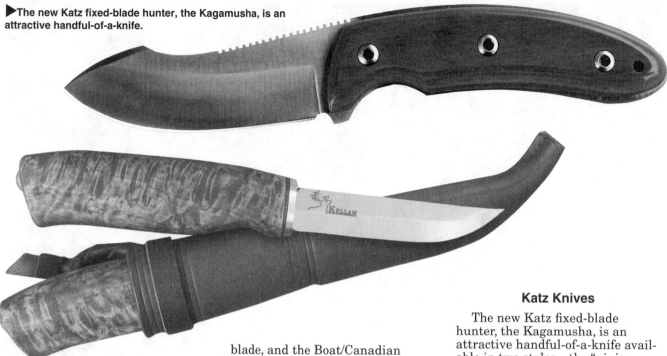

▶The new Katz fixed-blade hunter, the Kagamusha, is an attractive handful-of-a-knife.

▲Recently released from Kellam, well known for Scandinavian knives, is the handmade Puukko dressed up in a dyed-curly-birch handle and a 3-3/4-inch polished carbon steel blade.

Grohmann Knives Ltd.

If there's an instantly recognizable hunting knife in the world, it has to be the Grohmann Canadian Belt Knife. An award-winning fixed blade that needs no improvement, the Canadian Belt Knife has excelled in the field for more years than most of us want to remember.

It has, however, been tweaked for 2003. The original design, available in either high carbon or stainless steel, has been standard for years with a rosewood handle. Standard versions include the original design with a 4-inch blade, the Trout & Bird with a 3-7/8-inch

blade, and the Boat/Canadian Army/Yachtsman with a 4-inch blade.

New for 2003, are stag and red- or black-linen-Micarta® handles for the threesome of knives, as well as the addition of a small Mini Skinner with a 2-inch drop-point blade.

Ka-Bar Knives Inc.

Ka-Bar's Precision Hunters series has been expanded to include 11 models in varying blade lengths. The Drop Point, Game Hook and Skinner all have 2-1/8-inch blades. The Large Skinner and Large Drop Point employ 3-1/8-inch blades, and the Long Point Flex has a 4-inch blade. The Large Game Hook and the Classic feature 3-5/16-inch and 3-9/16-inch blades, respectively. All are hollow-ground 440A stainless steel complemented by Kraton G handles. Leather sheaths and wrist cords are standard with each knife.

Katz Knives

The new Katz fixed-blade hunter, the Kagamusha, is an attractive handful-of-a-knife available in two styles—the "ninja-point" and the gut hook. The ninja-point is a skinner designed to allow the user's forefinger to rest comfortably just behind the point for precise cutting control. Both models incorporate 3-1/2-inch, hollow-ground XT80 stainless blades. Handles are of full tang construction with either Micarta or Kraton® slabs secured by Allen bolts. Handle slabs can be changed to suit the customer. These attractive knives come in top-quality, heavy duty, pouch-type sheaths.

Kellam Knives Co.

Recently released from Kellam, well known for Scandinavian knives, is the handmade Puukko dressed up in a dyed-curly-birch handle and a 3-3/4-inch polished carbon steel blade. Handmade in Finland, the 8-1/4-inch Puukko comes in a dark-brown leather sheath.

Kershaw Knives

Custom knifemaker Tom Veff designed the Kershaw Kaper and Majesty fixed blades. The Kaper features a 3-1/8-inch, AUS8A stainless steel blade with full-tang construction and a cocobolo wood handle. Overall length is 7-1/8 inches, and it weighs only 2 ounces. The Majesty parades a 3-1/4-

▲The ingenuity of custom knifemaker Tom Veff shows through on the Kershaw Kaper, a knife that features a 3-1/8-inch, AUS-8A stainless steel blade with full-tang construction and a cocobolo wood handle. Overall length is 7-1/8 inches, and it weighs only 2 ounces.

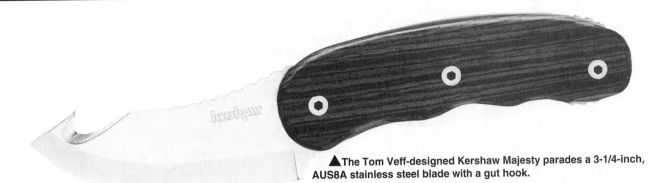

▲The Tom Veff-designed Kershaw Majesty parades a 3-1/4-inch, AUS8A stainless steel blade with a gut hook.

inch, AUS-8A stainless steel blade with a gut hook. It also has a full tang and a cocobolo handle. Overall length of the Majesty is 7-3/4 inches, and it weighs 5.2 ounces. A leather harness sheath is furnished with each knife.

Lone Wolf Knives, Inc.

If there's one knifemaker who has made the most impact on modern hunting knives, it has to be Bob Loveless. Lone Wolf Knives, in collaboration with Loveless, is producing two fixed-blade hunting knives classified as "classics," and that is just what Lone Wolf does—uilds classics. The Loveless Classic Utility and Semi-Skinner are two designs that have been copied by more knifemakers in the last 30 years than any other style of knife.

The Loveless Classic Utility has a 4-1/2-inch, flat-ground LV-04 stainless steel blade with an almost Bowie styled, dropped point. The blade, guard/bolster and tang are all closed-die forged from one piece of steel, and integral to the knife for maximum durability.

On the back of the blade is deep notching for a positive grip. Handle material is green canvas Micarta with red spacers between the guard and handle. Series 300 stainless steel lines the lanyard hole at the end of the handle.

Sharing the same features, except with a shorter, semi-skinner-type blade, the Loveless Classic Semi-Skinner sports a 3-3/4-inch blade with the Loveless-style drop point and a bit more sweep. Both knives come with top-grain cowhide sheaths with structural safety liners furnished, along with zippered cases and cleaning cloths. Each knife is also marked "R.W. LOVELESS" above "DESIGN" and "Lone Wolf Knives USA," in a manner that perfectly replicates the traditional Loveless logo. It goes without saying that these knives must be considered top of the line, probably instant collectibles, but like all Loveless-designed knives, practical to the utmost.

Meyerco USA

On its payroll, Meyerco keeps Blackie Collins, who's probably the most prolific knife designer in the world today. Blackie's new knife for Meyerco is the gut-hook model MCAMPHKGH. With a 4-inch 420 stainless steel blade and a rubber handle, overall length is 9 inches, and it weighs 5.48 ounces.

Two other Collins-designed pieces come in the form of the MAMEDSKIN medium skinner and the MALARGESKIN large skinner, both featuring T-shaped rubber handles and skinner-styled blades with gut hooks made from 440 stainless steel. The large skinner has a 3-1/4-inch blade, while

►Lone Wolf Knives burst onto the knife scene a couple years ago with a Bob Loveless-designed knife, the Loveless Classic Utility, and here it is for all to see and admire.

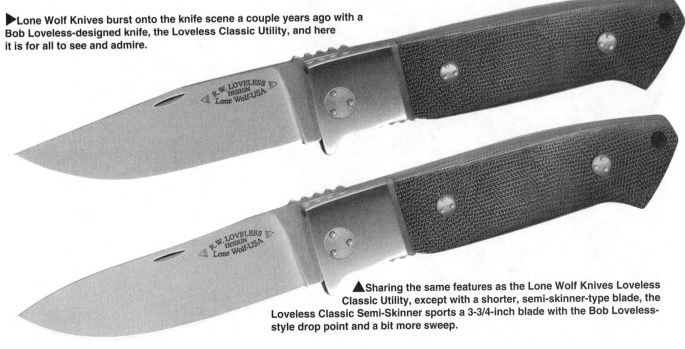

▲Sharing the same features as the Lone Wolf Knives Loveless Classic Utility, except with a shorter, semi-skinner-type blade, the Loveless Classic Semi-Skinner sports a 3-3/4-inch blade with the Bob Loveless-style drop point and a bit more sweep.

▼ A gut-hook model, this fixed blade is designed by none-other-than Blackie Collins, who's probably the most prolific knife designer in the world today.

▼ Here's a medium skinner with a T-shaped rubber handle, engineered for superior hand purchase, and a 440C blade that will hold an edge and resist rust.

Cool to look at are the Zytel handles of Schrade's new series of Badger fixed blades, and sharp are the European stainless steel blades.

the medium skinner's blade is 2 inches. The medium skinner weighs 2.24 ounces and the large skinner tips the scales at 4.32 ounces. Each knife comes with a belt sheath.

Schrade

The Badger series of fixed blades is Schrade's newest addition to its long line of hunting knives. There are three new knives in the Badger FX series—a Utility Skinner pattern with a half-serrated, 3-1/2-inch blade; a Drop Point, also with a 3-1/2-inch blade; and a Skinning-Clip model parading a 4-inch blade. All patterns feature European stainless steel and Zytel handles, and each Badger is delivered with a friction-fit, molded belt sheath.

SOG Specialty Knives

The SOG X-42 Field Knife and Field Pup share similarly shaped blades and handles, but the likenesses end there. The X-42 Field Knife incorporates a 5.4-inch BG-42 stainless steel blade and a Zytel handle, and the Field Pup has a 4-inch AUS-8A stainless steel blade and a Kraton handle. Overall length of the X-42 Field Knife is 10.65 inches, while the Field Pup stretches 8-1/2 inches. Both knives are practical outdoor knives, and BG-42 is one of the best stainless steels available for working knives.

▼SOG's X-42 Field Knife incorporates a 5.4-inch BG-42 stainless steel blade and a Zytel handle.

Tigersharp Technologies

One of the most innovative knives around is Tigersharp's replacement-cutting-edge Hunter. A replaceable 3-3/4 inch blade ensures that a sharp edge is always at the ready, and a high-impact ABS thermoplastic handle gives rigidity and durability. The steel of the K7 replaceable blade is hardened to 61 RC on the Rockwell Hardness scale, and one replacement blade is furnished with each knife, stashed in a pocket on its black nylon sheath. More replaceable-cutting-edge blades are available from Tigersharp at a nominal cost. This is the ideal knife for the man who absolutely insists on working with a sharp edge.

▲One of the most innovative knives around is Tigersharp's replacement-cutting-edge Hunter. A replaceable 3-3/4-inch blade ensures that a sharp edge is always at the ready, and a high-impact ABS thermoplastic handle gives rigidity and durability.

Timberline Knives

Alaskan guide and knife designer Terry Treutel designed Timberline's new Gut Hook Skinner, which sports a 3-1/4-inch AUS8A stainless steel blade, with, of course, a gut hook. The gut hook is extra-wide, 5/16-inches, for ease of use and re-sharpening. A trophy model Gut Hook Skinner is available with a Fibron Winewood handle, while the standard model sports a checkered, non-slip Kraton handle. Both knives incorporate full-tang construction for strength, and leather belt sheaths are furnished.

Fixed blade hunting knives are here to stay. There may be innovations in design and technology, but when the chips are down, nothing beats the tried and true. If it comes down to one knife, and one knife only, the fixed blade is the only way to go. ●

▲Alaskan guide and knife designer Terry Treutel designed Timberline's new Gut Hook Skinner, which sports a 3-1/4-inch AUS8A stainless steel blade, with, of course, a gut hook. The gut hook is extra-wide, 5/16-inches, for ease of use and re-sharpening.

Sharpeners, Sheaths, Lubes and Solutions

By Joe Kertzman

THE COMPANIES IN this section have grit — yes, this is the nitty-gritty. The leather smells like new and, mixed with the scents of oils, all is aromatic in the world of knife accessories. These are the products that help maintain knives, whether by storing them safely, keeping them keen, by lubing them to prevent rust or gumming up, or by making them easier to carry and use. It's an important end of the knife business, and some consider it not an end, but a beginning to understanding all edged tools.

The casual weekend household fixer-upper might throw his or her tools in the toolbox after done using them without another thought until there's a leaky faucet, whereas the learned handyman takes time to clean up the tools, bring them back to good working order and store them away from the elements. Such is also the difference between those who buy inexpensive knives for use only when the need arises, and others who depend on knives and frequently call them into action.

The accessories section of "Sporting Knives 2004" is meant to guide knife enthusiasts through the maze of knife-related products on the market and hit on key elements that might help distinguish sharpeners, sheaths, lubricants and solutions designed for specific purposes. Some knife sharpeners are meant to hone serrated blades, while others bring straight edges back to true. One grit texture might put a whole new edge on a knife, and another might just touch up or strop a blade bevel.

Toting factors include knife sheaths, holsters, packs and pouches. It's all well and good to buy the most expensive production knife on the market, sharpen it up and put it in a drawer, but having a useful system for carrying it makes all the difference out in the field, at work, in the barn, under the car in the garage or hanging from a cliff by your fingernails. Simply put, a practical means of carrying a blade is as important as lugging around the right kind of knife in the first place.

For years, people rubbed a little gun oil on their knife blade, spit on the handle, rubbed off the dirt and stuck the blade in the sand to bring it back to sharp. Then, into the leather belt sheath it went and was tossed under the bed until next hunting season. There are also a lot of rusty knives on flea market tables as a result of such carefree knife maintenance in days of yore.

Technology caught up to us. There are oils and lubricants out there that, when applied ever so lightly to knife blades, spread evenly across the steel like silk sheets across a mattress. Not only will such revolutionary lubes protect against rust, they don't taste oily the next time you use a lubed blade to slice an apple. Some lubricants actually add luster to already shiny steels. They don't build up like residue on wooden tables, and they don't rub off on your hands and clothing when accidentally coming into contact with the blades. In fact, most disintegrate into thin air after doing their jobs as to not cause undo cleaning stress.

There are more sheath rigs on the market today than you can shake a sharp stick at, and that means if you're left-handed, two fingered and double-jointed, you can carry a knife in just the right place to retrieve it in lightning-fast fashion. The body parts read like an anatomy lesson — small of the back, hip, leg, ankle, underarm, breast, chest, back — these are the places, and more, where knives can be carried, hidden and accessed using modern sheath systems.

Visionary knife companies have added clothing to their knife lines, jackets and vests with knife pockets, loops for carabineers and zippered pouches for other knives and accessories. Cargo pants have become as mainstream as baseball caps and blue jeans.

What it all boils down to is that knife enthusiasts are no different from car buyers, electronics customers or sporting goods consumers. All have a need to accessorize the main tools in their respective interest areas. It's considerably less expensive to accessorize knives than sports cars, audio equipment and mountain bikes, and half the fun of owning a knife or two is in handling and maintaining them. No surprise there, but what does amaze is the advancement in technology, workmanship and materials surrounding knife-care and accessory products.

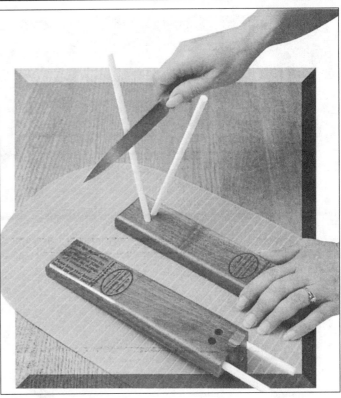

The long-tried and true A.G. Russell Field Sharpener and companion Ceramic Sharpener are fixed-angle units that rely on diamond and ceramic rods for establishing new blade bevels and polishing them up until they shave paper.

Knife sharpeners feature thousands of tiny diamonds fused onto metal substrates. Some include grooves for fishhook sharpening. Quite a few have preset angle guides that allow for sharpening factory edges the way they were applied. Sheaths are no longer just leather, but Kydex®, polyurethane, hard rubber, plastic, fiberglass-reinforced, resin-impregnated and practically bulletproof.

Without a doubt, the world of knives is better off for the accessories offered to conscientious consumers.

A.G. Russell Knives

You don't get to be one of the highest-regarded mail-order knife companies and cataloguers without selling quality products. A.G. Russell Knives has earned a good reputation for marketing high-performance knives and accessories to discerning clientele. Aimed at the gents and ladies, the knives A.G. Russell presents are higher-end than those offered in most knife catalogs, and the accessories are no different.

Starting with the long-tried and true A.G. Russell Field Sharpener

◀Knives are precious commodities to some, so A.G. Russell Knives has come up with a way to tote knives, hold them steady and protect them. The Double Wall Plastic Carrying Case is foam lined, hinged and double latched. So, relax, and enjoy the ride.

▶With accessory pouches, ambidextrous inside knife pockets, outside chest pockets and cargo pockets, wearing the Al Mar Tac-Jac is like donning cargo pants on your upper torso.

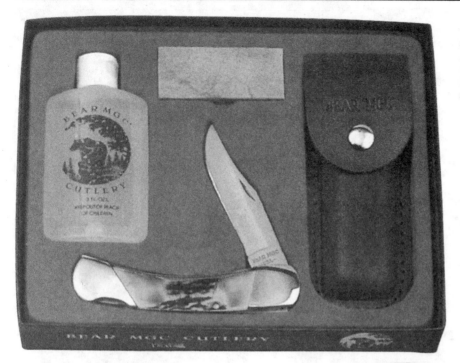

ments include higher-quality hinges and latches and an integral, molded-plastic handle.

Al Mar Knives

In case you need to speak to the president of the company, Gary Fadden is the well-over-6-foot giant hovering over the Al Mar Knives line wearing an extra-extra-large Al Mar Tac-Jac. The Tac-Jac's accessory pouches include ambi-dextrous inside knife pockets, out-side chest pockets with elastic for shotgun shells or small accessories, and cargo pockets with built-in elastic for holding rifle magazines or larger accessories. Wearing the jacket will help you stay on Fad-den's good side, too.

Bear MGC Cutlery

A division of Swiss Army Brands, Bear MGC Cutlery has won several BLADE Magazine Knife Of The Year Awards over the years, including Best Buy of the Year, Best Collector Value, the 1994 Excellence in Manufacturing Award and the 1996 Most Innova-tive Design Of The Year.

While some knife companies assemble parts brought in from various worldwide suppliers, Bear MGC claims to perform all work in its self-contained manufacturing plant, from building its own blank-ing dies to heat-treating, grinding and assembly.

Bear decided if it was to market knife accessories, it might as well offer a knife to potential customers along with the "extras." New in 2003 is a S597 Pattern set, includ-ing an India-stag-bone-handle lock-back folding knife, a bottle of Bear MGC Honing Oil, an Arkansas Sharpening stone and a leather sheath, all in a gift box. For a man-ufacturer's suggested retail price of $86.99, buyers get the knife, the lube, a sharpening stone and the sheath. It's not a bad deal at all.

Benchmade Knife Co.

What, Benchmade is selling accessories? Isn't that the company that offers the official Bali-Songs, police and military automatic

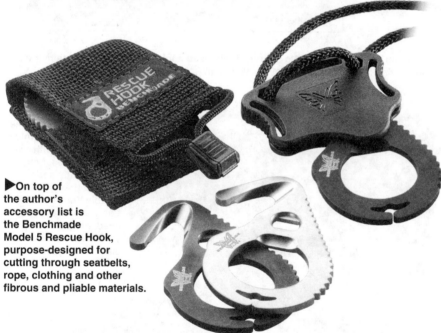

►On top of the author's accessory list is the Benchmade Model 5 Rescue Hook, purpose-designed for cutting through seatbelts, rope, clothing and other fibrous and pliable materials.

and companion Ceramic Sharp-ener, both are fixed-angle units that rely on diamond and ceramic rods for establishing new blade bevels and polishing them up until they shave paper.

Included in the A.G. Russell accessory line is also the Rust Eraser for cleaning the ceramic rods to remove metal deposits resulting from the honing process. A.G. Rus-sell himself puts his stamp of approval on Rust Free rust preven-tative solution, saying it's the best he's seen for deterring rust or stain-ing on high-carbon tool steel or any of the non-stainless steels.

The company also offers Happich Polishing Paste, touting it as the original knife collector's pol-ish for use on chrome, silver, brass, nickel silver and blade steels. Rus-sell claims he's used it for over 30 years and has never found a polish-ing paste that will replace it.

Russell has also reinvented the knife carrying case. The Double Wall Plastic Knife Carrying Case is a foam-lined case with a hinged lid and double latch capable of toting three hunting knives and six-to-eight pocketknives. A.G. Russell Knives sold the same type of case years ago, but modern improve-

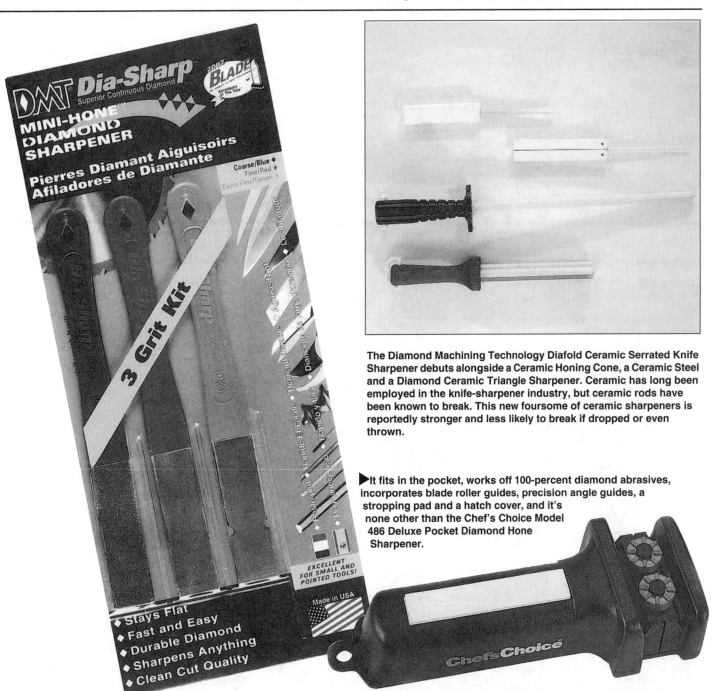

The Diamond Machining Technology Diafold Ceramic Serrated Knife Sharpener debuts alongside a Ceramic Honing Cone, a Ceramic Steel and a Diamond Ceramic Triangle Sharpener. Ceramic has long been employed in the knife-sharpener industry, but ceramic rods have been known to break. This new foursome of ceramic sharpeners is reportedly stronger and less likely to break if dropped or even thrown.

▶It fits in the pocket, works off 100-percent diamond abrasives, incorporates blade roller guides, precision angle guides, a stropping pad and a hatch cover, and it's none other than the Chef's Choice Model 486 Deluxe Pocket Diamond Hone Sharpener.

▲When DMT introduced the Diamond Mini-Hone, it became apparent that there was demand for the product in a hunting and outdoor environment. This led to the decision to package three Mini-Hones.

knives, and modern tactical folders and fixed blades? Isn't Benchmade the $100-and-up knife company for those who want blades that will stand up to hard use and abuse? Yes, but even the accessories have edges, or, at least one of them does.

It's reasonable to call the Model 5 Rescue Hook an accessory. It certainly isn't a knife, though it does have a blade and, more impor-

tantly, it would be an ideal accessory to other favorite edged tools. It's what the name implies — a rescue hook for cutting through seatbelts, rope, clothing and other fibrous and pliable materials. Integral to the piece is an oxygen-valve wrench for emergency medical team use, a bottle opener and a lanyard hole.

Benchmade also offers soft, polyballistic, denier nylon sheaths suited for folding knives with closed lengths of 5-to-5-1/4 inches or shorter. Each has a Velcro closure flap. The Benchmade Knife Attaché is a soft carry case that holds up to 12 folders. The shell is constructed

of a heavyweight, denier nylon and a plush interior lining for scratch-free knife storage. The Velcro flap closure is embroidered with the Benchmade logo.

Diamond Machining Technology

After 26 years in business, Diamond Machining Technology is still depending on the diamond's ability to abrade steel and other hard materials. It's always nice to see a sharpener line expanding and, thanks to dedication and a crack engineering and product development team, DMT's product offer-

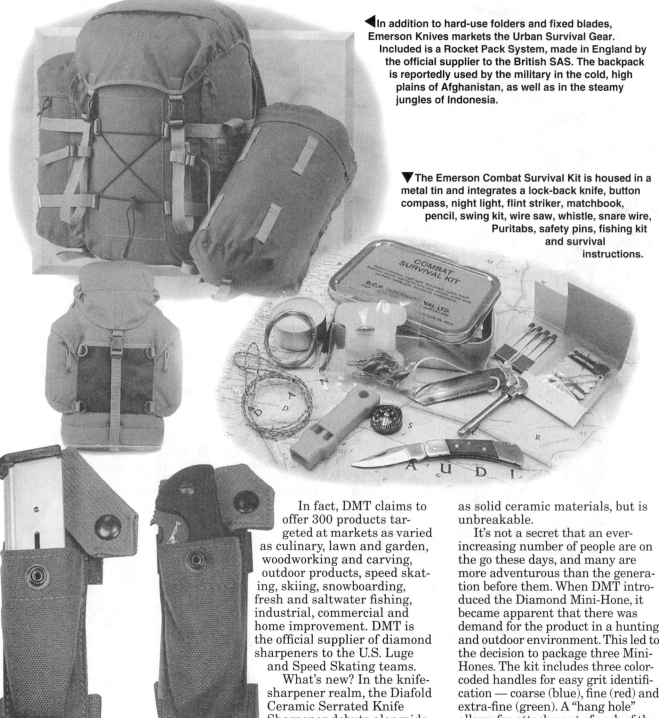

◀ In addition to hard-use folders and fixed blades, Emerson Knives markets the Urban Survival Gear. Included is a Rocket Pack System, made in England by the official supplier to the British SAS. The backpack is reportedly used by the military in the cold, high plains of Afghanistan, as well as in the steamy jungles of Indonesia.

▼ The Emerson Combat Survival Kit is housed in a metal tin and integrates a lock-back knife, button compass, night light, flint striker, matchbook, pencil, swing kit, wire saw, whistle, snare wire, Puritabs, safety pins, fishing kit and survival instructions.

▲ Aren't they just simple nylon ammo and knife sheaths? Yes, but the Emerson versions mount vertically or horizontally onto web belts, web gear systems and harnesses, and on civilian belts up to 1-3/4 inches wide.

ings have leapfrogged past hones for sharpening knives to include those that work on skis, snowboards, arrowheads, drill bits, shears and practically anything with an edge.

In fact, DMT claims to offer 300 products targeted at markets as varied as culinary, lawn and garden, woodworking and carving, outdoor products, speed skating, skiing, snowboarding, fresh and saltwater fishing, industrial, commercial and home improvement. DMT is the official supplier of diamond sharpeners to the U.S. Luge and Speed Skating teams.

What's new? In the knife-sharpener realm, the Diafold Ceramic Serrated Knife Sharpener debuts alongside a Ceramic Honing Cone, a Ceramic Steel and a Diamond Ceramic Triangle Sharpener. Ceramic has long been employed in the knife-sharpener industry, but ceramic rods have been known to break. This new foursome of ceramic sharpeners is reportedly stronger and less likely to break if dropped or even thrown. The patented Cerafuse process transforms the surface of aluminum to an extremely hard, dense aluminum oxide that has the same properties as solid ceramic materials, but is unbreakable.

It's not a secret that an ever-increasing number of people are on the go these days, and many are more adventurous than the generation before them. When DMT introduced the Diamond Mini-Hone, it became apparent that there was demand for the product in a hunting and outdoor environment. This led to the decision to package three Mini-Hones. The kit includes three color-coded handles for easy grit identification — coarse (blue), fine (red) and extra-fine (green). A "hang hole" allows for attachment of each of the three Mini-Hones to backpacks, fanny packs, belts or back quivers for those "on the go." The lightweight sharpeners are equally convenient to carry in a pocket or pouch.

For ultra-adventurous skiers and snowboarders, DMT suggests the Multi-Tuner, Fixed 90-Degree Tuner, Fixed Beveling Tuner, 4-Inch Diamond Stone and Mini Diamond Stone. The DMT Diamond stones are designed to remove burrs that chew up ordinary steel files, and the company suggests, for achieving the best performance on each ski or snowboarding run, carrying a DMT Diamond Stone on the slopes to touch up burrs as they occur. There is a full assortment of diamond tuning guides for maintaining the beveled edges of all shaped skis and snowboards.

EdgeCraft Corp.

EdgeCraft built a reputation around Chef'sChoice knife sharpeners. Electric kitchen-knife and scissors sharpeners continue, 19 years later, to make up the bulk of EdgeCraft's repertoire. Manual kitchen-knife sharpeners were soon to follow, making way for field-knife sharpening tools. Edge-Craft diamond steels, diamond stones and sharpening rods are now sold in over 50 countries.

Nowadays it seems that even pocket sharpeners have three stages of operation. The Chef'sChoice Model 486 Deluxe Pocket Diamond Hone Sharpener is no exception. Working off 100-percent diamond abrasives, it incorporates blade roller guides, precision angle guides, a stropping pad and a hatch cover.

The unit can fit into a pants pocket for carry while camping, boating, fishing, hunting or motor home traveling. Stage one is a sharpening stage in which the knife blade is inserted into a slot and pulled through along diamond abrasives and angle guides to remove weak blade edges and create bevels simultaneously on both sides of the blade. The second honing stage employs ultra-fine diamond abrasives to polish the edge at precisely the correct angle. A final, sharp edge is accomplished holding the knife at a 30-degree angle and drawing the blade over the stropping pad.

For those who prefer a flat stone, the EdgeCrafter 420 is a hone and file in one. A MagneLok magnetic holder allows for changing of diamond-grit plates quickly, and the diamond abrasives come in coarse, fine and extra-fine grits.

Emerson Knives

Maker of tactical and military knives, Emerson Knives is a company as dedicated to self-defense and knife-fighting training for military and Special Forces groups as it is to making dependable blades. Ernest Emerson is an accomplished trainer and says he's intimately involved in the war on terror, both

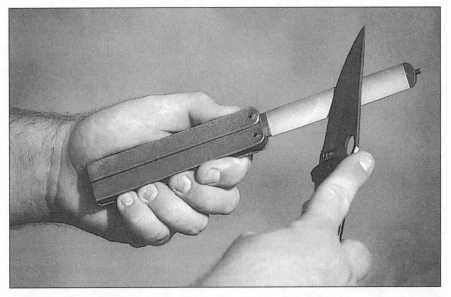

A new oval-shaped diamond sharpener for outdoorsmen manifests itself in the form of the Model 590 EZE-Lap EZE-Fold Sharpener. The super-fine diamond grit covers an oval shaft that can be used as a butcher's steel or as a file for touching up odd-shaped cutting blades.

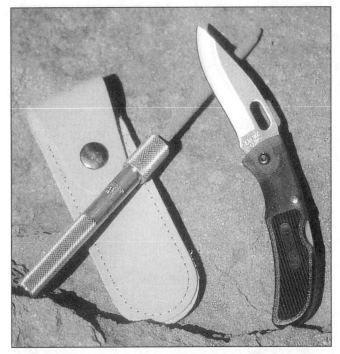

The EZE-Lap Model M Round Diamond Sharpener stows in any pocket and can hone most cutting edges. It measures just 3-1/4 inches long and features a cylindrical, fine-grit sharpening shaft, making short work of any dull hunting knife, fillet knife, pocketknife, fishhook or scissors. The round profile is well suited to serrated blades, and the sharpening shaft stores neatly within the unit's brass handle.

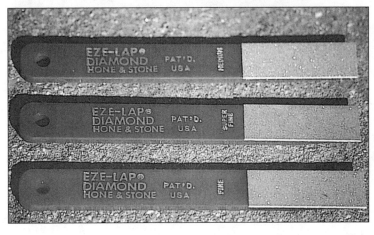

A set of three EZE-Lap grits — medium, fine and super-fine — combine to sharpen anything from knives and scissors to saw blades and wire cutters.

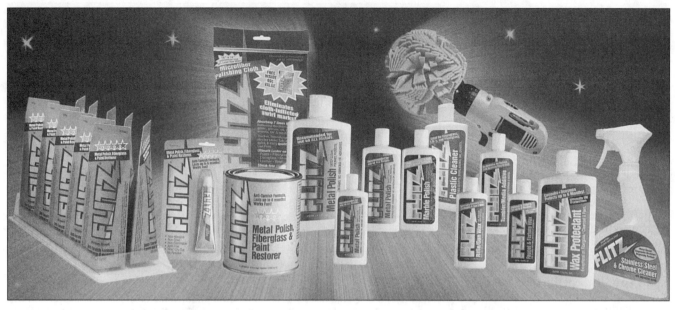

Flitz Polishing and Buffing Products are non-abrasive, yet they clean, polish, deoxidize and protect a great number of metals and non-metals.

with his knives and training programs. He pledges to continue to support the efforts of the U.S. Military and of the allied troops who have joined in a fight against evil and oppression worldwide.

In addition to hard-use folders and fixed blades, the company markets Emerson's Urban Survival Gear. Included is a Rocket Pack System, made in England by the official supplier to the British SAS. The backpack is reportedly used by the military in the cold, high plains of Afghanistan, as well as in the steamy jungles of Indonesia.

Just as intriguing is the Combat Survival Kit, another product made in England. The kit is housed in a metal tin and integrates a lockback knife, button compass, night light, flint striker, matchbook, pencil, swing kit, wire saw,

▼To use an AccuSharp handheld sharpener from Fortune Products, a knife is secured, by hand or clamp, spine down, edge up on a table or workbench, and the honing blades of an AccuSharp sharpener are run lengthwise along the edge of the blade.

Fortune Products' SturdyMount Knife Sharpener is easily secured to cutting boards, kitchen counters, fillet boards, workbenches, butcher blocks or cleaning tables.

whistle, snare wire, Puritabs, safety pins, fishing kit and survival instructions.

Emerson's Nylon Ammo/Knife Sheaths mount vertically or horizontally onto web belts, web gear systems and harnesses, and on civilian belts up to 1-3/4 inches wide. In addition to knives up to 6 inches long, the heavy-duty nylon snap pouches hold small flashlights, gun ammo magazines and other tools.

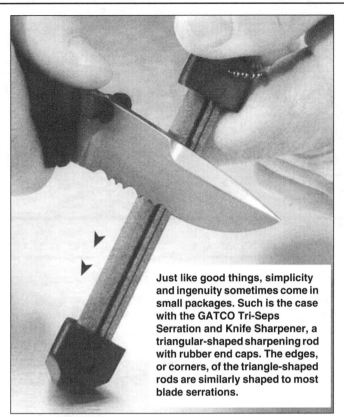

Just like good things, simplicity and ingenuity sometimes come in small packages. Such is the case with the GATCO Tri-Seps Serration and Knife Sharpener, a triangular-shaped sharpening rod with rubber end caps. The edges, or corners, of the triangle-shaped rods are similarly shaped to most blade serrations.

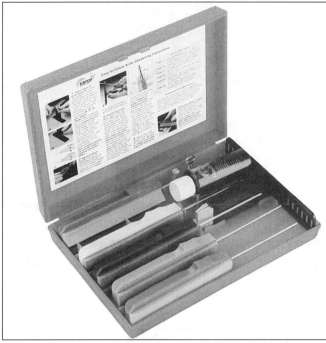

Many GATCO Sharpeners are complete honing systems, including knife clamps and angle guides for honing the correct angles on blade bevels, and the guides come in the form of rods with sharpening stones attached to hone handles.

EZE-Lap Diamond Products

It's a patented process of heat treatment that bonds industrial-grade diamond particles in a stainless alloy onto a precision-matched, metal substrate. It's what defines and sets apart EZE-Lap diamond hones. The resulting surface measures about 72Rc on the Rockwell C hardness scale, and the sharpeners to which the surface is applied are more than capable of honing carbide, ceramic, tool steel, hardened materials and the newer stainless steels that are used by most knife manufacturers today.

EZE-Lap diamond sharpeners include small, pocket-sized flat stones and compact, portable, round diamond sharpeners. Next in line are household and professional-size diamond steels for chefs, gourmets and meat cutters. The sharpeners employ five diamond grits, but EZE-Lap suggests that 98 percent of all sharpening can be performed using the fine, 600-grit diamond surface, which has the ability to hone a dull knife blade in less than a minute and bring the edge to a razor-sharp finish. The fine grit is offered on all EZE-Lap products, and the round sharpeners are only offered in fine grit.

Chainsaw sharpeners, needle files, flat hand files and oval sharpeners round out the product line.

A new oval-shaped diamond sharpener for outdoorsmen manifests itself in the form of the Model 590 EZE-Lap EZE-Fold Sharpener. The super-fine diamond grit covers an oval shaft that can be used as a butcher's steel or as a file for touching up odd-shaped cutting blades. The plastic handle folds over the metal shaft to protect it for carrying at home or in the woods.

The Model M Round Diamond Sharpener stows in any pocket and can hone most cutting edges. It measures just 3-1/4 inches long and features a cylindrical, fine-grit sharpening shaft, making short work of any dull hunting knife, fillet knife, pocketknife, fishhook or scissors. The round profile is well suited to serrated blades, and the sharpening shaft stores neatly within the unit's brass handle.

The Model L Pak is a set of three grits — medium, fine and super-fine — combining to sharpen anything from knives and scissors to saw blades and wire cutters.

Flitz Polishing & Buffing Products

Flitz Paste Metal Polish is a concentrated cream formulated to clean, polish, deoxidize and protect brass; copper; silver-plated surfaces; sterling silver; chrome; stainless steel; nickel; bronze; solid gold; aluminum; anodized aluminum; beryllium; magnesium; platinum; pewter; factory hot-gun bluing; painted surfaces; glass; Plexiglas; Fiberglass; and Armatel. It is non-abrasive and said to remove anything from tarnish to rust; water stains to chalking; lime deposits to heat discoloration; and bugs to tar.

The Flitz Liquid Metal Polish is a diluted version of the original paste formula for cleaning and polishing all but beryllium, magnesium, platinum, painted surfaces, glass, Plexiglas, Fiberglass and Armatel. It contains no ammonia or harsh abrasives.

Fortune Products

Ease of operation is what Fortune Products lays claim to with each of its AccuSharp handheld or workbench-mounting sharpeners. Most of the honing units involve plastic handles with finger guards and sharpening blades of diamond-tungsten carbide. To use a handheld unit, a knife is secured, by hand or clamp, spine down, edge up on a table or workbench, and the honing blades of an AccuSharp sharpener are run lengthwise along the edge of the blade.

The SturdyMount Knife Sharpener mounts to cutting boards, kitchen counters, fillet boards, workbenches, butcher blocks or cleaning tables. Diamond tungsten carbide sharpening blades are locked at preset angles, and straight or serrated knife blades are run through them.

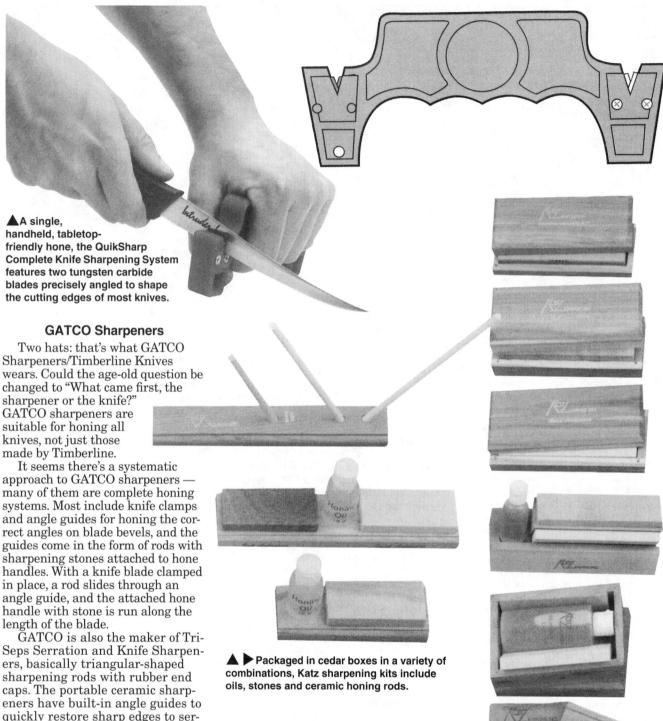

▲A single, handheld, tabletop-friendly hone, the QuikSharp Complete Knife Sharpening System features two tungsten carbide blades precisely angled to shape the cutting edges of most knives.

GATCO Sharpeners

Two hats: that's what GATCO Sharpeners/Timberline Knives wears. Could the age-old question be changed to "What came first, the sharpener or the knife?" GATCO sharpeners are suitable for honing all knives, not just those made by Timberline.

It seems there's a systematic approach to GATCO sharpeners — many of them are complete honing systems. Most include knife clamps and angle guides for honing the correct angles on blade bevels, and the guides come in the form of rods with sharpening stones attached to hone handles. With a knife blade clamped in place, a rod slides through an angle guide, and the attached hone handle with stone is run along the length of the blade.

GATCO is also the maker of Tri-Seps Serration and Knife Sharpeners, basically triangular-shaped sharpening rods with rubber end caps. The portable ceramic sharpeners have built-in angle guides to quickly restore sharp edges to serrations or plain blade edges. The edges, or corners, of the triangle-shaped rods are similarly shaped to most blade serrations.

Much larger than the Tri-Seps, but born of the same ingenuity, the 10-inch Scepter H/D Sharpener is an industrial-grade, unbreakable, solid-steel, triangle-shaped rod with dual-size radius corners for honing small and large serrations, and a flat side for plain-edge blades. Two sharpening grooves that run the length of the steel are purpose-designed for honing pointed instruments.

▲ ▶Packaged in cedar boxes in a variety of combinations, Katz sharpening kits include oils, stones and ceramic honing rods.

Gerber Legendary Blades

Knife companies are adding sharpeners to their existing lines faster than a customer can "hone in" on the new blades. Gerber is no exception. Several stones start out the accessories offerings, including small, rectangular fishhook and blade hones that pivot in and out of handy leather sheaths (via pins). Each sheath is complete with a lanyard hole, so these little sharpeners are as handy as one-hand-opening folders with dual thumb studs. The stones themselves are dual-grit sharpening steels. The diamond Steel model makes use of a diamond-coated surface, and the Honing Steel parades chromium-carbide-coated, dual-grit steel.

Gerber's Saf-T-Sharp is a hand-held unit with two finger holes, two ramps for resting the pinky and thumb, and twin tungsten-carbide blades to be run evenly along blade bevels. Gerber also offers a 3-In-1

▶ From Kershaw Knives is the Model 2535 Ultra-Tek Sharpener, a 600-grit, diamond-coated, oval honing rod in a self-containing handle.

stone with coarse, medium and fine grits on three sides of a hone paddle, complete with a Safe-Grip handle. Completing the accessories lineup is the Gerber Disc sharpener, a disc-shaped, handheld hone that fills the palm to reduce slipping. It looks rather like a fancy hockey puck with a handle for honing blades.

Intruder Inc.

The maker of fishing and hunting equipment added a knife sharpener to the inventory this year. The Intruder QuikSharp Complete Knife Sharpening System is a single, handheld, tabletop-friendly hone consisting of a plastic handle/base and two tungsten carbide sharpening blades precisely angled to shape the cutting edges of most knives. Two ceramic honing rods complete the process by putting fine, smooth edges on after initial honing. Both blades are reversible to double the life of the QuickSharp unit.

Katz Knives

Katz is a company that rarely wavers from its mission statement — to make well-built hunting, fishing and camp knives. No headline grabbing, no bells and whistles, just building quality knives and now sharpeners. Katz Knives separates itself from the competition by packaging knife sharpeners and honing oils in cedar boxes in a variety of combinations. For those who remember stereo-system/turntable care kits with needle brushes, cleaning solution and pads, the Katz sharpening kits have a similar look, only with oils, stones and ceramic rods.

Kershaw Knives

Some simple designs just deserve mention. From Kershaw Knives is the Model 2535 Ultra-Tek Sharpener, a 600-grit, diamond-coated, oval honing rod in a self-containing handle. The hollow 6061-T6 aircraft-aluminum grip holds the rod, but the rod also unscrews from the handle and can be turned upside down and inverted into the handle for storing.

Lansky Sharpeners

Life, or knives, would be dull without Crock Stick sharpeners from Lansky. Take one wooden

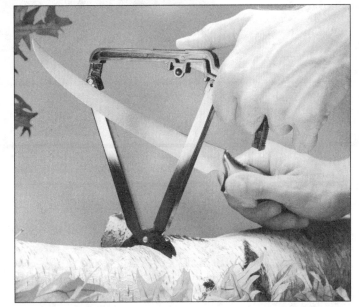

This is the perfect knife hone for hunters, campers, hikers, mountain bikers, climbers and outdoorsmen and women in general. The Lansky Fold-A-Vee boasts a curved base shaped to rest on logs, camp chairs, picnic tables, rocks or bumpy ground.

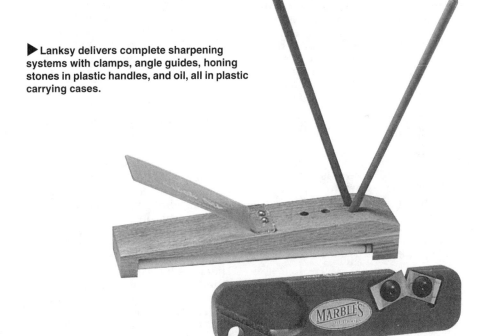

▶ Lanksy delivers complete sharpening systems with clamps, angle guides, honing stones in plastic handles, and oil, all in plastic carrying cases.

▶ The honing blades of the Marble's Redi-Edge Pro and Pocket Pro Hunting Knife sharpeners are composed of micro-grain carbide steel that is harder than cutlery steel.

base with a hand guard, insert two alumina-ceramic honing rods vertically from the base, angled so that together they form a vertical "V"

above the base. Then, hold a knife by the handle with the blade vertical and edge down, and run one side of the blade bevel down the inside of one of the rods, pulling the blade toward you as you descend the rod. Now, hone the other side of the bevel on the inside of the second rod, and repeat. When done, and the edge is sharp, the rods can be stored in the bottom of the base.

Another innovative design from Lansky is the Fold-A-Vee sharpener, an effective tool designed for field use. The curved base is shaped to rest on logs, camp chairs, picnic tables, rocks or bumpy ground. The sides of the sharpener form two sides of a vertical triangle, and the top composes the third side. By running a blade, one side at a time, down the inside walls of the vertical sides of the triangle, alumina-ceramic sharpening rods work their magic on each beveled edge. Pre-set sharpening angles of 17 and 23 degrees are ideal for fillet knives and other sporting knives, respectively. The entire unit is self-contained, compact and light-weight, with no parts to assemble.

In addition, Lanksy delivers complete sharpening systems with clamps, angle guides, honing stones in plastic handles, and oil, all in plastic carrying cases. Each features several stone grits and angle adjustments, with rods that slide into holes in vertical bases and descend at present angles to knife blades held in clamps. Attached to the rods are plastic handles holding stones that can be run along blade edges.

Three unusual sharpening stones for honing axes, swords, machetes, shovels and lawnmower blades are the Lansky Puck, Lawn & Garden Sharpener and Heavy Duty Sharpener. Each has a unique shape and design for getting at hard-to-reach or unusually angled blade edges.

Marble's Outdoors

From its earliest beginnings in the late 1800s making Safety Axes, Marble's has been committed to knives and the outdoors. Stacked-leather, stag and wood knife handles have always been the rule, not the exception, and only in modern times has the company switched some of its product line over from high-carbon blades to 420 HC stainless steel, and from the natural grips on some of the same knives to synthetic "Safe Grip" rubber-like handles.

The Marble's Redi-Edge Pro and Pocket Pro Hunting Knife sharpeners are thought-out designs that take the guesswork out of knife sharpening by ensuring consistent, sharp

With McGowan FireStone sharpeners, both sides of blade bevels are sharpened simultaneously with just a few strokes of edged steel through round, wheel-like fired stones.

▼ The FireStone RTS (Replace The Steel) Sharpener has a long, thin handle that fits into a typical kitchen knife block where the sharpening steel is usually kept.

edges. The honing blades of each sharpener are composed of micrograin carbide steel that is harder than cutlery steel. Each sharpener also has a hardened-ceramic honing surface that Marble's claims won't wear off, chemically bonded to its anodized-aluminum handle for use like a whetstone.

McGowan Mfg.

With McGowan FireStone sharpeners, both sides of blade bevels are sharpened simultaneously with just a few strokes of edged steel through round, wheel-like fired stones. The stones are made from a blend of aluminum silica and ceramic, and they are strategically placed in the sharpeners to guide each knife blade to a consistent angle every time. According to McGowan, because the stones interlock like gears, and because they rotate, the sharpening surface won't deteriorate.

The stones are color coded for grit texture and include medium-grit tan stones and fine-grit white stones. The FireStone 2-Stage Handheld sharpeners incorporate both stone grits for sharpening a blade and polishing it afterward. The FireStone RTS (Replace The Steel) Sharpener has a long, thin

▶ The heart of the Meyerco Sharpen-It is a set of three interlocking wheel-like hones for sharpening and polishing knife blades at predetermined angles.

handle that fits into a typical kitchen knife block where the sharpening steel is usually kept.

Meyerco

Blackie Collins is a knife designer who has worked with Meyerco since the 1995 Blade Show, when he demonstrated his new assisted-opening folding knife to Bill and John Meyer, proprietors of the company. The resulting Rascal and Speedster production folding knives are widely successful but, according to Collins, even more sales worthy is the Sharpen-It knife sharpener, also of his own design.

The heart of the Sharpen-It is a set of three interlocking wheel-like hones for sharpening and polishing knife blades at predetermined angles. The entire unit weighs 3-1/2 ounces and measures a mere 1-3/4-by-4-1/2 inches, fitting easily in a

▲Smith's Tri-Hone Sharpening System parades coarse, medium and fine Arkansas stones on a single triangular rod that rests one of three ways in a base. Depending on which way the rod is placed on the base determines which stone faces upward for honing a blade.

◄Unique to the Smith's 6-inch Diamond Bench Stones are multiple layers of micron-sized, mono-crystalline diamonds that do the honing.

◄Enter the Spyderco Tri-Angle Sharpmaker, a proven design with a couple recent updates, including new UltraFine Triangle (ceramic) and Diamond Triangle honing rods. Two sets of high-alumina-ceramic, triangular-shaped rods of different grits and a set of brass safety rods to protect the user's hand during sharpening. For honing plain edges, the flat sides of the stones are ideal and, for serrated edges, the corners work well.

pocket or belt sheath. Now, a lower-priced, more basic version of the Sharpen-It is available and appropriately named the Jr. Sharpen-It.

Smith's

Natural Arkansas stones are the backbone behind the Smith's sharpener business, yet the company also outfits its discerning customers with diamond abrasives, ceramics, bonded abrasives and carbides for honing knife blades.

Smith's Tri-Hone Sharpening System parades coarse, medium and fine Arkansas stones on a single triangular rod that rests one of three ways in a base. Depending on which way the rod is placed on the base determines which stone faces upward for honing a blade.

Multiple layers of micron-sized, mono-crystalline diamonds do the honing on the 6-inch Diamond Bench Stones, and each stone features a sharpening surface with an overlapping oval-hole design. This innovation speeds sharpening by collecting and holding the metal filings that ordinarily build up during the honing process.

Spyderco

Spyderco is largely credited for bringing one-hand-opening (with patented holes in the blades), partially serrated folding knives, complete with pocket clips, to the forefront of the knife industry. As Spyderco celebrates its silver anniversary of making knives, most with partial blade serrations, in 2003, what better company to have the know-how to design a sharpener for honing straight and fully or partially "scalloped" blades? Enter the Tri-Angle Sharpmaker, a proven design with a couple recent updates, including new UltraFine Triangle (ceramic) and Diamond Triangle honing rods.

The Tri-Angle Sharpmaker includes two sets of high-alumina-ceramic, triangular-shaped rods of different grits and a set of brass safety rods to protect the user's hand during sharpening. For honing plain edges, the flat sides of the stones are ideal and, for serrated edges, the corners work well. The stones fit into keyed holes and slots molded into a polymer base and have 40-degree and 30-degree sharpening angles for knives. ●

WEB DIRECTORY

MANUFACTURERS OF PRODUCTION & SEMI–PRODUCTION KNIVES

Compiled by Dexter Ewing

A

A.G. Russell Knives– http://www.agrussell.com
Al Mar Knives – http://www.almarknives.com/
Antoni Diving Knives – http://www.italpro.com/antoni/index.htm

B

Becker Knife & Tool – See Camillus Cutlery Co.
Benchmade Knife Co. – http://www.benchmade.com/
Benchmark – http://www.nkdi.com
Beretta Knives – http://www.beretta.com/home_2002.asp
Big Country Knives – http://www.knifeware.com
Blackjack Knives – http://www.knifeware.com
Blade Rigger – http://www.bladerigger.com/
Blue Grass Cutlery (Winchester Knives and John Primble Knives) – http://www.bluegrasscutlery.com/
Boker (Germany) – http://www.boker.de
Boker (USA) – http://www.bokerusa.com/
Boss Knives – http://www.wowinc.com
Browning Knives – http://www.browning.com/products/catalog/knives/knives.htm
Buck Knives – http://www.buckknives.com/
Busse Combat Knife Co. – http://www.bussecombat.com/

C

Camillus Cutlery Co. – http://www.camillusknives.com
C.A.S. Iberia – http://www.casiberia.com/
W.R. Case & Sons – http://www.wrcase.com/
Chris Reeve Knives – http://chrisreeve.com/
Coast Cutlery – http://www.coastcutlery.com
Cold Steel, Inc. – http://www.coldsteel.com
Columbia River Knife & Tool – http://www.crkt.com

D

David Boye Knives – http://www.boyeknives.com
Duel Knives – http://www.duelknives.co.nz/

E

Eickhorn – http://www.eickhorn-solingen.com/
Emerson Knives, Inc. – http://www.emersonknives.com/
Extrema Ratio – http://www.extremaratio.com

F

Fallkniven – http://www.fallkniven.com/
Fox Cutlery – http://www.italpro.com/fox/
Frost Cutlery – http://www.frostcutlery.com

G

GT Knives – http://www.gtknives.com/
Gerber Legendary Blades – http://www.gerberblades.com/
Grohmann Knives – http://www.grohmannknives.com/pages/index2.html
Gutmann Cutlery (Junglee Knives) – http://www.gutmanncutlery.com/

H

Hen & Rooster – http://www.fcdistributors.com
Himalayan Imports – http://www.himalayan-imports.com

I

Imagical Design – http://www.imagical-design.com/
Imperial Schrade Corp. – http://www.schradeknives.com/

J

John Primble Knives – See Blue Grass Cutlery
Joy Enterprises/Fury Cutlery – http://www.joyenterprises.com

K

KA-BAR – http://www.ka-bar.com/

Katz Knives – http://www.katzknives.com
Kellam Knives – http://www.kellamknives.com
Kershaw Knives – http://www.kershawknives.com
Klotzli – http://www.klotzli.com
Kopromed – See Wild Boar Blades
Knives of Alaska – http://www.knivesofalaska.com/
Kutmaster – http://www.kutmaster.com

L

Laguiole – http://www.laguiole.com/
Leatherman Tool Group – http://www.leatherman.com/
Lone Wolf Knives – http://www.lonewolfknives.com

M

Marble's Outdoors – www.marbleoutdoors.com
Master Cutlery, Inc. – http://www.mastercutlery.com
Masters Of Defense Knife Co.– http://www.mastersofdefense.com
Marttiini – http://www.marttiini.fi/
Maserin – http://www.italpro.com/maserin/index.htm
Meyerco Mfg. – http://www.meyercousa.com
Microtech – http://www.microtechknives.com
Mission Knives & Tools – http://www.missionknives.com/
Myerchin, Inc. – http://www.myerchin.com

O

Okapi – http://www.wildboarblades.com
Ontario Knife Co. – http://www.ontarioknife.com
Outdoor Edge Cutlery Corp. – http://www.outdooredge.com

P

P.J. Turner Knife Mfg. – http://www.dns1.silverstar.com/turnermfg/
Phantom Knives – http://www.phantomknives.com
Pro Tech Knives – http://www.protechknives.com
Puma – http://www.coastcutlery.com

Q

Queen Cutlery Co. – See Ontario Knife Co.

R

Randall Made Knives – http://www.randallknives.com/
Remington Knives – http://www.remington.com
Richartz – http://www.richartz.com

S

Schatt & Morgan – See Ontario Knife Co.
Seki Cut – http://www.sekidirect.com
Shepherd Hills Cutlery – http://www.casexx.com
Simonich Knives, LLC – http://www.simonichknives.com
Smith & Wesson Knives – See Taylor Cutlery
SOG Specialty Knives & Tools – http://www.sogknives.com/home.htm
Spyderco, Inc. – http://www.spyderco.com
Strider Knives – http://www.striderknives.com
Swamp Rat Knife Works – http://www.swamprat.com
Swiss Army Brands – http://www.swissarmy.com

T

Taylor Cutlery – http://www.taylorcutlery.com
Timberline Knives – http://www.timberlineknives.com
TiNives, Inc. – http://www.tinives.com
TOPS Knives – http://www.topsknives.com/

U

United Cutlery Brands – http://www.unitedcutlery.com/

V

Valor Corporation – http://www.valorcorp.com
Victorinox – http://www.victorinox.ch/

W

Wenger North America – http://www.wengerna.com
Wild Boar Blades – http://www.wildboarblades.com
William Henry Fine Knives – http://www.williamhenryknives.com/
Winchester Knives – See Blue Grass Cutlery

X

Xikar Knives – http://www.xikar.com

KNIFE RETAILERS AND PURVEYORS

2 The Hilt – http://www.2thehilt.com

A

A.G. Russell – http://www.agrussell.com/
Ajax Grips – http://www.ajaxgrips.com
Arizona Custom Knives – http://www.arizonacustomknives.com/
Arrow Dynamics – http://www.arrow-dynamics.com/
Atlanta Cutlery – http://www.atlantacutlery.com

B

Bayou LaFourche Knife Works- http://www.knifeworks.com/
Beck's Cutlery – http://www.beckscutlery.com/
BladeArt.com – http://www.bladeart.com/
Blade Runner Knives – http://www.brknives.com/
Blades For Less – http://www.uws.com/blades4less
Blowout Knives – http://www.blowoutknives.com/
Bob Neal Custom Knives – http://www.bobnealcustomknives.com
Brigade Quartermasters – http://www.actiongear.com/
Bud K Worldwide – http://www.budkww.com/
Bullman Cutlery – http://www.bullmancutlery.com/

C

Chesapeake Knife & Tool – http://www.chesapeakeknifeandtool.com/
Confederate Cutlery – http://www.confederatecutlery.com/
Cove Cutlery – http://www.covecutlery.com/
C.R. Specialties – http://www.crknives.com/
Cumberland Knives – http://www.cumberland-knives.com/
Cutlery Shoppe – http://www.cutleryshoppe.com/
Cutlery To Go – http://www.cutlerytogo.com/

D

Dantes Knife Works – http://www.dantesknife.com/
Discount Knives – http://www.discountknives.com/

E

Edge Pro Sharpeners – http://www.gorge.net/business/edgepro
Excalibur Cutlery – http://www.excaliburcutlery.com/
Exquisite Knives – http://www.exquisiteknives.com
Extremely Sharp – http://www.extremely-sharp.com/

G

Grand Prairie Knives – http://www.gpknives.com

I

IMS-Plus – http://www.imsplus.com/
Imperial Weapons – http://www.imperialweapons.com

K

KnifeArt.com – http://knifeart.com/
KnifeCenter of the Internet – http://www.knifecenter.com
Knife Outlet – http://www.knifeoutlet.com/
Knife Ware – http://www.knifeware.com
The Knife Professional – http://www.knifepro.com/
Knife Shop – http://www.knifeshop.com/

M

Maxon Systems – http://www.maxonsystems.com/

N

New Graham Knives – http://www.newgraham.com

O

One Stop Knife Shop – http://www.onestopknifeshop.com/
Oso Grande Knife & Tool – http://www.osograndeknives.com

P

Paragon Sports – http://www.paragonsports.com
Pete's Tactical – http://www.petestacticalknives.com
Phil's Fine Cutlery – http://www.philfine.com/
Phoenix Blades – http://www.phoenixblades.com
Pioneer Valley Knife & Tool – http://www.pvknife.com/
Plaza Cutlery – http://www.plazacutlery.com/
Premium Knives – http://www.premiumknives.com/

R

RayJay Knives – http://www.rayjayknives.com

Robertson's Custom Cutlery – http://www.robertsoncustomcutlery.com/
RP Sports – http://www.networksplus.net/rpsports/

S

Safe & Knife Company – http://www.safe-knife.com/
Santa Fe Stoneworks – http://www.santafestoneworks.com/
Sharper Things – http://www.sharperthings.com
Sharpknives.com – http://www.sharpknives.com/
Skylands Cutlery – http://www.skylandscutlery.com/
Smokey Mountain Knife Works – http://www.eknifeworks.com
Stidham's Knives – http://www.kmg.org/stidham/index.html
Straight River Knife Inc – http://www.srknife.com/

T

Tool Shop – http://www.tool-shop.com/
Top of Texas Knives – http://www.toptexknives.com/
Triple Aught Design – http://www.tripleaughtdesign.com/
True North Knives – http://www.truenorthknives.com

W

Wolf Den Knives – http://www.wolfdenknives.com

Y

Yukon Bay – http://www.yukonbay.com

KNIFE CARE & ACCESSORIES

A

Adam Unlimited – http://www.adamunlimited.com

B

Buck Knives – http://www.buckknives.com/

C

Cera Hone – http://www.cerahone.com
Chef's Choice Sharpeners – http://www.chefschoice.com/

D

Diamond Machining Technology (DMT) – http://www.dmtsharp.com/

E

Edge Craft – See Chef's Choice Sharpeners
Edge Maker – http://www.edgemaker.com/
Edge Pro Sharpeners – http://www.gorge.net/business/edgepro
EZE-Lap Diamond Products – http://www.eze-lap.com/

F

Flitz Metal Polish – http://www.flitz.com/

G

GATCO Sharpeners– http://www.timberlineknives.com

L

Lansky Sharpeners- http://www.lansky.com/

M

Meyerco USA – http://www.meyercousa.com/
Mission Knives & Tools – http://www.missionknives.com/

N

Normark – http://www.normark.com

R

Razor Edge Systems – http://www.razoredgesystems.com/

S

Sentry Solutions – http://www.sentrysolutions.com/
Smith Abrasives – http://www.smithabrasives.com/
Spyderco, Inc. – http://www.spyderco.com

T

Tomway, LLC – http://www.tomway.com
Tru Hone – http://www.truhone.com/

Commercial Knife Manufacturers and Distributors

(Companies that manufacture or are the primary importer of a knife brand)

A.G. Russell Knives Inc.

1920 N. 26th Street
Lowell, AR 72745
(800) 255-9034
(479) 631-0130
Fax: (479) 631-8493
www.agrussell.com
E-mail: ag@agrussell.com

Styles: Fixed blade and folding knives for hunting, camping and general use.

Sheaths: Leather and fiberglass-reinforced nylon.

Handles: Black pearl, mother of pearl, white bone, India stag, stainless steel, quince burl, carbon fiber, black Micarta® and fiberglass-reinforced nylon.

Features: Traditional designs with high-grade steel blades. Deer Hunter and Bird & Trout models feature extremely thin AUS 8A steel blades for precision cutting.

Retail prices: $29.95 to $225.00

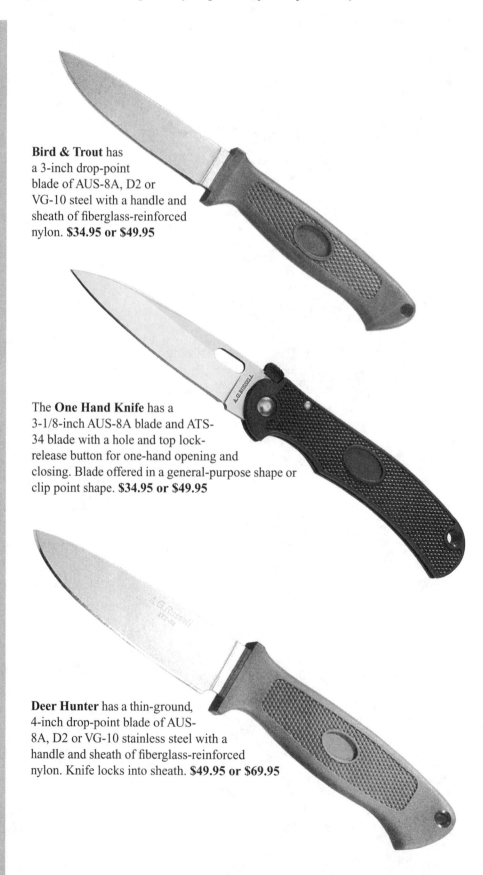

Bird & Trout has a 3-inch drop-point blade of AUS-8A, D2 or VG-10 steel with a handle and sheath of fiberglass-reinforced nylon. **$34.95 or $49.95**

The **One Hand Knife** has a 3-1/8-inch AUS-8A blade and ATS-34 blade with a hole and top lock-release button for one-hand opening and closing. Blade offered in a general-purpose shape or clip point shape. **$34.95 or $49.95**

Deer Hunter has a thin-ground, 4-inch drop-point blade of AUS-8A, D2 or VG-10 stainless steel with a handle and sheath of fiberglass-reinforced nylon. Knife locks into sheath. **$49.95 or $69.95**

Woodswalker is a lightweight non-folding pocketknife with a 2-1/4-inch blade of 8A stainless steel. The knife, which measures 6 inches and weighs 1.2 ounces, is now available with Kydex neck sheath or the original leather hip pocket sheath. **$19.95 and $24.95**

The **Drop Point Hunter** has a 4-inch ATS-34 blade of basic Loveless drop point design, deeply hollow ground. The knife, with an overall length of 8-1/8 inches and weight of 4-1/2 ounces, features a quince burl handle and includes a leather sheath. **$165.00**

A.G. Russell's **Premium Scout Knife** features a 2-3/4-inch 154CM high carbon stainless blade, a leather punch, bottle opener/screwdriver and can opener. The 3.8 ounce knife includes nickel silver bolsters. **$94.95**

Al Mar Knives Inc.

P.O. Box 2295
Tualatin, OR 97062
(503) 670-9080
Fax: (503) 639-4789
www.almarknives.com
E-mail: info@almarknives

Styles: Folding knives for tactical and general use.

Sheaths: N/A.

Handles: Micarta®, aluminum and G-10.

Features: All models have pocket clips; most have thumb studs for one-hand opening.

Retail Prices: $87.00 to $270.00

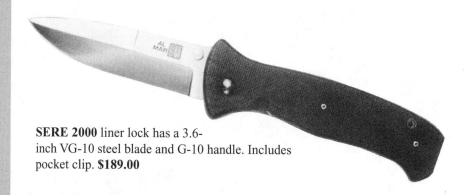

SERE 2000 liner lock has a 3.6-inch VG-10 steel blade and G-10 handle. Includes pocket clip. **$189.00**

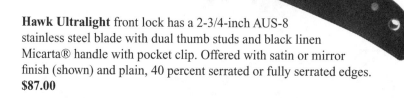

Hawk Ultralight front lock has a 2-3/4-inch AUS-8 stainless steel blade with dual thumb studs and black linen Micarta® handle with pocket clip. Offered with satin or mirror finish (shown) and plain, 40 percent serrated or fully serrated edges. **$87.00**

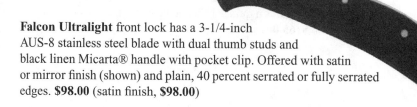

Falcon Ultralight front lock has a 3-1/4-inch AUS-8 stainless steel blade with dual thumb studs and black linen Micarta® handle with pocket clip. Offered with satin or mirror finish (shown) and plain, 40 percent serrated or fully serrated edges. **$98.00** (satin finish, **$98.00**)

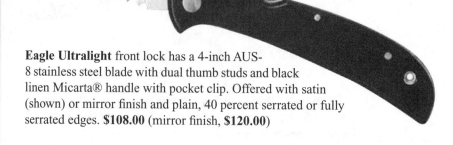

Eagle Ultralight front lock has a 4-inch AUS-8 stainless steel blade with dual thumb studs and black linen Micarta® handle with pocket clip. Offered with satin (shown) or mirror finish and plain, 40 percent serrated or fully serrated edges. **$108.00** (mirror finish, **$120.00**)

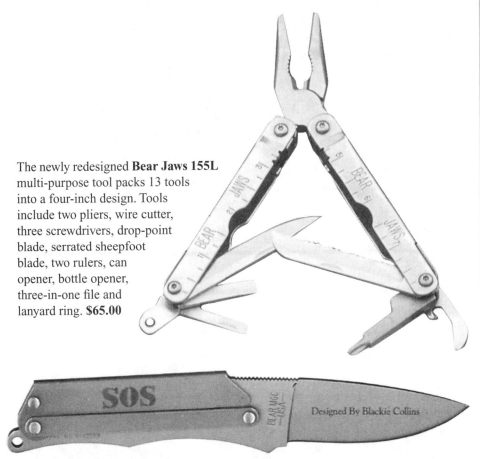

The newly redesigned **Bear Jaws 155L** multi-purpose tool packs 13 tools into a four-inch design. Tools include two pliers, wire cutter, three screwdrivers, drop-point blade, serrated sheepfoot blade, two rulers, can opener, bottle opener, three-in-one file and lanyard ring. **$65.00**

The Bear **S.O.S** survival knife was designed by Blackie Collins with a two-piece folding handle and stainless steel blade. The pocket-sized folder features built-in hex wrenches with English sizes of 1/2-inch, 7/16-inch, 3/8-inch and 11/22-inch. The handles are marked "S.O.S." and the blade has the words "Designed By Blackie Collins." **$39.99**

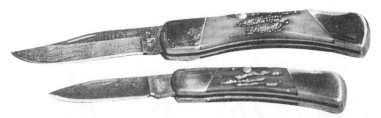

Eight lockback knives are included in the **Damascus Steel** collection, with folding blades of 3 inches to 3-3/4-inches. They feature oversized brass liners and hand-polished nickel silver bolsters with India stag-horn or mother of pearl handles and quality sheaths. **$90.00 and $150.00**. Damascus blades are available in limited quantities.

Bear MGC Cutlery

**1111 Bear Blvd.
Jacksonville, AL 36265
(800) 844-3034
or (256) 435-2227
Fax: (256) 435-9348
Web site: N/A
E-mail: N/A**

Styles: Fixed blade and folding models and multi-tools for hunting, fishing, camping and general use.

Sheaths: Leather and ballistic nylon.

Handles: India stag horn, Kraton™, oak, cocobolo, Zytel®, laminated zebra wood, mother of pearl, Micarta®, metal alloy and stainless steel.

Features: Many models offered with damascus steel blades; some models with gut hooks and saw blades; several models of butterfly knives.

Retail Prices: $23.00 to $455.00

A camping set is among several models of the of the 742 **Switch-A-Blade System**. This model features a handle with drop point and serrated blades as well as a can operner, fork and spoon, fillet blade, saw, master blade and gut hook, along with a camp roll for storage. **$35.99 to $89.99**

Benchmade Knife Co.

300 Beavercreek Road
Oregon City, OR 97045
(503) 655-6004
Fax: (503) 655-6223
www.benchmade.com
E-mail:
info@benchmade.com

Styles: Fixed blade and folding knives for hunting, rescue and tactical uses.

Sheaths: Kydex® and ballistic nylon.

Handles: Aluminum, G10, carbon fiber, stainless steel, rosewood/carbon fiber, titanium and Zytel®.

Features: Numerous collaborations with custom knifemakers Mel Pardue, Allen Elishewitz, Bill McHenry, Jason Williams, Warren Osborne and Robert Terzuola. Some models feature AXIS locking system, partially serrated blades, pocket clips, boron carbide or BT2® coatings and multi-colored or camouflage handles.

Retail Prices: $55.00 to $230.00

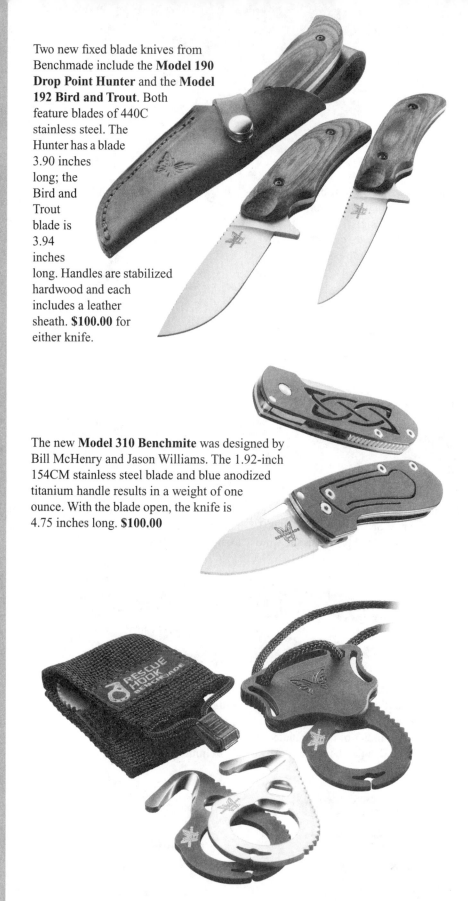

Two new fixed blade knives from Benchmade include the **Model 190 Drop Point Hunter** and the **Model 192 Bird and Trout**. Both feature blades of 440C stainless steel. The Hunter has a blade 3.90 inches long; the Bird and Trout blade is 3.94 inches long. Handles are stabilized hardwood and each includes a leather sheath. **$100.00** for either knife.

The new **Model 310 Benchmite** was designed by Bill McHenry and Jason Williams. The 1.92-inch 154CM stainless steel blade and blue anodized titanium handle results in a weight of one ounce. With the blade open, the knife is 4.75 inches long. **$100.00**

Model 5 Rescue Hook design incorporates an oxygen valve wrench for EMT use, a finger hole bottle opener and a lanyard hole. The 420HC stainless steel tool is 2.90 inches long and weighs 0.60-ounce. Blade finish choices are black oxide or satin. Nylon pouch sheath or hard Delrin neck sheath are optional. **$25.00 with soft sheath. $35.00 with hard molded snap sheath.**

Model 551 Griptilian has a 3.45-inch blade of 440C stainless steel with plain or ComboEdge partly serrated blade. Handle material is molded black or olive GTX. The carry clip is reversible. **$95.00 to $115.00**. **Model 556 Mini-Griptilian** has a 2.91-inch blade of 440C stainless steel and Velox handle material. The carry clip is reversible. **$85.00 or $95.00**

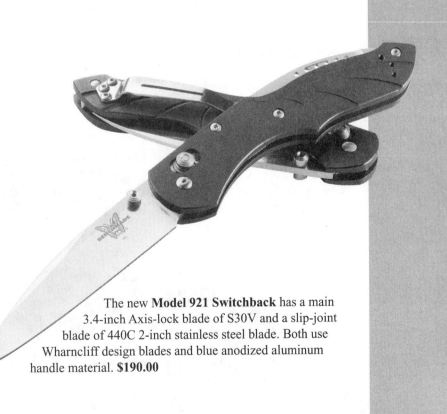

The new **Model 921 Switchback** has a main 3.4-inch Axis-lock blade of S30V and a slip-joint blade of 440C 2-inch stainless steel blade. Both use Wharncliff design blades and blue anodized aluminum handle material. **$190.00**

Beretta USA Corp.

17601 Beretta Dr.
Accokeek, MD 20607
(301) 283-2191
Fax: (301) 283-0189
Web site: www.beretta.com
E-mail:
wrice@berettausa.com

Styles: Tactical and multi-blade folders; fixed-blade hunting knives.

Sheaths: Tooled leather.

Handles: Camo or orange Zytel, black or brushed aluminum, stainless steel, black or green Micarta®, carbon fiber, cocobolo and stag.

Features: Most folders feature thumb stud on blade for one-hand opening and handle clip. Some Airlight models feature skeletonized blades. Blades offered in straight-edge or 30 percent serrated versions. Italian multi-use models include two- or four-blade versions with main blade, saw blade with screwdriver tip, skinning blade and fold-out corkscrew.

Retail Prices: **$49.95 to $469.95**

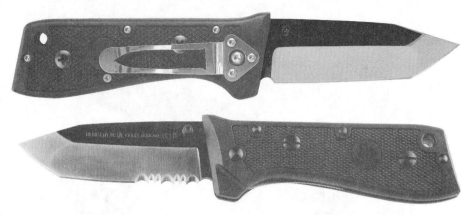

Model 92/Model 92 serrated feature one-hand operation of AUS-8 steel 3-1/2-inch tanto-style blade in VG-10 carbon fiber handle material. **$99.00**

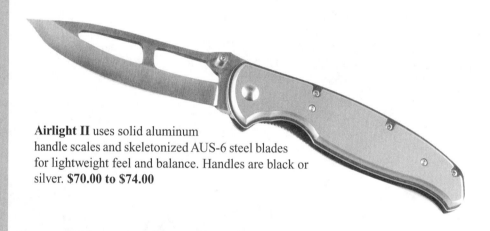

Airlight II uses solid aluminum handle scales and skeletonized AUS-6 steel blades for lightweight feel and balance. Handles are black or silver. **$70.00 to $74.00**

Beretta teamed with Bob Loveless to create the **Loveless Fixed Blade** knives using AUS-8 steel 8-inch blades with Zytel or figured quince handles. A leather sheath is included. **$66.00 to $198.00**

Fieldlight and Stag Folders feature AUS-8 steel blades in various shapes and configurations, single, double or triple. Four Fieldlight models have Zytel handles while the two Stag models feasture stag scales. All include nylon sheaths. **$50.00 to $110.00**

The new **Trident Cocobolo** joins **Trident G-10** with 2-3/4-inch Wharncliffe shape blades for slim pocket knives. **$110.00**

Boker USA Inc.

1550 Balsam St.
Lakewood, CO 80215-3117
(303) 462-0662
Fax: (303) 462-0668
www.BokerUSA.com
E-mail:
sales@bokerusa.com

Styles: Wide range of fixed blade and folding knives for hunting, military, tactical and general use.

Sheaths: Leather and Cordura nylon.

Handles: Sambar stag, rosewood, bone, mother of pearl, cocobolo, titanium, stainless steel, Zytel? and Delrin.

Features: Distributor for Boker, Klötzli and Opinel knives. Blade materials include carbon steel, 440C stainless steel, damascus steel, titanium and ceramic. Some models have interchangeable blades. Collaborations with Michael Walker, Walter Brend, the late Col. Rex Applegate and others. Many models with decorative handles, faux scrimshaw or etched blades. Some limited editions.

Retail Prices: $7.95 to $485.00

The **Boker Bowie** has a 7-3/4-inch blade that's one-fourth inch thick and features a full tang. European walnut handle with lanyard hole meets an "S" style brass guard. With leather sheath. $295.00

Model 2076 liner lock designed by Michael Walker has a 2-7/8-inch ATS-34 blade and cocobolo handle. **$115.00**

A-F 543DES Desert Storm is based on the original Applegate-Fairbairn A-F 12 fighting knife, with a 6-inch 440C stainless steel blade, forward-bending cross-guard and weighted Delrin® handle. Includes Kydex® sheath with desert camo finish. **$170.00**

Model 585AM is designed by U. Look of Germany, features 4-5/8-inch drop-point blade of 440C stainless steel, integral guard and pommel. Handle of Amboina wood. Includes leather sheath. **$350.00**

Opinel line imported from France by Boker includes this model with a 6-1/4-inch overall length (closed) and unique turning-ring design that locks the blade. All 12 models feature carbon-steel locking blades and pearwood or walnut handle. **$5.95 to $15.95**

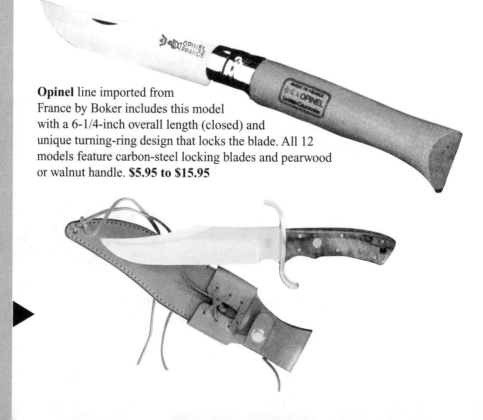

Lightweight Midlock Folder has hand-ground dendritic cobalt blade for high performance and no rust from seawater. Handle is glass filled nylon. **Price unavailable.**

Sunburst lockback folder has Boye dendritic cobalt blade for boating and general use. **$139.00**

Boye Knives

P.O. Box 1238
Dolan Springs, AZ 86441
(800) 853-1617
or (928) 767-4273
Fax: (928) 767-3030
www.boyeknives.com
E-mail:
info@boyeknives.com

Styles: Semi-production fixed-blade and folding knives for hunting and general use.

Sheaths: N/A

Handles: Ironwood, other hardwoods and glass filled nylon.

Features: Lightweight midlock folders for marine and general use.

Retail Prices: N/A

Browning

One Browning Place
Morgan, UT 84050-9326
(800) 333-3288
Fax: N/A
www.browning.com
E-mail: N/A

Styles: Fixed blade and folding hunting, fishing, camping and general-use knives.

Sheaths: Leather, nylon or Concealex®.

Handles: G-10 composite, carbon fiber, Zytel®, Zytel® with laminated-wood inserts, Zytel®/Kevlar® with checkered rubber, rosewood, cocobolo, quince, stag and mother of pearl.

Features: High-carbon, AUS-8A or ATS-34 blades.

Retail Prices: $25.00 to $152.00

Ice Storm is a brightly colored lightweight folder with VG-10 3-1/2-inch stainless steel blade and aluminum handle. Handle color choices are red, blue or green. **$79.95**

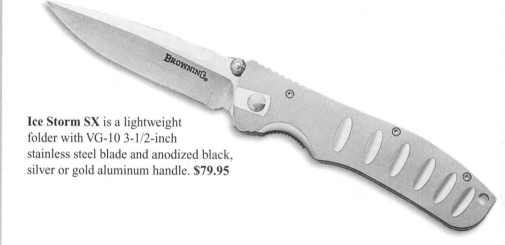

Ice Storm SX is a lightweight folder with VG-10 3-1/2-inch stainless steel blade and anodized black, silver or gold aluminum handle. **$79.95**

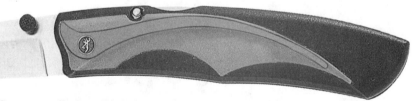

New **Sporter** series have 3-1/2-inch blades of AUS-8A stinless steel with one-hand operation and Zytel handle with colored rubber inlays. **$39.95**

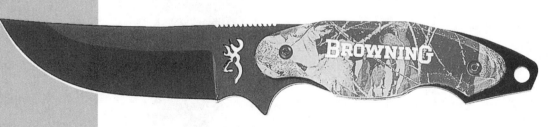

Buck Mark Silhouette is a full-tang fixed blade knive with 4-inch C-type stainless steel blade and camouflage handle. A Ballistic nylon sheath is included. **$95.00**

New **Coltar Bay** knives have blades of AUS-8A stainless steel with bead-blasted finish. Small Skinner with 2-3/4-inch blade, **$65.00**. Large Skinner with 3-3/4-inch blade, **$95.00**. Drop Point Skinner, **$115.00**

New **Extreme Field Dressing Tools** all feature 440C stainless steel blades secured by titanium locking liners for one-hand operation. Model 690, has 3-1/2-inch drop point blade and pocket clip, **$90.00**. Model 691 has 3-1/2-inch drop point blade with guthook and saw, **$115.00**. Model 692 has 3-1/2-inch drop point blade with guthook, saw and contoured drop point blade, **$130.00**.

Buck Knives

P.O. Box 1267
El Cajon, CA 92020
(800) 326-2825
Fax: (800) 729-2825
www.buckknives.com
E-mail: N/A

Styles: Wide range of fixed-blade and folding knives and multi-tools for hunting, fishing, camping and general use.

Sheaths: Leather, plastic, nylon and Kydex®.

Handles: Thermoplastic, G10, stainless steel, nylon /rubber, nylon, resin-impregnated Obechee wood, glass-reinforced nylon with rubber, Kraton™, aluminum, Zytel®, cocobolo, phenolic, hardwood, rosewood, cast resin Poly-Pearl and bonded malachite stone inlay.

Features: Ionfusion™ zirconium nitride coating on some blades provides a hard, long-lasting edge; some limited editions with laser-cut blades featuring elk or deer figures; full-color artwork on some handles; damascus-blade dagger; Crosslock® two-bladed knives with one-hand opening and closing design; many folders feature pocket clips and holes or studs in the blade for one-hand opening.

Retail Prices: $26.00 to $230.00

Strider™ Solution designed with Mick Strider and Duane Dwyer has a 4-1/4-inch ATS-34 stainless steel drop point blade, G-10 handle and Cordura sheath. **$230.00**

Buck's Alpha Hunter series includes both fixed blades and folding-blade models with a locking liner. The 4-1/4-inch drop-point blade is available with or without an inset gutting/skinning hook on the top edge. Steel for the wood-handle Alpha Hunter is ATS-34 and for the rubber-handle model it's 420HC stainless steel. Wood models come with a leather sheath and rubber models come with a Cordura sheath. **$70.00 to $124.00**

Vanguard® has a 4-1/8-inch drop-point 420 HC stainless steel blade with woodgrain handle, polished brass butt and handguard and leather sheath. **$92.00** (woodgrain handle). **$77.00** (rubber handle).

Mountaineer Peter Whittaker/Buck collaboration designed the **Approach**, which features one-hand operation of the 3-1/8-inch drop point, partially serrated blade. Large lanyard hole accommodates a carabiner. Available in black, blue, purple, lime green and burnt orange. **$50.00** (Approach) **$45.00** (Short Approach).

Metro is another Buck/Whittaker knife with locking 1-1/8-inch drop point blade with one-hand operation, bottle cap and can opener. Available in blue, purple, burnt orange, lime green or black. **$21.00**

Bird and Trout Skinner has a four-color etching of a Parker shotgun on the blade, stag handle. It was made for the Parker Gun Collectors Association. Includes leather sheath. **$55.00**

Clip-point Skinner has a 5-1/2-inch blade and a hardwood handle. Includes leather sheath. **$124.95**

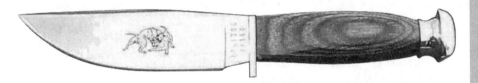

Upswept Skinner has a 4-3/4-inch blade and hardwood handle. Includes leather sheath. **$119.95**

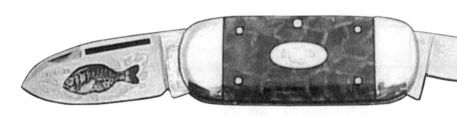

Baby Sunfish features a seven-color etching on the blade, "broken chain" celluloid handle. Overall length 3 inches (closed). Also offered in blue sapphire, India stag horn, oyster shell and pearl handles. **$99.99**

Double Doghead has a 4-inch, etched blade and India stag horn handle. Includes leather sheath. **$29.99**

Bulldog Brand Knives

P.O. Box 23852
Chattanooga, TN 37422
(423) 894-5102
Fax: (423) 892-9165
Web site: N/A
E-mail:
bbknives@bellsouth.net

Styles: Fixed-blade and folding knives for hunting and general use.

Sheaths: Leather.

Handles: Stag, hardwood, celluloid, other materials.

Features: Primarily traditional-design fixed-blade knives. Many blades have wildlife or other designs etched on them.

Retail Prices: $15.95 to $124.95

Busse Combat Knife Co.

11651 County Road 12
Wauseon, OH 43567
(419) 923-6471
Fax: (419) 923-2337
www.combatknives.com
E-mail:
info@bussecombat.com

Styles: Military-style fixed-blade knives and machetes.

Sheaths: Kydex®.

Handles: Canvas Micarta®, Resiprene C or skeletonized steel.

Features: Semi-production handmade.

Retail Prices: **$150.00 to $347.00**

Assault Shaker™ has a 2-1/2-inch blade of INFI™ steel and overall length of 5-1/2 inches, with ergonomic skeleton handle of INFI steel. **$117.00**

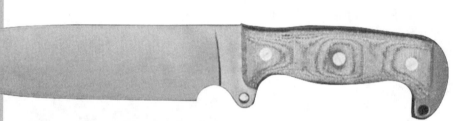

Steel Heart E™ has a 7-1/2-inch blade of INFI™ steel and a canvas Micarta® handle. Includes Kydex® sheath. **$297.00**

Battle Mistress™ has a 9-1/2-inch blade of INFI™ steel and a canvas Micarta® handle. Includes Kydex® sheath. **$347.00**

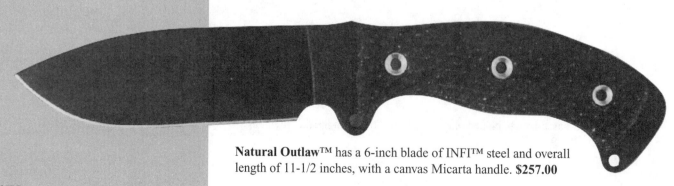

Natural Outlaw™ has a 6-inch blade of INFI™ steel and overall length of 11-1/2 inches, with a canvas Micarta handle. **$257.00**

Muela Rebeco Drop-Point Hunter
has a 3-1/2-inch moly-vanadium-
stainless steel blade and a hardwood handle.
Includes leather sheath. **$57.00**

Muela Small Game Knife has a 4-3/8-inch
moly-vanadium-stainless steel blade and a crown
stag handle. Includes leather sheath. **$41.00**

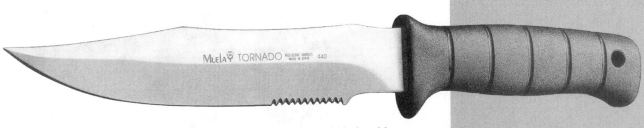

Muela Tornado has a 7-1/8-inch moly-vanadium-stainless steel blade with
partially saw-toothed edge and a synthetic handle. Includes nylon sheath. Also
offered in a black-coated blade. **$61.00**

CAS Iberia Inc.

650 Industrial Blvd.
Sale Creek, TN 37373
(423) 332-4700
Fax: (423) 332-7248
www.casiberia.com
E-mail: N/A

Styles: Extensive variety
of fixed-blade and folding
knives for hunting, diving,
camping, military and general
use.

Sheaths: Leather and nylon.

Handles: Thermoplastic,
stag, various hardwoods,
laminated wood and steel.

Features: Aitor and
Muela
knife lines made in Spain.

**Retail Prices: $5.00 to
$1,042.00**

Camillus Cutlery Co.

54 Main St.
Camillus, NY 13031
(315) 672-8111
Fax: (315) 672-8832
www.camillusknives.com
E-mail: camcut2@aol.com

Styles: Wide variety of pocketknives for hunting and general use.

Sheaths: Nylon, Kydex® and leather.

Handles: Laminated wood, Kraton™, Delrin®, Zytel®, stainless steel, leather, Valox®, circuit board, celluloid abalone and Micarta®.

Features: Sells Camillus, Western, Becker Knife & Tool and Cuda® brands.

Retail Prices: $10.95 to $199.95

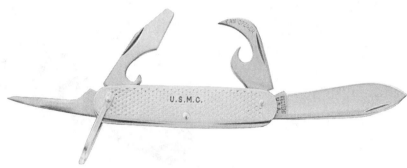

Marine Corps Camp Knife is approved by the U.S. military and built to government specifications. High-carbon stainless steel blade is 2-3/8 inches. Also has a can opener, punch, screwdriver and cap lifter. Stainless steel handle, springs and shackle. **$19.49**

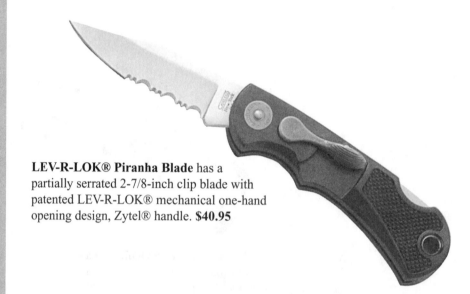

LEV-R-LOK® Piranha Blade has a partially serrated 2-7/8-inch clip blade with patented LEV-R-LOK® mechanical one-hand opening design, Zytel® handle. **$40.95**

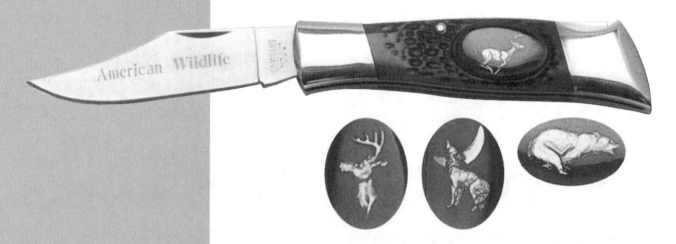

American Wildlife Series lockbacks have 3-1/8-inch high-carbon stainless steel clip blades with brown jigged Delrin® handles and a choice of running deer (shown), howling coyote, buck deer or charging bear gold-plated medallions in the handle. Includes leather sheath. Also offered in a two-blade trapper model. **$61.95**

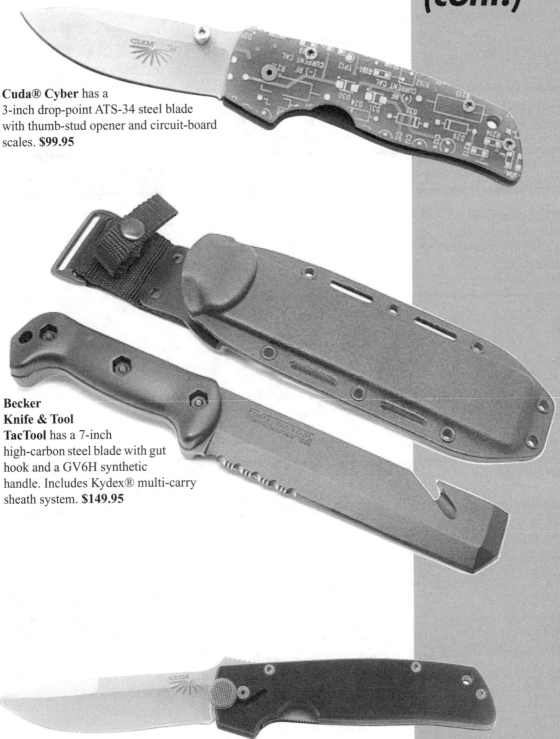

Cuda® Cyber has a 3-inch drop-point ATS-34 steel blade with thumb-stud opener and circuit-board scales. **$99.95**

Becker Knife & Tool TacTool has a 7-inch high-carbon steel blade with gut hook and a GV6H synthetic handle. Includes Kydex® multi-carry sheath system. **$149.95**

Cuda® Quik-Action Spear Blade has a 3-31/32-inch ATS-34 spear blade with bead-blasted finish that opens from its G-10 handle with the forward push of a button. Includes pocket clip. Cuda® models offered in a variety of blade lengths and points, as well as titanium nitride coating. **$169.95**

Case, W.R. & Sons Cutlery Co.

Owens Way
Bradford, PA 16701
(800) 523-6350
or (814) 368-4123
Fax: (814) 368-1736
www.wrcase.com
E-mail:
consumer-relations@
wrcase.com

Styles: Vast variety of fixed-blade knives and pocketknives (including limited editions) for hunting, camping, general use and collecting.

Sheaths: Leather.

Handles: Rosewood, amber bone, red bone, black bone, cranberry bone, vintage bone, natural bone, Staminawood™, leather, mother of pearl, plastic, Pakkawood, stainless steel and Zytel®.

Features: Some models feature RussLock™ one-hand opening mechanisms, multiple blades, exchangeable blades and nickel-silver Case logo imbedded in handle.

Retail Prices:
$17.50 to $249.30

Fixed Blade Hunter Model 321 has a mirror-polished 5-inch blade and a polished leather handle. Includes leather sheath. **$79.00**

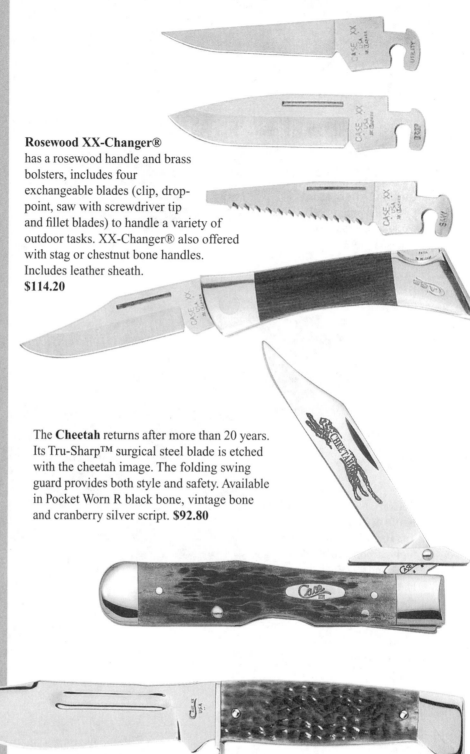

Rosewood XX-Changer® has a rosewood handle and brass bolsters, includes four exchangeable blades (clip, drop-point, saw with screwdriver tip and fillet blades) to handle a variety of outdoor tasks. XX-Changer® also offered with stag or chestnut bone handles. Includes leather sheath. **$114.20**

The **Cheetah** returns after more than 20 years. Its Tru-Sharp™ surgical steel blade is etched with the cheetah image. The folding swing guard provides both style and safety. Available in Pocket Worn R black bone, vintage bone and cranberry silver script. **$92.80**

Slab Side Hunter Model
370 has a 5-inch surgical steel blade and a chestnut bone handle. Includes leather sheath. Slab Side Hunters also offered with a 3-1/2-inch blade and stag or rosewood handles. **$107.10**

The **Mini Trapper with Golf Tool** is an enhanced version of its Mini-Trapper pocketknife. It includes a divot tool for golfers and a standard clip blade. Both blade and tool are made of Tru-Sharp™ surgical steel. Amber bone handle. **$56.80**

The **Seahorse Whittler** has a heavy-gauge Wharncliff blade for tough cutting and coping and pen blades for detailing. Available in mother of pearl, vintage bone or autumn bone small silver script. **$269.30**

The famous **Case Hobo** now featured a spoon in addition to the knife and fork. When opened the handle easily separates into three individual pieces: a clip blade, fork with bottle opener and a spoon. Slide the handle together and it folds up like a standard Trapper. Amber bone handle. **$99.50**

Chris Reeve Knives

11624 W. President Drive
No. B
Boise, ID 83713
(208) 375-0367
Fax: (208) 375-0368
www.chrisreeve.com
E-mail:
crkinfo@chrisreeve.com

Styles: Semi-custom fixed-blade military, survival, hunting and skinning knives and high-tech locking folders.

Sheaths: Leather and Cordura nylon.

Handles: A2 steel, titanium, canvas Micarta®.

Features: Fixed-blade knives of one-piece design; integral-lock folders use a slotted titanium handle scale that serves to lock the blade.

Retail Prices: $185.00 to $800.00

Project I and Project II have 7-1/2-inch blades with spear-point and clip-point blades, respectively, of A2 tool steel with integral handles that are hollow for storage. Nylon stud on supplied leather sheath prevents the knife from falling out. **$315.00**

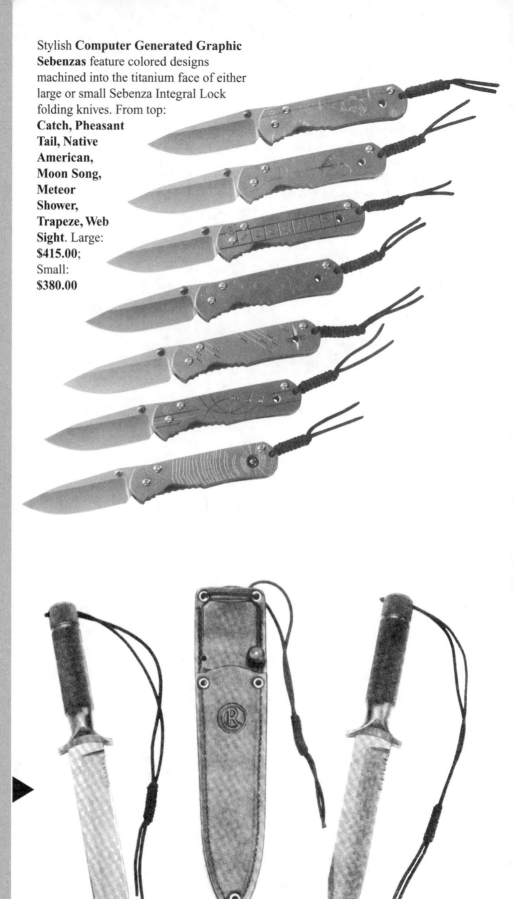

Stylish **Computer Generated Graphic Sebenzas** feature colored designs machined into the titanium face of either large or small Sebenza Integral Lock folding knives. From top: **Catch, Pheasant Tail, Native American, Moon Song, Meteor Shower, Trapeze, Web Sight**. Large: **$415.00**; Small: **$380.00**

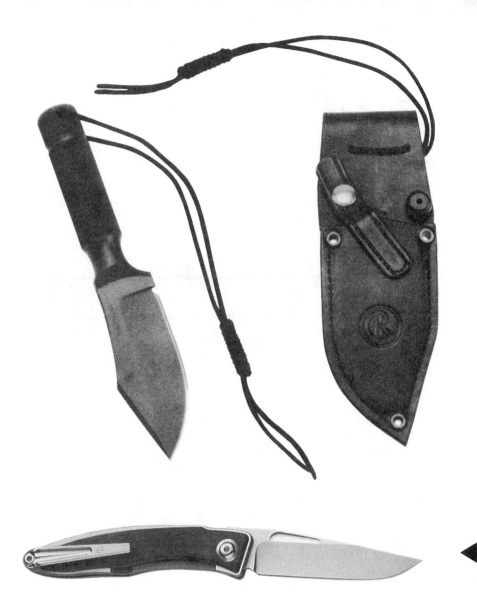

Skinner (Ubejane) is made of a single billet of A2 tool steel with no joint between handle and blade (as are all Chris Reeve fixed- blade models). Blade is 4-1/2 inches, hollow handle with threaded cap for storage. Includes leather sheath. **$265.00**

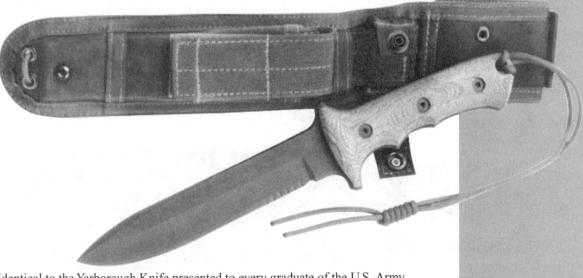

The **Mnandi** is an elegant and functional pocket knife, from the Zulu word meaning "very nice." The 2-3/4-inch blade of S30V stainless steel has titanium handles inlaid front and back with selected hardwoods and an Integral Lock mechanism. Its pocket clip can be placed on either side of the blade or removed. **$305.00**

Identical to the Yarborough Knife presented to every graduate of the U.S. Army Special Forces Qualification course, the **Green Beret Knife** is available to civilian market. Full tang, 7-inch blade workhorse made of CPM S30V steel with gray canvas Micarta handle. **$299.00**

Coast Cutlery

2045 SE Ankeny St.
Portland, OR 97214
(800) 426-5858
or (503) 234-4545
Fax: (503) 234-4422
www.coastcutlery.com
e-mail:
nancy@coastcutlery.com

Styles: Variety of fixed-blade and folding knives and multi-tools for hunting, camping and general use.

Sheaths: Leather and nylon.

Handles: Hardwoods, stag, mother of pearl, plastic and steel.

Features: Exclusive distributor for Puma knives.

Retail Prices: $35.00 to $190.00

Coast's **Ultimate Pocket Tool** has 15 functions, including main blade with partial serration, saw blade, scissors, screwdriver tips, file, cap lifter with wire stripper, toothpick and tweezers, key ring, punch tool, Phillips screwdriver and butane lighter. **$29.95**

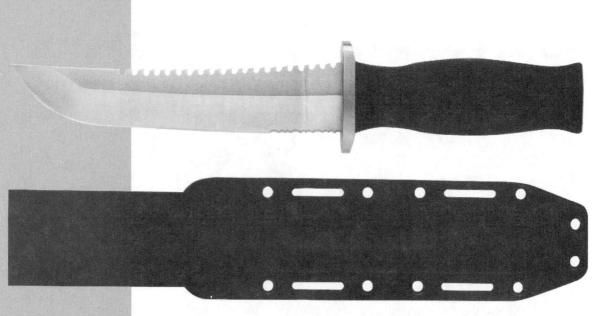

Coast's **Raptor** military tactical knife has a 6-inch 440C stainless steel blade with a saw back and triple-ground serrations. The carbide tip on the textured Krayton handle can break plexiglass, plastic or glass. Kydex molded sheath. **$59.95**

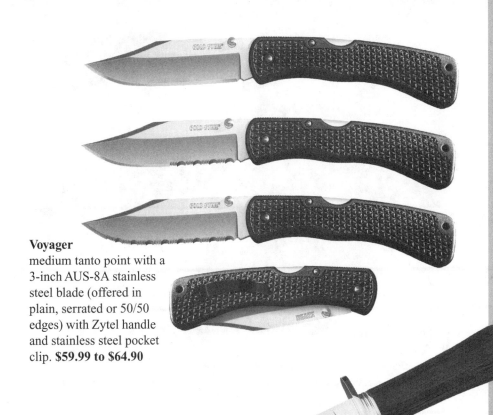

Voyager medium tanto point with a 3-inch AUS-8A stainless steel blade (offered in plain, serrated or 50/50 edges) with Zytel handle and stainless steel pocket clip. **$59.99 to $64.90**

Cold Steel Inc.

3036-A Seaborg Ave.
Ventura, CA 93003
(800) 255-4716 or
(805) 650-8481
Fax: (805) 642-9727
www.coldsteel.com
E-mail:
russell@coldsteel.com

Styles: Wide variety of folding lockbacks and fixed-blade hunting, fishing and neck knives, as well as bowies, kukris, tantos, throwing knives and kitchen knives.

Sheaths: Concealex® (plastic), polycarbonate, Cordura nylon and leather.

Handles: Zytel®, Kraton™, aluminum and steel.

Features: Extremely strong blades, many featuring the company's trademark tanto point. Blade steels include Carbon V (a high-carbon, low-alloy steel), AUS stainless, 5150 or San Mai III, a three-layered, laminated construction. Many collaborations with custom knifemakers.

Retail Prices: $24.99 to $799.99

Laredo Bowie is described as awesome, and it seems to be with its 10-1/2-inch Carbon V stainless steel blade and faux cocobolo handle. The knife is almost 16 inches long overall, weighing 16.3 ounces. A brown leather belt sheath is included. **$399.99** with a 10-percent discount for law enforcement, military, firefighters and other emergency personnel.

Bird and Trout knife with 2-1/4-inch Carbon V steel, black epoxy powder-coated blade. Comes with Concealex neck sheath and paracord lanyard. **$24.99**

All Terrain Hunter with 4-1/2-inch Carbon V steel, black epoxy powder-coated blade and Kraton handle. Comes with polycarbonate sheath. **$39.99**

Columbia River Knife & Tool

9720 S.W. Hillman Ct.
Ste. 885
Wilsonville, OR 97070-7712
(800) 891-3100
Fax: (503) 682-9680
www.crkt.com
E-mail: info@crkt.com

Styles: Large variety of fixed-blade and folding knives for hunting, fishing, camping, tactical and general use.

Sheaths: Leather, Zytel® and polypropylene.

Handles: Carbon fiber, zinc alloy, Zytel®, stainless steel, titanium and G-10 fiberglass laminate.

Features: Most folders include thumb studs and pocket clips. Many collaborations with custom knife makers, including Ed Halligan (K.I.S.S. and P.E.C.K. designs), Michael Walker, Steve Ryan, Brian Tighe, Russ Kommer, Gary Paul Johnston, Al Polkowski and others.

Retail Prices: $21.99 to $149.99

Rollock has as 2-1/4-inch blade of AUS-6M stainless steel and one-hand operation with a design by custom knifemaker Allen Elishewitz. Handle choices are black, blue, red, or clear. **$39.99**

Michael Walker **BladeLock 2** features Walker's lock-open, lock-shut mechanism on the 2-3/4-inch AUS-6M stainless steel blade. The folder weighs 3.8 ounces and has handle material of black Zytel®. **$79.99**

Bear Claw has a 2-inch AUS-6M blade with a Zytel® handle and sheath. Offered in straight or serrated edge. **$39.99**

M16 Carbon Fibre has a 2.6-inch ACUTO 440 stainless steel blade and carbon fiber handle, with an overall weight of 1.6 ounces. Offered in straight or partially serrated edge. M16 models also offered with aluminum and Zytel® handles, up to 3.9-inch blades of AUS-8 steel and Carson Flipper speed-openers. **$89.99** (shown)

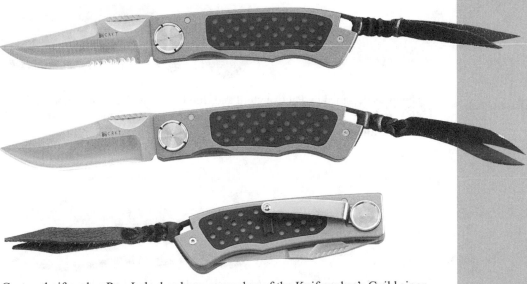

Custom knifemaker Ron Lake has been a member of the Knifemaker's Guild since 1972. **Lake Signature** features the Lake and Walker Knife Safety and interframe Zytel® handle inserts. The AUS-8 stainless steel blade is 3-1/4 inches long. **$99.99**

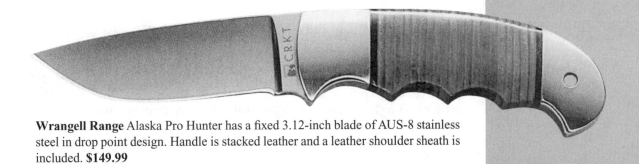

Wrangell Range Alaska Pro Hunter has a fixed 3.12-inch blade of AUS-8 stainless steel in drop point design. Handle is stacked leather and a leather shoulder sheath is included. **$149.99**

Pat Crawford Knives

205 N. Center
West Memphis, AR 72301
(870) 732-2452
www.crawfordknives.com
E-mail:
pat@crawfordknives.com

Styles: Semi-production folding knives for tactical and general use.

Sheaths: N/A

Handles: Stag, ivory, titanium and other materials.

Features: Most models have thumb studs for one-hand opening; some feature damascus steel blades.

Retail Prices: N/A

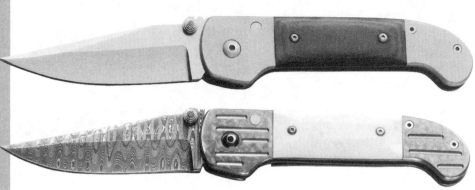

Recon has a 3-1/2-inch satin-finish 154CM steel blade, titanium bolsters and liners with black Micarta handles. **$475.00**. With Mike Norris fancy Damascus pattern blade and file work: **$850.00**

Point Guard Damascus locking liner has a 3-1/2-inch damascus blade with a titanium handle. **Price unavailable.**

Perfigo was designed by Pat Crawford and Bob Kasper with a choice of 4-1/2-inch 154CM or S30V steel blade, satin finish or blasted and a titanium bead-blasted handle. **Price unavailable.**

Point Guard locking liner has a 2-3/4-inch blade of ATS-34 stainless steel and a titanium handle. **Price unavailable.**

Falcon has a bead blast or satin finish with 3-inch or 3-7/8-inch 154cm blade with a handle of micarta, carbon fiber and titanium and a titanium guard and locking liner. It has grooves in micarta for grip, holes to tighten, wheel opener on the blade and a serrated thumb ramp. **$375.00 to $450.00**

Black Hawk Fighter has a 5-inch 154CM steel blade and controued black Micarta® handle. Choice of nylon or Kydex® sheath. **$350.00** Falcon has a bead blast or satin finish with 3-inch or 3-7/8-inch 154cm blade with a handle of micarta, carbon fiber and titanium and a titanium guard and locking liner. It has grooves in Micarta for grip, holes to tighten, wheel opener on the blade and a serrated thumb ramp. **$375.00 to $450.00**

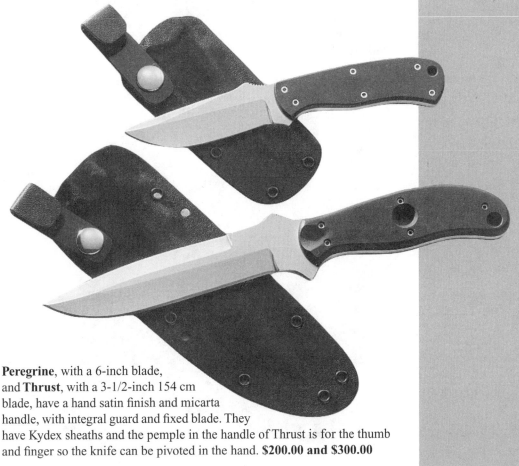

Peregrine, with a 6-inch blade, and **Thrust**, with a 3-1/2-inch 154 cm blade, have a hand satin finish and micarta handle, with integral guard and fixed blade. They have Kydex sheaths and the pemple in the handle of Thrust is for the thumb and finger so the knife can be pivoted in the hand. **$200.00 and $300.00**

Diamond Machining Technology

85 Hayes Memorial Drive
Marlborough, MA
01752-1892
(508) 481-5944
Fax: (508) 485-3924
www.dmtsharp.com
E-mail:
dmtsharp@dmtsharp.com

Styles: Wide range of knife and tool sharpeners all utilizing diamond-surfaced materials.

Features: More than 300 different sharpeners for all knife edges, chisels, scissors, broadheads, in various grits, plain edge or serrated. Products are many times winners of Blade Magazine's Accessory Of The Year Award.

Retail Prices: N/A

Broadhead Sharpener has two diamond whetstones on adjustable stand to sharpen 2, 3 or 4-blade broadheads. **Price unavailable.**

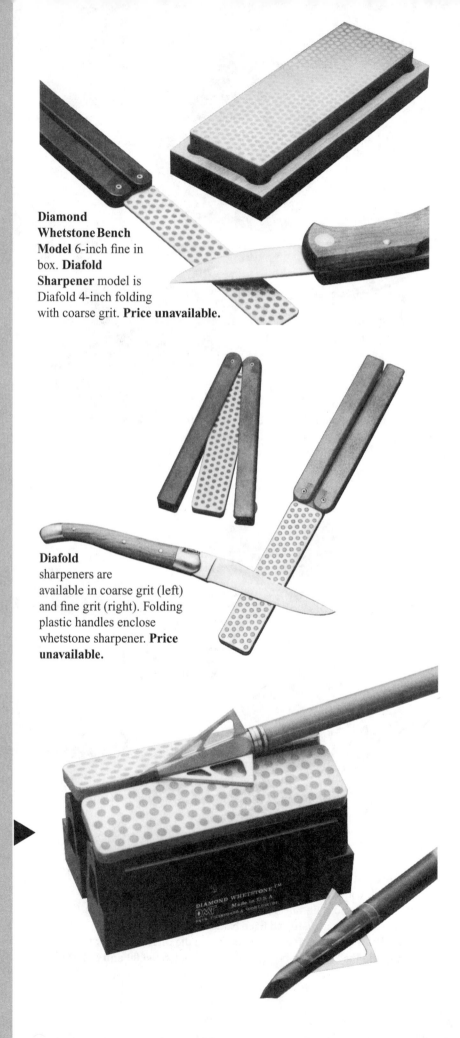

Diamond Whetstone Bench Model 6-inch fine in box. **Diafold Sharpener** model is Diafold 4-inch folding with coarse grit. **Price unavailable.**

Diafold sharpeners are available in coarse grit (left) and fine grit (right). Folding plastic handles enclose whetstone sharpener. **Price unavailable.**

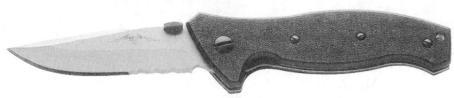

Specwar has a 3-1/2-inch 154 CM steel blade and G-10 epoxy/glass laminate handle. Offered with a tanto or spear point and satin or black finish. **$199.95**

The **Police-Sark** has a 3.6-inch blade of 154 CM steel with titanium and G-10 handle construction. Originally designed for the U.S. Navy, the Police-Sark is also a choice for law enforcement. Features Emerson's patented pocket deployment hook. **$189.95**

La Griffe has a 1-3/4-inch 154 CM blade with integral skeletonized handle. Includes Kydex® sheath and neck cord. **$71.95**

The **Commander** features a 3.7-inch blade of 154 CM steel. The handle is titanium and G-10 epoxy/glass laminate. The hook on the top of the blade is designed to quickly open the knife by catching on a pants pocket. **$219.95**

The **CQC-7** has a 3-1/4-inch blade of 154 CM steel with G-10 and titanium handle construction. The original tactical knife is available in original and mini versions. **$139.95-$169.95**

Fällkniven AB

Havrevagen 10
S-961 42 Boden
Sweden
US distributors:
Blue Ridge Knives
(onestop@
blueridgeknives.com)
Moten (info@moteng.com)
Fax: N/A
www.fallkkniven.com
E-mail: info@fallkniven.se

Styles: Fixed-blade hunting and survival knives.

Sheaths: Oxhide leather and Kydex®.

Handles: Kraton™ and Thermorun.

Features: Exceptionally strong laminated blades of VG10 steel. Ceramic coating available on most models. Two or three sheath choices.

Retail Prices: $79.95 to $178.95

WM1 has a 2-3/4-inch VG10 blade and Thermorun handle. Neck Kydex or leather belt sheath available. **$89.00**

G1 Garm Fighter with 3-1/2-inch VG10 double-edged blade and Thermorun handle. **$120.00**

F1 Pilot Survival knife has a 3.8-inch VG10 steel blade and Thermorun handle. **$104.00**

H1 Hunter's knife is a puukka design with 4-inch VG10 steel blade and Kraton handle. **$152.00**

S1 Forest knife has a 5-1/8-inch VG10 blade and Thermorun handle. Kydex or leather belt sheath available. **$134.00**

A1 Army Survival knife with 6.3-inch VG10 blade and Kraton handle. **$167.00**

Flying Falcon Tru-Line Tactical is 4-1/8 inches overall with a camo or black handle. **$11.50**

Marine Combat knife is 11-3/4 inches overall and includes sheath. **$16.95**

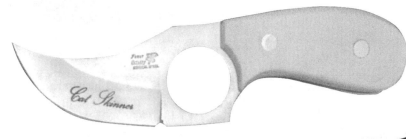

Cat Skinner is 6 inches overall and available with frostwood, smooth bone or wormgroove handle. **$22.95**

Piranha Bowie is 15 inches overall with a wormgroove handle. Includes sheath. **$80.00**

Lil' Handi-Mechanic has 13 functions in a 3-inch, stainless steel package. **$17.95**

Tobacco Congress offers four blades in a 4-1/4-inch package. **$16.95**

Frost Cutlery Co.

6861 Mountain View Road
Ooltewah, TN 37363
(800) 251-7768
or (423) 894-6079
Fax: (423) 894-9576
www.frostcutleryco.com
E-mail: frostcutlery@
mindspring.com

Styles: Wide range of fixed-blade and folding knives with a multitude of handle materials.

Sheaths: N/A

Handles: Bone, mother of pearl, laminated wood, thermoplastic, rubber, stainless steel, synthetic scrimshaw, stag, imitation ivory and numerous colors of celluloid.

Features: Fantasy-style Bowie knives; novelty pocketknives featuring western heroes and Masonic symbols; keychain novelty knives; general-use pocketknives and tactical folders; all-stainless Flying Falcon folders. Most models feature 440 Solingen steel blades, nickel silver bolsters and brass liners.

Retail Prices: **$3.00 to $239.95**

Gerber Legendary Blades — Fiskars

14200 SW 72nd Ave.
Portland, OR 97223
(503) 639-6161
Fax: (503) 684-7008
www.gerberblades.com
E-mail: N/A

Styles: Fixed-blade and folding knives and multi-tools for hunting, fishing, camping and general use.

Sheaths: Nylon, Concealex and plastic.

Handles: Santoprene® rubber/glass filled polypropylene, Kraton™, aluminum, G-10, carbon fiber, Zytel® and stainless steel.

Features: Multi-tools features include Torx wrench, saw coupler that takes standard jig saw blades, Fiskars® scissors, file, can opener, bottle opener, regular and Phillips screwdrivers, bit driver with bits, needlenose pliers with wire cutters, awl, standard and metric ruler, corkscrew, serrated and straight-edge knife blades. Some knife models have thumb studs or holes in the blade for one-hand opening.

Retail Prices: $20.00 to $240.00

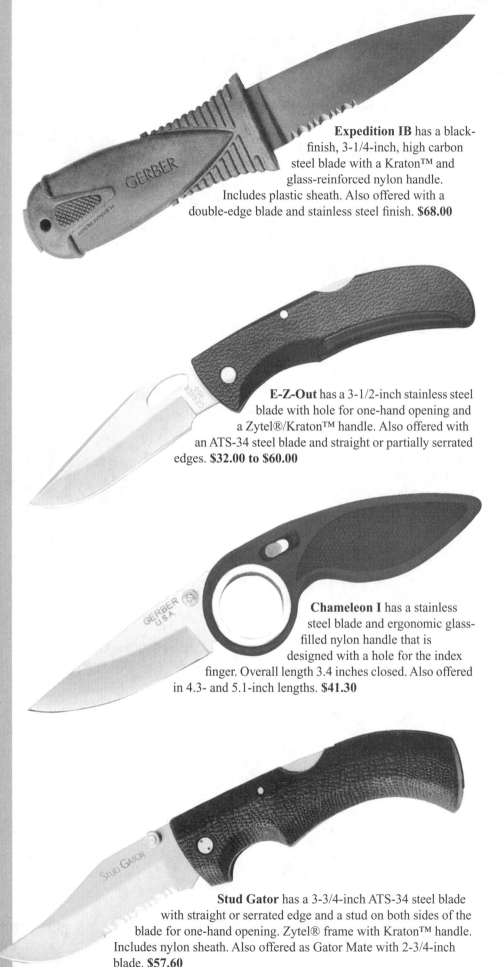

Expedition IB has a black-finish, 3-1/4-inch, high carbon steel blade with a Kraton™ and glass-reinforced nylon handle. Includes plastic sheath. Also offered with a double-edge blade and stainless steel finish. **$68.00**

E-Z-Out has a 3-1/2-inch stainless steel blade with hole for one-hand opening and a Zytel®/Kraton™ handle. Also offered with an ATS-34 steel blade and straight or partially serrated edges. **$32.00 to $60.00**

Chameleon I has a stainless steel blade and ergonomic glass-filled nylon handle that is designed with a hole for the index finger. Overall length 3.4 inches closed. Also offered in 4.3- and 5.1-inch lengths. **$41.30**

Stud Gator has a 3-3/4-inch ATS-34 steel blade with straight or serrated edge and a stud on both sides of the blade for one-hand opening. Zytel® frame with Kraton™ handle. Includes nylon sheath. Also offered as Gator Mate with 2-3/4-inch blade. **$57.60**

Gerber's **Air-Ti** gentleman's pocket knife, designed by William Harsey, has a 2-inch shallow drop point high carbon stainless steel blade. The handle is made by metal injection molding 6AL4V titanium. **$80.00**

The Sportster is a one-handed opening pocketknife with a 2.88-inch high carbon stainless steel blade and polycarbonate handle, covered by polyurethane. The pocket clip is replaceable. **$48.00**

Multi-Plier 650 Evolution is a new multi-function tool with interchangeable plier heads, including needlenose, bluntnose, technician and cable cutter heads, and all locking components. Other tools include Fiskars scissors, saw blade, Phillips screwdriver, bottle opener, can opener, and Simonds fine and coarse file. **$96.00**

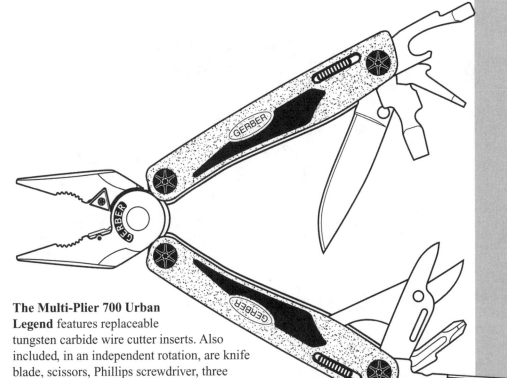

The Multi-Plier 700 Urban Legend features replaceable tungsten carbide wire cutter inserts. Also included, in an independent rotation, are knife blade, scissors, Phillips screwdriver, three screwdrivers, bottle opener and tweezers. **$104.00**

Gigand Company, Inc.

No. 4, Lane 130, Sec. 1
Kuang Fu Road
San Chung Taipei
Taiwan, R.O.C.
886-2-29952860
Fax: 886-2-29952860
www.gigand.com
E-mail:
gigand@ms39.hinet.net

Guardian neck knife has a 4-1/4-inch blade of AUS-8A stainless steel and an ABS plastic handle. Includes plastic sheath that holds knife with magnets. **Price unavailable.** ▶

Spectrum LT is a Carter-designed model with a 3-1/8-inch ATS-34 blade and aluminum handle with carbon fiber overlay. Also offered with G10 overlay and solid aluminum handle in blue, gold, green, red, black or silver. **Price unavailable.** ▶

Mosquito neck knife has a 2-inch blade of AUS-8A stainless steel and ABS plastic handle. Includes plastic sheath that holds knife with magnets. **Price unavailable.** ▶

Scrimshaw folder has a 2-7/8-inch blade of 420 J2 stainless steel and ABS plastic handle with laser scrimshaw in nine fish, wildlife and Indian patterns. **Price unavailable.** ▶

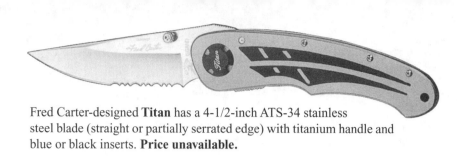

Fred Carter-designed **Titan** has a 4-1/2-inch ATS-34 stainless steel blade (straight or partially serrated edge) with titanium handle and blue or black inserts. **Price unavailable.**

Fred Carter-designed **Challenger Ti** has a 4-1/2-inch ATS-34 stainless steel blade (plain or partially serrated with tanto or plain point) and titanium-coated aluminum handle. Includes nylon sheath and clip. **Price unavailable.**

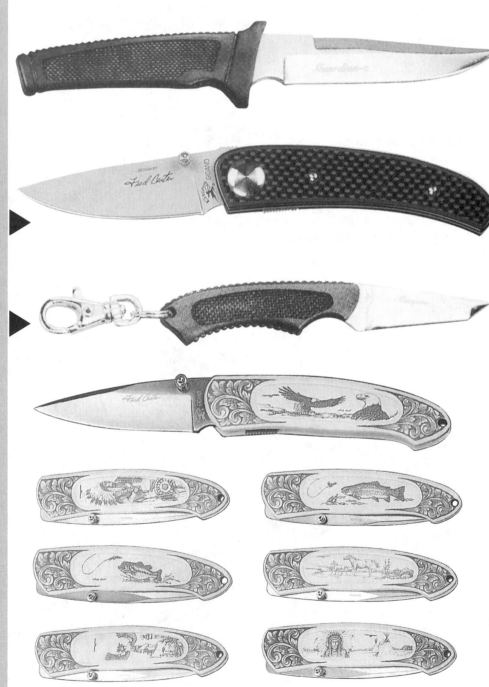

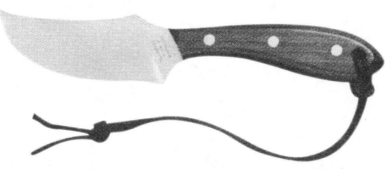

No. 103 Short Blade Skinner has a 3-1/2-inch carbon or high-carbon stainless steel blade with a rosewood (shown), resinwood or stag handle. Includes leather sheath (three models offered). **$91.00** (stainless with rosewood handle); **$96.00** (resinwood); **$166.00**

Grohmann Knives Ltd.

P.O. Box 40
116 Water St.
Pictou, Nova Scotia
Canada B0K 1H0
(888) 756-4837
or (902) 485-4224
Fax: (902) 485-5872
www.grohmannknives.com
E-mail: grohmann@
grohmannknives.com

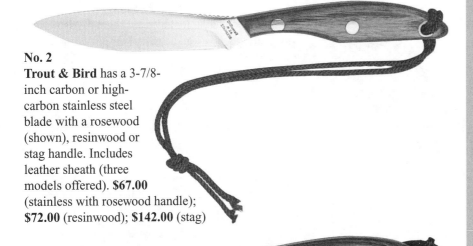

**No. 2
Trout & Bird** has a 3-7/8-inch carbon or high-carbon stainless steel blade with a rosewood (shown), resinwood or stag handle. Includes leather sheath (three models offered). **$67.00** (stainless with rosewood handle); **$72.00** (resinwood); **$142.00** (stag)

Styles: Fixed-blade belt knives for hunting and fishing; folding pocketknives for hunting and general use.

Sheaths: Leather.

Handles: Rosewood, stag, laminated hardwood (resinwood) and Zytel®.

Features: Made in Canada. D.H. Russell and Grohmann belt knives with high-carbon stainless steel or carbon steel blades (in traditional Russell elliptical blade designs or Grohmann skinning blade designs).

Retail Prices: $36.00 to $197.00

**No. 1
Original Design** has a 4-inch blade of carbon or high-carbon stainless steel and a rosewood (shown), water-resistant resinwood or stag handle. Includes oil-tanned leather sheath. Also offered with flap sheath and sheath with sharpening steel. **$72.00** (stainless with rosewood handle); **$77.00** (resinwood); **$147.00** (stag)

No. 4 Survival Knife has a 5-1/2-inch carbon or high-carbon stainless steel blade with a rosewood (shown), resinwood or stag handle. Includes leather sheath (three models offered). **$94.00** (stainless with rosewood handle); **$99.00** (resinwood); **$169.00** (stag)

GT Knives Inc.

7734 Arjons Dr.
San Diego, CA 92126-4365
(858) 530-8766
Fax: (858) 530-8798
Web site:
www.gtknives.com
E-mail:
gtknives@gtknives.com

Styles: Push-button and manual folding knives for sportsmen, law enforcement and the military.

Sheaths: N/A

Handles: Aircraft aluminum.

Features: ATS-34 stainless steel blades coated with titanium aluminum nitride. Most include pocket clip. Straight or serrated blades.

Retail Prices: **$53.95 to $219.95**

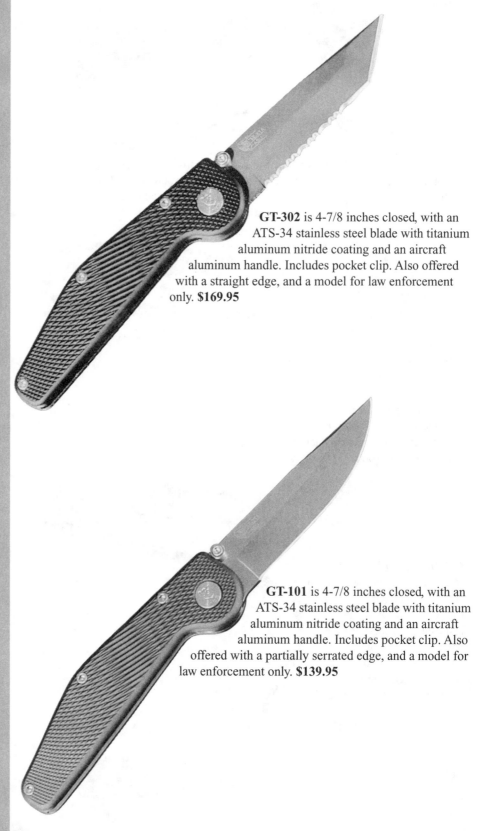

GT-302 is 4-7/8 inches closed, with an ATS-34 stainless steel blade with titanium aluminum nitride coating and an aircraft aluminum handle. Includes pocket clip. Also offered with a straight edge, and a model for law enforcement only. **$169.95**

GT-101 is 4-7/8 inches closed, with an ATS-34 stainless steel blade with titanium aluminum nitride coating and an aircraft aluminum handle. Includes pocket clip. Also offered with a partially serrated edge, and a model for law enforcement only. **$139.95**

Walther® Allied Forces™ has a 3-15/16-inch, 440A stainless steel black Teflon coated or matte grey bead blasted blade. The ADC12 aluminum handle is available with checkered rosewood or non-slip Kraton rubber inserts. Also available with a straight edge. **$49.95 to $59.95**

Junglee® Tri-Point™ has a partially serrated 3-1/2-inch AUS-10 stainless steel blade with a triangular hole for one-hand opening and a Zytel® handle. Also offered in a straight-edge or fully serrated blade. **$54.95**

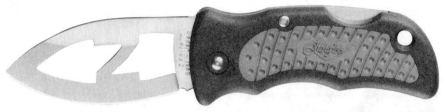

Junglee® "Z" Knife™ has a 2-1/4-inch AUS-6 stainless steel blade with Zytel® handle fitted with rosewood inserts. Includes stainless steel pocket clip. Also offered in a Zytel®-only handle. **$24.95** (scrimshaw models with numerous wildlife scenes, **$33.95**)

Junglee® Tactical Gurkha has a slightly reverse-swept, 5-inch AUS-8 stainless steel blade in the spirit of traditional Gurkha knives, as well as a Kraton™ rubber handle. Includes leather sheath. **$79.95**

Junglee® Tak Fukuta Signature Series Hunter has a 4-1/8-inch AUS-8 stainless steel blade with brushed nickel bolsters and Sambar stag handle. Includes leather sheath and Fukuta's trademark braided lanyard. **$131.95**

Junglee® Hattori Fighter® has a 7-3/4-inch MVS-8 stainless steel blade and a handle that combines nickel silver guards, polished hardwood and Kraton rubber. Includes top grain leather sheath. **$239.95**

Gutmann Cutlery Inc.

P.O. Box 2219
Bellingham, WA 98227
(800) 288-5379
or (360) 650-9141
Fax: (360) 676-1075
www.gutmanncutlery.com
E-mail: N/A

Styles: Wide range of folding and fixed-blade knives; multi-tools; compact pocket knives; Junglee folding and fixed hunting, military and fighting designs; axes; cleavers; cigar knives and kitchen knives.

Sheaths: Leather and ballistic nylon.

Handles: Kraton™ rubber, synthetic ivory, wood (some inlaid with turquoise or gemstones), aluminum, Zytel® and stag.

Features: Variety of scrimshaw handles; Explora survival knife; Stubby designs; some models with pocket clips, skeletonized blades, one-hand openers and Walther logo; Smith & Wesson multi-tools.

Retail Prices: $11.95 to $239.95

Historic Edged Weaponry

1021 Saddlebrook Dr.
Dept. BT
Hendersonville, NC 28739
(828) 692-0323
Fax: (828) 692-0600
Web site: N/A
E-mail: N/A

Styles: Antique knives from around the world; importer of puukko and other knives from Norway, Sweden, Finland and Lapland.

Sheaths: Leather.

Handles: Reindeer antler, curly birch and great sallow.

Features: Traditional puukko and Viking designs, most with Swedish carbon or stainless steel blades.

Retail Prices: $25.00 to $1,700.00

Reindeer horn **Puuko** by Lauri: **$225.00**. Large **Lapp Hunter** by Jarvenpaa: **$53.00**. **Laplander** knife with 8-1/2-inch blade: **$69.00**. **Bear Head Hunter**: **$63.00**. **Trofe Hunter**: **$89.00**

Three Helle Norwegian knives and one Finnish include: **Super Fjording Camp Knife: $39.00**. **Safari: $73.00**. 4-1/2-inch **Harding Hunter: $70.00**. Finnish made **Bronze Hunter** with 3-1/2-inch blade: **$46.00**

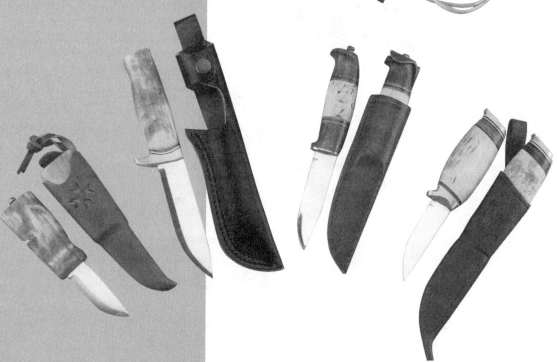

Swedish knives from EKA feature blades of Sandvik stainless steel and African Bubinga wood handle. **Nordic WII Hunter $93.00**. **Folding Fisherman $45.00**. **Nordic T8 Lockback Hunter $73.00**

Fury Black Hook is 3-5/8 inches in closed position with a matte aluminum overlay with shackle. **$8.00**

Fury Escape Black is 5 inches closed and an all-black handle and pocket clip and Damascene blade. **$6.00**

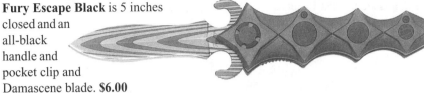

Fury Bald Eagle gifet set includes pocket knife and keychain in wood presentation box. **$13.00**

Fury Netsuke Bear is 9-3/4 inches long overall and ivory-like hand carved handle. Damascus blde is edged with bear design. **$15.00**

Fury Darius Eagle is 14-1/2 inches long overall with heavy sheath included. Accents designed with eagles. **$18.00**

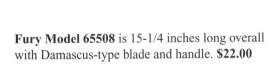

Fury Model 65508 is 15-1/4 inches long overall with Damascus-type blade and handle. **$22.00**

Joy Enterprises — Fury Cutlery

1104 53rd Court South
West Palm Beach, FL 33407
(800) 500-3879 or
(561) 863-3205
Fax: (561) 863-3277
www.joyenterprises.com or
www.furycutlery.com
E-mail:
mail@joyenterprises.com

Styles: Extensive variety of fixed-blade and folding knives for hunting, fishing, diving, camping, military and general use; novelty key-ring knives.

Sheaths: Leather and nylon.

Handles: Plastic, hardwoods, leather washers, rubber and stainless steel.

Features: Fury, Mustang, Hawg, Muela and Herbertz knife lines; models made in United States, Spain, Germany, Japan, Taiwan and China.

Retail Prices: **90 cents to $1,198.00**

KA-BAR Knives Inc.

1125 East State St.
Olean, NY 14760
(800) 282-0130
Fax: (716) 790-7188
www.ka-bar.com
E-mail: info@ka-bar.com

Styles: Military-style
fixed-blade knives (including
the Marine Corps fighting knife
design used in World War II),
fixed-blade hunting knives and
folding pocket and lockback
knives.

Sheaths: Leather, Kydex®
and nylon.

Handles: Leather washers,
Kraton thermoplastic,
Staminawood, Delrin,
stainless steel, ABS plastic,
Zytel, glass-filled
nylon and aluminum.

Features: High-
carbon, 440 stainless
steel, D2 tool steel or
Sandvik 12C27 stainless steel
blades; some models with black
epoxy powder or bead-blasted
blades; some with pocket
clips and thumb studs.

**Retail Prices: $4.21 to
$206.55**

Precision Hunter Long Point has a
4-inch, 440A stainless steel blade and Kraton G®
thermoplastic handle. Includes leather sheath and lanyard.
$47.02

Warthog has a 5-3/8-inch, epoxy powder-coated blade with a straight,
hollow-ground edge. Includes Kydex® sheath. **$82.03**

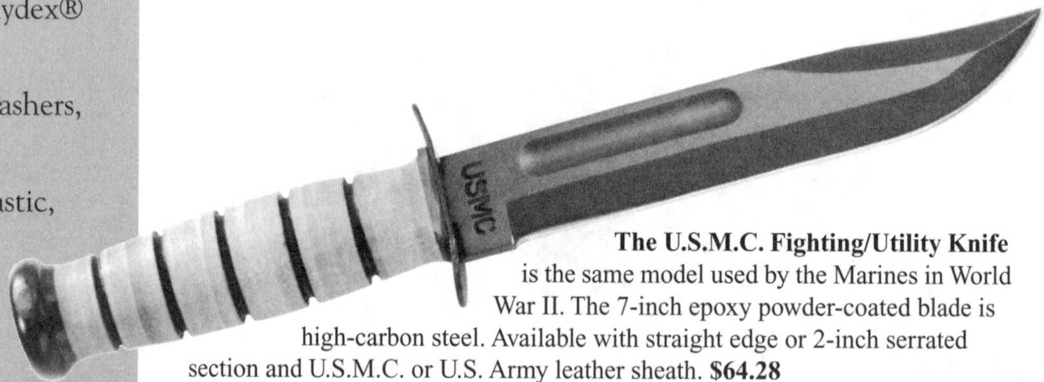

The U.S.M.C. Fighting/Utility Knife
is the same model used by the Marines in World
War II. The 7-inch epoxy powder-coated blade is
high-carbon steel. Available with straight edge or 2-inch serrated
section and U.S.M.C. or U.S. Army leather sheath. **$64.28**

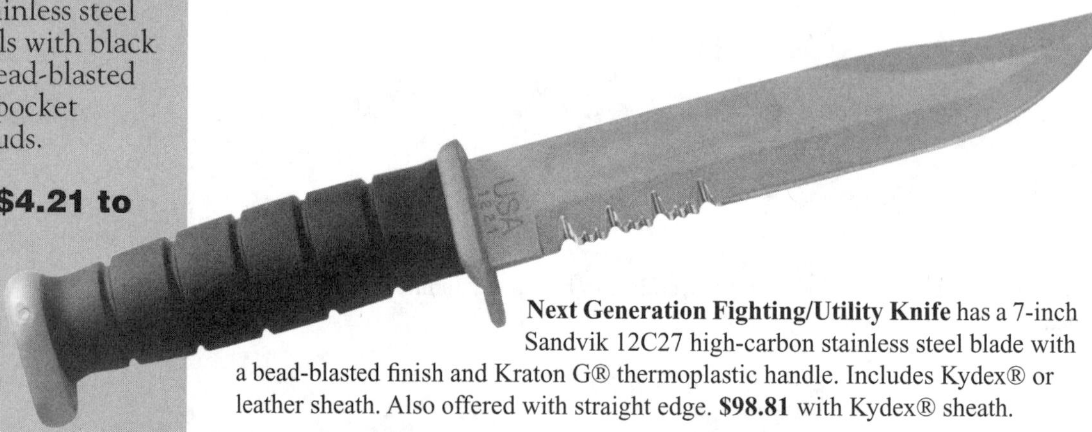

Next Generation Fighting/Utility Knife has a 7-inch
Sandvik 12C27 high-carbon stainless steel blade with
a bead-blasted finish and Kraton G® thermoplastic handle. Includes Kydex® or
leather sheath. Also offered with straight edge. **$98.81** with Kydex® sheath.

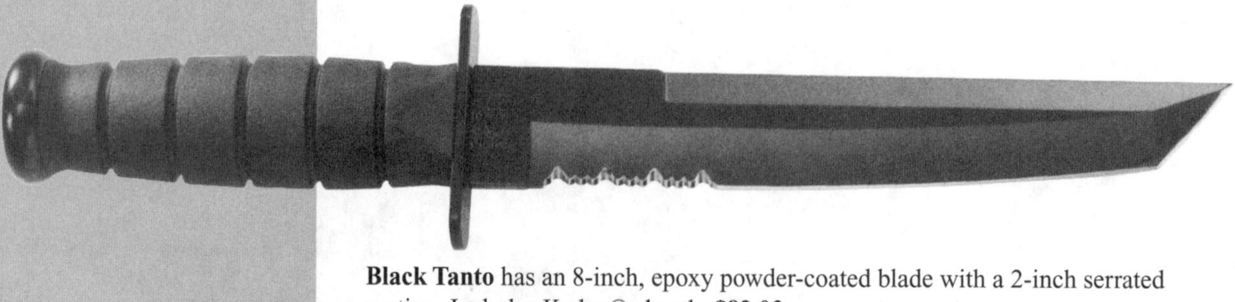

Black Tanto has an 8-inch, epoxy powder-coated blade with a 2-inch serrated
section. Includes Kydex® sheath. **$82.03**

Cheetah
K-900DP/CW has an XT80 stainless steel, 3-3/4-inch drop-point blade with cherrywood handle. Includes hip-hugger leather sheath. Also offered with a white Micarta® handle. **$149.99**

Black
Kat BK-900DP has an XT70 stainless steel, 3-3/4-inch drop-point blade with Katz One-Hand Opener thumb rest and Zytel® handle. Includes integral pocket clip. **$69.98**

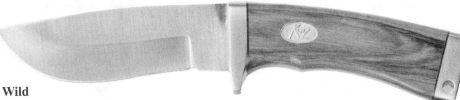

Wild
Kat K-103CW has a 4-5/8-inch XT80 stainless steel blade and a cherrywood handle. Includes Cordura® nylon sheath. Also offered with sambar stag, ivory Micarta® and Kraton™ handles. **$199.99**

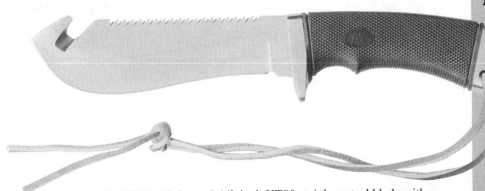

Hunter's Tool ™ Knife has a 5-1/2-inch XT80 stainless steel blade with a plain or partiazlly serrated edge, a gut hook and bone szaw. The handle is checkered Kraton™. Includes leather sheath and lanyard. **$224.00**

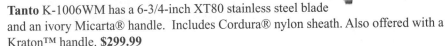

Tanto K-1006WM has a 6-3/4-inch XT80 stainless steel blade and an ivory Micarta® handle. Includes Cordura® nylon sheath. Also offered with a Kraton™ handle. **$299.99**

Katz Knives Inc.

P.O. Box 730
Chandler, AZ 85244-0730
(800) 848-7084
or (480) 786-9334
Fax: (480) 786-9338
www.katzknives.com
E-mail: Katzkn@aol.com

Styles: Folding and fixed-blade knives in hunting, fishing, tactical and general-use designs.

Sheaths: Cordura nylon and leather.

Handles: Zytel®, Kraton™, ivory Micarta®, cherrywood, Sambar stag and mother of pearl.

Features: XT80 or XT70 stainless steel blades; several models of military-style knives feature blades 5mm thick for extra strength; many folders feature pocket clips and one-hand opening.

Retail Prices: $20.55 to $299.99

Lion King K-302ST has a 6-1/8-inch XT80 stainless steel blade and sambar stag handle. Includes Cordura® nylon sheath. Also offered with cherrywood, ivory Micarta® and Kraton™ handles. **$310.00**

Kellam Knives Co.

902 S. Dixie Hwy.
Lantana, FL 33462
(800) 390-6918
or (561) 588-3185
Fax: (561) 588-3186
www.kellamknives.com
E-mail:
info@kellamknives.com

Styles: Finnish folding and fixed-blade knives for hunting, fishing, camping and general use.

Sheaths: Fitted hand-made leather, oxhide.

Handles: Reindeer antler, curly birch, African tuija wood.

Features: AUS-8, 440A or carbon stainless steel blades, several folding models with one-hand openers, lightweight and durable.

Retail Prices: $12.95 to $306.00

The F33 **Sailing Knife** has a 3-inch stainless steel blade with a laser cut shackle slot for one-handed opening. There is also a 2-inch marlinspike. Organically shaped handles are satin-finished blue aluminum. **$86.40**

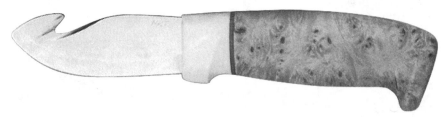

The **Marko-Hook** features a hand-forged carbon 3-1/2-inch blade that is easy to resharpen. The handle is carved from curly birch and reindeer antler. With hand-made leather sheath. **$306.00**

Shark fillet knives are available with flexible or stiffer blades with a serrated back for scaling fish. With plastic sheath. **$14.95**

The **KP-Hunter**, made by Kainuun Puukko of Finland, has a hand-forged 5-1/2-inch blade of tempered carbon steel. The handle is carved from curly birch and has a brass bolster and leather spacer. With hand-made leather sheath. **$198.00**

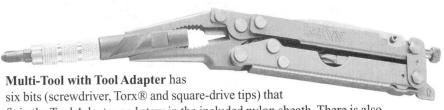

Kershaw Knives

25300 SW Parkway
Wilsonville, OR 97070
(800) 325-2891 or
(503) 682-1966
Fax: (503) 682-7168
www.kershawknives.com
E-mail: kershaw@
kershawknives.com

Styles: Fixed-blade and folding knives and multi-tools for hunting, fishing, camping and general use.

Sheaths: Nylon.

Handles: Polyamide, co-polymer, phenolic and brass, Kraton™ rubber, metal alloy with ABS plastic inlay, steel with sandalwood inlay, aluminum with co-polymer inlay and stainless steel.

Features: 440V or 440A stainless steel blades; several folding models feature Ken Onion Speed-Safe assisted opening mechanism for fast one-hand opening; one fillet knife has adjustable blade length.

Retail Prices: $24.95 to $299.00

Wade Officer has a 3-1/8-inch locking blade and a 2-1/8-inch serrated sheepfoot blade, both of 440A stainless steel, with a co-polymer handle available in black, blue, orange and yellow. **$49.95**

Ken Onion-designed **Boa Model** 1580 has a 3-3/8-inch blade of CPM-440V stainless steel coated with titanium-nitride and an aluminum handle. Features Speed-Safe assisted opening using index finger or thumb. Also offered in partially serrated blade. **$185.00**

Deer Hunter has a 4-inch AUS-8A drop-point blade and co-polymer handle. Includes leather sheath. **$150.00**

Multi-Tool with Tool Adapter has six bits (screwdriver, Torx® and square-drive tips) that fit in the Tool Adapter and stow in the included nylon sheath. There is also a hacksaw blade, more screwdrivers, file, can opener, ruler and locking pliers with wire cutter. **$119.95**

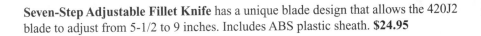

Seven-Step Adjustable Fillet Knife has a unique blade design that allows the 420J2 blade to adjust from 5-1/2 to 9 inches. Includes ABS plastic sheath. **$24.95**

Klotzli

CH 3400
Burgdorf, Switzerland
(800) 922-6537 (Boker USA)
or (800) 255-9034
(A.G. Russell)
Fax: N/A
www.klotzli.com
E-mail: info@klotzli.com

Styles: High-tech folding knives for tactical and general use.

Sheaths: N/A

Handles: Carbon fiber, G10 and titanium.

Features: Made in Switzerland. Blades of 440C stainless steel. Collaborations with Michael Walker and Christian Wimpff.

Retail Prices: $155.00 to $230.00

Model MW1-R-CST is a Michael Walker design with 2.9-inch, partially serrated blade of 440C stainless steel, black Teflon® coating and red carbon fiber handle. Includes pocket clip. **$220.00**

Model ACC1-CS has a 2.9-inch, partially serrated blade of 440C stainless steel, titanium liner and black carbon fiber handle. Includes pocket clip. **$220.00**

Model CHW1-CS is a Christian Wimpff design with a 3.6-inch, partially serrated blade of 440C stainless steel, titanium liner and black carbon fiber handle. Includes pocket clip. **$230.00**

Model CHW2-CS is designed by German knifemaker Christian Wimpff and has a 3.6-inch, partially serrated blade of 440C stainless steel, stainless steel liner and G10 handle. Includes pocket clip. **$175.00**

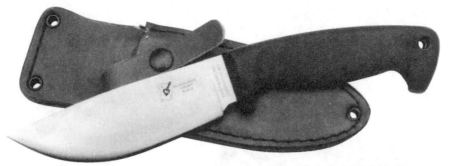

Blackjack Grunt offers convex-round cutting edge on 5-1/2-inch AUS-8 blade, Kraton handle. **$96.00**

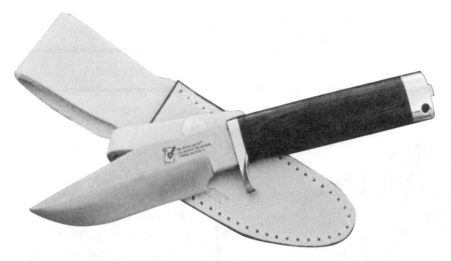

Blackjack Classic Trailguide II has 4-3/4-inch convex-ground high-carbon steel blade with stainless steel guard, aluminum pommel. **$132.00**

Blackjack Classic No. 5 subhilt in stacked leather handle with 5-1/2-inch 1095CRYO convex-ground blade. Available without subhilt with Micarta handle. **$170.00**

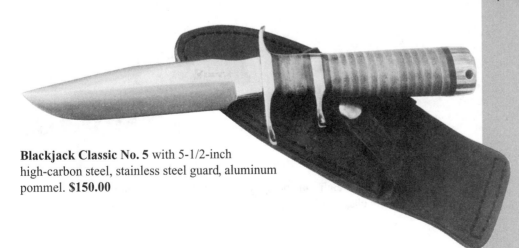

Blackjack Classic No. 5 with 5-1/2-inch high-carbon steel, stainless steel guard, aluminum pommel. **$150.00**

Knifeware Inc.

P.O. Box 3
Greenville, WV 24945
(304) 832-6878
Fax: (304) 832-6550
www.knifeware.com
E-mail:
knifeware@inetone.com

Styles: Blackjack and Big Country fixed-blade knives in hunting, military, tactical, and trail-and-camp patterns, all made to the designs or specifications of Ken Warner.

Sheaths: Leather in standard and in ambidextrous patterns.

Handles: Big Country Knives have Kraton™ handles over full tangs; Blackjack handles in laminated walnut, cocobolo, Micarta®, stacked leather, stag bone, and Kraton.

Features: All knives have convex-ground blades; Big Country knives are AUS-8 stainless steel; Blackjacks are high carbon steel … 52-100, 1095, and A-2 have been used. All blades are now labeled for steel type. Blade lengths run from 3 inches to 12 inches.

Retail Prices: $96.00 to $225.00; most around $100-$125

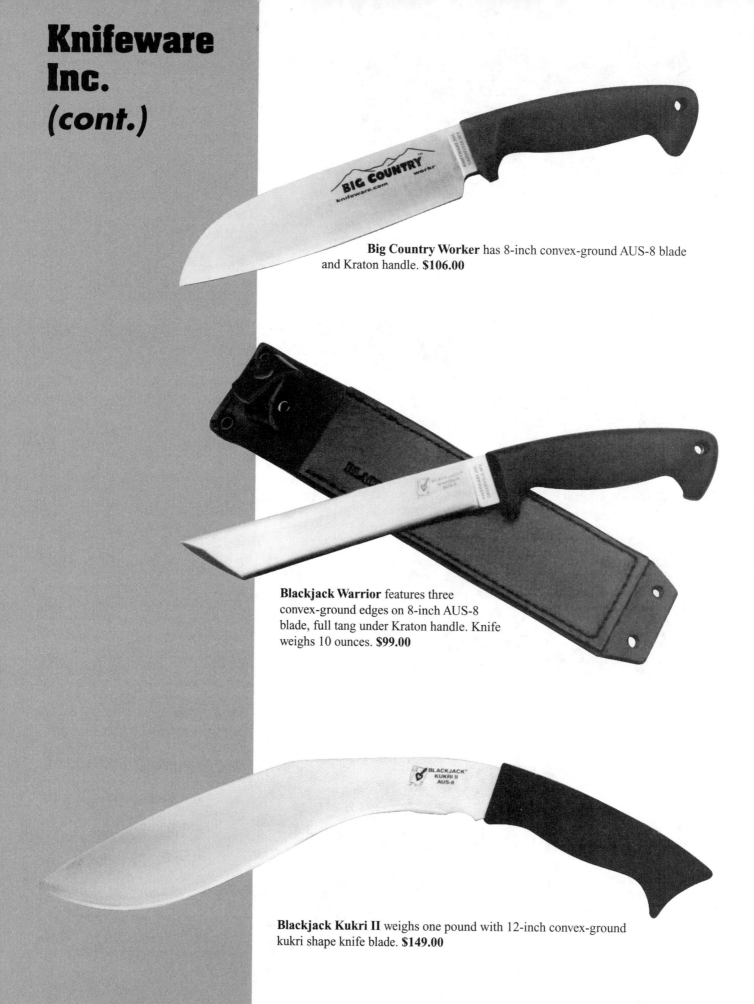

Big Country Worker has 8-inch convex-ground AUS-8 blade and Kraton handle. **$106.00**

Blackjack Warrior features three convex-ground edges on 8-inch AUS-8 blade, full tang under Kraton handle. Knife weighs 10 ounces. **$99.00**

Blackjack Kukri II weighs one pound with 12-inch convex-ground kukri shape knife blade. **$149.00**

Elite Damascus Hunter features a 3-1/2-inch Damascus steel blade and stag antler handle modeled after the German Black Forest hunting knives of the Middle Ages. Each knife includes a handmade leather sheath. **$245.00**

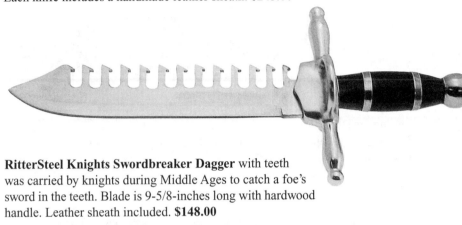

RitterSteel Knights Swordbreaker Dagger with teeth was carried by knights during Middle Ages to catch a foe's sword in the teeth. Blade is 9-5/8-inches long with hardwood handle. Leather sheath included. **$148.00**

RitterSteel Roman Gladius Sword has a hand-forged 22-inch blade with exotic wood pommel and guard. Sword is 30 inches long overall. Leather sheath included. **$186.00**

StageSteel Double-Handed Broadsword has a 28-inch carbon steel blade, 40 inches long overall and weighs 5-1/2 pounds. Grip is leather with wire wrapping. Sword is used by stunt and theater professionals. **$146.00**

Knights Edge Ltd.

5696 N. Northwest Highway
Chicago, IL 60646-6136
(773) 775-3888
Fax: (773) 775-3339
www.knightsedge.com
E-mail:
sales@KnightsEdge.com

Styles: Medieval weaponry, swords, suits of armor, helms, Oriental weaponry, daggers, katanas, stag hunting knives and swords, Civil War swords.

Sheaths: Leather, leather over wood, metal.

Handles: Cast brass, steel, wrought iron with leather, exotic hardwoods.

Features: Ritter steel blades authentically hand forged over hot coals, Stage steel live-action full-tang steel weaponry, Knightedge real stag handle hunting blades made in USA and Valiant Arms arms and armor. All high quality, functional replicas of Medieval weaponry and martial arts swords as well as accessories.

RitterSteel Sinbad Scimitar with a hand-forged blade that is almost 5 inches wide at its widest point and has an exotic hardwood handle. Length overall is 36 inches. **$178.00**

Knives of Alaska

3100 Airport Drive
Denison, TX 75020
(800) 572-0980 or
(903) 786-7366
Fax: (903) 786-7371
www.knivesofalaska.com
E-mail: info@
knivesofalaska.com

Styles: Folders, skinners, capers, fillet, cleavers, hatchets, unusual fixed-blade designs.

Sheaths: American leather.

Handles: Checkered rubberized, desert ironwood, Micarta®, carbon fiber, titanium, mammoth ivory, stag.

Features: Two- and three-knife combination sets with single sheaths; round-pointed Muskrat and Alaska Brown Bear skinner/cleaver; outfitter-grade products field-tested in the Alaskan bush.

Retail Prices: $39.97 to $695.00

Light Hunter mini-skinner/cleaver with 3-1/2-inch D-2 steel blade and rubberized Suregrip, stag or desert ironwood handle. **$112.97 to $161.97**

Alaska Brown Bear skinner/cleaver with 6-1/2-inch D-2 steel blade and stag handle. Other handle options include rubberized Suregrip and wood. **$112.97 to $179.97**

Muskrat skinning/fleshing knife has a 2-1/4-inch D-2 steel blade with rubberized handle. **$49.97**. Rubberized Suregrip, wood and stag handles available. **$49.97 to $103.97**

Presentation Series liner lock with 2-1/2-inch VG-10 steel blade and titanium, wood, G-10 Micarta, ivory Micarta, mammoth ivory handle. **$129.95 to $595.00** (scrimshaw additional)

Alaskan Super Cub liner lock with 2-5/8-inch VG-10 steel blade and wood, mammoth ivory or G-10 Micarta handle. **$99.97 to $158.97**

Handmade Series **Wolverine** clip point; 4-1/4-inch D-2 steel blade with stag handle. **$297.00** Other styles and handles available.

The **Hunter's Pro-Pack**, designed by Alaskan outfitter Charles Allen, includes a Hunter's Hatchet with hickory handle, **Bush Camp Knife**, **Cub Bear Caping Knife** and **Muskrat** fleshing and skinning knife. A Cordura® nylon pack holds the knives and hatchet. **$199.97**

Grayling Fisherman and Hunter's Boning Knife; 6-inch AUS-8A stainless steel blade with rubberized Suregrip, stag or desert ironwood handle. **$39.97 to $103.97**

The new **Hunter's Hatchet** by Knives of Alaska combines high-carbon S-7 tool steel and an oil-finished hickory handle. The sharp cutting edge is 2-1/2 inches and the total head length is 4-1/4 inches. Includes protective leather sheath. **$69.97**

Leatherman Tool Group Inc.

12106 NE Ainsworth Circle
Portland, OR 97220-9001
(800) 847-8665 or
(503) 253-7826
Fax: (800) 367-1355 or
(503) 253-7830
www.leatherman.com
E-mail:
mktg@leatherman.com

Styles: A dozen models of multi-tools, a category of knife launched by founder Tim Leatherman in 1983. All include either a pliers or scissors.

Sheaths: Nylon or leather.

Handles: Stainless steel or anodized aluminum.

Features: Blades include needlenose or regular pliers, wire cutters, scissors, drop-point knife, clip-point knife, diamond-coated file, cross-cut file, flat screwdriver, Phillips screwdriver, bottle opener, ruler, hex-bit driver, nail file, tweezers, awl, cocktail fork, spreader knife and corkscrew. Crunch features locking pliers. All models feature 100 percent stainless steel construction. Some models offered in black finish.

Retail Prices: $28.00 to $98.00

The smallest of Leatherman's new "Juice" line, the **C2** contains a needlenose pliers, knife and four screwdrivers as well as a corkscrew with assist. Contoured anodized aluminum handles keep it wrapped up in a compact package. **$60.00-$94.00**

Along with the basic pliers and four screwdrivers, the **KF4 Juice Tool** packs two knives, a file and a saw as well as a ruler, awl, wire cutters, diamond file and lanyard attachment. It's still small enough to be a pocket knife. **$60.00-$94.00**

Leatherman Tool Group Inc. (cont.)

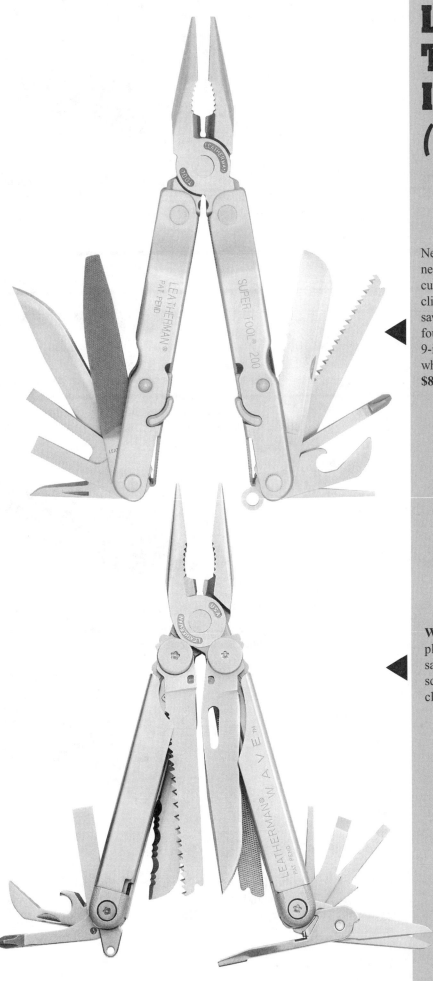

New **Super Tool 200** features include needle-nose and regular pliers, wire cutters and stripper, electrical crimper, clip-point and serrated knives, wood saw, metal/wood file, can/bottle opener, four screwdrivers, an awl/punch and a 9-inch ruler. It measures 4-1/2 inches when closed and weighs 9 ounces. **$80.00**

Wave features needle-nose and regular pliers, wire cutters and stripper, wood saw, serrated blade, scissors, file, five screwdrivers, a can/bottle opener and clip-point knife. **$100.00**

Marble's Outdoors

420 Industrial Park
Gladstone, MI 49837-0111
(906) 428-3710
Fax: (906) 428-3711
www.marblesoutdoors.com
E-mail:
info@marblesoutdoors.com

Styles: Traditional fixed-blade knives for hunting, camping and general use.

Sheaths: Leather.

Handles: Stacked leather, curly maple, cocobolo Dymond®, India stag, black Micarta® and impala horn.

Features: 52-100 carbon steel blades offered in clip and drop points.

Retail Prices: $85.00 to $275.00

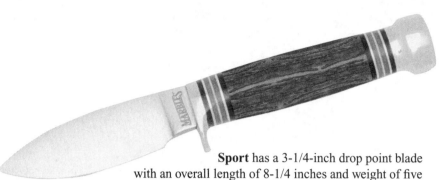

Sport has a 3-1/4-inch drop point blade with an overall length of 8-1/4 inches and weight of five ounces. **$66.99 to $93.99**

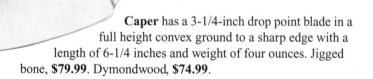

Caper has a 3-1/4-inch drop point blade in a full height convex ground to a sharp edge with a length of 6-1/4 inches and weight of four ounces. Jigged bone, **$79.99**. Dymondwood, **$74.99**.

Trailcraft™ has a 3-1/2-inch blade of 52-100 carbon steel and a stacked leather handle. Includes leather sheath. **$85.00**

Trailmaker features a 10-inch convex ground high carbon steel blade with an overall length of 15-1/2 inches and weight of 15 ounces. Jigged bone, **$198.99**. Stacked leather, **$188.99**.

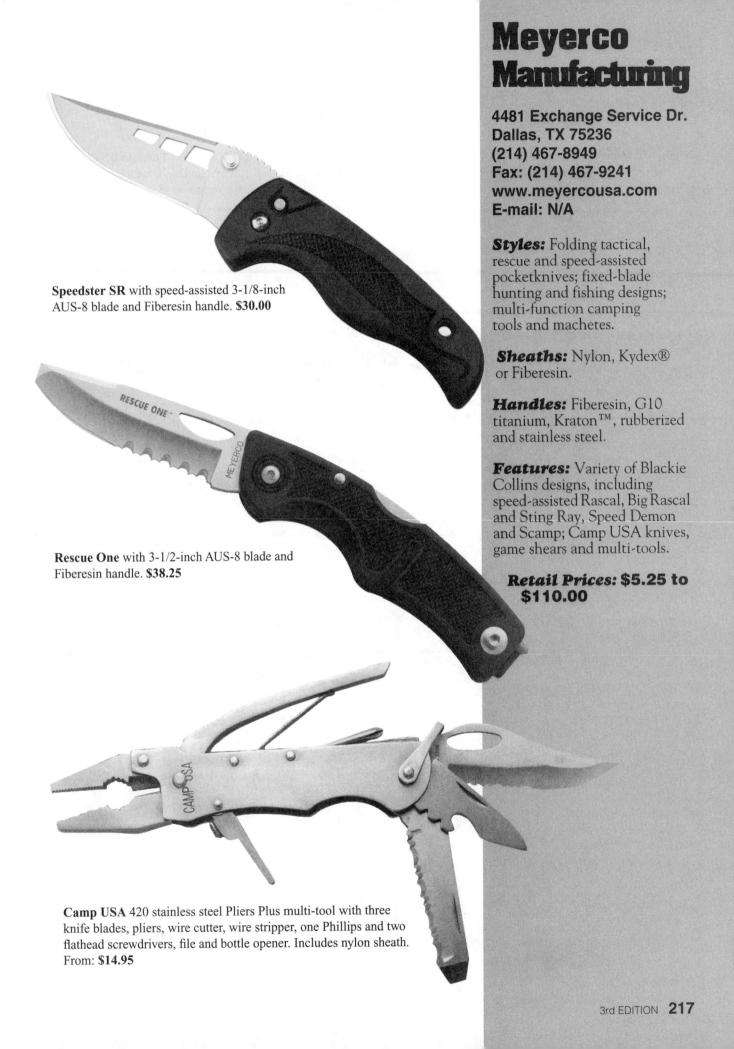

Meyerco Manufacturing

4481 Exchange Service Dr.
Dallas, TX 75236
(214) 467-8949
Fax: (214) 467-9241
www.meyercousa.com
E-mail: N/A

Speedster SR with speed-assisted 3-1/8-inch AUS-8 blade and Fiberesin handle. **$30.00**

Rescue One with 3-1/2-inch AUS-8 blade and Fiberesin handle. **$38.25**

Camp USA 420 stainless steel Pliers Plus multi-tool with three knife blades, pliers, wire cutter, wire stripper, one Phillips and two flathead screwdrivers, file and bottle opener. Includes nylon sheath. From: **$14.95**

Styles: Folding tactical, rescue and speed-assisted pocketknives; fixed-blade hunting and fishing designs; multi-function camping tools and machetes.

Sheaths: Nylon, Kydex® or Fiberesin.

Handles: Fiberesin, G10 titanium, Kraton™, rubberized and stainless steel.

Features: Variety of Blackie Collins designs, including speed-assisted Rascal, Big Rascal and Sting Ray, Speed Demon and Scamp; Camp USA knives, game shears and multi-tools.

Retail Prices: $5.25 to $110.00

Mission Knives & Tools Inc.

1251 N. Manassero St.,
Suite 402
Anaheim, CA 92807
(714) 777-7881
Fax: (714) 777-7258
www.missionknives.com
E-mail:
john@missionknives.com

Styles: Folding and fixed-blade survival, diving and battle knives.

Sheaths: Kydex®.

Handles: Molded Hytrel®/Kevlar®, titanium, A2 steel.

Features: Variety of models made entirely of titanium for military and cold-weather applications, including mine defusing; one-piece A2 or titanium multi-purpose dive and utility knives with skeletonized handles.

Retail Prices: $98.00 to $389.00

MPT-12 (Multi-Purpose Tactical) has 6-inch titanium blade and Hytrel/Kevlar handle. Includes Hytrel sheath. **$346.00**

MPK-12 (Multi-Purpose Knife) has 7-1/8-inch titanium blade and Hytrel/Kevlar handle. Includes Hytrel sheath. **$346.00**

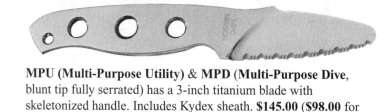

MPU (Multi-Purpose Utility) & **MPD (Multi-Purpose Dive,** blunt tip fully serrated) has a 3-inch titanium blade with skeletonized handle. Includes Kydex sheath. **$145.00** (**$98.00** for stainless steel) MPD **$157.00**

MPF (Multi-Purpose Folder) has a 4-inch titanium blade with drop or tanto point and partially serrated or straight edge. Titanium handles, screws, pins, thumb stud and pocket clip. All titanium. **$389.00**

MPS (Multi-Purpose Survival) has 5-inch titanium blade and skeletonized handle. Detachable handles available. Includes Kydex sheath. **$346.00**. For new bolt-on handles, add **$35.00**

MPK10 (Multi-Purpose Knife) has 5-3/4-inch titanium blade and Hytrel/Kevlar handle. Includes Hytrel sheath. **$336.00**

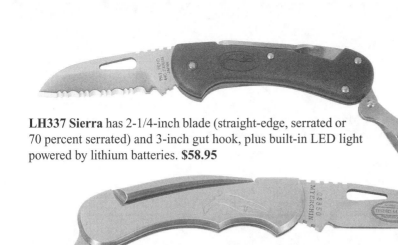

LH337 Sierra has 2-1/4-inch blade (straight-edge, serrated or 70 percent serrated) and 3-inch gut hook, plus built-in LED light powered by lithium batteries. **$58.95**

The **Model A377 Offshore Crew Knife** is designed for use by sailors, skydivers and backpackers. Its 2-1/4-inch 440C stainless steel blade secures with the DoubleLock system and has a stainless handle. Includes Ballistic nylon sheath. **$65.95**

B400 Alaska Guide has locking 440C stainless steel straight-edge and serrated blades. **$84.95**

LH 300 Yukon has 2.8-inch blade (straight-edge, serrated or 70 percent serrated) and 3-inch gut hook, plus built-in LED light. **$67.95**

One of the new Offshore System Pro models, **B001P**, has a 3-1/2-inch 440C stainless steel blade and a 6.65-inch spike. The black Micarta handle can be scrimshawed with white India ink and the Ballistic nylon sheath can be work on a belt vertically or horizontally. **$99.95**

B001 Offshore System includes 8-1/4-inch knife with black Micarta handle and 6.65-inch marlinspike in Cordura nylon sheath. Model used by U.S. Navy and U.S. Coast Guard. **$97.95**

Myerchin Inc.

**14185 Regina Drive, Suite G
Rancho Cucamonga, CA
91739
(800) 531-4890 or
(909) 463-6741
Fax: (909) 463-6751
www.myerchin.com
E-mail:
myerchin@myerchin.com**

Styles: Folding and fixed-blade hunting and offshore rigging knives.

Sheaths: Cordura® nylon.

Handles: Sandalwood, white Micarta®, black Micarta®, Zytel®.

Features: Blades of 440 high-carbon stainless steel; some models offered in a 70 percent serrated blade. Folders feature an oversized metal lanyard that unlocks the blade for one-hand closing. Many models feature a marlinspike for knot work or a gut hook for field dressing. Lightknife features built-in LED light.

Retail Prices: **$65.95 to $113.95**

A500 Safety/Dive knife is made from an 8-inch bar of steel with a sandblasted handle and 70 percent serrated blade. **$55.95**

Ontario Knife Co.

26 Empire St.
Franklinville, NY 14737
(800) 222-5233 or
(716) 676-5527
Fax: (800) 299-2618
www.ontarioknife.com
E-mail:
salesOKC@aol.com

Styles: Fixed-blade and folding knives and machetes for hunting, camping, military and general use.

Sheaths: Leather, nylon, molded plastic and Kydex®.

Handles: Leather and fiber washers, molded plastic, Kraton™ polymer

Features: Black powder-coated 1095 carbon-steel or 440A stainless steel blades; steel buttcaps.

Retail Prices:
$12.74 to $275.00

SPC21 Navy Mark I has a 4-3/4-inch, brushed-finish 1095 carbon-steel blade and a Kraton™ handle. Includes leather/nylon sheath. **$35.72**

SP17 Army Quartermaster has a 6-inch, 1095 carbon-steel blade with epoxy powder coating and a Kraton™ handle. Includes a leather/nylon sheath. **$60.00**

SP12 Tanto 6 has a 6-inch, 1095 carbon-steel blade with tanto point and a Kraton™ handle. Includes a leather/nylon sheath. Design also offered with an 8- or 10-inch blade. **$46.00**

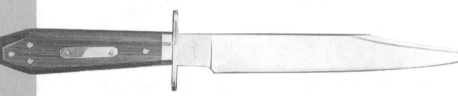

The **Gambler Bagwell Bowie** has a 9-3/8-inch blade of 440A stainless steel and a coffin-shaped wood handle. Includes leather sheath. **$175.00**

SP8 Machete has a 10-inch, 1095 carbon-steel blade with epoxy powder coating and a Kraton™ handle. Includes a combination leather/nylon sheath. **$65.00**

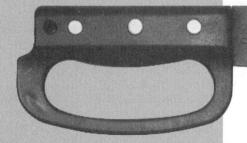

OKC22 Heavy Duty chopper has a 22-inch 1095 carbon-steel blade with zinc oxide phosphate finish and molded "D" handle. Blade lengths: 12-, 18- and 22-inch. **$25.25**

Wedge has a 2-3/8-inch 6M stainless steel blade with a Delrin handle and a button that locks and unlocks the Delrin sheath. Can be clipped to a belt loop (with included swivel clip) or worn around the neck on a cord (included). Also offered as a 3-inch-blade Wedge II model. **$19.50**

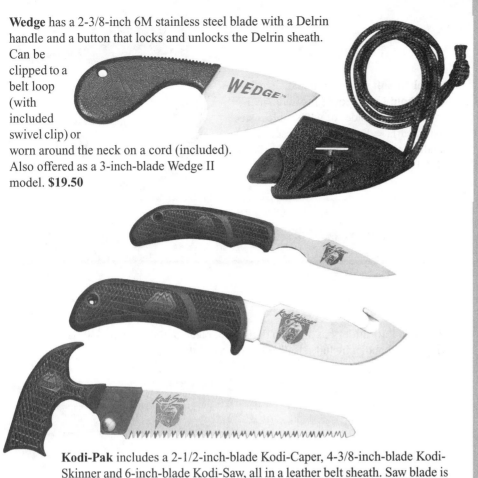

Kodi-Pak includes a 2-1/2-inch-blade Kodi-Caper, 4-3/8-inch-blade Kodi-Skinner and 6-inch-blade Kodi-Saw, all in a leather belt sheath. Saw blade is replaceable. **$119.70**

Field-Spear has a 3-5/8-inch AUS-8A stainless steel blade and Zytel handle. Also offered with 2-7/8-inch blade and 50-percent serrated edge. **$59.50**

Game-Processor is a 12-piece butchering set including 3-inch caping knife, 4-1/4-inch skinner, 5-1/2-inch boning/fillet knife, 8-inch bowie butcher knife, Smith's tungsten carbide V-sharpener, 10-inch wood/bone saw, 5-1/4-inch carving fork, game shears, steel stick/brisket spreader, 10- by 14-inch cutting board, set of six gloves and hard side carrying case. **$88.99**

Outdoor Edge Cutlery Corp.

4699 Nautilus Court So., Suite 503
Boulder, CO 80301
(303) 530-7667
(800) 447-3343
Fax: (303) 530-7020
www.outdooredge.com
E-mail:
info@outdooredge.com

Styles: Fixed blade and folding hunting, skinning and general-purpose knives.

Sheaths: Leather and Delrin®.

Handles: Delrin, aluminum, aluminum with Kraton™ inserts and Zytel®.

Features: Wedge and Wedge II fixed-blade knives are held in Delrin sheaths that lock and unlock by pushing a button; can be clipped to a belt or worn around the neck on a cord. Skinning knives and saws feature T-shaped handles. Some folding knives feature pocket clips and partially serrated blades.

Retail Prices: $19.95 to $105.50

Whitetail Skinner has a 2-5/8-inch AUS-8A stainless steel blade with hook and T-shaped handle. Includes leather belt sheath. Also offered with 3-inch blade and partially serrated blade. **$49.90**

Randall Made Knives

P.O. Box 1988
Orlando, FL 32802-1988
(407) 855-8075
Fax: (407) 855-9054
www.randallknives.com
E-mail:
grandall@
randallknives.com

Styles: Handmade fixed-blade knives for hunting, fishing, diving, military and general use.

Sheaths: Leather.

Handles: Stag; black, white or maroon Micarta®; walnut; maple; rosewood and leather.

Features: Tool or 440 stainless steel blades; brass, nickel silver or duralumin butt cap; choice of handle shape, hilt shape, compass embedded in handle and other options.

Retail Prices: $135.00 to $435.00 (standard models)

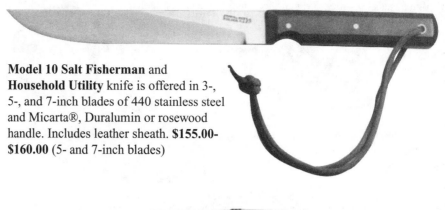

Model 10 Salt Fisherman and **Household Utility** knife is offered in 3-, 5-, and 7-inch blades of 440 stainless steel and Micarta®, Duralumin or rosewood handle. Includes leather sheath. **$155.00-$160.00** (5- and 7-inch blades)

Model 26 Pathfinder has a 4-inch drop-point blade of tool steel or 440 stainless steel with a stag handle. Includes leather sheath. **$245.00**

Model 11 Alaskan Skinner is offered in a 4-, 4-1/2- or 5-inch blade of tool steel or 440 stainless steel with a leather handle. Includes leather sheath. **$245.00** (4-inch blade) **$255.00** (4-1/2- and 5-inch blades)

Model 18 Attack-Survival knife has a 5-1/2- or 7-1/2-inch tool steel or 440 stainless steel blade with a stainless steel, hollow handle and threaded brass cap. Includes leather sheath. **$300.00** (6-inch blade) **$310.00** (7-1/2-inch blade)

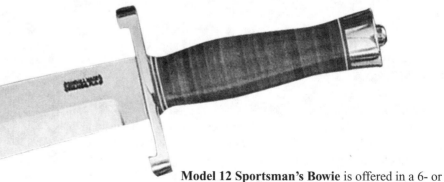

Model 12 Sportsman's Bowie is offered in a 6- or 9-inch blade of tool steel or 440 stainless steel with a leather handle, brass hilt and Duraluminun butt cap. **$260.00** (6-inch blade) **$405.00** (9-inch blade)

The **Falcon Fillet** comes with a plastic contoured sure-grip handle and finger guard for added safety and a 6-inch stainless steel blade. The Deluxe model includes a built-in Ceramic Stick sharpener. **Price unavailable**.

Rapala

**10395 Yellow Circle Drive
Minnetonka, MN 55343
(800) 874-4451
Fax: (952) 933-0046
www.rapala.com**

Styles: Rapala fillet knives.

Sheaths: Leather.

Handles: Birch or molded evoprene soft grip.

Features: Fillet knives of Scandinavian stainless steel in a variety of sizes.

The **Big Water Serrated Fillet** is a 8-inch long knife with a 5-inch blade. It's hand crafted and comes with a black evoprene soft-grip handle. **Price unavailable**.

The **Finn Thinn Fillet Knife** has an 8-inch thin blade designed for flexibility and strength, with a soft-grip handle. Included is a single-stage sharpener. **Price unavailable**.

The **Fish 'N Fillet** includes four blade sizes, from 4-inches to 9-inches, with progressively tapered, full-tang blades of Scandinavian stainless steel with a birch handle. Includes leather Laplander sheath and single-stage sharpener. **Price unavailable**.

Rapala Signature Series Knives are top-of-the-line with stained, waxed birch handles. Blades are double-tapered, hand-ground stainless steel of 4 inches, 6 inches or 7 inches, with flex for filleting. With oiled leather sheath. **Price unavailable**.

Remington Arms Co.

870 Remington Dr.
Madison, NC 27025
(800) 243-9700
Fax: (336) 548-7801
www.remington.com
E-mail:
info@remington.com

Styles: Fixed-blade and folding knives for hunting, fishing, camping and general use.

Sheaths: Leather and nylon.

Handles: G-10 composite, Delrin®, stainless steel, laminated wood and Kevlar®-impregnated nylon.

Features: ATS-34 tool or 440A stainless steel blades; some blades have oval cuts for one-hand opening; some models feature multiple blades, including screwdriver, can opener, saw, pin punch, gut hook and 12/20 ga. choke tool.

Retail Prices: $10.00 to $145.00

Delrin®-handle folding knife has a spear-point blade with hole for one-hand opening and a pen blade; 8-3/4-inches overall. Other models include a three-blade stockman; three-blade whittler; **Upland** with clip blade, 12/20 gauge choke tool and screwdriver, and gut hook; **Waterfowl** with clip blade, choke tool/screwdriver, pin punch and serrated bone blade; and **Camp** with four blades. **Price unavailable.**

2003 Pioneer Bullet Knife is a 2-blade trapper style design with cocobola wood handle. It features a 2-3/4-inch clip blade and a 2-3/4-inch spey blade with Remington tang stamp. Bullet shield, bolster, liners, pins and cap are made of nickel silver. 3-5/8 inches closed. **Price unavailable.**

The **Conquest** knife features a rosewood handle and a hollow-ground blade constructed of tough tool steel, with 4-inch cutting blade and full-length tang. Leather sheath included. **Price unavailable.**

Bird Hunter's Tool is the ultimate waterfowl/upland hunter's multi-tool. It folds to 4-1/2 inches long and features tough game shears, a bird gut hook, 3-inch clip-point blade, saw, flathead screwdriver, metric ruler and a patented 12 and 20 gauge choke tube wrench. It is 100 percent rust-resistant stainless steel and includes a ballistic sheath. **Price unavailable.**

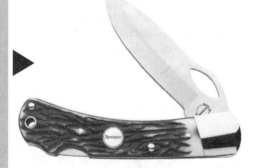

Deerhunter Series knives both feature stainless steel cutting-edge blade and all-weather Kraton™ handle with ferrule hole. **Deerhunter Clip** has an overall length of 8-1/8 inches and the Deerhunter Skinner has an overall length of 9-3/4 inches. **Price unavailable.**

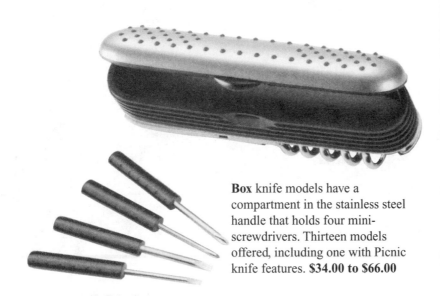

Box knife models have a compartment in the stainless steel handle that holds four mini-screwdrivers. Thirteen models offered, including one with Picnic knife features. **$34.00 to $66.00**

Structure maxi 9 has a stainless steel handle with rubber nubs for better grip, includes scissors, bottle opener, can opener, screwdriver, awl, corkscrew and knife blade. Thirteen other Structure models offered. **$85.00**

Blackwood maxi 9 has a blackwood handle and stainless steel blades. Thirteen other Blackwood models offered. **$90.00**

Richartz USA

1825 Walnut Hill Lane
Suite 120
Irving, TX 75038
(800) 859-2029
Fax: (972) 331-2566
www.richartz.com
E-mail: info@richartz.com

Styles: German-made, multi-blade folding knives for hunting, camping and general use.

Sheaths: N/A

Handles: Stainless steel with rubber nubs, sterling silver and rubber with stainless steel inlay.

Features: Box knives feature hollow handle with four mini-screwdrivers. Picnic knives separate into a knife and fork (with other blades included). Other blades include scissors, nail file, cuticle pusher, bottle opener, can opener, corkscrew, saw, pliers with wire cutter, Phillips and regular screwdrivers, awl and knife blade.

Retail Prices: $35.00 to $162.00

Santa Fe Stoneworks

3790 Cerrillos Road
Santa Fe, NM 87507
(800) 257-7625 or
(505) 471-3953
Fax: (505) 471-0036
www.santafestoneworks.
com
E-mail: knives@rt66.com

Styles: Camillus, Spyderco, Benchmade, Buck and other fixed-blade and folding knives enhanced with semi-precious stones, mother of pearl or inlaid woods.

Sheaths: N/A

Handles: Turquoise, malachite, azurite, lapis, chryscolla, apache gold, Picasso marble, mother of pearl and color-treated birch.

Features: Handle and bolster enhancements to factory knives.

Retail Prices: $41.00 to $330.00

These **Spyderco** models have enhancements that include turquoise, jet, mother-of-pearl and colored birch handle inlays.
$100.00 to $350.00

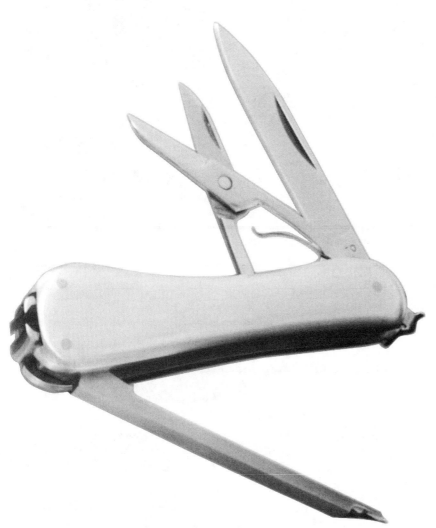

Sarco Cutlery LLC

115 Fairground Road
Florence, AL 35630
(256) 766-8099
Fax: (256) 766-7246
www.sarcoproducts.com
E-mail: sarco@hiwaay.net

Styles: Fixed-blade camping knife.

Sheaths: N/A

Handles: N/A

Features: N/A

Retail Prices: N/A

Tri Edge™ includes a file, clippers, manicure tip, scissors, and pen blade, with black Micarta® or Duraluminum handle. **$59.95**

Schrade Cutlery

7 Schrade Court
P.O. Box 7000
Ellenville, NY 12428-0981
(800) 272-4723
or (845) 647-7600
Fax: (845) 210-8670
www.schradeknives.com
E-mail:
info@schradeknives.com

Styles: Schrade, Old Timer, Uncle Henry and Imperial brands of fixed-blade and folding knives for hunting, fishing, camping, survival and general use; Schrade and Tradesman multi-tools; numerous other specialty knives, including Schrade Cliphanger folders with quick-release straps, the Schrade Iquip with altimeter, compass, and more.

Sheaths: Leather and ballistic nylon.

Handles: Stainless steel, oak, thermoplastic rubber, Delrin®, Staglon®, Zytel® and Kevlar®/Zytel®.

Features: High carbon or Schrade+ stainless steel blades; brass linings with nickel silver or brass bolsters; multi-tools allow access to all blades when opened or closed; most models offer limited lifetime warranty; some models offer one year replacement guarantee against loss.

Retail Prices: $21.95 to $500.00

Schrade Badger Lockbacks have 3-1/4-inch stainless steel blades and Zytel with thremoplastic handles with pocket clips. **SX4** with stainless steel blade and pocket clip **$24.95. SX4B** with blackened blade and pocket clip **$26.95**

Schrade Spitfire LTD has a one-hand operation 2-inch blade of ATS-34 stainless steel and handle of black G-10. Ambidextrous locking mechanism is treated with titanim. **$115.00**

Schrade Silhouette series have 2-7/8-inch stainless steel blades with 4-inch tempered aluminum handles. Anodized color options include black, fire engine red or cobalt. **$59.95**

Schrade Black Ice has a tapered 3-1/2-inch stainless steel blade and 4-1/4-inch black polycarbonate handle. **$64.95**

Schrade Viper features a tapered point 3-1/2-inch stainless steel blade with 4-1/2-inch anodized aluminum handle and ventilated steel pocket clip. **$59.95**

Schrade Cutlery (cont.)

Schrade Badger FX fixed blade knives have 3-1/2-inch blades (except SX23 model with 4-inch blade) with Zytel and thermoplastic rubber handles. SX20 with half serrated edge **$25.95,** SX21 with drop point blade **$24.95,** SX23 skinning blade **$24.95**

Winner of the 2001 Popular Mechanics Design and Engineering Award, **IQUIP** contains a computer module with altimeter, barometer, compass and clock modes, LED light, survival whistle, belt clip, Phillips and flathead screwdriver, cutting blade, scissors, saw, caplifter, can opener and corkscrew. It weighs 8.5 ounces. **$250.00**

Schrade Uncle Henry Golden Spike is 9-1/4 inches overall with Schrade+ stainless steel blade, Staglon handle and leather sheath. **$67.95**

SOG Specialty Knives Inc.

6521 212th St. SW
Lynnwood, WA 98036
(425) 771-6230
Fax: (425) 771-7689
www.sogknives.com
E-mail:
info@sogknives.com

Styles: Fixed-blade and folding knives and multi-tools for hunting, camping, tactical and general use.

Sheaths: Nylon, leather and Kydex®.

Handles: Zytel® glass-reinforced, Kraton™, lleather washers, Micarta® washers and stainless steel.

Features: Multi-tools feature pliers/wire cutters with an interlocking gear design that uses compound leverage for more gripping and cutting power. Titanium nitride finish on some multi-tools provides scratch and corrosion resistance. Many knife models feature semi-serrated edges, pocket clips and holes or thumb studs on the blades for one-hand opening.

Retail Prices: $24.95 to $274.95

Twitch I utilizes SOG's Assisted Technology for fast opening and locking of the 1.9-inch blade. Blade locks open and closed in the anodized aluminum handle. **$39.95**. **Twitch II** has a 2.7-inch blade. **$54.95**

Camo Flash II has a 3-1/2-inch blade of AUS 8 stainless steel and a camouflage Zytel handle with a new pocket clip for lowest carry position. **$64.95**

Mini Pentagon has a 3-1/2-inch, powder-coated blade of 440A stainless steel and a Zytel® glass-reinforced handle. Includes black leather sheath with mounting clip. **$54.95**

Recon Bowie has a 7-inch, gun-blued SK-5 carbon steel blade and a leather washer handle. Includes leather sheath and lanyard. **$225.00**

SEAL Pup has a partially serrated, scratch-resistant powder coated 4-3/4-inch blade of AUS-6 stainless steel and a Zytel handle. A Kydex sheath is included. **$74.95**

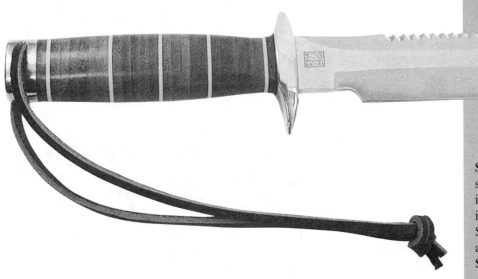

SEAL Revolver has a 4-3/4-inch blade of AUS-6 stainless steel and a Zytel handle. Pushing the locking lever and rotating the blade reveals a saw blade, readh to use. **$74.95**

X-42 Field Knife uses exotic BG-42 stainless steel for the 5.4-inch blade. Handle material is a deeply checkered Zytel. A black leather sheath is included. **$109.75**

SCUBA Demo has a 7-1/4-inch AUS-8 stainless steel blade and resin-impregnated leather washer handle, intended to revive the original Vietnam SOG fighting knife. A leather sheath and sharpening stone are include. **$230.00**

Spyderco Inc.

P.O. Box 800
Golden, CO 80402-0800
(800) 525-7770 or
(303) 279-8383
Fax: (303) 278-2229
www.spyderco.com
E-mail: custsvc@
spyderco.com

Styles: Primarily folding knives for law enforcement, hunting, fishing and general use. One style of fixed-blade hunting knife and SpydeRench multi-tool.

Sheaths: Concealex polymer.

Handles: Stainless steel, aluminum, fiberglass-reinforced nylon, G-10, G-10 with mother-of-pearl insets, Micarta®, Sermollan polymer, Kraton™ insets and titanium.

Features: Most models feature Spyderco's trademark hole in the blade for one-handed opening, fully or partially serrated blade and pocket clip. Numerous collaborations with custom knifemakers, including Bob Lum, Frank Centofante, Bill Moran, Bram Frank, Tim Zowada, James A. Keating, Howard Viele, Tim Wegner, Bob Terzuola and others.

Retail Prices: $26.95 to $349.95

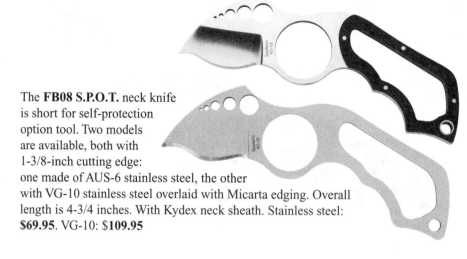

The **FB08 S.P.O.T.** neck knife is short for self-protection option tool. Two models are available, both with 1-3/8-inch cutting edge: one made of AUS-6 stainless steel, the other with VG-10 stainless steel overlaid with Micarta edging. Overall length is 4-3/4 inches. With Kydex neck sheath. Stainless steel: **$69.95**. VG-10: **$109.95**

The **C72 Pride Clipit** is the first one-hand open non-locking folder. It features a 2-inch AUS-6 stainless steel blade with a handle of brushed aluminum that has an embedded cloisonne enamel flag. Overall length is 5-5/8 inches and weight is 1.5 ounces. **$49.95**

C76 25-Year Anniversary Knife features a 3-inch VG-10 stainless steel blade, jig-bone handle and forged Damascus bolsters. No two are alike. **$349.95**

FB09 Ronin is a fixed blade neck knife designed by Michael Janich and Michael Snody with a 3-inch VG-10 blade in a modified Wharncliffe shape. The handle is of slate-colored linen Micarta. **$159.95**

Spyderco Inc. (cont.)

New from Spyderco is a set of **204D** diamond-coated triangular sharpening rods. Each rod is 7 inches and the three flat sides are 1/2-1/2-inch wide. Made of nickel-coated steel and plated with microscopic diamond particles, they are 400 mesh, with a channel for honing pointed items such as fishhooks, awls or darts. **$89.95**

The **FB05 Temperance** is Spyderco's newest entry into the fixed-blade market. The 4-inch blade of VG-10 stainless steel is 4 mm thick. A black fiberglass reinforced nylon handle is designed for cutting chores. Overall length is 9-5/8 inches, with a weight of 5.625 ounces. With Kydex sheath. **$119.95**

C77 SpyderHawk CLIPIT features a 3-3/8-inch VG-10 stainless steel serrated blade for fast cutting of line, rope or webbing, encased in a non-slip black fiberglass-reinforced nylong handle. It weighs 3 ounces. **$89.95**

T02 SpyderSaw is an unusual folding 5-inch pocket saw of high-carbon AUS-6 steel. The handle is black fiberglass-reinforced nylon with a non-slip grip. The clip permits the saw to be carried in a pocket, pack strap or waistband. **$59.95**

Taylor Cutlery

1736 N. Eastman Road
Kingsport, TN 37662-1638
(800) 251-0254 or
(423) 247-2406
Fax: (423) 247-5371
www.taylorcutlery.com
E-mail:
taylor@preferred.com

Styles: Fixed-blade and folding knives for tactical, rescue, hunting and general use.

Sheaths: Nylon and leather.

Handles: Stag, aluminum with rubber inserts, aluminum with turquoise inlays, Zytel® with aluminum inserts, Zytel®, skeletonized steel, fiberglass, G-10.

Features: Smith & Wesson and Cuttin' Horse brands. Many models feature decorative scrimshaw or printed-scene inserts in handle; most have thumb studs or blade holes for one-hand opening.

Retail Prices: $11.60 to $92.24

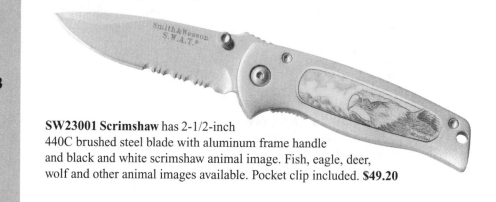

SW23001 Scrimshaw has 2-1/2-inch 440C brushed steel blade with aluminum frame handle and black and white scrimshaw animal image. Fish, eagle, deer, wolf and other animal images available. Pocket clip included. **$49.20**

SWHRTMGS Folder has 3.6-inch partly serrated 440C bead-blasted stainless steel blade and magnesium handle with pocket clip. Designed by Darrel Ralph and Mike Lamprey. **Price unavailable.**

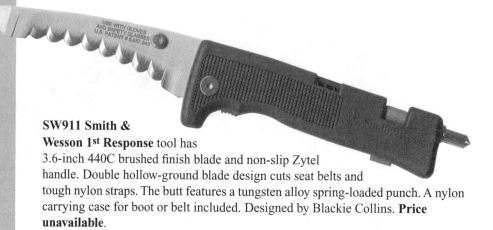

SW911 Smith & Wesson 1st Response tool has 3.6-inch 440C brushed finish blade and non-slip Zytel handle. Double hollow-ground blade design cuts seat belts and tough nylon straps. The butt features a tungsten alloy spring-loaded punch. A nylon carrying case for boot or belt included. Designed by Blackie Collins. **Price unavailable.**

SWFL1 Folder has 3-3/4-inch 440C stainless steel blade with thumb button, stainless steel handle and pocket clip. **Price unavailable.**

Tim Herman Wall Street Tactical™
gentlemen's folder has slender scales of
ivory or burgundy micarta, stainless
steel bolsters, 420-J stainless steel
liners and a 3-inch AUS-8M
stainless steel polished blade
with plain or combo edge.
$120.00

**Lightfoot Mini Pit
Bull™** a neck, belt and
boot knife, is 6.6 inches
long with Zytel® handle
scales and weighs 2.4
ounces. It has a plain or
combo edge 3-inch AUS-8
stainless steel blade and four-way
Kydex® sheath. **$39.99**

Timberline KickStart™ is a Butch
Vallotton design with perfect pivot-pin-
to-blade geometry and a Zytel® handle
with Kraton™ inserts. Bead-blasted 3-1/2-
inch AUS-8 blade is available in partially
serrated or plain edge. **$59.99**

Timberline Knives

P.O. Box 600
Getzville, NY 14068-0600
(800) 548-7427
or (716) 877-2200
Fax: (716) 877-2591
www.timberlineknives.com
E-mail:
gatco@buffnet.net

Styles: Fixed-blade and
folding knives for hunting,
camping, military and general
use; Frog Tool multi-tool.

Sheaths: Nylon and Kydex®.
Handles: Fiberglass-
reinforced nylon, aluminum,
Kraton™ and stainless steel.

Features: Folders have blade
stud or hole for one-hand
opening; some folders have
pocket clips; NeeleyLock™
opens and closes by pushing the
blade forward (no levers or
buttons); Discovery™ lock is
unlocked by sliding handle
button.

**Retail Prices: $23.99 to
$400.00**

TiNives

1725 Smith Road
Fortson, GA 31808
(888) 537-9991
Fax: (706) 322-2452
www.tinives.com
E-mail: info@tiknives.com

Styles: High-tech folding knives for tactical, law enforcement and general use.

Sheaths: N/A

Handles: Machined aluminum.

Features: Ball-bearing mechanism for smooth opening. Aluminum handles available in a wide variety of colors and milled to create a texture for improved grip.

Retail Prices: $249.00 to $800.00

TiNives 3.25 ball bearing knife has a 3-inch damasteel powdered stainless damascus blade with a 32 ball bearing mechanism and a milled 3-d aircraft aluminum handle. Law enforcement version also available. Prices start at **$249.00**

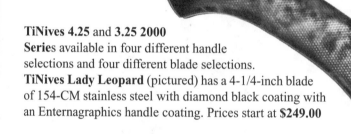

TiNives 4.25 and **3.25 2000**
Series available in four different handle selections and four different blade selections.
TiNives Lady Leopard (pictured) has a 4-1/4-inch blade of 154-CM stainless steel with diamond black coating with an Enternagraphics handle coating. Prices start at **$249.00**

TiNives 4.25 Tactical Speedroller has a 4-1/2-inch blade of 154-CM stainless steel and a 3-d milled aluminum handle. Available in manual, auto or DA. Price starts at **$249.00**

Uticryl Whitetail Deer Model with 2-1/4-inch stainless steel blade and clear Uticryl handle (offered with deer, ring-necked pheasant, mallard, bass, eagle, turkey, wolf and grizzly bear designs). **$36.74**

Teakwood Master Lockback with 2-1/4-inch stainless steel blade and laser-engraved teakwood handles (offered with eagle, deer, bass, mallard and trout designs). **$7.34**

Mountain Quest Laser Series lockback with 3-1/2-inch blade and laser-engraved handles (offered in turkey, deer, mallard and Lab designs). **$16.75**

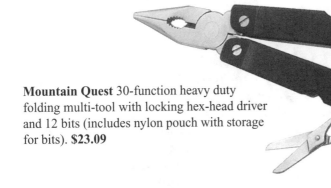

Mountain Quest 30-function heavy duty folding multi-tool with locking hex-head driver and 12 bits (includes nylon pouch with storage for bits). **$23.09**

Utica Cutlery Co.

820 Noyes St.
Utica, NY 13503-1527
(800) 888-4223
Fax: (315) 733-6602
Web site:
www.kutmaster.com
E-mail:
Sales@kutmaster.com

Styles: Wide range of folding and fixed-blade designs, multi-tools and steak knives.

Sheaths: Nylon and leather.

Handles: Stainless steel, thermoplastic, Delrin® Buckstag, hardwood, redwood, teakwood, brass, Uticryl.

Features: KutMaster and Mountain Quest brands; specialty multi-tools for archers, pruning shears/folding saw combo, folders with laser-engraved, scrimshaw or full-color wildlife scenes in clear handles; sculptured metal handles with die-struck wildlife scenes.

Retail Prices: **$6.25 to $75.25**

Victorinox

One Research Drive
P.O. Box 874
Shelton, CT 06484-0874
(800) 243-4045
Fax: (800) 243-4006
www.swissarmy.com
E-mail:
knife.repair@swissarmy.com

Styles: Folding multi-blade designs and multi-tools for hunting, fishing, camping, hiking, golfing and general use. One of the original makers (Victorinox) of Swiss Army knives.

Sheaths: Leather or nylon.

Handles: Stainless steel, sterling silver, solid plastic or translucent plastic.

Features: Wide variety of blades and tools (some removable), including straight-edge and serrated blades, saw blade, can opener, straight-edge screwdriver, Phillips screwdriver, file, scissors, ruler, hex socket with drive bits, pliers, wire cutter, awl, corkscrew, tweezers, toothpick, flashlight, hook, ball-point pen, hook disgorger, magnifying glass, sewing eye and digital altimeter.

Retail Prices: $10.00 to $175.00

Midnite MiniChamp® is available with a translucent red or blue handle and includes 16 features, including scissors, bottle opener, magnetic Phillips screwdriver, scraper, ruler, cuticle pusher, nail cleaner, retractable ball-point pen, flashlight and two blades. **$40.00**

Victorinox® SwissTool™ (shown) is made of stainless steel and has 24 tools, including five screwdriver blades, can opener, bottle opener, metal file, metal saw, ruler, pliers, wire cutter, wire stripper, electrical crimper, straight-edge blade and serrated blade. **$80.00**. **SwissTool Plus** includes the Swiss Tool, plus wrench and six drive bits. **$100.00**. **SwissTool CS** includes the SwissTool with detachable corkscrew. **$102.00/120.00**

SwissChamp XLT has a red translucent handle and 50 features, including a bit wrench, bit case with 10 bit points, pliers, magnifying lens, hook disgorger, ruler, wood saw, metal saw, metal file, wood chisel, ball-point pen, awl, straight pin, scissors and two knife blades. **$195.00**

CyberTool 29 (shown) has a translucent red or blue plastic handle and 29 tools, including hex driver with four bits (eight tips, including Torx, Phillips and regular screwdrivers), ball-point pen, can opener, bottle opener, two screwdriver blades, awl, tweezers, toothpick, eyeglasses screwdriver, straight pin, corkscrew and knife blade. **$60.00** **CyberTool 34** is offered in translucent red, blue or black handle and includes all the above features, plus pliers, wire cutter, wire crimper, scissors and hook. **$78.00** **CyberTool 41** is offered in translucent red or blue handle and includes all these features, plus wood saw, metal saw, metal file, nail cleaner, chisel/scraper and 2.5mm screwdriver. **$95.00**

Altimeter (shown) has a translucent red handle and 17 features, including scissors, bottle opener, can opener, awl, hook, corkscrew, mini-screwdriver, two knife blades, digital altimeter and digital thermometer. **$100.00**. Altimeter Plus has the same features, plus a wood saw and fine screwdriver. **$105.00**

Wenger North America

15 Corporate Drive
Orangeburg, NY 10962
(800) 431-2996 or
(914) 365-3500
Fax: (914) 425-4700
www.WengerNA.com
E-mail:
dplretra@wenger.com

Styles: One of the official makers of folding multi-blade Swiss Army Knives. Currently offers 81 models.

Sheaths: Nylon or leather pouch (some models).

Handles: Plastic (red, green, black), aluminum, stainless steel and titanium.

Features: Wide variety of stainless steel blades and tools (some removable) including straight edge and serrated blades, saw, ruler, fish hook disgorger, scissors, awl, can opener, flashlight, laser pointer, magnifier, fish hook file, nail file, compass, Allen wrenches, hex wrench, divot tool, cigar cutter and pliers.

Retail Prices: $15.00 to $125.00

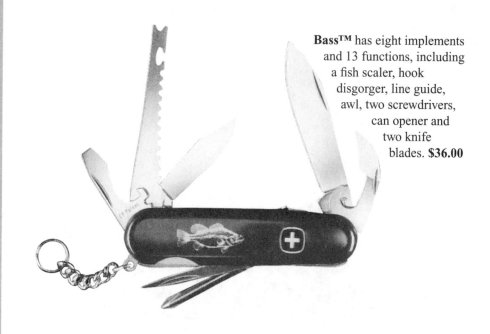

Bass™ has eight implements and 13 functions, including a fish scaler, hook disgorger, line guide, awl, two screwdrivers, can opener and two knife blades. **$36.00**

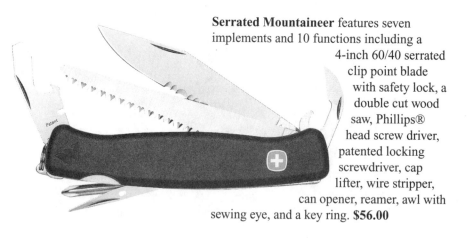

Serrated Mountaineer features seven implements and 10 functions including a 4-inch 60/40 serrated clip point blade with safety lock, a double cut wood saw, Phillips® head screw driver, patented locking screwdriver, cap lifter, wire stripper, can opener, reamer, awl with sewing eye, and a key ring. **$56.00**

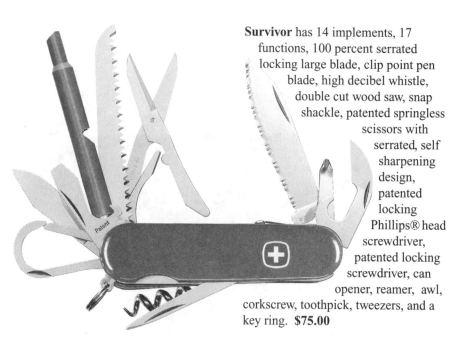

Survivor has 14 implements, 17 functions, 100 percent serrated locking large blade, clip point pen blade, high decibel whistle, double cut wood saw, snap shackle, patented springless scissors with serrated, self sharpening design, patented locking Phillips® head screwdriver, patented locking screwdriver, can opener, reamer, awl, corkscrew, toothpick, tweezers, and a key ring. **$75.00**

The **Highlander** with Advantage Timber™ camouflaged handles, has seven implements and 11 functions, including non-reflective stainless steel implements, a large blade, two screwdrivers (Phillips and patented locking flat head), cap lifter, wire stripper, can opener, nail file, nail cleaner, reamer, awl and key ring. **$32.00**

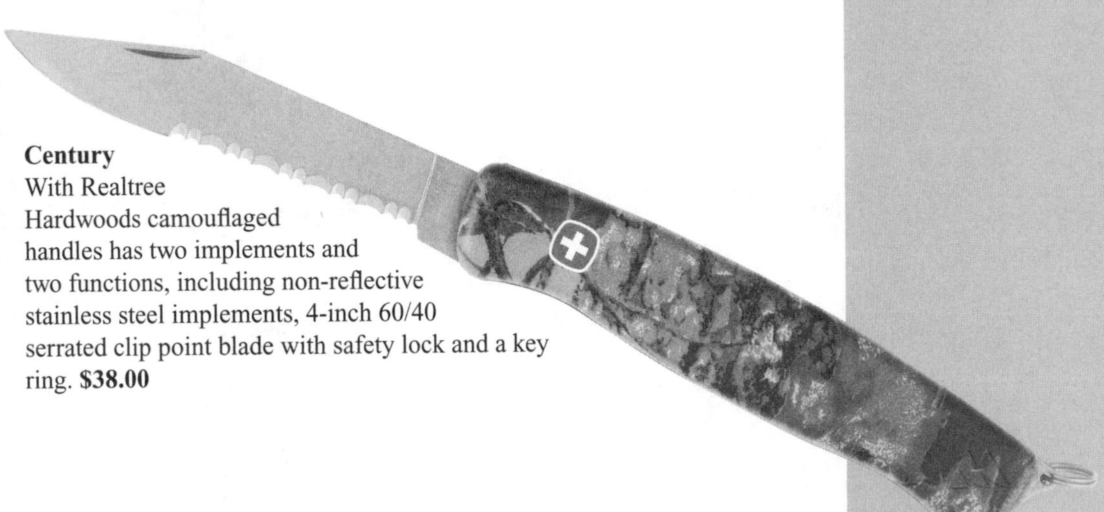

Century
With Realtree
Hardwoods camouflaged
handles has two implements and
two functions, including non-reflective
stainless steel implements, 4-inch 60/40
serrated clip point blade with safety lock and a key
ring. **$38.00**

Wild Boar Blades

P.O. Box 61485
Vancouver, WA 98666
(888) 735-8483 or
(360) 735-0570
Fax: (360) 735-0390
www.wildboarblades.com
E-mail:
info@wildboarblades.com

Styles: Fixed blade and folding hunting and general-use knives.

Sheaths: Natural, brown or black leather.

Handles: Deer antler, African wood or rubber-plastic composite.

Features: Made in Poland. Stainless-steel alloy blades are hand-ground and polished. Designs electrochemically etched on blades.

Retail Prices: $25.95 to $119.95
(also sold in sets)

The **Model 28, 29** and **29M** knives have 3-1/21/2-inch blades of 44-C stainless steel with a total length of 6-1/4 inches. **$49.95 to $75.95**

The **Model 24** has a 3-1/4-inch blade of 44-C stainless steel, a closed length of 4-5/8 inches and an open length of 8 inches. **$109.95**

The **Model 25, 26, 27** and **27M** all have 4-1/2-inch 44-C stainless steel blades, with a total length of 9-3/8 inches. Wood handles are made from African mahogany and all parts of the knives are made from 44-C stainless steel. **$55.95 to $95.95**

Spryte is an integral sculpted titanium-handled knife with ATS-34 blade. Button lock mechanism is inlaid with gemcut sapphire. **$300.00**

Amber Series Lancet Folder liner lock has a 2-5/8-inch ATS-34 stainless steel blade, titanium frame and jigged bone handle. Hidden thong attachment in the handle's spine. **$275.00**

Pearl Series Kestrel Folder liner lock has a 2-1/8-inch ATS-34 stainless steel blade, titanium frame and mother-of-pearl handle. Hidden thong attachment in the handle's spine. **$300.00**

Monarch has an ATS-34 blade with a button lock mechanism, desert Ironwood scales and integral titanium handle. **$395.00**

Westcliff features a stainless Damascus blade, integral mokume handle, mop scales and button locking mechanism. It has an opan inlaid thumbstud. **$105.00**

Carbon Fiber Series Spearpoint Folder liner lock has a 3-1/4-inch ATS-34 stainless steel blade, titanium liner and pocket clip, and carbon fiber handle. Weighs 1.6 ounces. **$220.00**

William Henry Fine Knives

2125 Delaware Ave.
Suite C
Santa Cruz, CA 95060
(831) 454-9409
Fax: (831) 454-9309
www.williamhenryknives.
com
E-mail: sales@
williamhenryknives.com

Styles: Semi-custom folding knives for hunting and general use; some limited editions.

Sheaths: Leatherslip sheath. ClipCase optional.

Handles: Jigged bone, genuine motgher of pearl, carbon fiber, exotic woods, fossil ivories, silver granulation and koftgari (inlaid 24K gold).

Features: Blades of ATS-34 or Norris stainless Damascus steel; locking liner or button lock mechanisms.

Retail Prices: $120.00 to $1100.00

Wuu Jau Co. Inc.

2600 S. Kelly Ave.
Edmond, OK 73013
(800) 722-5760
or (405) 359-5031
Fax: (877) 256-4337
or (405) 340-5965
www.WuuJau.com
Email:
wuujau@direcway.com

Styles: Wide variety of imported fixed-blade and folding knives for hunting, fishing, camping, and general use.

Sheaths: Nylon or leather.

Handles: Cast metal, plastic, synthetic ivory, stainless steel and hardwood.

Features: Many models have thumb studs or holes in blades for one-hand opening. Variety of wildlife scenes scrimshawed on handles of some models.

Retail Prices: N/A

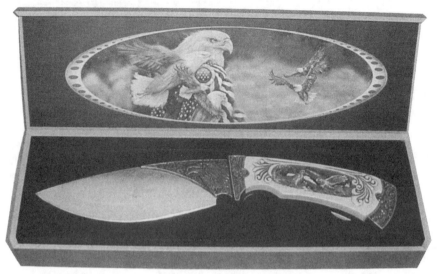

Model K8202 Eagle has a Damascus-type blade, carved-simulated ivory handle with wildlife scents. Gift box included. **Price unavailable**.

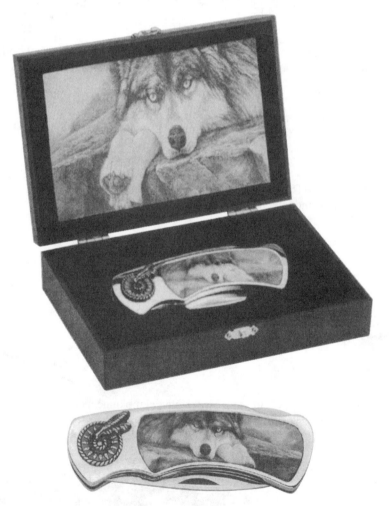

Model YC8774 has a stainless steel blade and a handle laminated with wildlife scene insert. Gift box included. **Price unavailable**.

Model **55801** has 3 functions for an economical pocket knife. **$12.00**

Model **55803** has 4 functions in its pocket knife configurations. **$20.00**

Model **55804** moves up to 10 functions. **$25.00**

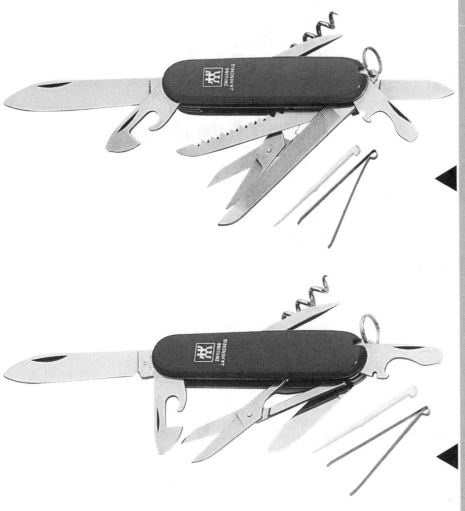

Zwilling J.A. Henckels Inc.

**171 Saw Mill River Road
Hawthorne, NY 10532-1529
(914) 747-0300
Fax: (914) 747-1850
www.j-a-henckels.com
E-mail:
info@jahenckels.com**

Styles: Folding multi-blade utility knives for hunting, fishing, camping and general use.

Sheaths: Leather.

Handles: Plastic and stainless steel.

Features: Stainless steel blades and liners.

Retail Prices: **$12.00 to $52.00**

Model **55807** has seven tools and 14 functions, including can opener, two screwdrivers, bottle opener, corkscrew, awl, tweezers, toothpick, fish scaler and two knife blades. **$52.00**

Model **55817** has nine tools and 13 functions, including can opener, bottle opener, two screwdrivers, corkscrew, awl, scissors, tweezers, toothpick and two knife blades. **$45.00**

MISCELLANEOUS COMPANIES

Beck's Cutlery & Specialties

SHP CENTER No. 109
McGregor Village
107 Edinburgh South Dr.
Cary, NC 27511
(919) 460-0203
Fax: (919) 460-7772

National Knife Distributors

P.O. Box 188
Forest City, NC 28043
800-447-4342
or (828) 245-4321
Fax: (828) 245-5121

Features: Bench Work pocketknives from Solingen, Germany.

Lakota (Brunton USA)

620 E. Monroe
Riverton, WY 82501-4997
(307) 856-6559
Fax: (307) 856-1840

Features: AUS-8A high-carbon stainless steel blades.

Masters of Defense Knife Co.

1941 Camp Branch Road
Waynesville, NC 28786
(828) 452-4158
Fax: (828) 452-4158
www.mastersofdefense.com

Styles: Fixed-blade and folding knives for tactical and general use.

Sheaths: Nylon or Kydex®.

Handles: Hardened 6061-T6 aluminum.

Features: Plain or serrated edge; satin polished, matte bead blasted, satin gloss black titanium carbo nitride or matte black titanium carbo nitride finish; plunge lock mechanism; some models have pocket clips; one model has auxiliary cutter in handle.

Queen Cutlery Co.

P.O. Box 500
Franklinville, NY 14737
(800) 222-5233
Fax: (800) 299-2618
www.cutlery.com
E-mail: salesOKC@aol.com

Quikut

P.O. Box 29
Airport Industrial Park
Walnut Ridge, AR 72476
(870) 886-6774
Fax: (870) 886-9162

Round Eye Knife & Tool

P.O. Box 818
Sagel, ID 83860
(208) 265-8858
Fax: (208) 263-0848
www.roundeye.com
E-mail: roundeye@nidlink.com

Styles: Folding and fixed-blade knives for hunting and general use.

Sheaths: Kydex®.

Handles: G-10 or carbon steel.

Features: Rolling Lock™ with slide-bar operation is considered one of the strongest locking mechanisms for a folding knife. All R.E.K.A.T. folders feature this lock.

Retail Prices: $54.95 to $224.95

sporting cutlers

The firms listed here are special in the sense that they make or market special kinds of knives made in facilities they own or control either in the U.S. or overseas. Or they are special because they make knives of unique design or function. The second phone number listed is the fax number.

A.G. RUSSELL KNIVES INC
1920 North 26th St
Lowell, AR 72745-8489
479-631-0130 800-255-9034
749-631-8493
ag@agrussell.com
www.agrussell.com
The oldest knife mail-order company, highest quality. Free catalog available. In these catalogs you will find the newest and the best. If you like knives, this catalog is a must.

AHERN GROUP, THE/EXECUTIVE EDGE
3462 Cascade Ive Drive
Buford, GA 30519
678-482-8116 or 800-334-3790
6784829421; 800-334-3790
www.executiveedge.com
tahern@bellsouth.net
Pen style shirt pocket knives ideal for carry or gift giving. Several sizes and style available

AL MAR KNIVES
PO Box 2295
Tualatin, OR 97062-2295
503-670-9080; 503-639-4789
www.almarknives.com
Featuring our ultralight™ series of knives. Sere 2000™ Shirke, Sere™, Operator™, Nomad™, and Ultralight series™

ALCAS COMPANY
1116 E State St
Olean, NY 14760
716-372-3111; 716-373-6155
twarner@kabar.com
www.cutco.com
Household cutlery / sport knives

ANZA KNIVES
C Davis
PO Box 710806
Santee, CA 92072
619-561-9445
619-390-6283
sales@anzaknives.com
www.anzaknives.com

B&D TRADING CO.
3935 Fair Hill Rd.
Fair Oaks, CA 95628

BARTEAUX MACHETES, INC.
1916 SE 50th St.
Portland, OR 97215
503-233-5880
barteaux@machete.com
www.machete.com
Manufacture of machetes, saws, garden tools

BEAR MGC CUTLERY
1111 Bear Blvd. SW
Jacksonville, AL 36265
256-435-2227; 256-435-9348
Lockback, commemorative, multi tools, high tech & hunting knives

BECK'S CUTLERY & SPECIALTIES
Mcgregor Village Center
107 Edinburgh South Dr
Cary, NC 27511
919-460-0203
919-460-7772
beckscutlery@mindspring.com
www.beckscutlery.com

BENCHMADE KNIFE CO. INC.
300 Beaver Creek Rd.
Oregon City, OR 97045
503-655-6004; 503-655-6223
info@benchmade.com
www.benchmade.com
Sports, utility, law enforcement, military, gift and semi custom

BERETTA U.S.A. CORP.
17601 Beretta Dr.
Accokeek, MD 20607
800-528-7453
www.berettausa.com
Full range of hunting & specialty knives

BLACKJACK KNIVES
PO Box 3
Greenville, WV 24945

BLUE GRASS CUTLERY CORP
20 E Seventh St PO Box 156
Manchester, OH 45144
937-549-2602; 937-549-2709 or 2603
sales@bluegrasscutlery.com
www.bluegrasscutlery.com
Manufacturer of Winchester Knives, John Primble Knives and many contract lines

BOKER USA INC
1550 Balsam St
Lakewood, CO 802014-5917
303-462-0662
303-462-0668
sales@bokerusa.com
www.bokerusa.com
Wide range of fixed blade and folding knives for hunting, military, tactical and general use

BROWNING
One Browning Pl
Morgan, UT 84050
801-876-2711; 801-876-3331
www.browning.com
Outdoor hunting & shooting products

BUCK KNIVES INC
1900 Weld Blvd.
El Cajon, CA 92020
800-735-2825; 619-562-2285
www.buckknives.com
Sports cutlery

BULLDOG BRAND KNIVES
PO Box 23852
Chattanooga, TN 37422
423-894-5102
423-892-9165
Fixed blade and folding knives for hunting and general use

BUSSE COMBAT KNIFE CO.
11651 CO Rd 12
Wauseon, OH 43567
419-923-6471; 419-923-2337
www.bussecombat.com
Simple & very strong straight knife designs for tactical & expedition use

CAMILLUS CUTLERY CO.
54 Main St.
Camillus, NY 13031
315-672-8111; 315-672-8832
customerservice@camillusknives.com
www.camillusknives.com

CAS IBERIA INC
650 Industrial Blvd.
Sale Creek, TN 37373
423-332-4700
423-332-7248
www.casiberia.com
Extensive variety of fixed-blade and folding knives for hunting, diving, camping, military and general use

CASE CUTLERY
W R & Sons
Owens Way
Bradford, PA 16701
800-523-6350; 814-368-1736
consumer-relations@wrcase.com
www.wrcase.com
Folding pocket knives

CHICAGO CUTLERY CO.
9234 W Belmont Ave
Franklin Park, IL 60131
847-678-8600
www.chicagocutlery.com
Sport & utility knives

CHRIS REEVE KNIVES
11624 W President Dr. No.B
Boise, ID 83713
208-375-0367
208-375-0368
crknifo@chrisreeve.com

www.chrisreeve.com
Makers of one-piece range of fixed blades, sebenza and folding knives

COAST CUTLERY CO
2045 SE Ankeny St.
Portland, OR 97214
800-426-5858 or 503-234-4545
503-234-4422
www.coastcutlery.com
Variety of fixed-blade and folding knives and multi-tools for hunting, camping and general use

COLD STEEL INC
3036 Seaborg Ave. Suite A
Ventura, CA 93003
800-255-4716 or 805-650-8481
805-642-9727
art@coldsteel.com
www.coldsteel.com
Wide variety of folding lockbacks and fixed-blade hunting, fishing and neck knives, as well as bowies, kukris, tantos, throwing knives and kitchen knives

COLONIAL CUTLERY INTERNATIONAL
K.M. Paolantonio
PO Box 960
North Scituate, RI 02857
866-421-6500
401-421-6500
colonialcutlery@aol.com
Custom design, sport and camp knives

COLUMBIA RIVER KNIFE & TOOL
9720 SW Hillman Ct.
Wilsonville, OR 97070
800-891-3100
503-682-9680
info@crkt.com
www.crkt.com
Complete line of sport, work and tactical knives

CRAWFORD KNIVES
205 N Center
West Memphis, AR 72301
870-732-2452
Folding knives for tactical and general use

CRIPPLE CREEK KNIVES
Rt. 1, Box 501B
Oldfort, TN 37362

DAVID BOYE KNIVES
PO Box 1238
Dolan Springs, AZ 86441
800-853-1617 or 520-767-4273
520-767-3030
www.boyeknives.com
Semi-production fixed-blade and folding knives for hunting and general use

DUNN KNIVES
Steve Greene
PO Box 204
Rosville, KS 66533
785-584-6856
785-584-6856

EMERSON KNIVES, INC.
PO Box 4180
Torrance, CA 90510-4180
310-212-7455
310-212-7289
www.emersonknives.com
Hard use tactical knives; folding & fixed blades

FALLKNIVEN AB
Havrevagen 10
S-96142 Boden
SWEDEN
46-92154422
46-92154433
info@fallkniven.se
www.fallkniven.com
High quality stainless knives

FROG TOOL CO
PO Box 600
Getzville, NY 14068-0600
716-877-2200; 716-877-2591
gatco@buffnet.net
www.frogtool.net
Precision multi tools

Sporting Cutlers, continued

FROST CUTLERY CO
PO Box 22636
Chattanooga, TN 37422
800-251-7768 or423-894-6079
423-894-9576
www.frostcutleryco.com
Wide range of fixed-blade and folding knives with a multitude of handle materials

GATCO SHARPENERS
PO Box 600
Getzville, NY 14068
716-877-2200; 716-877-2591
gatcosharpeners.com
Precision sharpening systems, diamond sharpening systems, ceramic sharpening systems, carbide sharpening systems, natural Arkansas stones

GENUINE ISSUE INC.
949 Middle Country Rd.
Selden, NY 11784
631-696-3802; 631-696-3803
gicutlery@aol.com
Antique knives, swords

GERBER LEGENDARY BLADES
14200 SW 72nd Ave.
Portland, OR 97223
503-639-6161
www.gerberblades.com
Knives, multi-tools, axes, saws, outdoor products

GIGAND USA
701 Penhoun Ave.
Secaucus, NJ 07094
201-583-5968
Imports designed by Fred C.

GROHMANN KNIVES LTD.
PO Box 40
Pictou Nova Scotia B0K 1H0
CANADA
888-756-4837 or 902-485-4224
902-485-5872
Fixed-blade belt knives for hunting and fishing, folding pocketknives for hunting and general use

GT KNIVES
7734 Arjons Dr.
San Diego, CA 92126
858-530-8766; 858-530-8798
gtknives@gtknives.com
www.gtknives.com
Law enforcement & military automatic knives

GUTMANN CUTLERY INC
PO Box 2219
Bellingham, WA 98227
800-288-5379
Junglee knives, Smith & Wesson tools and optics, Walther knives and optics

H&B FORGE CO.
235 Geisinger Rd.
Shiloh, OH 44878
419-895-1856
Tomahawks & throwing knives

HISTORIC EDGED WEAPONRY
1021 Saddlebrook Dr
Hendersonville, NC 28739
828-692-0323
828-692-0600
histwpn@bellsouth.net
Antique knives from around the world; importer of puukko and other knives from Norway, Sweden, Finland and Lapland

HONEYCUTT MARKETING, INC., DAN
3165 C-4 S Campbell
Springfield, MO 65807
417-886-2288; 417-887-2635
ozk_knife_gun@hotmail.com
All kinds of cutlery, military, Randalls

IMPERIAL SCHRADE CORP.
7 Schrade Ct.
Ellenville, NY 12428
800-2-Schrade
www.schradeknives.com

JOY ENTERPRISES-FURY CUTLERY
1104 53rd Court South
West Palm Beach, FL 33407
800-500-3879 or 561-863-3205
561-863-3277
mail@joyenterprises.com
www.joyenterprises.com; www.furycutlery.com
Extensive variety of fixed-blade and folding knives for hunting, fishing, diving, camping, military and general use; novelty key-ring knives

KA-BAR KNIVES INC
1125 E State St.
Olean, NY 14760
800-282-0130
www.info@ka-bar.com

KATZ KNIVES, INC.
PO Box 730
Chandler, AZ 85224-0730
480-786-9334; 480-786-9338
katzkn@aol.com
www.katzknives.com

KELLAM KNIVES CO.
902 S Dixie Hwy.
Lantana, FL 33462
800-390-6918; 561-588-3185; 561-588-3186
info@kellamknives.com
www.kellamknives.com
Largest selection of Finnish knives; handmade & production

KERSHAW/KAI CUTLERY CO.
25300 SW Parkway
Wilsonville, OR 97070

MESSEV KLOTZLI
Hohengasse E Ch 3400
Burgdorf
SWITZERLAND
(34) 422-2378
(34) 422-7693
info@klotzli.com
www.klotzli.com
High-tech folding knives for tactical and general use

KNIFEWARE INC
PO Box 3
Greenville, WV 24945

KNIGHTS EDGE LTD.
5696 N Northwest Highway
Chicago, IL 60646-6136
773-775-3888
773-775-3339
sales@knightsedge.com
www.knightsedge.com
Medieval weaponry, swords, suits of armor, katanas, daggers

KNIVES OF ALASKA, INC.
Charles or Jody
3100 Airport Dr.
Denison, TX 75020 8623
903-786-7366, 800-752-0980; 903-786-7371
info@knivesofalaska.com
www.knivesofalaska.com
High quality hunting & outdoorsmen's knives

KUTMASTER KNIVES
Div of Utica Cutlery Co
820 Noyes St.
Utica, NY 13502
315-733-4663; 315-733-6602
www.kutmaster.com
Manufacturer and importer of pocket, lockback, tool knives and multi-purpose tools

LAKOTA
620 E Monroe
Riverton, WY 24945
307-856-6559
307-856-1840
AUS 8-A high-carbon stainless steel blades

LEATHERMAN TOOL GROUP, INC.
PO Box 20595
Portland, OR 97294
503-253-7826; 503-253-7830
mktg@leatherman.com
www.leatherman.com
Multi-tools

LONE WOLF KNIVES
Doug Hutchens
17400 SW Upper Boones Ferry Rd. Suite 240
Portland, OR 97224
503-431-6777

MARBLE'S OUTDOORS
420 Industrial Park
Gladstone, MI 49837
906-428-3710; 906-428-3711
marble@up.net
www.marblesoutdoors.com

MASTERS OF DEFENSE KNIFE CO
256 A Industrial Park Dr.
Waynesville, NC 28786
828-452-4158
828-452-7327
info@mastersofdefense.com
www.mastersofdefense.com
Fixed-Blade and folding knives for tactical and general use

MEYERCO MANUFACTURING
4481 Exchange Service Dr.
Dallas, TX 75236
214-467-8949
214-467-9241
www.meyercousa.com
Folding tactical,rescue and speed-assisted pocketknives; fixed-balde hunting and fishing designs; multi-function camping tools and machetes

MCCANN INDUSTRIES
132 S 162nd PO Box 641
Spanaway, WA 98387
253-537-6919; 253-537-6993
McCann.machine@worldnet.att.net
www.mccannindustries.com

MICRO TECHNOLOGY
932 36th Ct. SW
Vero Beach, Fl 32968
772-569-3058
772-569-7632
sales@microtechknives.com
www.microtechknives.com
Manufacturers of the highest quality production knives

MORTY THE KNIFE MAN, INC.
4 Manorhaven Blvd.
Pt Washington, NY 11050
516-767-2357; 516-767-7058

MUSEUM REPLICAS LTD.
PO Box 840 Dept PQ
Conyers, GA 30012
800-883-8838
www.museumreplicas.com
Historically accurate & battle-ready swords & daggers

MYERCHIN MARINE CLASSICS
14185 Regina Dr Ste. G
Rancho Cucamonga, CA 91739
909-463-6741; 909-463-6751
myerchin@myerchin.com
www.myerchin.com
Rigging/ Police knives

NATIONAL KNIFE DISTRIBUTORS
PO Box 188
Forest City, NC 28043
800-447-4342; 828-245-4321 or 828-245-5121
Benchmark pocketknives from Solingen, Germany

NORMARK CORP
10395 Yellow Circle Dr.
Minnetonka, MN 55343
800-874-4451
612-933-0046
Hunting knives, game shears and skinning ax

ONTARIO KNIFE CO.
26 Empire St.
Franklinville, NY 14737
800-222-5233; 800-299-2618
salesokc@aol.com
www.ontarioknife.com
Fixed blades, tactical folders, military & hunting knives, machetes

OUTDOOR EDGE CUTLERY CORP.
4699 Nautilus Ct. S
Boulder, CO 80301
800-447-EDGE; 303-530-7020
outdooredge@plinet.com
www.outdooredge.com

Sporting Cutlers, continued

PARAGON CUTLERY CO.
2015 Asheville Hwy.
Hendersonville, NC 28791
828-697-8833; 828-697-5005
www.paragonweb.com
Knifemaking furnaces

PILTDOWN PRODUCTIONS
Errett Callahan
2 Fredonia Ave.
Lynchburg, VA 24503

QUEEN CUTLERY COMPANY
PO Box 500
Franklinville, NY 14737
800-222-5233; 800-299-2618
salesokc@aol.com
www.queencutlery.com
Pocket knives, collectibles, Schatt & Morgan, Robeson, club knives

QUIKUT
PO Box 29
Airport Industrial Park
Walnut Ridge, AR 72476
870-886-6774
870-886-9162

RANDALL MADE KNIVES
PO Box 1988
Orlando, FL 32802-1988
407-855-8075
407-855-9054
grandall@randallknives.com
www.randallknives.com
Handmade fixed-blade knives for hunting, fishing, diving, military and general use

REMINGTON ARMS CO., INC.
870 Remington Drive
PO Box 700
Madison, NC 27025

RICHARTZ USA
1825 Walnut Hill Lane Suite 120
Irving, TX 78038
800-859-2029
972-331-2566
info@richartz.com
www.richartz.com
German-made, multi-balde folding knives for hunting, camping and general use

ROUND EYE KNIFE & TOOL
PO Box 818
Sagel, ID 83860
208-265-8858
208-263-0848
roundeye@nidlink.com
www.roundeye.com
Folding and fixed-blade knives for hunting and general use

SANTA FE STONEWORKS
3790 Cerrillos Rd.
Santa Fe, NM 87507
800-257-7625; 505-471-0036
knives@rt66.com
www.santafestoneworks.com
Gem stone handles

SARCO CUTLERY LLC
449 Lane Dr.
Florence, AL 35630
256-766-8099
256-766-7246
sarcoknives@earthlink.net
www.sarcoknives.com
Fixed-blade camping knife

SOG SPECIALTY KNIVES & TOOLS, INC.
6521 212th St. S.W.
Lynwood, WA 98036
425-771-7689
425-771-7681
info@sofknives.com
www.sogknives.com
ARC-LOCK advantage, automatic tools. Specialized fixed blades, folding knives, multi-tools

SPYDERCO, INC.
PO Box 800
Golden, CO 80402-0800
800-525-7770; 303-278-2229
sales@spyderco.com
www.spyderco.com
Knives and sharpeners

SWISS ARMY BRANDS INC.
PO Box 874
One Research Dr.
Shelton, CT 06484-0874
800-243-4045
800-243-4006
www.swissarmy.com
Folding multi-blade designs and multi-tools for hunting, fishing, camping, hiking, golfing and general use. One of the original brands (Victorinox) of Swiss Army Knives

TAYLOR CUTLERY
1736 N Eastman Rd.
PO Box 1638
Kingsport, TN 37662-1638
800-251-0254 or 423-247-2406
423-247-5371
taylor@preferred.com
www.taylorcutlery.com
Fixed-blade and folding knives for tactical, rescue, hunting and general use

TIGERSHARP TECHNOLOGIES
1002 N Central Expwy Suite 499
Richardson, TX 75080
469-916-2861
972-907-0716
claudettehead@hotmail.com

TIMBERLINE KNIVES
PO Box 600
Getzville, NY 14068-0600
716-877-2200; 716-877-2591
gatco@buffnet.net; timberlineknives.com
High Technology production knives for professionals, sporting, tradesmen & kitchen use

TINIVES
1725 Smith Rd.
Fortson, GA 31808
888-537-9991
706-322-9892
info@tinives.com
www.tinives.com
High-tech folding knives for tactical, law enforcement and general use

TRU-BALANCE KNIFE CO.
PO Box 140555
Grand Rapids, MI 49514

TURNER, P.J., KNIFE MFG., INC.
PO Box 1549
Afton, WY 83110
307-885-0611
pjtkm@silverstar.com
www.eknife.net

UTICA CUTLERY CO
820 Noyes St.
Utica, NY 13503-1537
800-888-4223
315-733-6602
sales@kutmaster.com
Wide range of folding and fixed-blade designs, multi-tools and steak knives

WARNER, K.
PO Box 3
Greenville, WV 24945
304-832-6878

WENGER NORTH AMERICA
15 Corporate Dr.
Orangeburg, NY 10962
800-431-2996 or 845-365-3500
845-365-3558
www.wengerna.com
One of the official makers of folding multi-blade Swiss Army knives

WILD BOAR BLADES
1701 Broadway PMB 282
Vancouver, WA 98666
888-735-8483 or 360-735-0570
360-735-0390
Wild Boar Blades is pleased to carry a full line of Kopromed knives and kitchenware imported from Poland

WILLIAM HENRY FINE KNIVES
2125 Delaware Ave. Suite C
Santa Cruz, CA 95060
831-454-9409
831-454-9309
www.williamhenryknives.com
Semi-custom folding knives for hunting and general use; some limited editions

WORLD SURVIVAL INSTITUTE
C. Janowsky
PO Box 394
Tok, AK 99780
907-883-4243

WUU JAU CO INC
2600 S Kelly Ave.
Edmond, OK 73013
800-722-5760 or 405-359-5031
877-256-4337 or 405-340-5965
www.wuujau.com
Wide variety of imported fixed-blade and folding knives for hunting, fishing, camping, and general use

WYOMING KNIFE CORP.
101 Commerce Dr.
Ft. Collins, CO 80524

XIKAR INC
PO Box 025757
Kansas City, MO 64102
888-266-1193
info@xikar.com
www.xikar.com

importers & foreign cutlers

A. G. RUSSELL KNIVES INC
1920 North 26th St.
Lowell, AR 72745-8489
479-631-0130; 800-255-9034
479-631-8493
ag@agrussell.com
www.agrussell.com
The oldest knnife mail-order company, highest quality. Free catalog available. In these catalogs you will find the newest and the best. If you like knives, this catalog is a must.

ADAMS INTERNATIONAL KNIFEWORKS
8710 Rosewood Hills
Edwardsville, IL 62025
Importers & foreign cutlers

AITOR-BERRIZARGO S.L.
P.I. Eitua PO Box 26
48240 Berriz Vizcaya
SPAIN
946826599
94602250226
info@aitor.com
www.aitor.com
Sporting knives

ATLANTA CUTLERY CORP.
2143 Gees Mill Rd.
Box 839Fd
Conyers, GA 30207
770-922-3700
770-388-0246
www.atlantacutlery.com

BAILEY'S
PO Box 550
Laytonville, CA 95454

directory

Importers & Foreign Cutlers, continued

BELTRAME, FRANCESCO
Flli Beltrame F&C SNA
Via Dei Fabbri As/3
33085 Maniago PN
ITALY
switches@iol.it
www.italianstiletto.com

BOKER USA, INC.
1550 Balsam St.
Lakewood, CO 80214-5917
303-462-0662
303-462-0668
sales@bokerusa.com
www.bokerusa.com
Ceramic blades

CAMPOS, IVAN DE ALMEIDA
Custom and Old Knives Trader
R. Stelio M. Loureiro, 206
CENTRO, TATUI
BRAZIL

C.A.S. IBERIA, INC.
650 Industrial Blvd.
Sale Creek, TN 37373
423-332-4700
423-332-7248
cas@casiberia.com
www.casiberia.com
Paul Chen/Hanwei Swords, Muela, Ajtor,
Replica weaponry

CATOCTIN CUTLERY
PO Box 188
Smithsburg, MD 21783

CLASSIC INDUSTRIES
1325 Howard Ave., Suite 408
Burlingame, CA 94010

COAST CUTLERY CO.
2045 SE Ankeny St.
Portland, OR 97214

COLUMBIA PRODUCTS CO.
PO Box 1333
Sialkot 51310
PAKISTAN

COLUMBIA PRODUCTS INT'L
PO Box 8243
New York, NY 10116-8243
201-854-3054
201-854-7058
nycolumbia@aol.com
http://columbiaproducts.homestead.com/cat/html
Pocket, hunting knives and swords

COMPASS INDUSTRIES, INC.
104 E. 25th St.
New York, NY 10010

CONAZ COLTELLERIE
Dei F.Lli Consigli-Scarperia
Via G. Giordani, 20
50038 SCARPERIA (FIRENZE)
ITALY
conaz@dada.it
www.conaz.com

CONSOLIDATED CUTLERY CO., INC.
696 NW Sharpe St.
Port St. Lucie, FL 34983

CRAZY CROW TRADING POST
PO Box 847 Dept 96
Pottsboro, TX 75020
903-786-2287
903-786-9059
info@crazycrow.com
www.crazycrow.com
Solingen blades, knife making parts & supplies

DER FLEISSIGEN BEAVER
(THE BUSY BEAVER)
Harvey Silk
PO Box 1166
64343 GRIESHEIM
GERMANY
4961552231
49 6155 2433
Der.Biber@t-online.de

EMPIRE CUTLERY CORP.
12 Kruger Ct.
Clifton, NJ 07013

EXTREME RATIO SAS
Mauro Chiostri
Maurizio Castrat, Viale
Montegrappa 298
59100 Prato
ITALY
0039 0574 58 4639
0039 0574 581312
chios@iol.it
www.extremaratio.com
Tactical & military knives manufacturing

FALLKNIVEN AB
Havrevagen 10
S-96142 Boden
SWEDEN
46 92154422
4692154433
info@fallkniven.se
www.fallkniven.com
High quality knives

FREDIANI COLTELLI FINLANDESI
Via Lago Maggiore 41
I-21038 Leggiuno
ITALY

GIESSER MESSERFABRIK GMBH, JOHANNES
Raiffeisenstr 15
D-71349 Winnenden
GERMANY
49-7195-18080
49-7195-64466
info@giesser.de
www.giesser.de
Professional butchers and chef's knives

HIMALAYAN IMPORTS
3495 Lake Side Dr
Reno, NV 89509
775-825-2279
himimp@aol.com
httpillmembers.aol.com/himinp/index.html

IVAN DE ALMEIDA CAMPOS-KNIFE DEALER
R. Xi De Agosto
107, Centro, Tatui, SP 18270
BRAZIL
55-15-2518092
55-15-251-4896
campos@bitweb.com.br
Custom knives from all Brazilian knifemakers

JOY ENTERPRISES
1104-53rd Court
South West Palm Beach, FL 33407
561-863-3205/800-500-3879
561-863-3277
mail@joyenterprises.com
www.joyenterprises.com
Fury™, Mustang™, Hawg Knives, Muela

KELLAM KNIVES CO.
902 S Dixie Hwy.
Lantana, FL 33462
561-588-3185; 800-390-6918
561-588-3186
info@kellamknives.com
www.kellamknives.com
Knives from Finland; own line of knives

KNIFE IMPORTERS, INC.
PO Box 1000
Manchaca, TX 78652
800-561-5301
800-266-2373
Wholesale only

KNIGHTS EDGE
5696 N Northwest Hwy.
Chicago, IL 60646
773-775-3888
773-775-3339
Exclusive designers of our Rittersteel,
Stagesteel and Valiant Arms lines of weaponry

LEISURE PRODUCTS CORP.
PO Box 1171
Sialkot-51310
PAKISTAN

L. C. RISTINEN
Suomi Shop
17533 Co. Hwy. 38
Frazee, MN 56544
218-538-6633
icrist@scta.net
Scandinavian cutlery custom antique

LINDER, CARL NACHF.
Erholungstr. 10
42699 Solingen
GERMANY
212 330856
212 337104
info@linder.de
www.linder.de

MARTTIINI KNIVES
PO Box 44 (Marttiinintie 3)
96101 Rovaniemi
FINLAND

MATTHEWS CUTLERY
4401 Sentry Dr., Suite K
Tucker, GA 30084

MESSER KLÖTZLI
PO Box 104
Hohengasse 3, Ch-3402 Burgdorf
SWITZERLAND
034 422 2378
034 422 7693
info@klotzli.com
www.klotzli.com

MURAKAMI, ICHIRO
Knife Collectors Assn. Japan
Tokuda Nishi 4 Chome, 76 Banchi, Ginancho
HASHIMAGUN, GIFU
JAPAN
81 58 274 1960
81 58 273 7369
www.gix.orjp/~n-resin/

MUSEUM REPLICAS LIMITED
2147 Gees Mill Rd., Box 840 PQ
Conyers, GA 30012
800-883-8838
www.museumreplicas.com

NICHOLS CO.
PO Box 473, #5 The Green
Woodstock, VT 05091
802-457-3970
802-457-2051
janjesse@sover.net
Import & distribute knives from EKA (Sweden),
Helle (Norway), Brusletto (Norway), Roselli
(Finland). Also market Zippo products and
snow & Neally axes.

NORMARK CORP.
Craig Weber
10395 Yellow Circle Dr.
Minnetonka, MN 55343

PRO CUT
9718 Washburn Rd.
Downey, CA 90241
562-803-8778
562-803-4261
sales@procutdist.com
Wholesale only. Full service distributor of
domestic & imported brand name cutlery.
Exclusive U.S. importer for both Marto Swords
and Battle Ready Valiant Armory edged
weapons.

PRODUCTORS AITOR, S.A.
Izelaieta 17
48260 Ermua
SPAIN
943-170850
943-170001
info@aitor.com
Sporting knives

SCANDIA INTERNATIONAL INC.
5475 W Inscription Canyon Dr.
Prescott, AZ 86305
928-442-0140
928-442-0342
frosts@cableone.net
www.frosts-scandia.com
Frosts Knives of Sweden

STAR SALES CO., INC.
1803 N. Central St., PO Box 1503
Knoxville, TN 37901

SVORD KNIVES
Smith Rd., Rd 2
Waiuku, South Auckland
NEW ZEALAND

Importers & Foreign Cutlers, continued

SWISS ARMY BRANDS LTD.
The Forschner Group, Inc.
One Research Drive
Shelton, CT 06484
203-929-6391
203-929-3786
www.swissarmy.com

TAYLOR CUTLERY
PO Box 1638
1736 N. Eastman Rd.
Kingsport, TN 37662
Colman Knives along with Smith & Wesson, Cuttin Horse, John Deere, Zoland knives.

UNITED CUTLERY CORP.
1425 United Blvd.
Sevierville, TN 37876
865-428-2532
865-428-2267
order@unitedcutlery.com

www.unitedcutlery.com
Harley-Davidson™, Colt™, Stanley™ hunting, camping, fishing, collectible & fantasy knives

UNIVERSAL AGENCIES INC
4690 S Old Peachtree Rd., Ste C
Norcross, GA 30071-1517
678-969-9147; 678-969-9148
678-969-9169
info@uai.org
www.knifesupplies.com; www.thunderforged.com;
www.uai.org
Serving the cutlery industry with the finest selection of India Stag, Buffalo Horn, Thurnderforged™ Damascus. Mother of Pearl, Knife Kits and more

VALOR CORP.
1001 Sawgrass Corp Pkwy.
Sunrise, FL 33323-2811
954-377-4925
954-377-4941
www.valorcorp.com
Wide variety of imported & domestic knives

WENGER N. A.
15 Corporate Dr.
Orangeburg, NY 10962
800-431-2996
www.wengerna.com
Swiss Army™ Knives

WILD BOAR BLADES
1701 Broadway, Suite 282
Vancouver, WA 98663
888-735-8483; 360-735-0570
360-735-0390
usakopro@aol.com
www.wildboarblades.com
Wild Boar Blades is pleased to carry a full line of Kopromed knives and kitchenware imported from Poland.

ZWILLING J.A.
Henckels Inc
171 Saw Mill River Rd.
Hawthorne, NY 10532

mail order sales

A. G. RUSSELL KNIVES INC.
1920 North 26th St
Lowell, AR 72745-8489
479-631-0130
479-631-8493
ag@agrussell.com
www.agrussell.com
The oldest knife mail-order company, highest quality. Free catalog available. In these catalogs you will find the newest and the best. If you like knives, this catalog is a must.

ADAMS BILL
PO Box 666
Conyers, GA 31078
912-836-4195

ARIZONA CUSTOM KNIVES
Jay and Karen Sadow
8617 E. Clydesdale
Scottsdale, AZ 85258
480-951-0699
sharptalk@aol.com
www.arizonacustomknives.com
Color catalog $5 U.S. / $7 Foreign

ATLANTA CUTLERY CORP.
2147 Gees Mill Rd., Box 839DY
Conyers, GA 30012
800-883-0300
www.atlantacutlery.com
Special knives & cutting tools

ATLANTIC BLADESMITHS/PETER STEBBINS
50 Mill Rd.
Littleton, MA 01460
978-952-6448
j.galt1100@verizon.ent
www.atlanticbladesmiths.com
Sell, trade, buy; carefully selected handcrafted, benchmade and factory knives

BALLARD CUTLERY
1495 Brummel Ave.
Elk Grove Village, IL 60007

BECK'S CUTLERY SPECIALTIES
Macgregor Village #109
107 Edinburgh S
Cary, NC 27511
919-460-0203
www.beckscutlery.com
Knives

BLUE RIDGE KNIVES
166 Adwolfe Rd.
Marion, VA 24354-6664
276-783-6143
276-783-9298
www.blueridgeknives.com
Wholesale distributor of knives

BOB NEAL CUSTOM KNIVES
PO Box 20923
Atlanta, GA 30320
770-914-7794
770-914-7796
bob@bobnealcustomknives.com
www.bobnealcustomknives.com
Exclusive limited edition custom knives-sets & single

BOONE TRADING CO., INC.
PO Box 669
Brinnon, WA 98320
800-423-1945
www.boonetrading.com
Ivory scrimshaw horns

CARMEL CUTLERY
Dolores & 6th; PO Box 1346
Carmel, CA 93921
831-624-6699
831-624-6780
ccutlery@ix.netcom.com
www.carmelcutlery.com
Quality custom and a variety of production pocket knives, swords; kitchen cutlery; personal grooming items

CORRADO CUTLERY
Otto Pomper
1630 Payne St
Chicago, IL 60602
847-329-9770
847-329-9770
www.corradocutlery.com
Knives, Nippers, Scissors, Gifts, Optical Goods

CREATIVE SALES & MFG.
Box 111
Whitefish, MT 59937
406-849-5174
406-849-5130
www.creativesales.com

CUTLERY SHOPPE
357 Steelhead Way
Boise, ID 83704
800-231-1272
208-672-8588
www.cutleryshoppe.com
Discount pricing on top quality brands

CUTTING EDGE, THE
1920 North 26th St.
Lowell, AR 72745-8489
479-631-0055
479-631-8734
editor@cuttinedge.com
www.cuttingedge.com
After-market knives since 1968. We offer about 1,000 individual knives for sale each month. Subscription by first class mail, in U.S. $20 per year, Canada or Mexico by air mail, $25 per year. All overseas by air mail, $40 per year.

The oldest and the most experienced in the business of buying and selling knives. We buy collections of any size, take knives on consignment. Every month there are 4-8 pages in color featuring the work of top makers

DENTON, J.W.
102 N. Main St., Box 429
Hiawassee, GA 30546
706-896-2292
706-896-1212
jwdenton@alltel.net
Loveless knives

DUNN KNIVES INC
PO Box 204
Rossville, KS 66533
785-584-6856
785-584-6856

EDGE CO. KNIVES
17 Kit St.
Keene, NH 03431-7125
603-357-9390
edgeco.com

FAZALARE, ROY
PO Box 1335
Agoura Hills, CA 91376
818-879-6161 after 7pm
ourfaz@aol.com
Handmade multiblades; older case; Fight'n Rooster; Bulldog brand & Cripple Creek

FROST CUTLERY CO.
PO Box 22636
Chattanooga, TN 37422

GENUINE ISSUE, INC.
949 Middle Country Rd.
Selden, NY 11784
516-696-3802
516-696-3803
g.l._cutlery.com
All knives

GODWIN, INC., G. GEDNEY
2139 Welsh Valley Rd.
Valley Forge, PA 19481
610-783-0670
610-783-6083
www.gggodwin.com
18th century reproductions

GUILD KNIVES
320 Paani Place 1A
Paia, HI 96779
808-877-3109
808-877-3524
donguild@aol.com
www.donguild1@aol.com
Purveyor of Custom Art Knives

HAWTHORN GALLERIES, INC.
PO Box 6071
Branson, MO 65616
417-335-2170
417-335-2011
hg_inc@hotmail.com

Mail Order Sales, continued

HERITAGE ANTIQUE KNIVES
Bruce Voyles
PO Box 22171
Chattanooga, TN 37422
423-894-8319
423-892-7254
bruce@jbrucevoyles.com
www.jbrucevoyles.com
Knives, knife auctions

HOUSE OF TOOLS LTD.
#136, 8228 Macleod Tr. SE
Calgary, Alberta, Canada
T2H 2B8

HUNTER SERVICES
Fred Hunter
PO Box 14241
Parkville, MD 64152

JENCO SALES, INC.
PO Box 1000
Manchaca, TX 78652
800-531-5301
800-266-2373
jencosales@sbcglobal.net
Wholsale only

KELLAM KNIVES CO.
902 S Dixie Hwy.
Lantana, FL 33462
561-588-3185; 800-390-6918
561-588-3186
info@kellamknives.com
www.kellamknives.com
Largest selection of Finnish knives; own line of folders and fixed blades.

KNIFEART.COM
13301 Pompano Dr
Little Rock, AR 72211
501-221-1010
501-221-2695
www.knifeart.com
Large internet seller of custom knives & upscale production knives.

KNIFE IMPORTERS, INC.
PO Box 1000
Manchaca, TX 78652

KNIFEMASTERS CUSTOM KNIVES/J&S FEDER
PO Box 208
Westport, CT 06881
(203) 226-5211
(203) 226-5312
Investment grade custom knives

KNIVES PLUS
2467 I 40 West
Amarillo, TX 79109
800-687-6202
Retail cutlery and cutlery accessories since 1987

KRIS CUTLERY
PO Box 133 KN
Pinole, CA 94564
510-223-8968
kriscutlery@attbl.com
www.kriscutlery.com
Japanese, medieval, Chinese & Philippine

LDC CUSTOM KNIVES
PO Box 20923
Atlanta, GA 30320
770-914-7794
770-914-7796
bob@bobnealcustomknives.com
Exclusive limited edition custom knives - sets & single

LES COUTEAUX CHOISSIS DE ROBERTS
Ron Roberts
PO Box 273
Mifflin, PA 17058

LONE STAR WHOLESALE
PO Box 587
Amarillo, TX 79105
806-356-9540
806-359-1603
Wholesale only; major brands and accessories

MATTHEWS CUTLERY
4401 Sentry Dr., Suite K
Tucker, GA 30084

MORTY THE KNIFE MAN, INC.
4 Manorhaven Blvd.
Port Washington, NY 11050

MUSEUM REPLICAS LTD.
2143 Gees Mill Rd., Box 840PQ
Conyers, GA 30207
800-883-8838
www.museumreplicas.com
Historically accurate and battle ready swords & daggers

NORDIC KNIVES
1634CZ Copenhagen Dr.
Solvang, CA 93463
805-688-3612
info@nordicknives.com
www.nordicknives.com
Custom and Randall knives

PARKER'S KNIFE COLLECTOR SERVICE
6715 Heritage Business Court
Chattanooga, TN 37422
423-892-0448
423-892-0448
bbknife@bellsouth.net

PEN AND THE SWORD LTD., THE
PO Box 290741
Brooklyn, NY 11229 0741
(718) 382-4847
(718) 376-5745
info@pensword.com
Custom folding knives, engraving, scrimshaw, Case knives, English fruit knives, antique pocket knives

PLAZA CUTLERY, INC.
3333 S. Bristol St., Suite 2060
South Coast Plaza
Costa Mesa, CA 92626
714-549-3932
plazacutlery@earthlink.net
www.plazacutlery.com
Largest selection of knives on the west coast. Custom makers from beginners to the best. All customs, reeves, randalls & others available online by phone.

ROBERTSON'S CUSTOM CUTLERY
PO Box 1367
Evans, GA 30809-1367
706-650-0252
706-860-1623
customknives@comcast.net
www.robertsoncustomcutlery.com
Limited edition exclusive designs, Vanguard knives and world class custom knives.

ROBINSON, ROBERT W.
1569 N. Finley Pt.
Polson, MT 59860

SHAW, GARY
24 Central Ave.
Ridgefield Park, NJ 07660
201-641-8801
201-641-0872
gshaw@carroll.com
Investment grade custom knives

SMOKY MOUNTAIN KNIFE WORKS
2320 Winfield Dunn Pkwy.
Sevierville, TN 37876
865-453-5871; 800-251-9306
info@smkw.com
www.eknifeworks.com
The world's largest knife showplace, catalog and website

STIDHAM'S KNIVES
PO Box 570
Roseland, FL 32957-0570
772-589-0618
772-589-3162
rstidham@gate.net
www.randallknifesociety.com
Randall, Loveless, Scagel, custom and antique knives

STODDARD'S, INC.
Copley Place 25
100 Huntington Ave.
Boston, MA 02116
617-536-8688
617-536-8689
Cutlery (Kitchen, pocket knives, Randall-made knives, custom knives, scissors & manicure tools) Binoculars, lwo vision aids, personal care items (hair brushes, manicure sets mirrors)

organizations & publications

organizations

AMERICAN BLADESMITH SOCIETY
c/o Jim Batson
PO Box 977
Peralta, NM 87042

AMERICAN KNIFE & TOOL INSTITUTE***
Dave Kowalski, Comm. Coordinator
AKTI, Dept BL2
PO Box 432
Iola, WI 54945-0432
715-445-3781
715-445-5228
communications@akti.org
www.akti.org

AMERICAN KNIFE THROWERS ALLIANCE
c/o Bobby Branton
4976 Seewee Rd.
Awendaw, SC 29429

ART KNIFE COLLECTOR'S ASSOCIATION
c/o Mitch Weiss, Pres.
2211 Lee Road, Suite 104
Winter Park, FL 32789

AUSTRALIAN KNIFEMAKERS GUILD INC.
PO Box 659
Belgrave 3160
Victoria, AUSTRALIA

CALIFORNIA KNIFEMAKERS ASSOCIATION
c/o Clint Breshears, Membership Chairman
1261 Keats St.
Manhattan Beach CA 90266

CANADIAN KNIFEMAKERS GUILD
c/o Peter Wile
RR # 3
Bridgewater N.S.
B4V 2W2
902-543-1373
www.ckg.org

CUTTING EDGE, The
1920 N 26th St.
Lowell AR 72745
479-631-0055
479-631-8734
buyer@cuttingedge.com
After-market knives since 1968. We offer about 1,000 individual knives each month. Subscription by first class mail, in U.S. $20 per year, Canada or Mexico by air mail, $25 per year. All overseas by air mail, $40 per year. The oldest and the most experienced in the business of buying and selling knives. We buy collections of any size, take knives on consignment or we will trade. Every month there are eight pages in color featuring the work of top makers.

JAPANESE SWORD SOCIETY OF THE U.S.
PO Box 712
Breckenridge, TX 76424

KNIFE COLLECTORS CLUB INC, THE
1920 N 26th St.
Lowell AR 72745
479-631-0055
479-631-8734
ag@agrussell.com
Web:www.club@k-c.com
The oldest and largest association of knife collectors. Issues limited edition knives, both handmade and highest quality production, in very limited numbers. The very earliest was the CM-1, Kentucky Rifle.

KNIFE WORLD
PO Box 3395
Knoxville, TN 37927

KNIFEMAKERS GUILD
c/o Al Pendray, President
13950 N.E. 20th St.
Williston FL 32696
352-528-6124
352-528-6124
bpendray@aol.com

KNIFEMAKERS GUILD OF SOUTHERN AFRICA, THE
c/o Carel Smith
PO Box 1744
Delmars 2210
SOUTH AFRICA
carelsmith@therugby.co.za
Web:www.kgsa.co.za

KNIVES ILLUSTRATED
265 S. Anita Dr., Ste. 120
Orange, CA 92868
714-939-9991
knivesillustrated@yahoo.com
Web:www.knivesillustrated.com
All encompassing publication focusing on factory knives, new handmades, shows and industry news.

MONTANA KNIFEMAKERS' ASSOCIATION, THE
14440 Harpers Bridge Rd.
Missoula, MT 59808
406-543-0845
Annual book of custom knife makers' works and directory of knife making supplies; $19.99

NATIONAL KNIFE COLLECTORS ASSOC.
PO Box 21070

Chattanooga, TN 37424
423-892-5007
423-899-9456
nkca@aol.com Web: nationalknive.org

NEO-TRIBAL METALSMITHS
PO Box 44095
Tucson, AZ 85773-4095

NEW ENGLAND CUSTOM KNIFE ASSOCIATION
George R. Rebello, President
686 Main Rd.
Brownville, ME 04414
Web:www.kinvesby.com/necka.html

NORTH CAROLINA CUSTOM KNIFEMAKERS GUILD
c/o Tommy McNabb, Pres.
4015 Brownsboro Rd.
Winston-Salem, NC 27106
tommy@tmcnabb.com
Web:www.ncknivequild.org

PROFESSIONAL KNIFEMAKERS ASSOCIATION
2905 N. Montana Ave., Ste. 30027
Helena, MT 59601

RESOURCE GUIDE AND NEWSLETTER / AUTOMATIC KNIVES
2269 Chestnut St., Suite 212
San Francisco, CA 94123
415-731-0210
Web:www.thenewsletter.com

TACTICAL KNIVES
Harris Publications
1115 Broadway
New York, NY 10010

TRIBAL NOW!
Neo-Tribal Metalsmiths
P.O. Box 44095
Tucson, AZ 85733-4095

TWO KNIFE GUYS PUBLISHING
Ken Warner/J Bruce Voyles
PO Box 24477
Chattanooga, TN 37422
423-894-6640

UNITED KINGDOM BLADE ASSOCIATION (UKBA)
PO Box 1
Brampton, CA67GD
ENGLAND

WEYER INTERNATIONAL BOOK DIVISION
2740 Nebraska Ave.
Toledo, OH 43607-3245

publications

BLADE MAGAZINE
Krause Publications
700 E. State St.
Iola, WI 54990
(800) 272-5233

Editor: Steve Shackleford. Monthly. Official magazine of the Knifemakers Guild. $3.25 on newsstand; $19.95 per year. Also publishes Blade Trade, a cutlery trade magazine; Dream Teams; Tek-Knives; Knives of Europe and knife books.

KRAUSE PUBLICATIONS
700 E. State St.
Iola, WI 54990
(715) 445-2214
(715) 445-4087

In addition to this Knives annual, Krause and its DBI Books division publish many knife books, including American Premium Guide to Knives and Razors by Jim Sargent; IBCA Price Guide to Antique Knives by J. Bruce Voyles; Levine's Guide to Knives and Their Values by Bernard Levine; The Wonder of Knifemaking by Wayne Goddard; How To Make Knives by Richard W. Barney and Robert W. Loveless; The Tactical Folding Knife by Bob Terzuola; How to Make Folding Knives by Ron Lake, Frank Centofante and Wayne Clay; Complete Book of Pocketknife Repair by Ben Kelly Jr.; Knife Talk by Ed Fowler; Collins Machetes and Bowies 1845-1965 by Daniel E. Henry; and Collecting Indian Knives by Lar Hothem.

KNIFE WORLD
P.O. Box 3395
Knoxville, TN 37927
(800) 828-7751

Editor: Mark Zalesky. Monthly. Tabloid size on newsprint. Covers custom knives, knifemakers, collecting, old factory knives, etc. General coverage for the knife enthusiast. Subscription $15 year.

KNIVES ILLUSTRATED
265 S. Anita Dr., Ste. 120
Orange, CA 92868
(714) 939-9991

Editor; Bruce Voyles. $3.99 on newsstands; $16.95 for six issues. Bi-monthly; plenty of four-color, all on cutlery; concentrates on handmade knives.

RESOURCE GUIDE AND NEWSLETTER / AUTOMATIC KNIVES
2269 Chestnut St., Suite 212
San Francisco, CA 94123
(415) 731-0210
415-664-2105 for 24/hr. ordering info.

Editor: Sheldon Levy. In its 10th year as a quarterly. Deep coverage of automatic folders. $30 year by mail.

TACTICAL KNIVES
Harris Publications
1115 Broadway
New York, NY 10010

(212) 807-7100
(212) 627-4678

Editor: Steve Dick. Aimed at emergency-service knife designs and users, this new publication has made a great start. Price $5.95; $14.95 for six issues. On newsstands.

TRIBAL NOW!
Neo-Tribal Metalsmiths
P.O. Box 44095
Tucson, AZ 85733-4095

Editor: Bill Randall. (See Neo-Tribal Metalsmith under Organizations.) Price: $10 per year for four issues with two- to four-page supplements sent out on a regular basis.

UK BLADE
United Kingdom Blade Associations
P.O. Box 11
Brampton CA67GD
ENGLAND

WEYER INTERNATIONAL BOOK DIVISION
2740 Nebraska Ave.
Toledo, OH 43607-3245
(800) 448-8424
(419) 534-2020
(419) 534-2697
law-weyerinternational@msn.com
www.weyerinternational.com

Publishers of the Knives: Points of Interest series. Sells knife-related books at attractive prices; has other knife-publishing projects in work.

Essential References for Knife Makers

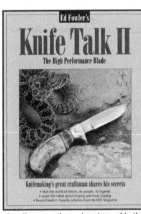

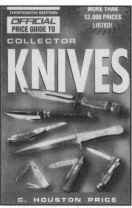
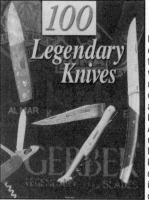
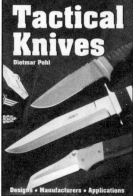
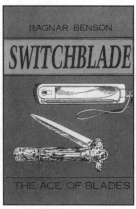